For some sixty years, commencing in 1260, the Mamluk state in Egypt and Syria was at war with the Īlkhānid Mongols based in Persia. This is the first comprehensive study of the political and military aspects of the early years of the war, the twenty-one-year period commencing with the battle of ʿAyn Jālūt in Palestine in 1260 and ending in 1281 at the battle of Homs in northern Syria. Between these major confrontations, which resulted from Mongol invasions into Syria, the Mamluk–Īlkhānid struggle was continued in the manner of a 'cold war' with both sides involved in border skirmishes, diplomatic maneuvers, psychological warfare, ideological posturing, espionage and other forms of subterfuge. Here, as in the major battles, the Mamluks usually maintained the upper hand, establishing themselves as the major Muslim power at the time. Using primarily contemporary Arabic and Persian sources, Reuven Amitai-Preiss sheds new light on the confrontation, examining the war within the context of Īlkhānid/Mamluk relations with the Byzantine Empire, the Latin West and the crusading states, as well as with other Mongol states.

Cambridge Studies in Islamic Civilization

Mongols and Mamluks

Cambridge Studies in Islamic Civilization

Titles in the series

B.F. MUSALLEM. *Sex and society in Islam: birth control before the nineteenth century*

SURAIYA FAROQHI. *Towns and townsmen of Ottoman Anatolia: trade, crafts and food production in an urban setting, 1520–1650*

PATRICIA CRONE. *Roman, provincial and Islamic law: the origins of the Islamic patronate*

STEFAN SPERL. *Mannerism in Arabic poetry: a structural analysis of selected texts, 3rd century AH/9th century AD – 5th century AH/11th century AD*

BEATRICE FORBES MANZ. *The rise and rule of Tamerlane*

AMNON COHEN. *Economic life in Ottoman Jerusalem*

PAUL E. WALKER. *Early philosophical Shiism: the Ismaili Neoplatonism of Abū Yaʿqūb al-Sijistānī*

BOAZ SHOSHAN. *Popular culture in medieval Cairo*

STEPHEN FREDERIC DALE. *Indian merchants and Eurasian trade, 1600–1750*

AMY SINGER. *Palestinian peasants and Ottoman officials: rural administration around sixteenth-century Jerusalem*

MICHAEL CHAMBERLAIN. *Knowledge and social practice in medieval Damascus, 1190–1350*

Mongols and Mamluks

The Mamluk–Īlkhānid War, 1260–1281

REUVEN AMITAI-PREISS

PUBLISHED BY THE PRESS SYNDICATE OF THE UNIVERSITY OF CAMBRIDGE
The Pitt Building, Trumpington Street, Cambridge, United Kingdom

CAMBRIDGE UNIVERSITY PRESS
The Edinburgh Building, Cambridge CB2 2RU, UK
40 West 20th Street, New York NY 10011–4211, USA
477 Williamstown Road, Port Melbourne, VIC 3207, Australia
Ruiz de Alarcón 13, 28014 Madrid, Spain
Dock House, The Waterfront, Cape Town 8001, South Africa

http://www.cambridge.org

First published 1995
Reprinted 1996
First paperback edition 2004

A catalogue record for this book is available from the British Library

Library of Congress Cataloguing in Publication data
Amitai–Preiss, Reuven, 1955–
Mongols and Mamluks: the Mamluk-Īlkhānid War, 1260–1281 / Reuven Amitai–Preiss.
p. cm. – (Cambridge Studies in Islamic civilization)
Includes bibliographical references and index.
ISBN 0 521 46226 6 hardback
1. Islamic Empire – History – 1258–1516. I. Title. II. Series.
DS38.7.A46 1995
909′.097671–dc20 94-21441 CIP

ISBN 0 521 46226 6 hardback
ISBN 0 521 52290 0 paperback

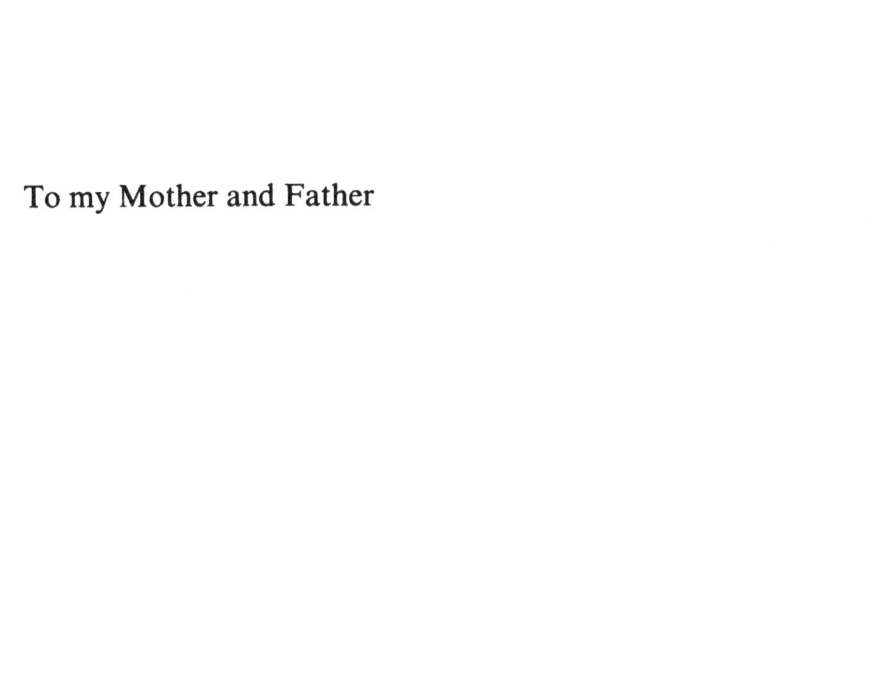

To my Mother and Father

Contents

Illustrations

Plates *page*

Figure *page*

Maps *page*

Dynastic and genealogical tables *page*

Preface

This present study had its genesis as a Ph.D. dissertation, which was submitted to the Senate of the Hebrew University of Jerusalem in February 1990. I wish to take this opportunity to express my deep gratitude to my supervisors, Professor David Ayalon and Dr. Peter Jackson, for having given unstintingly of their time and knowledge over a period of many years, even after my formal status as a student was ended. I would also like to thank the following: Dr. D.O. Morgan, for his sound advice and helping hand; Professor M. Sharon, for his encouragement and counsel over the years; Mr. A.H. Morton, who first introduced me to the Īlkhānid sources; Mr. R. Irwin, who contributed both helpful criticism and countenance, perhaps more than he is willing to admit; Professor U. Haarmann, who supplied me with an important microfilm at very short notice; Professor A. Khazanov, who read a very early version of chapter 1; Professor R.P. Lindner, for reading a draft of chapter 10. I would also like to acknowledge the assistance of Professor E. Kohlberg for his advice regarding publishing this work. In addition, my thanks are due to Dr. Ellenblum for his translations from Latin, Professor M. Erdal for his help in transliterating Turkish and Mongolian names and terms, and Mr. D. Dector for assistance with Russian material. I am also grateful to Ms. Tamar Sofer and Ms. Noa Nachum of the Cartographic Laboratory of the Hebrew University of Jerusalem, for the maps which they produced for this volume, as well as to Ms. Sally Ayrton and Ms. Roza el-Eini for their careful reading of this study and their judicious comments. My wife Nitzan deserves special thanks for her continuous encouragement and support, along with her careful and critical reading of my text. The oft-repeated but ever-valid warning applies here: I alone am responsible for any mistakes or shortcomings contained in this study.

I am grateful to the staffs of the following institutions for assisting my research: the Jewish National and University Library (Jerusalem); Hebrew University Map Library; Library of the School of Oriental and African Studies (London); Institute of Historical Research (London); Dept. of Oriental Manuscripts and Printed Books, the British Library; Bodleian Library (Oxford); Chester Beatty Library (Dublin); Topkapı Sarayı, Süleymaniye and

Köprülüzade Libraries (Istanbul); the Bibliothèque Nationale (Paris); the Vatican Library; Princeton University Library; and the University of Pennsylvania Library (Philadelphia). Much of the revision of this work was done during the 1990–1 year as a visiting research fellow at the Department of Near Eastern Studies at Princeton University. I would like to thank the staff of the Department and its then chairman, Professor A. Udovitch, as well as Professor M.A. Cook, for helping to make my stay there so profitable. I would also like to express my gratitude to the following bodies which assisted in the financing of the research and writing of this study: the Institute of Asian and African Studies, Hebrew University of Jerusalem; Central Research Fund, Hebrew University; Golda Meir Fund (Jerusalem); Council for Higher Education in Israel.

I am grateful to the following for permission to reproduce photographs: Professor M. Sharon, editor of *Corpus Inscription Arabicarum Palaestinae* (Jerusalem); Ms. Habie Schwarz (London); Libraire Orientaliste Paul Geuthner (Paris); Dr. T.A. Sinclair (London and Nicosia). I would also like to acknowledge the permission of Dr. D.O. Morgan to reproduce genealogical tables from his *The Mongols* (Oxford: Basil Blackwell, 1986). I cite in this book sections from two of my articles, and express my gratitude to the publishers for permission to do so: *al-Masāq: Studio Arabo-Islamica Mediterranea* (vol. 3 [1990]), and *Tārīḫ* (vol. 2 [1992]). Finally, it is a special pleasure to thank the staff at Cambridge University Press, particularly the series editor, Marigold Acland, and the sub-editor, Margaret Sharman, for their diligent and professional work, as well as their patience and good grace.

In conclusion, I would like to evoke the memory of the late Burton Barsky, my English teacher at Central High School in Philadelphia. The resemblance that this text has to standard written English is due largely to his stern teachings, for which I am ever grateful.

Abbreviations

AAS	*Asian and African Studies*
AEMA	*Archivum Eurasiae Medii Aeivi*
AOL	*Archives de l'orient latin*
BEO	*Bulletin d'études orientales*
BSOAS	*Bulletin of the School of Oriental and African Studies*
CAJ	*Central Asiatic Journal*
CHIr, 5	*Cambridge History of Iran.* Vol. 5: Ed. J.A. Boyle. *The Saljuq and Mongol Periods.* Cambridge, 1968.
Dozy	R. Dozy. *Supplément aux dictionnaires arabes.* Leiden, 1881. 2 vols.
DOP	*Dumbarton Oaks Papers*
EI[1]	*Encyclopaedia of Islam*, 1st edition. Leiden and London, 1913–36.
EI[2]	*Encyclopaedia of Islam*, 2nd edition. Leiden and London, 1960–.
EIr	*Encyclopaedia Iranica.* London, Boston and Henley, 1985–.
Faḍl	Shāfiᶜ b. ᶜAlī. *Al-Faḍl al-ma'thūr min sīrat al-sulṭān al-malik al-manṣūr.* MS. Bodleian Marsh 424.
HJAS	*Harvard Journal of Asiatic Studies.*
Ḥusn	Shāfiᶜ b. ᶜAlī. *Ḥusn al-manāqib al-sirriyya al-muntazaᶜa min al-sīra al-ẓāhiriyya.* Ed. ᶜA-ᶜA. al-Khuwayṭir. Riyad, n.d.
IOS	*Israel Oriental Studies*
JA	*Journal asiatique*
JAOS	*Journal of the American Oriental Society*
JSS	*Journal of Semitic Studies*
JESHO	*Journal of the Economic and Social History of the Orient*
JRAS	*Journal of the Royal Asiatic Society*
Lane	E.W. Lane. *An Arabic-English Lexicon.* Rpt. Cambridge, 1984. 2 vols.
MHR	*Mediterranean Historical Review*
Rawḍ	Ibn ᶜAbd al-Ẓāhir. *Al-Rawḍ al-zāhir fī sīrat al-malik al-ẓāhir.* Ed. ᶜA-ᶜA al-Khuwayṭir. Riyad, 1396/1976.
RCEA	*Répertoire chronologique d'épigraphie arabe.* Ed. E. Combe, J. Sauvaget and G. Wiet. Cairo, 1931–. 17 vols. to date.

REI	*Revue des études islamiques*
RHC, Ar	*Recueil des historiens des croisades, documents armeniens*. Paris, 1869–1906.
RHC, Occ	*Recueil des historiens des croisades, historiens occidentaux*. Paris, 1844–95.
RHC, Or	*Recueil des historiens des croisades, historiens orientaux*. Paris, 1872–1906.
ROL	*Revue de l'orient latin*
SI	*Studia Islamica*
Tashrīf	Ibn ʿAbd al-Ẓāhir. *Tashrīf al-ayyām wa'l-ʿuṣūr fī sīrat al-malik al-manṣūr*. Ed. M. Kāmil. Cairo, 1961.
TMEN	G. Doerfer. *Türkische und mongolische Elemente im Neupersisichen*. Wiesbaden, 1963–75. 4 vols.
Tuḥfa	Baybars al-Manṣūrī. *Kitāb al-tuḥfa al-mulūkiyya fī dawla al-turkiyya*. Ed. ʿA-R. Ḥamdān. Cairo, 1987.
Zubda	Baybars al-Manṣūrī. *Zubdat al-fikra fī ta'rīkh al-hijra*. MS. British Library Add. 23325

Notes on dates and transliteration

1 Dates are generally given according to the *hijrī* calendar, followed by the Western (i.e., AD) equivalent. When *hijrī* dates are given alone, as in the notes, they are prefixed by AH. Western dates are sometimes found on their own, particularly when discussing events in Europe or among the Franks of Outremer.

2 Arabic words, titles and names have been transliterated according to the system used in the *International Journal of Middle Eastern Studies*. Words and names of Persian origin have usually been transliterated as if they were Arabic (e.g., ʿAlīzādah, not ʿAlīzāde; Juwaynī, not Juvaynī); the same applies to the titles of Persian books. One exception to this rule is the title *pervāne*, which is preferable to its rendering in Arabic sources, *barwānāh*. Common words of Arabic origin, such as mamluk, amir and sultan, are written without diacritical points. "Mamluk" and "Mamluks" with capital letters specifically refer to the Sultanate established in Egypt in AD 1250, while "mamluks" without a capital letter refers to military slaves in a general sense.

3 Place names are generally given in their Arabic forms. Frankish, Armenian or Modern Turkish variants are also given in parenthesis, at least for the first time the location is named. Well-known place names are given in their accepted English forms: e.g., Cairo, Damascus, Jerusalem, Homs, Aleppo, Mosul.

4 Names and terms of Mongolian origin are generally rendered in the Middle Mongolian form, while Turkish words and names (including those of mamluks) are transcribed in a manner which will hopefully approximate their pronunciation in the Mamluk Sultanate. Instead of *č* in Mongolian and ç in Turkish, I have used the diagraph *ch*; in lieu of *γ* used by linguists for both languages, I have adopted *gh*; *j* has replaced the *ǰ* of Mongolian and the *c* of modern Turkish; *š* in Mongolian and ş in Turkish have been replaced by *sh*. Turkish and Mongolian names are not given with the long vowels found in their Arabic and Persian transcriptions, e.g., Qalawun, not Qalāwūn. Purists might find fault with my usage of *īlkhān* instead of *ilkhan* or even *elkhan*, as well as *bahādur* instead of *baghatur*, but since these terms were thoroughly Arabized, I have permitted myself to adopt the form favored by historians of medieval Islam.

Introduction

> The Mongols conquered the land and there came to them
>   From Egypt a Turk, who sacrificed his life.
> In Syria he destroyed and scattered them.
>   To everything there is a pest of its own kind.
>
> Abū Shāma (d. 1267)[1]

For sixty years, commencing in AD 1260, the Mamluks of Egypt and Syria were involved in a more or less constant struggle with the Īlkhānid Mongols of Persia. During this period, the Mongols made several concerted efforts to invade Syria: in AD 1260, 1281, 1299, 1300, 1303 and 1312. With one exception, all the Mongol expeditions were failures. Even the one Mongol victory on the field, at Wādī al-Khaznadār in AD 1299, did not lead to the permanent Mongol occupation of Syria and the ultimate defeat of the Mamluks, as the Mongols evacuated Syria after an occupation lasting only a few months. Between these major campaigns, the war generally continued in a form which in modern parlance might be described as a "cold war": raids over both sides of the border, diplomatic maneuvers, espionage and other types of subterfuge, propaganda and ideological posturing, psychological warfare, use of satellite states, and attempts to build large-scale alliances against the enemy. Here, as in the major battles, the Mamluks usually maintained the upper hand. Yet, in spite of a conspicuous lack of success on the part of the Mongols, they continued to pursue their goals of conquering Syria and subjecting the Mamluks, until their efforts began to peter out towards the end of the second decade of the fourteenth century. It was only then that the Mongols initiated negotiations which led to a formal conclusion of a peace agreement in AD 1323.

The study of this conflict is essential to understanding both the Mamluk and Īlkhānid states. The early history of the Mamluk Sultanate is inextricably bound up with the Mongols. As will be seen, the establishment of the Sultanate was indirectly influenced by the early Mongol invasions of the Islamic world

[1] *Dhayl ʿalā al-rawḍatayn* (Cairo, 1947), 208.

and the steppe region north of the Black Sea. The Mongols were the Mamluks' greatest concern in the realm of foreign relations during the formative first decades of the Mamluk Sultanate. This was not only because the Īlkhānid Mongols were its greatest enemies, but also because the Mongols of the Golden Horde were its most important allies, not the least because it was from the territory of the latter that the vast majority of young mamluks were imported to the Sultanate.[2] It is thus impossible to understand the development of the Sultanate without first analyzing the nature of the relationship with the Mongols. The Īlkhānids, on the other hand, may have had more pressing matters on their minds than their conflict with the Mamluks, yet over the years it still remained a major concern, to which they repeatedly returned. If nothing else, an analysis of their failure to defeat the Mamluks should lead to a greater understanding of the Īlkhāns and their army.

Both the Mamluks and Mongols were military elites of Eurasian Steppe origin who ruled over large sedentary Muslim populations, and based their armies on disciplined masses of mounted archers. Yet fundamental differences existed between the two groups. First, the Mongols continued to maintain a tribal and pastoral nomadic way of life, whereas the Mamluks, born as pagans, had been plucked out of the nomadic environment, converted to Islam and functioned as an urban military caste. While the Mamluks were Muslims, the Mongols entered the Islamic world holding a mixture of Shamanistic, Buddhist and Eastern Christian beliefs. The Mamluk sultans saw themselves as defenders of Islam and the Muslims, and portrayed themselves as such, whereas the early Īlkhāns blithely killed the Caliph, destroyed mosques and sought alliances with local and Western Christians against the Muslims. Even with the eventual conversion of the Mongols to Islam, towards the end of the thirteenth century, the religious dimension of the conflict did not completely disappear.

The purpose of this study is to present a political and military history of the Mamluk–Īlkhānid war from the first clash, at the battle of ʿAyn Jālūt in AD 1260, until the second battle of Homs in 1281. The plethora of evidence and the lack of space precluded dealing in a single volume with the entire war to 1320 and its subsequent resolution. It is my hope that in the future I will be able to publish further studies which will deal with Mamluk–Īlkhānid relations from 1281 to the demise of the Īlkhānid state in the 1330s.

Previous scholarship

For all the interest and importance of the Īlkhānid–Mamluk war, it has until now only been partially studied. The general works on Mamluk history in European languages – most noteworthy being those by G. Weil,[3] P.M. Holt[4]

[2] These comments are based on the remarks in D. Ayalon, "The Great Yāsa of Chingiz Khān. A Re-examination," Pt. C1, *SI* 36 (1972):117. See n. 13 below.

[3] G. Weil, *Geschichte des Abbasidenchalifats in Egypten* (Stuttgart, 1860–2), vol. 1.

[4] P.M. Holt, *The Age of the Crusades: The Near East from the Eleventh Century to 1517* (London, 1986).

and R. Irwin[5] – usually mention the war only in passing, perhaps discussing at length one of the battles or certain other aspects. The same can be said of the surveys of Īlkhānid history, such as those works by A.C.M. D'Ohsson,[6] J.A. Boyle,[7] B. Spuler[8] and D.O. Morgan.[9] The standard narrative histories of the Crusades – by R. Grousset,[10] S. Runciman[11] and J. Prawer[12] – discuss the Mongols only in as far as they are relevant to their central subject. This does not mean that these works are without value. They provide a historical framework in which to view the Mamluk–Īlkhānid war, and offer much information and many insights into the conflict itself. They do not, however, fill the need for a detailed study on the subject.

There are several specialized studies which have proved invaluable for this work. D. Ayalon, in a series of articles on the *yasa*, or Mongol law code,[13] discussed some of the salient features of the conflict, while analyzing possible Mongol influence, including the *yasa*, on the Mamluks. Many of Ayalon's other studies supplied important relevant information. P. Jackson has given us two lengthy studies,[14] which provide a clearer understanding of some of the important aspects of the early stages of the war. J.M. Smith, Jr.'s article on ʿAyn Jālūt[15] is actually a wide-ranging study of the tactical and strategic sides of the war, among which he discusses Mongol logistical problems. D.O. Morgan[16] has also written on this latter topic. A.P. Martinez[17] has published a long and detailed study of the Īlkhānid army and the transformations it may have undergone. Finally, P. Thorau's recent biography of Baybars[18] has been extremely helpful, both in providing much useful background information and discussing Mongol–Mamluk relations. A preliminary study of the Īlkhānid–Mamluk war is F.Ḥ. ʿĀshūr's *al-ʿAlāqāt al-siyāsiyya bayna al-mamālīk wa'l-mughūl fī al-dawla al-mamlūkiyya al-ūlā* ("The Political Relations between the Mamluks and the Mongols during the First Mamluk Dynasty").[19] Other studies will be mentioned in the course of this work.

5 R. Irwin, *The Middle East in the Middle Ages: The Early Mamluk Sultanate, 1250–1382* (London, 1986).

6 A.C.M. D'Ohsson, *Histoire des Mongols* (rpt., Tientsin, China, 1940, of The Hague, 1834), vol. 3.

7 J.A. Boyle, "Dynastic and Political History of the Īl-Khāns," in *CHIr*, 5:303–421.

8 B. Spuler, *Die Mongolen in Iran* (4th ed., Leiden, 1985).

9 D.O. Morgan, *The Mongols* (Oxford, 1986), 145–74.

10 R. Grousset, *Histoire des croisades* (Paris, 1934–6), vol. 3.

11 S. Runciman, *A History of the Crusades* (rpt., Harmondsworth, 1971), vol. 3.

12 J. Prawer, *Histoire du royaume latin de Jérusalem*, tr. J. Nahon (Paris, 1970), vol. 2.

13 Besides the part mentioned in n. 2 above, see *SI* 33 (1971):97–140; 34 (1971):151–80; 38 (1973):107–56.

14 P. Jackson, "The Dissolution of the Mongol Empire," *CAJ* 32 (1978):186–244; *idem*, "The Crisis in the Holy Land in 1260," *English Historical Review* 95 (1980):481–513.

15 J.M. Smith Jr., "ʿAyn Jālūt: Mamlūk Success or Mongol Failure?," *HJAS* 44 (1984):307–45.

16 D.O. Morgan, "The Mongols in Syria, 1260–1300," in P.W. Edbury (ed.), *Crusade and Settlement* (Cardiff, 1985), 231–5.

17 "Some Notes on the Īl-Xānid Army," *AEMA* 6 (1986 [1988]):129–242.

18 P. Thorau, *Sultan Baibars I. von Ägypten* (Wiesbaden, 1987); trans. by P.M. Holt as *The Lion of Egypt: Sultan Baybars I and the Near East in the Thirteenth Century* (London, 1992). In the present work I have referred to the English translation.

19 Cairo, 1976. This work, although useful, is basically a compilation of Arabic sources.

Although I have at times disagreed with some of the points raised by several of these scholars, they are responsible for shedding much light on the conflict and helping to clarify my own thinking.

Sources[20]

This study is based primarily on contemporary or near-contemporary sources composed in the Mamluk (in Arabic) and Īlkhānid realms (in Persian, Armenian and – to a much smaller extent – Syriac and Arabic). Both Mamluk and Īlkhānid sources have been analyzed elsewhere,[21] and therefore a lengthy discussion here would be superfluous. The following survey will be limited to remarks outlining the way in which the present study was conducted.

First and foremost, there are three contemporary biographies of the Sultan Baybars, by Muḥyī al-Dīn Ibn ʿAbd al-Ẓāhir (d. 692/1292), his nephew Shāfiʿ b. ʿAlī (d. 730/1330), and Ibn Shaddād al-Ḥalabī (d. 684/1285). These works are rich in information relating to the conflict with the Mongols, but they are not without their problems. Ibn ʿAbd al-Ẓāhir, a high government official, was essentially an official biographer of his employer. Shāfiʿ's work is more independent, but much of the time it is merely a compendium of his uncle's work. Ibn Shaddād, also a high official, is much less explicitly panegyrical than Ibn ʿAbd al-Ẓāhir, and his work contains much unique information. Unfortunately, only the later part of his work is extant. This is partially compensated for by the extracts from his work found in later chronicles. Ibn ʿAbd al-Ẓāhir and Shāfiʿ both wrote biographies of Qalawun, which were also of some use.

Mamluk chroniclers can be divided into several groups. First there are those writers who could be described essentially as late Ayyūbid historians who continued to write into the Mamluk period: Ibn al-ʿAmīd (d. 672/1273), Abū Shāma (d. 665/1267), and Ibn Wāṣil (d. 697/1298). The work of the last mentioned writer, who concluded his chronicle in AH 660 (1261–2), was continued by his kinsman, Ibn ʿAbd al-Raḥīm up to AH 695 (1295–6). Next, there are two Mamluk writers who in their youths lived through the period dealt with in this study, but who wrote their works only at a later date: Baybars al-Manṣūrī (d. 725/1325) and al-Yūnīnī (d. 726/1326). These two authors relate information from earlier writers (those mentioned above), eye-witness reports, and their own youthful experiences of the conflict with the Mongols. Al-Yūnīnī was one of the earliest of what could be called the Syrian school of

[20] Full bibliographic references to sources mentioned below are found in the Bibliography.

[21] For the Mamluk sources, see C. Cahen, *La Syrie du nord* (Paris, 1940), 68–93; D.P. Little, *An Introduction to Mamlūk Historiography* (Wiesbaden, 1970); U. Haarmann, *Quellenstudien zur frühen Mamlukenzeit* (Freiburg, 1970); P.M. Holt, "Three Biographies of al-Ẓāhir Baybars," in D.O. Morgan (ed.), *Medieval Historical Writing in the Christian and Islamic Worlds* (London, 1982), 19–29. For the pro-Mongol sources, see Spuler, *Iran*, 3–15; D.O. Morgan, "Persian Historians and the Mongols," in Morgan, *Medieval Historical Writing*, 109–24; *idem*, *Mongols*, 5–27; M. Weiers (ed.), *Die Mongolen: Beiträge zu ihrer Geschichte und Kultur* (Darmstadt, 1986), 3–28; T.S.R. Boase (ed.), *The Cilician Kingdom of Armenia* (Edinburgh, 1978), 187–8.

fourteenth-century historians, a group which includes al-Jazarī (d. 739/1338), al-Birzālī (d. 739/1339), al-Dhahabī (d. 748/1348), al-Kutubī (d. 764/1363), and Ibn Kathīr (d. 775/1373). I used extensively only the last three of these works. While repeating much of the evidence found in al-Yūnīnī's work, all three add interesting information. Most of the relevant parts of al-Jazarī's work have been lost,[22] while the one manuscript of al-Birzālī[23] remained inaccessible to me. This is unfortunate, since these are both seminal works and had a direct influence on the rest of the Syrian historians, including al-Yūnīnī. The inaccessibility of these two manuscripts was partially mitigated by the extensive citation of these works, often by name, by both Syrian and other writers.[24]

Two other later chroniclers deserve mention: al-Nuwayrī (d. 732/1332) and Ibn al-Furāt (d.807/1405). For his annals relating to Baybars's reign, al-Nuwayrī relies heavily on Ibn ʿAbd al-Ẓāhir's biography. In a separate volume of his work, *Nihāyat al-arab*, he also provides a treatise on the Mongols, which contains important information. Ibn al-Furāt was one of the main sources of this study. Although he is a relatively late writer, he cites extensively, often naming his sources, both earlier writers and eyewitnesses. One of his most important sources was Shāfiʿ b. ʿAlī's no longer extant *Naẓm al-sulūk*, which appears to have been a vast repository of information on the events during the early Mamluk Sultanate. Ibn al-Furāt also cited at length lost portions of *Nuzhat al-anām*, written by his younger contemporary Ibn Duqmaq (d. 809/1406).

The importance of Ibn al-Furāt's work is clearly seen when compared to *Kitāb al-sulūk* of al-Maqrīzī (d. 845/1442). The latter work has long been a mainstay of modern research in Mamluk and Crusader history, due to a large extent to both M.E. Quatremère's pioneering translation and M.M. Ziyāda's excellent edition. However, a systematic comparison between the two works for twenty-two years of annals (AH 658–80), shows that, for this period at least, al-Maqrīzī's work is virtually a precis of Ibn al-Furāt's vast chronicle.[25] This in itself would not be a bad thing, but al-Maqrīzī often did his work in a haphazard manner, distorting the meaning of his source. This phenomenon will be seen to occur several times in this study.

Among the other Mamluk authors repeatedly cited are the early fourteenth-century writers, Ibn al-Dawādārī and Qirtay al-Khaznadārī, and the mid-fifteenth-century al-ʿAynī (d. 855/1451) and Ibn Taghrī Birdī (d. 874/1470).

[22] I am grateful to Prof. U. Haarmann, who kindly sent me a microfilm of those extant folios of Jazarī, *Ḥawādith al-zamān*, MS. Gotha 1560, which are relevant to this study.

[23] *Al-Muqtafā li'l-ta'rīkh al-shaykh shihāb al-dīn abī shāma*, MS. Topkapı Sarayı, Ahmet III 2951.

[24] Little, *Introduction*, 46–64; Haarmann, *Quellenstudien*, 94–116.

[25] The possibility of a common source cannot be discounted, although none has come to light. Nuwayrī's *Nihāyat al-arab*, MS. Leiden Univ. Or. 2m, is not the common source, because the material therein is arranged somewhat differently in both works and is less detailed than in Ibn al-Furāt's chronicle. See the comments in R. Amitai-Preiss, "In the Aftermath of ʿAyn Jālūt: The Beginnings of the Mamlūk–Īlkhānid Cold War," *al-Masāq* 3 (1990):12–13; *idem*, "ʿAyn Jālūt Revisited," *Tārīḫ* 2 (1991):129–30.

The former two writers were useful sources, but both (especially Qirtay), suffer from a credibility gap, as will be seen below. Professor Little,[26] basing his study on research conducted on annals from a later period, has drawn attention to the importance of al-ᶜAynī's work. Without detracting from this view, in the period covered in this study al-ᶜAynī generally cited known sources, especially Baybars al-Manṣūrī's *Zubdat al-fikra*. This, however, is at times an advantage, for it helps us to reconstruct lost passages of this latter work. Ibn Taghrī Birdī is important for his citation of passages from the lost parts of Ibn Shaddād's biography and the unavailable work of al-Jazarī.

This is not an exhaustive survey of all the Mamluk chronicles which have been used, but only of the most significant ones. Additional annalistic works are cited on occasion, and provide important details. Besides the biographies and annalistic sources, extremely useful works include Ibn Shaddād al-Ḥalabī's historical geography *al-Aᶜlāq al-khaṭīra*, the relevant sections of the encyclopedias by al-ᶜUmarī (d. 749/1349) and al-Qalqashandī (d. 821/1418), and the biographical dictionaries of Ibn al-Ṣuqāᶜī (d. 726/1326) and al-Ṣafadī (d. 764/1363).

It is not uncommon for a piece of information which appears in one Mamluk source to be copied more or less exactly in several others. If every appearance of a particular detail or story were to be faithfully recorded, the result might be an unwieldy list of authorities. Thus, in the notes I have usually given what seems to me to be the original source for a story and two or three additional sources which transmit it. These are generally arranged in rough chronological order; to emphasize the dependence of a particular writer on another, I use the word "whence." In the case of Ibn al-Furāt's chronicle, most of which – at least for the part relevant to this study – is still only in manuscript form, I have always given the parallel (and generally shorter) passage in al-Maqrīzī's *Sulūk*. This is because of the wide availability of the edition of the latter, and the extensive use which it hitherto has enjoyed.

The pro-Mongol sources are divided into three groups. First are the Persian sources, the most important being Rashīd al-Dīn (d. 718/1318). This writer served as a wazir to the Īlkhāns, and it is clear that his work is not unaffected by his desire to please his employers. A second source is Waṣṣāf (fl. 698–723/1299–1323), also employed by the Mongols, albeit in a more modest capacity. Waṣṣāf provides some information on the war with the Mamluks, but it generally seems of a somewhat exaggerated or even fictional nature. This author's convoluted style makes the use of this work difficult at best. Other Persian sources of importance are Ibn Bībī (fl. 681/1283), for events in Seljuq Rūm (Anatolia), and Juwaynī (d. 681/1283), for background.

The second group of pro-Mongol sources comprises the Armenian authors. These works have been consulted either in English and French translations from Armenian, or in the Old French originals of certain works. The sources

[26] Little, *Introduction*, 80–7.

are especially important for the discussion of the role of Lesser Armenia. On occasion, however, they provide information on wider matters. The third group consists of two non-Persian sources from inside the Īlkhānid Empire: Bar Hebraeus (d. AD 1286) and the Arabic work questionably attributed to Ibn al-Fuwaṭī (d. 723/1323).[27] The former, a Jacobite prelate, originally wrote his chronicle in Syriac (which was read here in translation), and later prepared a condensed version in Arabic. Finally, additional details have been provided from Frankish (i.e. European Christian) sources.

As a final note, I should mention that most of the information at our disposal on the Mamluk–Īlkhānid conflict is derived from the pro-Mamluk Arabic sources. It is true that the corpus of Mamluk historical works is much larger than its pro-Mongol counterpart, and this might be one reason for this phenomenon, but I would suggest that other explanations are involved. I will return to this point in chapters 5 and 10.

[27] See F. Rosenthal, "Ibn al-Fuwaṭī," *EI*² 3:769.

CHAPTER 1

The historical background

Another decree is that [the Mongols] are to bring the whole world into subjection to them, nor are they to make peace with any nation unless they first submit to them . . .

John of Plano Carpini (ca. 1247)[1]

The Mongols and their conquest of southwest Asia

The Mongol Empire was founded in the late twelfth and early thirteenth centuries by Temüchin, later known as Chinggis Khan (died AD 1227), who united the Mongolian and Turkish-speaking tribes of the eastern Eurasian steppe and forged an empire which within the span of two generations was to stretch across Asia. Having put the Inner Asian steppe under his sway and obtained the submission of the Tanguts of the Hsi-Hsia state in northwest China, Tibet and Chinese Turkestan (1209), Chinggis Khan commenced his campaign against the north Chinese state of the Chin in 1211. While this conquest was not yet completed by the end of the decade, it was well enough along for Chinggis Khan to turn his attention to the west. One of his generals had already defeated the ruler of the Qara-Khitai in western Turkestan, obliterated this state and integrated its territory into the Mongol Empire.[2]

In 1219, Chinggis Khan launched a massive offensive against the Khwārazm-shāh, who controlled most of the eastern Islamic world. The campaign had been sparked off by the Khwārazm-shāh's truculent attitude towards the Mongols and by his governor's murder of several hundred Muslim merchants under Mongol protection. This, however, was only a pretext, and it would seem – as Barthold has suggested – that once the Mongols had definitely established themselves on the steppes bordering the Khwārazm-shāh's kingdom, "they could not but become aware of its internal weakness and under such circumstances a nomad invasion of the much richer lands of the civilized

[1] "History of the Mongols," in C. Dawson (ed.), *The Mission to Asia* (London, 1980), 25; original text in A. Van den Wyngaert, *Sinica Fransciscana*, vol. 1 (Quaracchi-Firenze, 1929), 64.

[2] For Chinggis Khan and his early conquests, see P. Ratchnevsky, *Genghis Khan*, tr. and ed. T.N. Haining (Oxford, 1991); Morgan, *Mongols*, 55–73; J.J. Saunders, *The History of the Mongol Conquests* (rpt., London, 1977), 44–70.

peoples was inevitable."[3] By 1223, the Khwārazm-shāh was dead, the lands and cities of this empire were in ruins and Chinggis Khan was on his way back to Mongolia, having left behind a small part of his army in the conquered territory.

Mongol administration of the newly conquered area was of a limited nature, its primary goals being the prevention of rebellion and the extraction of maximum taxes and tribute. In spite of its relatively small size, this Mongol force – first under Chormaghun and then Baiju (with a brief interruption in which Eljigidei was in command) – slowly but steadily expanded the realm of Mongol control, reaching as far as Seljuq Rūm (Anatolia), which was subjugated in the aftermath of the battle of Köse Dagh in 641/1243.

Areas independent of Mongol control, however, continued to exist, such as the Ismāᶜīlī strongholds in Iran and the local dynasties in southern Iran. In addition, the Jazīra (the region divided today among northern Iraq, northeastern Syria and southeastern Turkey) and the Caliph's state in Iraq had yet to be conquered, although the Mongols had raided the former area several times. Even before Hülegü's arrival in the mid-1250s in Iran, potentates large and small in the as yet unconquered parts of southwest Asia had begun to realize that some type of accommodation had to be made with this strange but very real menace from the East, and many rulers had already dispatched missions to ascertain its nature and to request its mercy.[4]

A recurring theme in early Mongol history is the idea of Mongol imperial destiny. According to this belief, which may be called the Mongol imperial ideology, Chinggis Khan had been given a divinely inspired mission to conquer the world and place it under Mongol domination. Thus the Mongols were not only pursuing a campaign of self-aggrandizement, but were also carrying out a heaven-ordained task to bring order to the world by placing it under the aegis of Chinggis Khan and his family. Those who totally submitted were *el* (written *īl* in Persian and Arabic texts), which literally meant "to be at peace or in harmony," but really connoted the state of unconditional loyalty to the Mongols. On the other hand, all those who resisted the Mongols and refused to submit were *bulgha* (literally "to be in a confused or disordered state") or *yaghı* ("enemy"); both terms expressed the state of being "unsubmitted" or "rebellious" and thus being at war with the Mongols. There was no intermediate state and those who resisted were to be annihilated accordingly.[5]

[3] W. Barthold, *Turkestan down to the Mongol Invasion* (4th ed., London, 1977), 400.

[4] For Chinggis Khan's campaign against the Khwārazm-shāh and the subsequent period up to Hülegü's dispatch by Möngke, see Barthold, *Turkestan*, 381–483; Spuler, *Iran*, 16–44; Morgan, *Mongols*, 145–7; Boyle, "Īl-Khāns," 303–40; R.S. Humphreys, *From Saladin to the Mongols* (Albany, 1977), 220–1, 227, 310, 334–41.

[5] J.F. Fletcher, "The Mongols: Ecological and Social Perspective," *HJAS* 46 (1986):19, 30–5; I. de Rachewiltz, "Some Remarks on the Ideological Foundations of Chingis Khan's Empire," *Papers on Far Eastern History* 7 (1973):21–36; K. Sagaster, "Herrschaftsideologie und Friedensgedanke bei den Mongolen," *CAJ* 17 (1973):223–6; E. Voegelin, "The Mongol Orders of Submission to European Powers, 1245–1255," *Byzantion* 15 (1940–41):378–413; Spuler, *Iran*, 20; T.T. Allsen, *Mongol Imperialism* (Berkeley, 1987), 42; P. Jackson and D.

This concept of divinely inspired mission played an important role in the Mongol conquests. The seemingly endless Mongol victories and resulting wealth evidently proved the validity of the ideology. This in turn strengthened the resolve of the soldiers and officers to fight and led to more victories, thereby consolidating further the belief in the ideology. It is difficult to judge how far this belief permeated the Mongol ranks, that is, did every soldier of Turco-Mongol origin know or really believe it? This ideal must certainly have been held by members of the Mongol ruling strata, thus welding them to Chinggisids and helping to propel the Mongols towards conquest.[6] In addition, there is some evidence in a Chinese source from the 1230s that this ideology was known and internalized by the rank and file of the Mongol army.[7]

This is not to say that the belief in the ideal of Mongol "manifest destiny" was the only or even primary reason for the ongoing Mongol expansion under Chinggis Khan and his successors.[8] Other factors favoring Chinggis Khan's rise to power were the particular relations within the steppe at his time, especially China's relative inability to interfere with steppe politics, as well as plain luck.[9] On a more fundamental level, territorial expansion into neighboring areas was a *sine qua non* of nomadic states in the Eurasian steppes, motivated as they were by the desire to control the manufactured and agricultural goods which could only be found there.[10] Expansion was also the justification for the existence of the nomadic ruler, and one who did not succeed in this endeavor was soon abandoned by his followers.[11] The flexible nature of Turco-Mongolian tribal society made possible both the rapid construction of larger tribal entities and the absorption of foreign nomadic groups,[12] thus giving the tribal leader the power to launch his campaigns of

Morgan (tr. and ed.), *The Mission of Friar William of Rubruck* (London, 1990), 25–6. For a discussion of the terms *el/īl*, *bulgha* and *yaghı*, see M. Erdal, "Die Türkisch-mongolischen Titel *elxan* und *elči*," *Proceedings of the Permanent International Altaistic Conference (Berlin, 1991)*, forthcoming; *TMEN*, 2:197, 317–19; 4:99–102.

6 Allsen, *Mongol Imperialism*, 79, and B. Spuler, *The Muslim World*, vol. 2: *The Mongol Period* (Leiden, 1960), 4–5, emphasize the impact of this belief on the Mongol elite.

7 Peng Da-ya and Xu Ting, *Hei-da shi-lue*, in Wang Guo-wei (ed.), *Meng-gu shi-liao si-zhong* (Taipei, 1975), 488, as cited in T. Allsen, "Changing Forms of Legitimation in Mongol Iran," in G. Seaman and D. Mark (eds.), *Rulers from the Steppe* (Los Angeles, 1991), 223.

8 This point is made by Fletcher, "Mongols," 32.

9 O. Lattimore, "The Geography of Chinggis Khan," *The Geographical Journal* 129/1 (1963):1–7; *idem*, Review of F. Grenard, *Genghis-Khan* (Paris, 1935), in *Pacific Affairs* 10/4 (Dec. 1937):466–8.

10 See A.M. Khazanov, *Nomads and the Outside World*, tr. J. Crookenden (Cambridge, 1984), 228–30; cf. D. Sinor, "Horse and Pasture in Inner Asian History," *Oriens Extremus* 19 (1972):180.

11 Khazanov, *Nomads*, 161, 229; J.M. Smith, Jr., "Turanian Nomadism and Iranian Politics," *Iranian Studies* 11 (1978):63–4; Morgan, *Mongols*, 38–9; Fletcher, "Mongols," 19–20.

12 A.M. Khazanov, "Characteristic Features of Nomadic Communities in the Eurasian Steppes," in W. Weissleder (ed.), *The Nomadic Alternative* (The Hague, 1978), 123; R.P. Lindner, "What Was a Nomadic Tribe?," *Comparative Studies in Society and History* 24 (1982):693–711; Morgan, *Mongols*, 37. On the similarities and differences between Turks and Mongols, see Fletcher, "Mongols," 39; L. Krader, "The Cultural and Historical Position of the Mongols," *Asia Major*, NS 3 (1952–3):175–6.

expansion. The warrior culture and ethos of the tribesmen must also have contributed to Turco-Mongol irredentism.[13] Finally, the archery and riding skills of the tribesmen, along with their toughness and endurance, made for excellent soldiers who constituted the conquering armies.[14] It was Chinggis Khan's genius to weld the various Mongol, and later Turkish, tribes into a united military machine, and provide the leadership and vision to engage in a series of victorious campaigns. As he became increasingly successful, more and more tribesmen either flocked to his banner of their own free will or were compelled to join his army.

It is clear that without these factors the Mongol imperial ideology would have had little if any impact, and it is even doubtful that it ever would have been conceived. But this ideology cannot be discounted merely as a rationalization for unbridled nomadic egoism. At the least, it helped in the formation of a more united and motivated Mongol soldiery, let alone leadership, which in turn contributed to Mongol successes.

Dr. Morgan has expressed some doubts as to whether the Mongol imperial ideology was conceived in Chinggis Khan's reign, and has raised the point that there is only concrete evidence for its existence in the years subsequent to the great leader's death.[15] The resolution of this question is not germane to the subject of the present book, although it might be mentioned that Temüchin's adoption of the title Chinggis Khan, which has been translated as "Oceanic" or "Universal Khan,"[16] may be an indication that some form of this ideology was current in his lifetime. Be this as it may, it is important to note that the "imperial idea" was later to find repeated expression in the context of the Mamluk–Īlkhānid war. As will be seen, this belief is found to varying degrees in the many missives sent to the Mamluk rulers from 1260 onward. I would suggest that it was one of the reasons behind the ongoing war with the Mamluks; this point will be discussed in chapter 10.

The phase of slow but steady Mongol expansion in the Islamic world came to an end in the middle of the 1250s, when Hülegü Khan came into the region at the head of a large army. Hülegü had been ordered to campaign in southwestern Asia in 1251 by his brother Möngke, the newly elected Qa'an (the supreme Mongol ruler). Hülegü, after making the necessary arrangements, left Mongolia in 1253. Travelling slowly through the steppe, Hülegü only began his campaign in earnest in the spring of 1256.[17] According to Rashīd al-Dīn,

[13] Fletcher, "Mongols," 33. [14] See Morgan, *Mongols*, 84–5.

[15] Morgan, *Mongols*, 14; *idem*, "The Mongols and the Eastern Mediterranean," *MHR* 4 (1987):200; see also the comments in Jackson and Morgan's introduction to William of Rubruck, tr. Jackson, 25–6. It might be added that one could take this line of reasoning to an extreme, and suggest that we can know nearly nothing of Chinggis Khan's life and work, since almost all the sources for his biography are posthumous.

[16] On the meaning of this title, see Ratchnevsky, *Genghis Khan*, 89–90. But see now I. de Rachewiltz, "The Title Činggis Qan," in W. Heissig and K. Sagaster (eds.), *Gedanke und Wirkung* (Weisbaden, 1989), 221–8, who suggests that the title should be translated as "fierce khan." [17] Boyle, "Īl-Khāns," 340–2; Morgan, *Mongols*, 147–9.

Hülegü's mission was first to eliminate the Ismāʿīlī sect, concentrated in eastern Iran and south of the Caspian Sea, and having completed that he was to continue on to Iraq and put down the rebellious Kurds and Lurs. As for the Caliph, if he submitted, he was to be well treated; if not, he was to be attacked. Möngke also took the opportunity to commission his brother to "conquer the lands of the enemies . . . until you have many summer and winter camps." In addition, Hülegü was to enact the laws of Chinggis Khan in the lands from the River Oxus (Jayḥūn) up to the edge of the land of Egypt.[18]

Rashīd al-Dīn's evidence should be approached with some care, as he was writing more than half a century after the events he describes, and like Juwaynī, he might be retelling history in a tendentious fashion for the sake of his employers, the Toluids.[19] There is, however, nothing in the above brief which rings false. Quite the contrary: the large size of Hülegü's army (see below) indicates that his mission was more than just the subjugation of the Ismāʿīlīs, and that a goal of his campaign was to enlarge the Mongol Empire. This is confirmed by information in the *Yüan Shih* (compiled in 1369), where Hülegü (Hsuh-lieh) is sent to subject the "Western countries and the various lands of the Sultan."[20]

Möngke's dispatch of Hülegü was part of a larger effort to expand the Mongol Empire. A third brother, Qubilai, was also sent at this time to expand Mongol territory in China.[21] There is a parallelism between Hülegü's and Qubilai's missions: Rashīd al-Dīn writes that Möngke simultaneously ordered the two to set out on campaign, and Juwaynī reports that the Qa'an allocated armies of equal size to each prince.[22] Mustawfī (ça. 730/1329–30) equates the two campaigns, stating that the two brothers were dispatched in order to expand Mongol-ruled territory,[23] while the *Yüan shih* also describes together the dispatch of the two expeditions, indicating that they were conceived as parallel campaigns.[24] Möngke's plans to enlarge the empire were certainly influenced by the traditional Mongol desire for expansion, of which the imperial ideology discussed above was surely a component. In addition, there

[18] Rashīd al-Dīn, *Jāmiʿ al-tawārīkh*, ed. ʿA. ʿAlīzādah, vol. 3 (Baku, 1957):23. For the reasons behind the decision to destroy the Ismāʿīlīs, see Morgan, *Mongols*, 147–8; see also ʿUmarī, *Das Mongolische Weltreich*, ed. and tr. K. Lech (Wiesbaden, 1968), 2, 17 (of Arabic text). For Hülegü's brief *vis-à-vis* the Caliph, see below, p. 16.

[19] On Juwaynī's tendentiousness, see Ayalon, "Yāsa," pt. B, 152–66. See also Jackson, "Dissolution," 188–9. Tolui was the fourth son of Chinggis Khan, and the father of Möngke, Hülegü, Qubilai and Arigh Böke.

[20] W. Abramowski, "Die chinesischen Annalen des Möngke. Übersetzung des 3. Kapitel des Yüan-chih," *Zentralasiatische Studien* 13 (1979):21. It is not specified to whom "Sultan" here refers.

[21] On his expedition, see M. Rossabi, *Khubilai Khan: His Life and Times* (Berkeley, 1988), 22–8.

[22] Rashīd al-Dīn, ed. ʿAlīzādah, 3:21. Cf. Juwaynī (*Ta'rīkh-i jahān-gushā*, ed. M.M. Qazwīnī [London and Leiden, 1912–37], 3:90; trans. in J.A. Boyle, *The History of the World Conqueror* [Manchester, 1958], 2:607), where Möngke first orders Qubilai to go, and only subsequently, in AH 650/1252–3, gives his command to Hülegü.

[23] Mustawfī, *Ta'rīkh-i guzīda*, ed. A. Nawā'ī (Teheran, 1958–61), 587–8.

[24] Abramowski, "Annalen," 21; see also Pai-nan Rashid Wu, "The Fall of Baghdad and the Mongol Rule in al-Iraq, 1258–1335," Ph.D. diss., Univ. of Utah (1974), 69–70.

was a political aspect to the expansionist policy: this was a way of dealing with the crisis which struck the Mongol elite after the death of Güyük and the election of Möngke in 1251, by keeping "the Mongol ruling class ... continuously involved in the preparation and execution of military operations."[25]

In conclusion, Möngke gave Hülegü the mission to expand the Mongol empire to the southwest, the first stage of which was to eliminate the Ismāʿīlīs. Thereupon, Hülegü was to continue as he thought fit, although he was given general instructions. Already at the planning stage in Mongolia, it is hinted that Egypt was within the sights of the Mongol ruler.[26]

One matter which remains unclear is the nature of Möngke's ultimate plans for Hülegü and whether he intended him to set up his own dynasty in the Islamic world. Professor Allsen has suggested that this was the case, and Qubilai was to do the same in China. Möngke's plan was to establish sub-qa'anates in order to strengthen his position and that of his immediate family *vis-à-vis* the other branches of the Mongol royal family. Möngke bestowed the title *īlkhān* ("subservient *khan*"; see below) on Hülegü, to indicate the latter's clearly defined subordinate status to the Qa'an.[27] On the other hand, Dr. Jackson has shown that the evidence on Möngke's mandate to his brother is far from unequivocal. In fact, there are indications that Hülegü may have been exceeding his brother's instructions, both by setting up a dynasty and "usurping" the rights of the Jochid Mongols, rulers of the Golden Horde, who had some type of authority over the pasture areas of northern Iran.[28]

It is beyond the scope of this study to attempt to resolve this question. I will limit myself therefore to three comments. First, on the basis of the evidence at our disposal, it is impossible to determine with certainty whether Hülegü was sent merely as the commanding general of the expeditionary force or had a mandate to establish a dynasty. Yet, whatever his original status, it does appear that sometime after the conquest of Baghdad and probably after hearing of the death of Möngke (who died August 1259), Hülegü probably took advantage of the prevailing confusion in the Mongol empire to increase his authority.[29] Qubilai, needing Hülegü's support in his war with Arigh-böke, could do little to contest this; according to Rashīd al-Dīn, Qubilai sent a *yarligh* (royal decree) to Hülegü ca. 661/1263, giving him the kingship over the land from the Oxus "up to the extremities of Syria and Egypt."[30]

25 Allsen, *Mongol Imperialism*, 77–79 (77 for quote); Fletcher, "Mongols," 39.

26 On the general nature of instructions given to Mongol generals or princes before they set out on a campaign of conquest, see D. Sinor, "On Mongol Strategy," in *idem*, *Inner Asia and its Contacts with Medieval Europe* (London, 1977), art. XVI, 241.

27 Allsen, *Mongol Imperialism*, 48–9. In his subsequent article "Legitimation in Mongol Iran," Allsen has adopted a position closer to Jackson and Morgan, as cited in the next note.

28 Jackson, "Dissolution," 220–22; cf. Morgan, *Mongols*, 148–9 for a more moderate version of this thesis. Jochi was Chinggis Khan's first son, whose descendants ruled over the Qipchaq steppe of southern Russia; their kingdom came to be known as the Golden Horde. Jochid claims on Iran will be discussed in ch. 4.

29 Jackson, "Dissolution," 232–5; Morgan, *Mongols*, 149.

30 Rashīd al-Dīn, ed. ʿAlīzādah, 3:90. See also Jackson, "Dissolution," 234.

Secondly, there is no evidence that Möngke actually bestowed the title *īlkhān* on Hülegü, and it is possible that he adopted the title of his own volition. It is true that this title is used in the Arabic version of the *Chronography* of Bar Hebraeus (d. 1286) to describe Hülegü *sub anno* 651/1253, but this may well be anachronistic.[31] The earliest references whose dating leaves little doubt are from 657/1259.[32] The first example of the title on a coin would appear to be on a specimen struck in 658/1259–60.[33] At this point, the circumstances of the adoption by Hülegü of the title *īlkhān* are still unknown.[34]

Thirdly, there is some question regarding the exact meaning of title *īlkhān* (thus in Persian and Arabic transcription < *elkhan*/*elqan* in Mongolian). Until recently, most scholars were in agreement that the term should be translated as "subservient or submissive *khan* (ruler)" and it referred to the subservient status of Hülegü and his descendants towards the Qa'an in the east.[35] Other possible translations, such as "*khan* of the tribe" or "peaceful *khan*," have been suggested but were not widely accepted.[36] Recently, Dr. Krawulsky has suggested that the term should be glossed as "the *khan* who brings peace (*īl*)." Little evidence, however, is adduced to prove this proposal.[37] On the other hand, Prof. Erdal has cogently argued that the term is derived from the old Turkic title *elkhan*, which in turn is a contraction of *eligkhan*. The original meaning of both these titles is merely "ruler," and thus it may have been understood by the Mongols. It is also possible, Erdal adds, that the Mongols may have associated the title with the term *el*/*īl* and thus modified the original meaning of the title.[38]

In spite of the obscurity of the title *īlkhān*'s etymology, translation and the circumstances in which it was adopted, there is clear evidence that it was in use during Hülegü's reign, at least as early as 657/1259. Hülegü's successors continued using the *īlkhān*, showing that, whatever its origins, they attributed great importance to it, surely serving to provide legitimization to the dynasty.[39] The title has also supplied modern historians with a convenient name for the dynasty.

[31] Ibn al-ʿIbrī, *Ta'rīkh mukhtaṣar al-duwal*, ed. A. Ṣāliḥānī (Beirut, 1980), 460. For other uses of *īlkhān* before 658/1260, see R. Amitai-Preiss, "Evidence for the Early Use of the Title *īlkhān* among the Mongols," *JRAS*, 3rd ser. 1 (1991):353 n. 4.

[32] See Amitai-Preiss, "Evidence," 353–61.

[33] N. Amitai-Preiss and R. Amitai-Preiss, "Two Notes on the Protocol on Hülegü's Coinage," *Israel Numismatic Journal* 10 (1988–9 [1991]):126. Certain colleagues have questioned our reading of the date on this coin and even have suggested that "Hülegü Īlkhān" is only found on posthumous strikes. This question will have to be resolved by further study.

[34] Some speculation is offered in *ibid.*, 120–1; Allsen, "Legitimation," 234.

[35] The literature is reviewed in Amitai-Preiss, "Evidence," 353, n. 2. This translation is also adopted in Amitai-Preiss, "Protocol," 117, 120–1; Allsen, "Legitimation," 234; Ratchnevsky, *Genghis Khan*, 274.

[36] *TMEN*, 2:207–9, reviews these and other suggestions.

[37] D. Krawulsky, "Die Dynastie der Ilkhâne. Eine Untersuchung zu Regierungsbeginn, Dynastie- und Reichsname," in *idem*, *Mongolen Ilkhâne und Ideologie Geschichte* [*sic*] (Beirut, 1989), 93–8. In light of the literary and numismatic evidence mentioned above, the author's assertion that *īlkhān* was adopted by Hülegü only in 1264 cannot be accepted.

[38] Erdal, "Titel," forthcoming.

[39] Allsen, "Legitimation," 227–34; Amitai-Preiss, "Protocol," 120–1.

The large size of Hülegü's army has been alluded to above, and calls for additional comment. Some idea of the enormous nature of Hülegü's forces is found in Juwaynī's statement that his army was composed of two out of every ten soldiers in the Mongol army, that is, the adult male population of Inner Asia.[40] This evidence, however, should perhaps not be taken too literally, because the expression "two out of every ten" may have merely been a way of saying very many troops or contingents from all the princes. This expression is already found in AD 1246, when Güyük sent Eljigidei to the Islamic world.[41] It is difficult to imagine that then also 20 percent of the Mongol army was dispatched to that corner of the Mongol empire.

Some scholars have attempted to calculate a more exact figure for Hülegü's army: 15–17 *tümens* (units of theoretically 10,000 men), ca. 150–170,000 Mongol and Turkish troops to which a slightly smaller number of local auxiliaries was eventually added, for a grand total of some 300,000 troops under Hülegü's command.[42] Even if these figures are questioned,[43] they still give an idea of the general scale of the forces at Hülegü's disposal. It is noteworthy that two ninth/fifteenth-century sources give figures for these forces: Naṭanzī writes that 70,000 troops actually accompanied Hülegü from Mongolia;[44] and, the fifteenth-century anonymous *Shajarat al-atrāk* reports that Möngke gave Hülegü "one fifth of all able-bodied" Mongols (see above), and this equalled 120,000 men.[45]

By the end of 1256, Hülegü had successfully completed the first stage of his campaign. The Ismāʿīlī "state" had been destroyed, the vast majority of its castles taken and its grand master captured and later executed.[46] Hülegü thereupon turned his attention to the next stage: expanding and consolidating the areas under Mongol control.[47] Most of the remaining rulers of Iran had

40 Juwaynī, 3:90 (= tr. Boyle, 2:607); whence Rashīd al-Dīn, ed. ʿAlīzādah, 22.

41 Juwaynī, 1:211–12 (= tr. Boyle, 1:256).

42 J.M. Smith Jr., "Mongol Manpower and Persian Population," *JESHO* 18 (1975):270–99, esp. 274–8; Allsen, *Mongol Imperialism*, 2, 203–7.

43 The calculations are based on the assumption that each Mongol commander named in the sources was a *tümen* commander and each *tümen* numbered exactly 10,000 soldiers. Even if we accept the first assertion, other research has shown that *tümens* were rarely up to their theoretical strength; Hsiao Ch'i-ch'ing, *The Military Establishment of the Yuan Dynasty* (Cambridge, MA, 1978), 170–1 n. 27, cited in Morgan, *Mongols*, 89; Allsen, *Mongol Imperialism*, 193–4.

44 Naṭanzī, *Muntakhab al-tawārīkh-i muʿīnī*, ed. J. Aubin (Teheran, 1957), 133. U. Schamiloglu ("Tribal Politics and Social Organization in the Golden Horde," Ph.D. diss., Columbia Univ. (New York, 1986), pp. 165–8) criticizes Naṭanzī's veracity, at least as far as the Golden Horde is concerned.

45 *Shajarat al-atrāk*, tr. Miles (London, 1838), 213; I was unable to check this evidence in the original Persian text (MSS. British Library Or.8106 and Add. 26190).

46 See Morgan, *Mongols*, 149–59; Boyle, "Īl-Khāns," 342–5; M.G.S. Hodgson, "The Ismāʿīlī State," *CHIr*, 5:479–482.

47 The Georgian historian edited and translated by M. Brosset, *Histoire de la Géorgie*, vol. 1 (St. Petersburg, 1849), 544, writes: "S'étant ainsi rendu maître d'Alamout et de tout de Khorasan, Houlagou résolut de marcher contre tous les peuples non soumis ..."

made their submission to the Mongols previous to Hülegü's campaign and upon his arrival presented themselves or sent representatives to reaffirm their loyalty.[48] One figure who had yet to submit was al-Mustaᶜṣim, the Caliph in Baghdad. While his political authority scarcely went beyond Baghdad and the surrounding countryside, the Caliph still commanded a great deal of religious and moral prestige in the Islamic world and some political influence. His claim to universal sovereignty, albeit far from the political reality of the day, must have annoyed the Mongols. Hülegü's anger must have been aroused by the Caliph's refusal to send troops to fight the Ismāᶜīlīs as ordered, and his subsequent unwillingness to show any obeisance to the Mongols,[49] even though as early as 1246 envoys had come from the Caliph to the Qa'an, who – it appears – performed some expression of submission.[50] Hülegü and his armies proceeded westward, approaching Baghdad from the north. Before drawing close to the city, a number of letters were sent back and forth between the two rulers, but the Caliph refused to submit. The Mongol forces then converged on Baghdad at the start of 1258 and in early February the city wall was breached. The Caliph was taken prisoner and subsequently put to death. The city itself was given over to slaughter. Hülegü, after sending an army south to complete the conquest of southern Iraq, moved north, first to Hamadhān, and then into Azerbaijan, where he remained for more than a year, until the commencement of his campaign in Syria.[51]

Hülegü (and Möngke) probably had the vague idea of pushing on to Syria and Egypt in mind all along. This goal would have become more defined as Hülegü drew closer to the Mediterranean. Certainly by the time he reached Baghdad this aim was set in his mind. Even before the capture of that city, there is evidence that Hülegü had his eyes set on the Syrian coast when he told the general Baiju, hitherto the commander of the Mongol forces in Anatolia and Iran: "You must set out, in order to deliver those countries up to the coast of the western sea, from the hands of the sons of France and England(?)."[52] He was also thinking of Egypt at this time. During the siege of Baghdad itself, Hülegü sent back to the city two officers who had submitted to him, so that they would bring out their followers; these were to join him in the fight against Egypt.[53] After taking the city, Hülegü sent part of the booty captured to

[48] Rashīd al-Dīn, ed. ᶜAlīzādah, 3:25.

[49] Naṣīr al-Dīn al-Ṭūsī in J.A. Boyle, "The Death of the Last ᶜAbbāsid Caliph: A Contemporary Muslim Account," *JSS* 6 (1961):151–2; Ibn al-ᶜIbrī, 471; trans. in G.M. Wickens, "Naṣīr al-Dīn Ṭūsī on the Fall of Baghdad: A Further Study," *JSS* 7 (1962):32.

[50] Bar Hebraeus, *The Chronography of Gregory Abû 'l-Faraj*, tr. E.A.W. Budge (London, 1932), 1:411 (= Ibn al-ᶜIbrī, 448); John of Plano Carpini, tr. Dawson, 62 (= ed. Van den Wyngaert, 118). On early relations between the Caliphs and the Mongols, see: Wu, "Fall of Baghdad," 73–6, 131.

[51] Boyle, "Īl-Khāns," 345–50; Morgan, *Mongols*, 151–4.

[52] Rashīd al-Dīn, ed. ᶜAlīzādah, 3:39; cf. the earlier edition of E. Quatremère, *Histoire de Mongols de la Perse* (Paris, 1836), 224, who read *az kuffār* instead of *l-n-k-t-'-r*, which has been read here as a corrupted form of *ingiltera*. See P. Jackson, "Crisis," 481–513, 495, cf. *idem*, "Bāyjū," *EIr*, 4:1, where it is suggested that this conversation is apocryphal.

[53] Rashīd al-Dīn, ed. ᶜAlīzādah, 3:58. This was, however, only a ruse to get the two officers to bring out their troops and dependents. They were subsequently all killed.

Möngke, along with a message telling him of his victories and how he intended to ride on to Egypt and Syria.[54] Around 657/1258–9, Hülegü ordered the two Seljuq sultans of Rūm to Tabrīz, in order to take part in the invasion of Syria and Egypt.[55] Before he set out westward, Hülegü wrote to Badr al-Dīn Lu'lu', ruler of Mosul, that he should send his son al-Ṣāliḥ Ismāʿīl to accompany him to Syria and Egypt.[56] His letters to the premier Syrian prince, al-Nāṣir Yūsuf (see below), and his subsequent letter to Sultan Qutuz of Egypt give additional proof that his sights were set on these countries.

Hülegü's appetite for Syria was probably whetted by reports that he must have received of the fractured state of politics in that area, and in particular of the conflict between the Ayyūbid princes and the new Mamluk state in Egypt.[57] Why he waited a year and a half before setting off again on the offensive is unknown, but by the end of the summer of 657/1259 Hülegü rode out from Azerbaijan. Before moving onto Syria, he tarried in the Jazīra, putting most of it under his direct control by the end of the year, with the exception of Mayyāfāriqīn, which was to hold out until the spring of 658/1260. By the end of 657/1259, Hülegü and his army were on the verge of invading Syria.[58]

Egypt and Syria on the eve of the Mongol invasion

In 1250, the Baḥrī Mamluks deposed the Ayyūbid prince of Egypt and Damascus, al-Muʿaẓẓam Tūrānshāh b. al-Ṣāliḥ Ayyūb. With this, the Ayyūbid dynasty in Egypt was brought to an end, although it was another decade until the Baḥrīs were firmly to establish their rule in this country. In Syria, on the other hand, Ayyūbid rule continued for an additional ten years until it was obliterated by the Mongols. R. Irwin has aptly called this interim period "the turbulent decade,"[59] for it was a period of civil disorder, conspiracies, *coups d'état*, battles and political confusion. It was only in the face of the Mongol menace that some semblance of unity was achieved, and this only in Egypt.

The mamluks were slave-soldiers, mostly of Turkish origin, who had been brought when young from the wild, pagan areas to the north of the Islamic world. Upon coming to their new homes, they were converted to Islam and then underwent a rigorous religious and military training, until they were manumitted and then enrolled as mounted archers in the army of their patron. Separated as they were from their families and land of origin, on the one hand,

[54] *Ibid.*, 3:65.1
[55] Ibn Bībī, *Histoire des Seldjoucides d'Asie Mineur*, ed. T. Houtsma (Leiden, 1902), 294; trans. in H.W. Duda, *Die Seltschukengeschichte des Ibn Bībī* (Copenhagen, 1959), 281.
[56] Rashīd al-Dīn, ed. ʿAlīzādah, 3:68.
[57] See below, in the next section. Boyle's suggestion ("Īl-Khāns," 350) that Hülegü may have been motivated into invading Syria by Christian influence or his own pro-Christian feelings is not convincing; see Jackson, "Crisis," *passim*.
[58] Humphreys, *Saladin*, 344–5; Boyle, "Īl-Khāns," 349–50.
[59] The title of chapter 2 of his *The Middle East in the Middle Ages*.

and the local population, on the other, they maintained a strong loyalty to both their patron and their comrades in slavery. Mamluk society was a continually replicating one-generation military aristocracy, that is, the sons of mamluks could not become mamluks. The mamluk ranks were replenished by the influx of new, young slave recruits.[60]

From the beginning of the Ayyūbid period, even during Saladin's reign, Mamluk units and *amīrs* (officers) played an important and often decisive role in both the military campaigns and political events.[61] It was the last important Ayyūbid sultan in Egypt, al-Ṣāliḥ Ayyūb (637–47/1240–9), who unwittingly laid the foundations of the Mamluk Sultanate. Distrustful of his non-mamluk troops and taking advantage of the flooded slave-markets, an indirect result of the Mongol invasions of southern Russia, he founded the Baḥriyya mamluk regiment. This unit, numbering some 800–1000 men, was to save the day against the Franks at the battle of al-Manṣūra in 647/1250. They were the driving force behind the ending of the Ayyūbid regime and the establishment of the Mamluk Sultanate.[62]

It is worth dwelling on the impact of the Mongol campaigns in the steppe of southern Russia on the formation of the Baḥriyya. The Mamluk writers were certainly aware of this connection. The earliest writer whom I have found to make this link is al-Nuwayrī (d. 732/1332), who writes after describing the difficulties that the early Ayyūbids had in procuring mamluks from the Qipchaq Turkish tribes of the southern Russian steppes, that:

> The [Mongols] fell upon [the Qipchaqs] and brought upon most of them death, slavery and captivity. At this time, merchants bought [these captives] and brought them to the [various] countries and cities. The first who demanded many of them and made them lofty and advanced them in the army was al-Malik al-Ṣāliḥ Najm al-Dīn Ayyūb . . .[63]

In other words, the Mongols unintentionally and indirectly helped create the force which was to stop them at ʿAyn Jālūt in 1260 and was to frustrate their plans to conquer Syria in the succeeding years.

The end of Ayyūbid rule in Egypt came about soon after the victory at al-

[60] This sketch is based on the articles of Prof. D. Ayalon, most of which have been collected in two books: *Studies on the Mamlūks of Egypt* (London, 1977); *The Mamlūk Military Society* (London, 1979). See also R. Amitai, "The Rise and Fall of the Mamlūk Military Institution: A Summary of David Ayalon's Works," in M. Sharon (ed.), *Studies in Islamic History and Civilization in Honour of Professor David Ayalon* (Jerusalem and Leiden, 1986), 19–30, esp. 20.

[61] D. Ayalon, "Aspects of the Mamlūk Phenomenon: Ayyūbids, Kurds and Turks," *Der Islam* 54 (1977):1–32.

[62] Ayalon, "Aspects," 23–5. A discussion of al-Ṣāliḥ Ayyūb's mamluk policy is found in A. Levanoni, "The Mamluks' Ascent to Power in Egypt," *SI* 72 (1990):122–6; Thorau, *Baybars*, 14–23.

[63] Nuwayrī, *Nihāyat al-arab*, MS. Leiden Univ., MS. Or. 2m, fol. 114a. See also Ibn Khaldūn, *Kitāb al-ʿibar* (Bulāq, 1284/1867–8), 5:371–2; Ibn al-Duqmaq [Duqmāq], *Kitāb al-jawhar al-thamīn* (Mecca, n.d.), 255; Qalqashandī, *Ṣubḥ al-aʿshā* (Cairo, 1913–19), 4:458; Ayalon, "Yāsa," pt. C1, 117–24; *idem*, "The Wafidiya in the Mamluk Kingdom," *Islamic Culture* 25 (1951):88; R.S. Humphreys, "The Emergence of the Mamluk Army," *SI* 45 (1977):95–6.

Manṣūra. Al-Ṣāliḥ Ayyūb had died just prior to this battle and was replaced by his son al-Muʿaẓẓam Tūrānshāh, who quickly succeeded in alienating the military elite in general, and the mamluks of his father, the Baḥriyya, in particular.[64] The latter group spearheaded the conspiracy that led to Tūrānshāh's death. But the Baḥriyya, who were strong enough to depose the sultan, were unable to gain control of the state. True, another former mamluk of al-Ṣāliḥ, the amir Aybeg, gained ascendency, but he showed himself to be an active opponent of the Baḥriyya, as did his mamluk and eventual successor Qutuz, the other strong sultan of this decade. Only with the victory at ʿAyn Jālūt was the Baḥriyya, led by Baybars al-Bunduqdārī, able to assert itself as the leading group within the Egyptian and Syrian military elite.[65]

Two points interest us here. The first is that Baybars and most of the Baḥriyya, totalling some 700 mamluks, were forced to abscond to Syria in 652/1254. The Sultan Aybeg, afraid of their power, had felt strong enough to confront them, and began by murdering their leader, Fāris al-Dīn Aqtay. Baybars and his comrades fled for fear of their lives, and spent the next several years alternately serving al-Nāṣir Yūsuf, ruler of Aleppo and Damascus, and al-Mughīth ʿUmar, ruler of Karak.[66] Only on the eve of the Mongol invasion of Syria did Baybars and several of his comrades return to Egypt, both alienated by al-Nāṣir Yūsuf's inability to adopt a decisive policy towards the Mongols and aware that serving the Syrian Ayyūbids had little future.

The second point is the rise to power of Qutuz, originally a mamluk of the recently assassinated Aybeg (655/1257). Ruling first through the son of the latter, Qutuz at the end of 657/1259 succeeded in deposing this puppet-sultan and placed himself on the throne, using as a pretext the need for a strong leader in the face of the Mongol advance, certainly a cogent argument. It was soon after this that Baybars and Qutuz, actual killer of the late Baḥrī leader Aqtay, were reconciled and Baybars returned to Egypt.[67]

On the eve of the Mongol invasion, Muslim Syria was essentially divided up among three Ayyūbid princes. Most important was al-Nāṣir Yūsuf b. al-ʿAzīz Muḥammad, ruler of Aleppo and Damascus. Aleppo had long been in his family, but it was only in 648/1250, with the assassination of Tūrānshāh, also ruler of Damascus, that al-Nāṣir Yūsuf was able to gain control of that city. In Hama ruled al-Manṣūr Muḥammad b. al-Muẓaffar Maḥmūd. He was, however, completely subservient to al-Nāṣir Yūsuf. In Karak, al-Mughīth

[64] This was a common phenomenon in Mamluk society; see D. Ayalon, "Studies on the Structure of the Mamlūk Army," pt. 1, *BSOAS* 15 (1953):217–20.

[65] On the end of the Ayyūbid rule in Egypt and events during the subsequent decade, see: Irwin, *Middle East*, 21–9; Humphreys, *Saladin*, 302–30; Holt, *Crusades*, 82–89; Thorau, *Baybars*, 33–58; Levanoni, "The Mamluks' Ascent to Power," 121–44.

[66] D. Ayalon, "Le régiment Bahriya dans l'armée mamelouke," *REI* 19 (1951):135–6; Humphreys, *Saladin*, 326–33, 341–4; Irwin, *Middle East*, 30.

[67] Irwin, *Middle East*, 29, 32–3; Humphreys, *Saladin*, 345; Thorau, *Baybars*, 51–66. See also below.

ʿUmar b. al-ʿĀdil Abū Bakr b. al-Kāmil Muḥammad had established himself in the same year that al-Nāṣir Yūsuf took Damascus. He not only maintained his independence from Damascus, but with the support of the Baḥriyya and other freebooters attempted several times to take both it and even Egypt. During al-Ṣāliḥ Ayyūb's reign, several smaller Ayyūbid principalities – Bosra, Baalbek and Banias – had been eliminated and integrated into the united sultanate of Egypt and Damascus. These were also absorbed by al-Nāṣir Yūsuf when he gained control of Damascus. The last prince of Banias, al-Saʿīd Ḥasan, was still alive and languishing in prison in the fortress of al-Bīra on the Euphrates. We are to meet him again in the service of the Mongols. Likewise, the former prince of Homs, al-Ashraf Mūsā b. al-Manṣūr Ibrāhīm, deposed by al-Nāṣir Yūsuf in 646/1248 and given the very minor principality of Tall Bāshir instead, was also to throw in his lot with the Mongols. In fact, after 651/1253–4, out of hatred for al-Nāṣir Yūsuf, al-Ashraf was corresponding with the Mongols. He evidently encouraged them to invade Syria, thus hoping he would be able to win back his own principality or even take al-Nāṣir's place.[68]

Grousset has described al-Nāṣir Yūsuf as "une personage médiocre et sans courage."[69] Perhaps this is overstating the case somewhat, but al-Nāṣir reveals himself, at least in the later part of his regime, to be extremely irresolute in times of crisis, and his "indecision and lack of personal courage"[70] during the Mongol invasion of Syria was to have far-reaching consequences for Muslim Syria, let alone for himself. Al-Nāṣir had formally submitted to the Mongols many years before Hülegü's arrival on the scene. As early as 641/1243–4, there is information that al-Nāṣir, still only prince of Aleppo, as well as the current Ayyūbid ruler of "Syria" (evidently meaning Damascus, that is, al-Ṣāliḥ Ismāʿīl) sent an envoy to Arghun Aqa, the newly arrived Mongol viceroy in the conquered areas of the Islamic world, then at Tabrīz.[71] It is reported that from the subsequent year (642/1244–5) al-Nāṣir Yūsuf was paying tribute to the Mongols.[72] This may or may not be identical with the annual tribute which he paid to Baiju, commander of Mongol forces in western Asia since 1241.[73] In 643/1245–6, al-Nāṣir sent a relative as an envoy to Güyük Qa'an in Mongolia, who returned with *yarlighs* defining al-Nāṣir's obligations to the Qa'an.[74]

68 For al-Ashraf's pro-Mongol sympathies, see Yūnīnī, *Dhayl mir'at al-zamān* (Hyderabad, 1954–61), 2:311–12. For events in Syria in the decade before the Mongol invasion, see Humphreys, *Saladin*, ch. 9; Thorau, *Baybars*, 51–8.

69 R. Grousset, *L'Empire des steppes* (rpt., Paris, 1949), 434; cited in Boyle, "Īl-Khāns," 350.

70 Humphreys, *Saladin*, 321.

71 Juwaynī, 2:244 (= tr. Boyle, 2:508); Boyle, "Īl-Khāns," 338.

72 Ibn Shaddād, *al-Aʿlāq al-khaṭīra*, vol. 3: *Ta'rīkh al-jazīra*, ed. Y. ʿAbbāra (Damascus, 1978), 485; summary in H.F. Amedroz, "Three Arabic MSS on the History of the City of Mayyāfāriqīn," *JRAS* (1902):806. Previously, Ibn Shaddād (*Aʿlāq*, 3:472–3) reported that the Mongols raided the environs of Aleppo in AH 641–2. This was surely connected to the sending of tribute and possibly the dispatch of the embassy the previous year.

73 Ibn al-ʿAmīd, *Kitāb al-majmūʿ al-mubārak*, in C. Cahen (ed.), "La 'Chronique Ayyoubides' d'al-Makīn b. al-ʿAmīd," *BEO* 15 (1955–7):163.

74 Ibn Shaddād, *Aʿlāq*, 3:237–42 (summarized by Amedroz, "Arabic MSS," 803); Juwaynī, 1:205, 212 (= tr. Boyle, 1:250, 257); Bar Hebraeus, 411 (= Ibn al-ʿIbrī, 448); Simon de Saint-

Some years later, in 648/1250, al-Nāṣir Yūsuf dispatched another mission to the Mongol capital of Qaraqorum. The mission, which was to express submission to the soon-to-be elected Möngke Qa'an, was led by al-Zayn al-Ḥāfiẓī, who later played an important role in dissuading al-Nāṣir Yūsuf from resisting Hülegü in 1260. It was probably at this time that al-Zayn al-Ḥāfiẓī began secretly serving the Mongols. The mission returned to Damascus late in 649/1251, bringing tokens of Möngke's recognition of al-Nāṣir's submission and his confirmation as a Mongol vassal.[75] This same year (649/1251–2), there is mention of envoys sent by Baiju to demand what appears to be additional tribute.[76]

From this time until the conquest of Baghdad by Hülegü in 656/1258, there is no explicit record of additional missions between al-Nāṣir Yūsuf and the Mongols. Other Ayyūbids, however, felt it wise to dispatch envoys or even to go personally before the Qa'an in order to express their submission and to arrange their position in the emerging Mongol order. Al-Kāmil Muḥammad b. al-Muẓaffar Ghāzī, ruler of Mayyāfāriqīn, arrived at Möngke's court at the end of 650/February 1253, as part of a pledge to end a Mongol siege of his city. When al-Kāmil reached the Qa'an's court he found there the heirs apparent of Mosul and Mārdīn, as well as Leon (Layfūn), prince of Cilician Armenia.[77] Al-Kāmil, however, was to throw off allegiance to the Mongols as soon as he returned to his city in early 655/1257.[78] William of Rubruck reports that when he arrived at Möngke's court at the end of AD 1253, he met a Christian from Damascus who claimed he was on a mission for the Sultan of Mont Real (= Shawbak) and Crac (= Karak), "who wished to become a tributary and friend of the Tartars."[79] This "sultan" is al-Mughīth ᶜUmar, who evidently thought it expedient to ingratiate himself with the Mongols at this time, although he was not yet in any immediate danger from them.

For some unknown reason, with the coming of Hülegü to Iraq, al-Nāṣir Yūṣuf changed his mind about the wisdom of his submissive policy. Al-Nāṣir had probably been called upon, like all the other princes of the Muslim world who had already submitted in one form or another, to assist Hülegü in his conquest. This demand was made even before Hülegü crossed the Oxus.[80] Ibn al-ᶜAmīd writes that al-Nāṣir paid no attention to Hülegü when he conquered Iran, not sending him an envoy or gifts. This especially galled the Khan, since previously al-Nāṣir had sent gifts to Baiju, now his subordinate.[81]

When news that Baghdad had been taken reached Damascus, al-Nāṣir Yūsuf again reversed his policy, and sought to reconcile Hülegü by sending

Quentin, *Histoire des Tartares*, ed. J. Richard (Paris, 1965), 112 (I am grateful to Dr. Jackson for this last reference).

75 Ibn al-ᶜAmīd, 163; Ibn al-Furāt, *Ta'rīkh al-duwal wa'l-mulūk*, MS. Vatican Ar. 726, fol. 145b; Rashīd al-Dīn, ed. ᶜAlīzādah, 3:67–8; Humphreys, *Saladin*, 334–5, and 466 nn. 40–1.

76 Ibn Shaddād, *Aᶜlāq*, 3:237–8; Amedroz, "Arabic MSS," 802–3.

77 Yūnīnī, 1:431; 2:75–6; Ibn Shaddād, *Aᶜlāq*, 3:476–81; trans. in C. Cahen, "La Djazira au milieu du treizième siècle d'après ᶜIzz ad-Din Ibn Chaddad," *REI* 8 (1934):121–2; Humphreys, *Saladin*, 335, 466 n. 42.

78 Ibn Shaddād, *Aᶜlāq*, 3:481, 484.

79 Tr. Jackson, 184 (= ed. Van den Wyngaert, 253); see n. 1 there.

80 Rashīd al-Dīn, ed. ᶜAlīzādah, 3:67–8.

81 Ibn al-ᶜAmīd, 163, 167–8.

him gifts and submissive messages. It appears that al-Nāṣir hoped, at least for a while, to prevent a Mongol attack by tendering his submission, although in an equivocal manner. Al-Nāṣir's ambivalent policy and his frequent changes of heart were a mixture of his own indecisive nature plus the divided opinions of those around him. On the one hand, there were the "defeatists," who counselled a submissive policy to the Mongols. Prominent members of this group were the Ayyūbid al-Ṣāliḥ Nūr al-Dīn Ismāᶜīl b. Shīrkūh and the high bureaucrat al-Zayn al-Ḥāfiẓī, both secretly loyal to the Mongols.[82] Other members of this "peace-party" were the previously mentioned Ayyūbid al-Ashraf Mūsā, also in contact with the Mongols, Najm al-Dīn Muḥammad b. al-Iftikhār Yāqūt, the *amīr ḥājib* (Chief Chamberlain), and the merchant, Wajīh al-Dīn Muḥammad al-Takrītī.[83] The Kurdish amirs (probably the Qaymariyya) were also known for their "defeatist" opinions.[84] On the other hand, the militant approach was represented by Baybars al-Bunduqdārī (at least from mid-657/1260, when he returned to al-Nāṣir's service), the amir ᶜImād al-Dīn Ibrāhīm b. al-Mujīr (?), and the amirs from the Nāṣiriyya, that is, al-Nāṣir Yūsuf's own mamluks.[85]

According to Rashīd al-Dīn, envoys of al-Nāṣir Yūsuf arrived in Baghdad as early as 19 Rabīᶜ I 656/26 March 1258. Hülegü, however, had already left the city on 23 Ṣafar/12 March for his *ordo* (camp) in Azerbaijan, so they set out after him.[86] Upon arriving they were given a letter written in Arabic by the Shīᶜī scholar, Nāṣir al-Dīn al-Ṭūsī, now in Hülegü's entourage.[87] Rashīd al-Dīn gives the text of a letter,[88] but this may be a rendition of a later missive (see below), since the first line of both are similar. The text of the actual letter may be the first of three letters sent by Hülegü to al-Nāṣir Yūsuf, which are related in the admittedly late source *Ta'rīkh al-khulafā'* by al-Suyūṭī (d. 911/1505). This letter, transmitted only by al-Suyūṭī, was perhaps also composed by al-Ṭūsī. It describes how Hülegü came to Iraq, conquered Baghdad and killed the Caliph because of his falsehood. Al-Nāṣir Yūsuf is commanded to give his answer: does he submit to or will he resist Hülegü. As a final note, al-Nāṣir is told to level his fortresses.[89] Although it is not stated so here, it would seem that it was conveyed to al-Nāṣir, either in writing or verbally, that he was to come to Hülegü.

Still in 656/1258–9, al-Nāṣir Yūsuf responded to Hülegü's letter by dis-

[82] Yūnīnī, 2:126–7; on al-Zayn al-Ḥāfiẓī, see n. 90 below.

[83] Ibn al-ᶜAmīd, 170; Ibn Shaddād, *Aᶜlāq*, 3:486; *idem*, *Ta'rīkh al-malik al-ẓāhir*, ed. A. Ḥuṭayṭ (Wiesbaden, 1983), 48.

[84] Ibn al-Furāt, MS. Vatican, fols. 220b–221a.

[85] Yūnīnī, 2:127; 3:243, plus the sources cited in ch. 2, nn. 59–60. On the struggle between the "defeatists" and "militants" among the Syrian amirs and officials, see Ayalon, "Aspects," 27–8.

[86] Rashīd al-Dīn, ed. ᶜAlīzādah, 3:62–3. Ibn al-Kathīr, *Bidāya wa'l-nihāya*, (rpt., Beirut, 1977), 13:203, writes that Hülegü left Baghdad in Jumādā I 656/May-June 1258.

[87] On this scholar, see: R. Strothmann, "al-Ṭūsī," *EI*[1], 4:980–1.

[88] Rashīd al-Dīn, ed. ᶜAlīzādah, 3:63.

[89] Suyūṭī, *Ta'rīkh al-khulafā'* (Miṣr [Cairo], 1351/1932), 314; trans. in H.S. Jarrett, *History of the Caliphs*, (Calcutta, 1881), 499.

patching his young son al-ʿAzīz, along with al-Zayn al-Ḥāfiẓī and several amirs. They brought with them gifts of various kinds. When Hülegü asked why al-Nāṣir had not come himself, the excuse was offered that he could not leave Syria in the face of the Frankish threat. Hülegü, however, was not placated by this answer, although publicly he pretended that he accepted it, and treated al-ʿAzīz well. During his stay, al-Zayn al-Ḥāfiẓī spoke several times secretly with Hülegü and urged him to invade Syria. This mission stayed some time with the Mongols: Ibn al-ʿAmīd writes that they only returned on 15 Shaʿbān 657/7 August 1259. They reported that Hülegü had received the present, and was in good spirits and was no longer angry with al-Nāṣir Yūsuf.[90] They also brought another letter from Hülegü. Again it is recounted that the Caliph was killed for his falsehoods. When al-Nāṣir received this letter, he was to come with his soldiers and his wealth in order to submit to the "sultan of the world, supreme king of the face of the earth" (*sulṭān al-arḍ shāhinshāh-i rūy-i zamīn*). Al-Nāṣir was not to delay his envoys as previously. The letter states that there is nowhere to hide from the Mongols. Like the previous letter, this one is accompanied by citations from the Qur'ān and Arabic poetry. The message, however, is purely Mongolian: submit to the lawful ruler of the earth or be prepared to be destroyed.[91]

Also early in 657/1258–9, al-Nāṣir Yūsuf sent another envoy, the author ʿIzz al-Dīn ibn Shaddād al-Ḥalabī. His mission was to travel to the besieged city of Mayyāfāriqīn, in order to meet with the Mongol commander Yoshmut, the son of Hülegü, and to get him to desist from attacking the city. Soon after he set out, Ibn Shaddād ran into Mongol envoys at Hama, presumably on their way to al-Nāṣir Yūsuf. Ibn Shaddād eventually reached Yoshmut, although he and his companions suffered from Mongol depredations en route. He was unsuccessful in convincing the Mongol commander to give up the siege. Instead, the Mongols tried to use Ibn Shaddād to draw out the ruler of Mayyāfāriqīn, al-Kāmil, from his besieged city. After some wrangling and threats, Ibn Shaddād agreed, but nothing came of this intervention. He subsequently returned to Syria with no message.[92]

The third extant letter was brought probably at some point in late 657/1259 by Mongol envoys (*ilchis*). The letter is addressed to al-Nāṣir and his amirs, two of whom are named. It opens with a recapitulation of the taking of

[90] Ibn al-ʿAmīd, 168; Ibn Wāṣil, *Mufarrij al-kurūb*, MS. Bibliothèque Nationale, ar. 1703, fol. 140a–b; Ibn al-Furāt, MS. Vatican, fols. 203b, 217b; Maqrīzī, *Kitāb al-sulūk*, ed. M.M. Ziyāda and S.ʿA-F. ʿĀshūr (Cairo, 1934–73), 1:410–11; Ibn al-Ṣuqāʿī, *Tālī kitāb wafayāt al-aʿyān*, ed. J. Sublet (Damascus, 1974), 78, 167; Ibn Kathīr, 13:215.

[91] Qirtay [Qirṭāy] al-Khaznadārī, *Ta'rīkh al-nawādir*, MS. Gotha 1655, fol. 57a–b; cited in Ibn al-Furāt, MS. Vatican, fol. 218b; Maqrīzī, 1:415–16. A parallel letter, with both similar and convergent parts, is found in Suyūṭī, 315 (= tr. Jarrett, 499–500), who calls this the "second letter." See also W. Brinner, "Some Ayyūbid and Mamlūk Documents from Non-archival Sources," *IOS* 2 (1972):121.

[92] Ibn Shaddād, *Aʿlāq*, 3:491–9. For a discussion and partial translation of this passage, see Amitai-Preiss, "Evidence," 354–7; see also Y. Koch, "ʿIzz al-Dīn ibn Shaddād and his Biography of Baybars," *Annali dell'Istituto Universitario Orientale* 43 (1983):251 and n. 9.

Baghdad and the reason the Caliph was killed. Then comes a long description of Mongol might, their right to conquer the world and the fate of those who resist. Finally, there is a call to submit or face the consequences.[93]

By now, however, al-Nāṣir Yūsuf had adopted a defiant attitude towards the Mongols. He sent off a belligerent answer to Hülegü, contrasting the latter's disbelief with his own Islam. Hülegü's call for submission was spurned and he declared himself ready for war.[94] Towards the end of 657/1259, having heard of the Mongol advance towards Syria, al-Nāṣir both sent an envoy to Egypt to ask for help,[95] and set up camp at Barza, some 5 km to the north of Damascus. It is said that besides his army he was joined by bedouins, Persians, Kurds, Türkmen and volunteers of unspecified origin (*mutaṭawwiʿa*).[96] Al-Nāṣir's new-found resolve, however, was short-lived, and his natural indecisiveness soon got the better of him, leading in the end to the disintegration of his army, the end of his kingdom and his own capture and eventual death.

Two other political entities were found in or near Syria at this time. The first of these were the Crusader states, namely the Principality of Antioch and County of Tripoli in the north and the so-called Kingdom of Jerusalem centered at Acre. Already in 1246, it is reported that Bohemond V of Antioch, along with King Hetʿum of Cilician Armenia (see below), had become a tributary of the Mongols.[97] In 1259, as the Mongols approached Antioch, his son and successor, Bohemond VI, went with his father-in-law, the same Hetʿum, and made his submission to Hülegü. From here on, Antioch was to pursue a distinctly pro-Mongol policy, without, however, being able to enjoy any significant Mongol protection.[98] Further south, the Kingdom at Acre, ruled by the barons, heads of the military orders, and the local representatives of the Italian communes, adopted a much less sanguine approach towards the Mongols. As early as the end of 1256, they had been expecting a Mongol invasion of Syria and were quite disconcerted by the prospect. At this date at least, the Franks of the Syrian coast saw no advantage to be gained by the intrusion of the Mongols into their country and sought neither to make an alliance with them nor to tender their submission.[99]

[93] Ibn al-ʿIbrī, 484 (cf. Bar Hebraeus, 434); Waṣṣāf, *Tajziyat al-amṣār wa-tazjiyat al-aʿṣār* (rpt., Teheran, 1338/1959–60 of ed. Bombay, 1269/1852–3), 43–4; Brinner, "Documents," 127–36 (esp. 120–1, for a discussion of Ṭūsī's authorship of the letter). This text was used, with appropriate changes, by Hülegü in his letter to Qutuz in 658/1260; see below in chap. 2. A shorter and somewhat different version of this letter is found in Suyūṭī, 314–15 (= tr. Jarrett, 500), who lists this as Hülegü's "third letter." This last mentioned version is also found in Dhahabī, *al-Mukhtār min ta'rīkh al-jazarī*, MS. Köprülü 1147, fol. 83b, but it is stated there that this was a letter from Hülegü which was read to the people of Damascus after al-Nāṣir Yūsuf had fled. The short Arabic text in Rashīd al-Dīn, ed. ʿAlīzādah, 3:63, is apparently based on this third letter, as the opening sentence is the same in both.

[94] Waṣṣāf, 44–5; Brinner, "Documents," 136–43; Amitai-Preiss, "Evidence," 360.

[95] See Humphreys, *Saladin*, 345.

[96] Ibn Wāṣil, MS. 1703, fol. 146b; Kutubī, *ʿUyūn al-tawārīkh*, vol. 20, ed. F. Sāmir and N. Dāwūd (Baghdad, 1980), 214.

[97] Jackson, "Crisis," 488; Prawer, *Histoire*, 2:421–2.

[98] Runciman, *Crusades*, 3:306; Cahen, *Syrie*, 702–3.

[99] Jackson, "Crisis," 489–90; Cahen, *Syrie*, 708–9 and n. 22.

The second force, not centered in Syria proper, was the Kingdom of Cilicia or Lesser Armenia, with its capital at Sīs. Its king, Hetʿum, quickly made his submission to the Mongols after the defeat they had dealt his neighbors, the Seljuqs of Rūm, in 1243. Four years later, Hetʿum sent his brother, the constable (and historian) Smpad, to the Qa'an at Qaraqorum. Smpad returned in 1250. In 1253 Hetʿum himself went to the Mongol court and was absent for three years. His namesake and relative, the historian, Hetʿum, would have us believe that it was the Armenian king himself who prevailed on Möngke to send Hülegü west, in order to conquer Baghdad and liberate the Holy Land, which would then be returned to the Christians. This report can be questioned, not least because of the historian Hetʿum's well-known tendency to rewrite history as he would have liked to have seen it.[100] On the other hand, as Professor Cahen has suggested, perhaps King Hetʿum brought to Möngke's attention the Mediterranean areas about which he had not yet given any serious thought. King Hetʿum was a major influence in bringing his son-in-law, Bohemond VI of Antioch, into the Mongol camp, although political realities also must have played their part. From the beginning, the Armenians were the main pro-Mongol boosters among the Christians, and from an early date both Armenian rulers and writers made attempts to interest the Christian west in a Mongol–Christian alliance against the Muslims. After the first Mongol setbacks in Syria in 1260, the pro-Mongol policy of the Armenian king as well as his raids into northern Syria were to target his kingdom for attack by the Mamluks.[101]

[100] Hetʿum (Hayton or Hethoum), "La Flor des estories de la Terre d'Orient," *RHC, Ar*, 2:163–5; Jackson, "Crisis," 485–6.

[101] Runciman, *Crusades*, 294; T.S.R. Boase, "The History of the Kingdom," in *idem* (ed.), *The Cilician Kingdom of Armenia* (Edinburgh, 1978), 25–6; S. Der Nersessian, "The Kingdom of Cilician Armenia," in K.M. Setton, *History of the Crusades*, vol. 2 (Philadelphia, 1962), 652–3; Cahen, *Syrie*, 696, 700–1; M. Canard, "La royaume d'Arménie-Cilicie et les Mamelouks jusqu'au traité de 1285," *Revue des études arméniennes* 4 (1967):217–19.

CHAPTER 2

The battle of ᶜAyn Jālūt

Then when Ḳôtâz the Turk, who reigned in Egypt, heard that the King of Kings [Hülegü] had gone away . . . and that Kît Bôghâ alone with ten thousand men remained in Palestine, he collected the armies of Egypt and sallied forth and met the Tatars in battle in the plain of Baishân . . .

Bar Hebraeus[1]

The Mongol invasion of Syria

At the beginning of AH 658 (the year commencing on 18 December 1259), Mongol troops under Hülegü, accompanied by Georgian, Armenian and Rūmī Seljuq contingents, crossed the Euphrates and took up position outside Aleppo.[2] Already at the end of the previous *hijrī* year a Mongol force had penetrated Syria, raided as far as Aleppo, inflicting a severe beating on a local force before withdrawing.[3] This time, however, the Mongols had more than a transitory raid in mind. Al-Nāṣir Yūsuf's governor, the venerable al-Malik al-Muᶜaẓẓam Tūrānshāh (a son of Saladin), was called upon to surrender. His refusal led to the investment of the city on 2 Ṣafar/18 January. It was taken a week later, and was subjected to the usual slaughter and looting. The defenders of the citadel continued to resist and it took another month before it capitulated. Surprisingly enough, Hülegü let the defenders live, although the citadel itself was subsequently destroyed.[4] Thereupon Hülegü marched west-

1 Tr. Budge, 437 (= Ibn al-ᶜIbrī, 489).

2 Ibn Wāṣil, MS. 1703, fol. 149a, who also speaks of Persians; Kutubī, 20:214; Canard, "Arménie," 219, also cites Ibn Shaddād, *al-Aᶜlāq al-khaṭīra*, vol. 1, pt. 1: *Ta'rīkh ḥalab*, ed. D. Sourdel (Damascus, 1953), 36; Cahen, *Syrie*, 705. On the Seljuq contingents, led by the joint sultans ᶜIzz al-Dīn Kaykāwūs and Rukn al-Dīn Qilich Arslan, see Ibn Bībī, 294–5 (= tr. Duda, 281); *Zubda*, fols. 35b–36a; Qalqashandī, 5:361.

3 Ibn Wāṣil, MS. 1703, fol. 148a–b; Nuwayrī, *Nihāyat al-arab*, vol. 27 (Cairo, 1984):386; Kutubī, 20:215.

4 For these dates and details of the siege itself, see Abū Shāma, *Dhayl ᶜalā al-rawḍatayn* (Cairo, 1947), 203; Ibn Wāṣil, MS. 1703, fols. 149a–150a; Yūnīnī, 1:349; 2:312; Nuwayrī, 27:387–8; Ibn Shaddād, *Aᶜlāq*, vol. 1, pt. 1:36 (city taken on 10 Ṣafar). For different dates, see Ibn al-ᶜAmīd, 171 (the city was taken at the end of Muḥarram; the citadel on 10 Ṣafar/26 January); and in his aftermath, Ibn al-Furāt, MS. Vatican, fols. 226b–227a; Maqrīzī, 1:422–3. Also cf.

ward and obtained the surrender of Ḥārim, which was still sacked for temporizing,[5] and then apparently returned to the neighborhood of Aleppo,[6] where he received delegations of notables from Hama and Homs who tendered the submission of their cities. The Ayyūbid ruler of Hama, al-Manṣūr Muḥammad, had already left his city to join al-Nāṣir Yūsuf at Damascus and eventually made his way to Egypt with his army.[7] Homs had been under the direct control of al-Nāṣir Yūsuf. Al-Ashraf Mūsā, the former ruler of Homs who had long been secretly loyal to the Mongols, now came to Hülegü from Damascus in order to submit personally and received his old principality in return.[8]

Even before the taking of Aleppo's citadel, Hülegü had sent south a corps under one of his most trusted generals, Ketbugha.[9] Hülegü himself did not remain in Aleppo for long. Taking with him the vast majority of his army, he began to move eastward, leaving Ketbugha in charge,[10] along with those troops he had previously assigned to him.[11] It appears that Ketbugha's force numbered in the region of 10–12,000 troops, although the possibility of a larger number cannot be dismissed.[12]

Hülegü left Syria by the northeast, passing Sarūj some time in mid-spring

Qirtay, fols. 58b–59a (cited also in Ibn al-Furāt, fol. 231a), who writes that Aleppo was captured in Ṣafar, after a seven-day siege, and the citadel was taken after another seven days. For the Mongol view, see Rashīd al-Dīn, ed. ʿAlīzādah, 3:67–9 (who says that the city was taken in Dhū 'l-ḥijja 657!). For the Mongol administration of the city, see *ibid.*, 69; Ibn al-Fuwaṭī, *al-Ḥawādith al-jamīʿa*, ed. M. Jawād (Baghdad, 1351/1232–3), 342.

5 Abū 'l-Fidā', *al-Mukhtaṣar fī ta'rīkh al-bashar* (Istanbul, 1286/1869–70), 3:212; Rashīd al-Dīn, ed. ʿAlīzādah, 3:69; Bar Hebraeus, 436 (= Ibn al-ʿIbrī, 487).

6 The Arabic and contemporary Persian sources are virtually unanimous that Hülegü stayed in north Syria. Only Maqrīzī, 1:423 claims that Hülegü subsequently advanced to Damascus; this sentence is not found in the parallel passage in Ibn al-Furāt, MS. Vatican, fol. 233a, and appears to be an unjustified extrapolation by Maqrīzī. Various Armenian sources write that Hülegü went to Damascus and Jerusalem: Kirakos, in E. Dulaurier, "Les Mongols d'après les historiens arméniens," *JA* 5 ser., 11 (1858):498; Grigor of Akancʿ [Akner], "History of the Nation of the Archers," tr. and ed. R.P. Blake and R.N. Frye, *HJAS* 12 (1949):349; Stepʿanos Orbellian, in M. Brosset, *Histoire de la Siounnie* (St. Petersburg, 1860–4), 1:227, but this surely must be understood to mean that Mongol troops reached these cities.

7 Ibn Wāṣil, MS. 1703, fols. 150a, 151a–b. For the Mongol administration in Hama, see Nuwayrī, 27:388–9. 8 Ibn Wāṣil, MS. 1703, fol. 150a.

9 As seen above, the citadel of Aleppo was taken on 29 Ṣafar/14 February, while Ketbugha entered Damascus on the same date; see below, p. 30.

10 Maqrīzī's statement (1:427) that Baydarā (= Baydar in Rashīd al-Dīn) was appointed co-governor with Ketbugha in Syria (Baydarā in Damascus, Ketbugha in Aleppo) is surely incorrect; see Amitai-Preiss, "ʿAyn Jālūt," 124–5.

11 Nuwayrī, 27:390, explicitly states that Hülegü left Ketbugha in Syria with the same number of troops which he had originally sent with him to the south.

12 These sources state that Ketbugha was left as commander and give the following numbers. 10,000: Bar Hebraeus, 1:436 (= Ibn al-ʿIbrī, 489); Hetʿum, 173; *Faḍl*, fol. 55a, who states that Ketbugha commanded a *tümen*, "that is to say, 10,000 men." 12,000: *Zubda*, fol. 37b; *Tuḥfa*, 43; Nuwayrī, 27:390 (follows Baybars, *Zubda*). 20,000: Kirakos, tr. Dulaurier, 498; Vardan, in R.W. Thomson, "The Historical Compilation of Vardan Arewelcʿi," *DOP* 43 (1989):218. For a discussion of these and other figures, and the reasoning behind the adoption of 10–12,000, see Amitai-Preiss, "ʿAyn Jālūt," 123–5. Cf. Smith, "ʿAyn Jālūt," 309–11.

658/1260[13] and then Akhlāṭ on 26 Jumādā II/7 June 1260,[14] and eventually established his camp in Azerbaijan, in the environs of Tabrīz.[15] Scholars have traditionally explained Hülegü's withdrawal from Syria as a response to the news of the death of Möngke Qa'an, Hülegü's brother (in August 1259), and the subsequent struggle over the succession.[16] There is certainly evidence for this suggestion. Rashīd al-Dīn connects Hülegü's withdrawal from Syria with the sorrow he felt at Möngke's death as well as the news of Arigh-böke's "rebellion," but does not hint at his plans.[17] It is possible that Hülegü thought himself a candidate for the throne,[18] but considering what appears to be a leisurely march from Syria, this seems unlikely. More probable in prompting Hülegü to set out eastward were reports which reached him of the struggle between the two other brothers, Arigh-böke and Qubilai, over the succession.[19]

Recently, an alternative explanation has been offered by Dr. Morgan: Hülegü withdrew because of the lack of adequate pasture land in Syria for his enormous army, mostly composed of cavalry.[20] The main basis for this suggestion is the letter sent by Hülegü to King Louis IX of France in 1262, in which it is claimed that the withdrawal of the majority of his forces from Syria was due to the lack of fodder and grazing there.[21] This would seem a reasonable explanation, although a certain amount of caution must be taken with excuses for failure: it was, after all, Hülegü's withdrawal that led to the defeat at ʿAyn Jālūt. Be that as it may, logistics may explain why Hülegü departed with a large portion of his army, but it does not explain why he withdrew with the overwhelming majority of his troops and left such a small force.

We must look elsewhere for the reason as it would seem that Syria's resources, at least those which interested the Mongols – fodder, grazing land

[13] It was in Sarūj, according to Ibn Shaddād, *Aʿlāq*, 3:504, that Hülegü interviewed and executed al-Kāmil Muḥammad, prince of Mayyāfāriqīn, which was captured on 23 Rabīʿ II/7 April; al-Kāmil's head was sent to Syria where it arrived on 27 Jumādā I/10 May; Abū Shāma, 205.

[14] Rashīd al-Dīn, ed. ʿAlīzādah, 3:70.

[15] Boyle, "Īl-Khāns," 351. For additional evidence that Hülegü was in Azerbaijan later in AH 658, see: Qirtay, fol. 66a–b; Ibn al-ʿIbrī, 488–9; ʿAynī, *ʿIqd al-jumān*, MS. Topkapı Sarayı, Ahmet III 2912, fol. 81a.

[16] Besides Prawer, *Histoire*, 2:431–2, see R. Grousset, *The Empire of the Steppes*, tr. N. Walford (New Brunswick, 1970), 363; L. Kwanten, *Imperial Nomads* (Philadelphia, 1979), 159; Saunders, *Mongol Conquests*, 114. For a recent reformulation of this approach, see Fletcher, "Mongols," 47.

[17] Rashīd al-Dīn, ed. ʿAlīzādah, 70–1; Rashīd al-Dīn's pro-Qubilai partisanship is revealed by his describing Arigh Böke's claim to the throne as a "rebellion" (*bulghaq*).

[18] Hetʿum, 172, cited in Jackson, "Dissolution," 230 n. 196. Nuwayrī, 27:390 (whence, evidently, ʿAynī, fol. 80a), writes that Hülegü returned to Qaraqorum to demand the Qa'anate for himself.

[19] Jackson, "Dissolution," 230, who cites Ibn al-ʿAmīd, 173; *Zubda*, fol. 37b. See also Ibn al-Furāt, MS. Vatican, fol. 224a; ʿAynī, fol. 80a.

[20] Morgan, "The Mongols in Syria," 231–3.

[21] P. Meyvaert, "An Unknown Letter of Hulagu, Il-Khan of Persia, to King Louis IX of France," *Viator* 11 (1980):258.

and water – were far from having been exhausted. Certainly the Mongols would have had little compunction about grazing their animals on farm lands during a campaign, using grain supplies and grazing lands belonging to local nomads. In addition, whole areas of Syria had yet to be touched.[22]

Two explanations suggest themselves. First, Hülegü may have felt that he needed most of his forces in Iran upon hearing of Möngke's death and the subsequent troubles. The usual explanation offered for Hülegü's movements is that he went to Azerbaijan to await upon developments in Inner Asia. Had this been the case, however, it seems likely he would have continued eastward, at least to Khurasān. From the vantage point of Mongolia, Azerbaijan and Syria were fairly much the same thing. It would seem that Hülegü went to Azerbaijan because he was concerned about something there. As Dr. Jackson has shown, Īlkhānid claims to that area appear to have been weak, and there is some evidence that the pasture lands in northwest Iran, at least, belonged to the Jochids by right.[23] The reaction of Berke, Khan of the Golden Horde, to this usurpation was as yet unknown. As Hülegü had now lost his protector, Möngke, it made sense to be at a possible trouble spot with the bulk of his army.[24] Perhaps the lion's share of Hülegü's army had been left in Iran all along, as Professor Smith has suggested.[25] Still, Hülegü might have thought that in the post-Möngke era, both he and more of his army should be nearer a potential trouble spot.

The second reason for Hülegü's leaving such a small force with Ketbugha appears to have been faulty intelligence: Hülegü simply underestimated the numbers, quality and willpower of his opponents in Egypt. He was perhaps misled here by Syrian captives. The attribution of this disinformation to al-Nāṣir Yūsuf,[26] however, is anachronistic, because – as will be shown below – al-Nāṣir reached Hülegü several months after the latter had withdrawn from Syria. In any event, Hülegü's decision to leave only 10–12,000 soldiers with Ketbugha was based on a misreading of the situation, and this was to have disastrous consequences for the Mongols.

Initially, Ketbugha did not have to worry about encountering any serious opposition in Syria: on 15 Ṣafar 658/31 January 1260 al-Nāṣir Yūsuf had fled in panic with his troops from his camp at Barza near Damascus upon hearing of the quick Mongol conquest of Aleppo, and headed towards Gaza. On his way south, al-Nāṣir stopped at Nablus for several days, leaving behind there a a rearguard.[27] He then camped at Gaza for a while, where he met up with the

[22] See the discussion in ch. 10.

[23] Jackson, "Dissolution," 208–22; cf. Morgan, *Mongols*, 148–9. See ch. 4, pp. 78–9.

[24] This was suggested by both Canard, "Arménie," 222, and Boyle, "Īl-Khāns," 351.

[25] Smith, "ʿAyn Jālūt," 328.

[26] For al-Nāṣir's belittling of the Egyptian danger, see: *Zubda*, fols. 37b, 40a; Nuwayrī, 27:390; MS. 2m, fol. 105b. Cf. also the comment in Thorau, *Baybars*, 73 n. 56.

[27] Ibn al-ʿAmīd, 172; Abū Shāma, 203; Ibn Wāṣil, MS. 1703, fol. 150a–b; Abū 'l-Fidā', 3:210; Kutubī, 20:222; Ibn al-Furāt, MS. Vatican, fol. 232a–b; Maqrīzī, 1:423.

Shahrazūrī Kurds,[28] Türkmen, assorted deserters from his army and his brother al-Ẓāhir. Heading this ragtag force al-Nāṣir continued on to Qaṭyā. Instead of marching on to Cairo, however, al-Nāṣir's fear of Qutuz got the better of him and he turned around and rode into the desert with a small entourage. Eventually he reached Birkat al-Zayzā', some two days' ride to the north of Karak, where he was captured by the Mongols. As for his army, they continued on to Cairo, where they were integrated into the Egyptian army. Among the new refugees was the Ayyūbid al-Manṣūr Muḥammad, prince of Hama.[29]

Ketbugha arrived in Damascus, according to Ibn Kathīr, at the end of Ṣafar 658 (14 February 1260). He had been preceded into the city by envoys of the Mongols who had been in al-Nāṣir Yūsuf's camp at Barza when the latter had fled. These envoys had entered the city on 19 Ṣafar/4 February and established, albeit only in a formal manner, Mongol sovereignty. The local notables wisely decided to accept the inevitable and submitted of their own free will. This decision was reached with the help of al-Zayn al-Ḥāfiẓī, who had long been busy undermining Muslim morale and trying to foster a pro-Mongol policy. Ketbugha decamped a few days later to Marj Barghūth, on the road south between Damascus and Jisr Yaʿqūb.[30] On 17 Rabīʿ I/2 March 1260 Hülegü's *nuwwāb* (representatives or governors) came to the city to set up a regular Mongol administration. These *nuwwāb* surely refer to the *shaḥna*[31] Il-Shiban and associates, who are also mentioned as arriving at Damascus around this time.[32]

[28] For the coming of the Shahrazūrī Kurds, who fled from the Mongols previous to the taking of Baghdad, see Rashīd al-Dīn, ed. ʿAlīzādah, 65; Ibn al-ʿAmīd, 165; Ibn al-Furāt, MS. Vatican, fol. 205a; Maqrīzī, 1:411. See also Ayalon, "Wafidiya," 97; Thorau, *Baybars*, 62–3. For the Shahrazūr region from which these Kurds hailed, see W. Barthold, *An Historical Geography of Iran* (Princeton, 1984), 207–9.

[29] Ibn Wāṣil, MS. 1703, fols. 150b–151a, 154a–b; Ibn al-ʿAmīd, 172, 174–5; Abū Shāma, 205; *Zubda*, fol. 37b; Kutubī, 20:223; Ibn al-Furāt, MS. Vatican, fols. 233a, 237a–238a; Maqrīzī, 1:423, 427; Humphreys, *Saladin*, 352–3, 356–7; Thorau, *Baybars*, 68–9. The sources are not in complete agreement about al-Ẓāhir's adventures and the exact circumstances of al-Nāṣir's capture. On Birkat al-Zayzā''s location, see: Ibn Wāṣil, MS. 1703, fol. 144b; D. Krawulsky, *Īrān – Das Reich der Īlḫāne* (Wiesbaden, 1978), 596.

[30] The exact location of Marj Barghūth is not clear; see Maqrīzī, 1:585 n. 3.

[31] The *shaḥna* (or *shiḥna*, but see Lane, s.v. *sh-ḥ-n*) was the senior Mongol official in a conquered city who oversaw the local administration. It is the equivalent of the Turkish *basqaq* and the Mongolian *darugha(chi)*, and is also rendered by Arabic *nā'ib*; see A.K.S. Lambton, "Mongol Fiscal Administration in Persia," *SI* 64 (1986):80 n. 2.

[32] Abū Shāma, 203; Ibn al-ʿAmīd, 173; Ibn Kathīr, 13:219; Ibn al-Furāt, MS. Vatican, fols. 233a, 234a–235a; Rashīd al-Dīn, ed. ʿAlīzādah, 3:70 (who writes of the arrival of an unnamed Mongol *shaḥna* and three Persian retainers – *nökers*). There is some confusion about the date of Ketbugha's arrival. Maqrīzī, 1:424, states that he came on 16 Rabīʿ I/1 March, along with the *nuwwāb* of Hülegü; see also Humphreys, *Saladin*, 353; Thorau, *Baybars*, 68. But Abū Shāma and Ibn al-Furāt write respectively that on 17 or 16 Rabīʿ I only *nuwwāb* of Hülegü arrived, without any mention of Ketbugha. This is an example of Maqrīzī's distortions of Ibn al-Furāt. For additional mention of Il-Shiban's activities in Damascus, see Abū Shāma, 208–9; Nuwayrī, 27:389–90; Yūnīnī, 1:357, 363–3; Ibn al-Furāt, MS. Vatican, fol. 234b (cf. editor's

There is a singular report in *Gestes des Chiprois* that Ketbugha was accompanied into Damascus by Prince Bohemond VI of Antioch and King Het'um of Lesser Armenia, and that the former turned a mosque into a church and destroyed several others.[33] While this report certainly cannot be taken literally,[34] it may contain a grain of truth. Armenian troops were part of Ketbugha's force,[35] while some time during the Mongol occupation Bohemond visited Baalbek and even intended to ask Hülegü for possession of the town. The inhabitants were spared this ordeal by the Mongol defeat at ʿAyn Jālūt.[36] If this prince reached as far as Baalbek, it is most probable that he also passed through Damascus. All of this taken together, along with the information we have on the disestablishment of Islam as the official religion of the newly conquered territory and the pro-Christian sympathies of certain Mongol officers (including Ketbugha),[37] may have given rise to this story of Bohemond and Hetʿum.

It was around this time that al-Ashraf Mūsā returned to the scene. This prince, who had been secretly in contact with Hülegü for some time, had left Damascus to make his submission to the Khan the evening before al-Nāṣir Yūsuf left the city. Al-Ashraf Mūsā was well received at Aleppo by Hülegü and soon returned with both his old principality of Homs back (it had previously been taken away from him by al-Nāṣir) plus the vague title of ruler over all of Syria. What exactly this title meant is not clear, since power remained in the hands of the Mongols and their agents. But it evidently served their needs to have titular local leaders with whom, at least, they could consult on regional problems. Al-Yūnīnī adds that Hülegü also granted al-Ashraf an *iqṭāʿ* (revenues of a land assignment) large enough to maintain 100 horsemen, indicative of the extent of power that he really enjoyed.[38]

Early on, and perhaps even before he had entered Damascus, Ketbugha had dispatched a force south, whose mission appears to have included reconnaissance, looting and the striking of terror into the hearts of the local population. This force, either as one column or smaller separate parties, made a sweep through Palestine and Trans-Jordan, wreaking havoc and taking booty as it

insertion in Maqrīzī, 1:425); Baybars, *Zubda*, fol. 37b; Ghāzī b. al-Wāsiṭī, in R. Gottheil, "An Answer to the Dhimmis," *JAOS* 41 (1921):409–10. Ibn Bībī, 295 (tr. Duda, 281) says that ʿAlā' al-Dīn [al-]Kāzī was appointed *shaḥna*, but according to the Arabic writers, he was just one of the associates of Il-Shiban. [33] *RHC, Ar*, 2:751.

[34] Jackson, "Crisis," 486–7, and Thorau, *Baybars*, 68–9, doubt the veracity of this report.

[35] Kirakos, tr. Dulaurier, 498; G. Dédéyan (tr.), *La Chronique attribuée au Connétable Smbat* (Paris, 1980), 106 ; S. Der Nersessian, "The Armenian Chronicle of Constable Smpad or of the Royal Historian," *DOP* 13 (1959):160.

[36] Yūnīnī, 3:92–3; Ibn Kathīr, 13:269. See R. Irwin, "The Mamluk Conquest of the County of Tripoli," in Edbury (ed.), *Crusade and Settlement*, 246; cf. *idem*, *Middle East*, 31.

[37] Yūnīnī, 1:362–3; 2:34–5.

[38] Ibn al-ʿAmīd, 172–3; Ibn Shaddād, in A-M. Eddé, "La description de la Syrie du Nord de ʿIzz al-Dīn ibn Šaddād," *BEO* 32–3 (1981–2):378; Nuwayrī, 27:289; MS. 2m, fol. 112b; Yūnīnī, 1:377; 2:312; Ibn Kathīr, 13:221; Ibn al-Furāt, MS. Vatican, fols. 233a, 235a; Maqrīzī, 1:423, 425–6; cf. Humphreys, *Saladin*, 350–1.

went, finally reaching as far as Gaza and the area just north of Karak. In Palestine, Bayt Jibrīl/Jibrīn, Hebron, Ascalon, Jerusalem and Nablus are mentioned as targets of these raiders. Near the last mentioned town the Mongols came upon the rearguard left by al-Nāṣir Yūsuf and completely annihilated it before proceeding to enter the city proper and slaughtering many of its inhabitants. By Rabīʿ II 658/March-April 1260, the raiders returned to the Damascus area, bringing with them captives, livestock and other booty.[39]

Ketbugha's itinerary can be roughly established. As said above, he left Damascus after a few days and set up camp at Marj Barghūth to the south.[40] It was there that he apparently received a delegation from the Franks on the coast, who brought him presents out of fear that the Mongols wanted to attack their country.[41] In mid-Jumādā I/end of April, Ketbugha was back in Damascus, putting down the rebellion of the garrison there.[42] It is uncertain whether this was an actual rebellion or whether the garrison had actually never submitted. The former explanation seems more likely because it is doubtful that Ketbugha would have left Damascus with a recalcitrant force controlling the citadel. Having taken the citadel on 15 Jumādā I/28 April, he ordered its partial destruction. Ketbugha then moved west to Baalbek; the inhabitants had submitted, but there also the citadel's garrison had taken an independent attitude and hitherto had refused to surrender. A vigorous siege soon brought the defenders round, and they asked for an *amān* (guarantee of safety) which was granted. The citadel was subsequently destroyed.[43] From Baalbek, Ketbugha went on to the fortress of al-Ṣubayba in the Golan which was taken with the assistance of al-Saʿīd Ḥasan b. al-ʿAzīz ʿUthmān, its former ruler, whom Hülegü had released from al-Nāṣir Yūsuf's jail in al-Bīra on the Euphrates. Al-Saʿīd had encouraged Hülegü to attack al-Nāṣir Yūsuf and was reinstated as ruler of al-Ṣubayba and Banias. Much to his later regret, al-Saʿīd became a most loyal supporter of the Mongol cause in Syria.[44]

From al-Ṣubayba, Ketbugha went to the fortress of ʿAjlūn which he put

[39] R. Amitai, "Mongol Raids into Palestine (AD 1260 and 1300)," *JRAS* 1987:236–42; on Ascalon, see Jackson, "Crisis," 491. Yūnīnī, 3:205, tells of how his brother and a companion went to Damascus to ransom Muslim prisoners taken in this raid.

[40] Ibn al-ʿAmīd, 173; Ibn al-Furāt, MS. Vatican, fol. 235a; Maqrīzī, 1:425; Abū Shāma, 204.

[41] *Zubda*, fol. 38a; Nuwayrī, 27:390; Ibn al-Furāt, MS. Vatican, fol. 235a (= *Ayyubids, Mamlukes and Crusaders. Selections from the Tārīkh al-Duwal wa'l-Mulūk of Ibn al-Furāt*, tr. U. and M.C. Lyons, intro. and notes J.S.C. Riley-Smith [Cambridge, 1971], 1:50). These sources write only that Ketbugha went to the Marj. This may refer to the large plain east of Damascus (s.v. "Ghūṭa," *EI*², 2:1105a), but given the sources mentioned in the previous note, it appears to be a shortened form of Marj Barghūth.

[42] Ibn al-ʿAmīd, 174; Abū Shāma, 204; Ibn Wāṣil, MS. 1703, fol. 152b; Yūnīnī, 1:351–2; Ibn al-Furāt, MS. Vatican, fol. 235b; Maqrīzī, 1:426.

[43] Ibn Wāṣil, MS. 1703, fol. 152b; Yūnīnī, 1:354–5; 2:34 (cited by Ibn Kathīr, 13:227), who saw Ketbugha in his hometown of Baalbek. No date for the capture of Baalbek is given. For the Mongol administration of this city, see Yūnīnī, 1:353–4; 3:49–50.

[44] Ibn Wāṣil, MS. 1703, fol. 154a; Abū 'l-Fidā', 3:213; Yūnīnī, 2:16–17. The last writer saw al-Saʿīd in Baalbek and wrote that his enthusiasm for the Mongols extended to his wearing of Mongol garb and hat.

under siege. He was spared the need of a lengthy investment by the appearance of al-Nāṣir Yūsuf early in Rajab/June 1260. As will be remembered, he had been captured at Birkat al-Zayzā' in the Trans-Jordan desert. Al-Nāṣir obliged his captors by fulfilling their request to order the surrender of ᶜAjlūn. Whereupon, he was sent off to Hülegü, then somewhere east of the Euphrates. Al-Nāṣir was well received, but later was put to death when news of the defeat at ᶜAyn Jālūt reached Hülegü.[45] After their capture, al-Ṣubayba and ᶜAjlūn were then despoiled and destroyed as much as time and means allowed, as were other forts in Trans-Jordan over which the Mongols had gained possession: al-Ṣalt, Bosra and Ṣarkhad.[46] Their intention was thus to eliminate potential centers of rebellion and resistance.

Evidently some time during this campaign in the Golan and north Trans-Jordan, Ketbugha also made a quick advance to Safad, where the local Franks sent down supplies and built a giant tent for him.[47] It was also during this operation that a Mongol force was probably dispatched southward towards Gaza, in order – according to Ibn Wāṣil – to prevent the Egyptians from sending assistance to the Franks on the coast.[48] This was probably the advance guard (*yazak*) mentioned by Rashīd al-Dīn in Gaza under the command of Baydar (Baydarā in the Arabic sources).[49] It would seem that this unit had the mission of watching developments in Egypt and preventing a surprise attack from that direction. This was to confront the Mamluk advance guard under Baybars in the upcoming summer. In spite of the presence of this force in Gaza and the Mongol raids throughout the country, there is no evidence of the establishment of a Mongol administration in Palestine as there was in central and northern Syria, with the exception of that of their client in Banias, al-Saᶜīd Ḥasan. In fact, with the disintegration of al-Nāṣir Yūsuf's kingdom, there seems to have been no real authority in Palestine, excluding the Frankish-held coast, in the months before ᶜAyn Jālūt. Had the Mongol conquest gone on, however, certainly Palestine would have been more firmly integrated into the Mongol administrative system.

[45] Abū Shāma, 205; Ibn Wāṣil, MS. 1703, fol. 154b; Ibn al-Furāt, MS. Vatican, fols. 237a–238a; Maqrīzī, 1:426–7. See also Humphreys, *Saladin*, 356–7. Ibn al-Shaddād, *al-Aᶜlāq al-khaṭīra*, vol. 2, pt. 2, *Ta'rīkh lubnān, al-urdunn wa-filasṭīn*, ed. S. Dahhān (Damascus, 1963):89–90, gives the date for the taking of ᶜAjlūn as Rajab 658/June-July, but this must have been quite early in the month, because al-Nāṣir reached Damascus on 6 Rajab/17 June and was sent off to Hülegü on 14 Rajab/25 June; Abū Shāma, 206; Yūnīnī, 1:358–9. Ibn al-ᶜIbrī, 489, has al-Nāṣir coming to Hülegü at Jabal al-Ṭāgh (= Ala Tagh, so it would seem) in Azerbaijan. For al-Nāṣir's death, see Thorau, *Baybars*, 86 n. 17.

[46] Abū Shāma, 206; Yūnīnī, 1:358; Ibn Wāṣil, MS. 1703, fol. 154a; ᶜUmarī, *Masālik al-abṣār ... mamālik miṣr wa'l-shām wa'l-ḥijāz wa'l-yaman*, ed. A.F. Sayyid (Cairo, 1985), 120.

[47] Dhahabī, *Ta'rīkh al-islām*, MS. Bodleian Laud 305, fol. 252b; *ibid.*, MS. Aya Sofya 3015, fol. 222b. See below for the attitude of the Franks to the Mongols. This short hop to Safad may be the basis for the phrase in Ibn Wāṣil, MS. 1703, fol. 154a: "Then the Mongols turned towards [or turned their attention towards] the Franks on the coast ... "; cf. wording in Ibn al-Furāt, MS. Vatican, 237b (= ed. Lyons, 1:50).

[48] Ibn Wāṣil, MS. 1703, fol. 154a.

[49] Rashīd al-Dīn, ed. Quatremère, 346–7; cf. ed. ᶜAlīzādah, 3:73. For the identity of the commander of the Mongol force, see Amitai, "Mongol Raids," 250 n. 31.

The Mongols also obtained the submission of the ruler of Karak, al-Mughīth ᶜUmar, or rather resubmission, since as has been seen al-Mughīth had officially tendered his submission to the Mongols many years before. Mongol raids to the north of Karak were evidently sufficient to convince al-Mughīth to submit when called to do so by a Mongol envoy. Al-Mughīth sent back with this envoy his son al-ᶜAzīz. Hülegü in turn sent a *shaḥna* (commissioner) to watch over al-Mughīth. This official, however, never reached his destination. While stopping en route at Damascus, news arrived of the Mongol defeat at ᶜAyn Jālūt, and he escaped with the local Mongol officials.[50]

Hülegü had left Ketbugha in Syria with a relatively small force, and we are told by sources close to the Mongols,[51] as well as by the Mamluk historian Baybars al-Manṣūrī,[52] that he was to guard the conquests and to garrison the country. Ibn al-ᶜAmīd reports that, in addition to this mission, Ketbugha was to keep a watchful eye on the Franks of the coast.[53] Hülegü himself, in his letter to King Louis IX of France in 1262, writes that Ketbugha was ordered to reduce the Ismāᶜīlī fortresses of northern Syria.[54]

There are a number of indications that in the near future Hülegü intended to renew the conquest in the direction of Egypt, by sending or personally leading a larger force; not the least of these are the general expansionist plans of the Mongols, which have been examined in chapter 1. As has also been seen, the further Hülegü penetrated into the Islamic world, the more explicit became his desire to conquer Syria and Egypt. In addition, it is reported that Hülegü promised al-Nāṣir Yūsuf, who had been brought before him somewhere in the environs of Azerbaijan, that he would make him ruler of Syria when the Mongols conquered Egypt.[55] Finally, some time during the months preceding

[50] Ibn Wāṣil, MS. 1703, fol. 152b; Yūnīnī, 1:358; Ibn al-Furāt, MS. Vatican, fol. 238b; Ibn Shaddād, *Aᶜlāq*, 2, pt. 2:76, 242; Nuwayrī, MS. 2m, fols. 107a, 132b; Qirtay, fols. 65b–66a. See also Amitai, "Mongol Raids," 238; L. Hambis, "La lettre mongole du governeur de Karak," *Acta Orientalia Academiae Scientarum Hungaricae* 15 (1962):143–6; R. Amitai-Preiss, "Hülegü and the Ayyūbid Lord of Transjordan," *AEMA*, forthcoming.

[51] Rashīd al-Dīn, ed. ᶜAlīzādah, 3:70; Kirakos, tr. Dulaurier, 498; Vardan, tr. Thomson, 218. Mustawfī, 589, writes that Hülegü had ordered Ketbugha to "liberate" Syria and Egypt, but the veracity of this statement is brought into question by both the above evidence and the author adding that Hülegü was in Damascus when he received word of Möngke's death and that it was from there that he gave this order. Ṣārim al-Dīn Özbeg's statement (in Levi della Vida [ed. and tr.], "L'Invasione dei Tartari in Siria nel 1260 nei ricordi di un testimone oculare," *Orientalia* 4 (1935):365, from Ibn al-Furāt, MS. Vatican, fol. 241a–b; also cited, with differences in Ibn al-Dawādārī, *Kanz al-durar*, vol. 8, ed. U. Haarmann [Freiburg-Cairo, 1971], 56–7) that Hülegü ordered Ketbugha (and Baydarā) to invade Egypt is also doubtful; see Amitai, "Mongol Raids," 239–42; cf. Jackson, "Crisis," 502–3.

[52] *Zubda*, fol. 37b (but cf. his *Tuḥfa*, 43). This is cited by Ibn al-Furāt, MS. Vatican, fol. 239b, who does not name his source.

[53] Ibn al-ᶜAmīd, 173 (whence Ibn al-Furāt, MS. Vatican, fol. 235a, who does not name his source), who subsequently mentions Baydarā with Ketbugha. It is clear from the context that Baydarā is subordinate to Ketbugha, and certainly does not share a joint command with him.

[54] Meyvaert, "Letter," 258.

[55] Rashīd al-Dīn, ed. ᶜAlīzādah, 3:70; Ibn al-Fuwaṭī, 342–3; Bar Hebraeus, 437 (= Ibn al-ᶜIbrī, 488–9); Baybars, *Zubda*, fol. 40a; Ibn Kathīr, 13:240; Ibn al-Furāt, MS. Vatican, fol. 252a, writes that al-Nāṣir was given a *farmān* (royal order) for the rulership of both Syria and Egypt

ʿAyn Jālūt, Hülegü's letter reached Sultan Qutuz in Egypt, unequivocally calling on the Mamluks to submit or face destruction (see below).[56]

Mamluk countermeasures

Events in Egypt were in the meanwhile coming to a head. From the beginning of his reign, Qutuz had pursued an unequivocal anti-Mongol policy. He had used the need to resist the Mongols as the justification for his disposal of al-Manṣūr ʿAlī b. Aybeg and his own accession to the throne (28 Dhū 'l-qaʿda 657/16 November 1259). The story is told that Qutuz claimed that he was descended from the Khwārazm-shāh ʿAlā' al-Dīn Muḥammad, and thus his emerging struggle with the Mongols also had an element of personal revenge in it.[57]

Qutuz's resolve was certainly strengthened with the steady influx of troopers from Syria as al-Nāṣir's army began to disintegrate in the late winter and spring of 658/1260. Of tremendous importance was the return of Baybars to the Mamluk fold, in spite of the old hatred occasioned by Qutuz's role in the murder of Aqtay, former leader of the Baḥriyya regiment. This enmity had been exacerbated by the numerous raids and invasion attempts made into Egypt from Ayyūbid Syria under Baybars's prodding and leadership. But now in the face of the Mongol threat, past differences were forgotten. Qutuz needed Baybars's leadership abilities and his following of Baḥrīs (whose ranks, however, must have been somewhat depleted by years of fighting as mercenaries and imprisonments). Baybars had clearly seen that his continued allegiance to al-Nāṣir Yūsuf or any other Ayyūbid prince in Syria had little to commend itself. After sending a trusted subordinate and obtaining an oath of safety, Baybars made his way to Egypt from Gaza, reaching it on 22 Rabīʿ I 658/7 March 1260, at the time when the Mongol raiders were harrying Palestine.[58]

The Mamluk sources contain stories of Baybars's anti-Mongol resolve both before and after his return to Egypt. He had wanted to take three or four thousand horsemen to hold the fords of the Euphrates against the Mongols, but al-Nāṣir Yūsuf did not permit it.[59] During a discussion of the policy to be adopted towards the approaching Mongols, Baybars is credited with having both verbally rebuked and physically beaten al-Zayn al-Ḥāfiẓī, the main

(when it would be conquered). The sources do not tell us how this promise was to be reconciled with Hülegü's earlier appointment of al-Ashraf Mūsā as governor of Syria.

56 The Armenian historian Smpad (d. 1276) reports that Ketbugha may have jumped the gun by initiating an invasion with those troops under his command; Smpad, tr. Der Nersessian, 160 (= tr. Dédéyan, 106). This evidence is discussed in detail, and rejected, in Amitai, "Mongol Raids," 239–42.

57 Yūnīnī, 1:368; Ibn al-Dawādārī, 8:39–40: both cite Jazarī. This story is discussed by Irwin, *Middle East*, 32–3.

58 Humphreys, *Saladin*, 345–8; A.A. Khowaiter, *Baibars the First* (London, 1978), 18–20; Thorau, *Baybars*, 65–6.

59 *Rawḍ*, 61–2; Yūnīnī, 3:243; Kutubī, *Fawāt al-wafayāt* (Bulāq, 1299/1881–2), 1:86; Ṣafadī, *al-Wāfī bi'l-wafayāt*, ed. H. Ritter *et al.* (Wiesbaden, 1931), 10:332.

proponent of submission to Hülegü among al-Nāṣir Yūsuf's advisors.[60] After his return to Egypt, Baybars strengthened Qutuz's resolve and denigrated the might of the Mongols.[61] While there may be a large dose of post-Qutuz panegyric here, both intentional and otherwise, these reports seem to contain at least some truth. Rashīd al-Dīn, certainly no booster of Baybars, reports his major role in convincing Qutuz to go out and fight the Mongols.[62] And Baybars's vigorous anti-Mongol policy during his own sultanate hints at a similarly strong attitude beforehand.

Some time in 658/1260, probably towards the summer, Hülegü sent envoys to Qutuz bringing a letter calling on him to submit.[63] This letter, although couched in Islamic terms, and even containing verses from the Qur'ān, expresses the traditional Mongol world view: the Mongols have a heaven-given right to rule the world. All those who resist are rebels who will be destroyed. There is no possibility of escaping, so he is counseled to submit at once. The letter also specifically refers to Qutuz and disparages his mamluk origins: "He is of the race of mamluks who fled before our sword into this country, who enjoyed its comforts and then killed its rulers."[64]

The threats and insults, however, did not work, and Qutuz obtained the agreement of the amirs to execute the Mongol envoys; they were cut in half and their heads were displayed at Bāb al-Zuwayla in Cairo, and "these were the first Mongol heads to be hung [there]."[65] The Mamluks were now committed to a military confrontation with the Mongols.

Qutuz and his armies left Cairo for Ṣāliḥiyya, the staging area some 120 km to the north-east of Cairo, on 15 Shaʿbān/26 July.[66] The regular Egyptian army had been swollen by the influx of refugee Syrian troops,[67] and assorted Türkmen, bedouins (*al-ʿurbān*) and Shahrazūriyya Kurds, who had also fled to Egypt.[68] Exact numbers for this combined force are not given in any of the Mamluk sources. The later Persian historian Waṣṣāf offers the figure of 12,000 men, but his source is unknown, and the possibility of pure imagination on his part should not be discounted.[69] This number, however, is not totally

60 Ibn al-Furāt, MS. Vatican, fol. 220a–b; Maqrīzī, 1:419 (s.a. 657).
61 Yūnīnī, 1:365; Ibn al-Furāt, MS. Vatican, fol. 238b.
62 Rashīd al-Dīn, ed. ʿAlīzādah, 3:73.
63 Cf. Nuwayrī, 27:391; MS. 2m, fol. 131b, who writes that Ketbugha actually sent the envoys.
64 Ibn al-Furāt, fol. 243b–244a, whence Maqrīzī, 1:427–8; trans. of the latter in B. Lewis, *Islam: From the Prophet Muhammad to the Capture of Constantinople* (New York, 1974), 1:84–5. As mentioned in ch. 1, this letter is based on the last of Hülegü's letters sent to al-Naṣir Yusuf, although appropriate changes were made. Cf. the version in Rashīd al-Dīn, ed. ʿAlīzādah, 3:71, which, although shorter and in Persian, conveys the same aggressive message.
65 Ibn al-Furāt, MS. Vatican, fol. 244a; Maqrīzī, 1:429.
66 Ibn al-Dawādārī, 8:49; Yūnīnī, 1:365; Ibn al-Furāt, MS. Vatican, fol. 244b; Maqrīzī, 1:429.
67 Among these was al-Manṣūr of Hama: Ibn Wāṣil, MS. 1703, fol. 160a. Ibn Kathīr, 13:220, 226, says that the majority of the Syrian army entered Egypt; see also Ibn al-Ṣuqāʿī, 168.
68 Ibn al-ʿAmīd, 175; *Ḥusn*, 30; Ibn al-Furāt, MS. Vatican, fol. 244b (whence Maqrīzī, 1:429, but he omits the Kurds). Cf. Abū Shāma, 207; *Zubda*, fol. 38b. For a further discussion of the composition of the army, see Amitai-Preiss, "ʿAyn Jālūt," 126–7.
69 Waṣṣāf, 47. This figure was cited by D'Ohsson, *Histoire*, 334. This in turn was misread by H.H. Howorth, *The History of the Mongols* (rpt., New York, 1965), 3:167, who gave the

unreasonable. We have figures of 10,000 and 12,000 horsemen for the Egyptian army under the last Ayyūbids.[70] These numbers, however, should be used with care, especially since the Mamluk army in Egypt surely underwent many changes in the first years of its existence, but they provide at least some idea of the size of this army. It is difficult to give even a rough estimation of the size of the total army under Qutuz's command, since there are no figures for the Syrian and auxiliary forces. On the other hand, some writers assert in a different context that at ʿAyn Jālūt the Muslim army was larger than that of their Mongol adversaries.[71] This claim makes sense if we accept the figure of 10–12,000 for the Mongols (see above), while the Mamluks may well have had a hard core of about 10,000 Egyptian troops, plus the additional forces mentioned above.[72]

Qutuz's troubles, however, were far from over. Having reached Ṣāliḥiyya, he was confronted with the amirs' unwillingness to advance into Syria. There is some indication that in order to get the amirs to mobilize and leave Cairo, Qutuz had at first agreed with them to wait for Ketbugha at Ṣāliḥiyya. But Qutuz certainly knew that a prolonged wait would bring about the weakening of their will to fight the Mongols, not particularly strong in any case. Through the use of religious exhortation, personal example and the judicious application of guilt feeling, he was able to cajole the amirs into following him into Syria. At one point, exasperated by the amirs' refusal to move, he is reported to have said, "I am going to fight the Mongols alone." The amirs, shamed by their cowardice, had no choice but to follow him.[73] In spite of the probable tendency of the sources to glorify Qutuz as the great holy warrior, there is little doubt that here, as elsewhere, Qutuz's personal example and resolute leadership were a major factor in the course of these events. Qutuz was certainly well served by a small group of close associates, and as has been seen Baybars – now reinstated among the senior amirs – was also pushing for a decisive and speedy advance into Syria.

It is perhaps not obvious why Qutuz decided to attack the Mongols in Syria rather than wait for them in Egypt. In fact, at first glance, the second option may have more to commend itself: Qutuz and his army would be waiting – rested and near their base – for a Mongol army which had just finished an

number of 120,000 [!]. This last figure was evidently the basis for that used in B. Lewis, "ʿAyn Djālūt," *EI*², 1:786; see Jackson in *BSOAS* 50 (1987):552.

70 See ch. 3, p. 71.

71 Ibn al-Dawādārī, 8:68; Mufaḍḍal ibn Abī 'l-Faḍā'il, in E. Blochet, "Histoire des sultans mamlouks," *Patrologia Orientalis* 12, 14, 20 (1919–28):75 [of consecutive pagination].

72 The question of Mamluk numbers is discussed in Amitai-Preiss, "ʿAyn Jālūt," 127–9; cf. Thorau, "The Battle of ʿAyn Jālūt: A Re-examination," in Edbury (ed.), *Crusade and Settlement*, 236–7; Smith, "ʿAyn Jālūt," 311–13.

73 Ibn al-Furāt, MS. Vatican, fols. 244a–245a, who quotes the now lost *Naẓm al-sulūk* by Shāfiʿ b. ʿAlī and other, unnamed works, each giving a slightly different version of these events. Maqrīzī, 1:429–30, presents an edited version of Ibn al-Furāt. As a result of his deletions, the original sense is not always faithfully conveyed, e.g., the bottom paragraph in Maqrīzī, 1:429 (which continues on to p. 430) is actually the beginning of one account and the end of a second in Ibn al-Furāt, fol. 244a–b.

exhausting ride through the desert. In addition, it could always be hoped that the Mongols would not realize their threat to invade Egypt.

Other considerations, however, were to lead to another decision. First, Qutuz was aware that only a small part of the Mongol army was now in Syria, and thus he had an opportunity to confront the Mongols with some chance of success.[74] Qutuz may well have been aware of the psychological importance of a victory over the Mongols in strengthening both his own position and the morale of his army. Second, by moving into Syria, he was seizing the initiative from the Mongols, an important strategic consideration. Third, if he was defeated in Syria, there was a chance that he could withdraw back to Egypt to reorganize; a defeat in Egypt left him without a fallback position. Fourth, Qutuz knew his officers and troops too well. Perhaps he feared that with the approach of the Mongols many would either be paralyzed by fear or willing to "negotiate." Possibly the best way to preempt such defeatist attitudes was to adopt an aggressive mien and to try to inculcate it within the army.

Baybars's anti-Mongol resolve and the trust that Qutuz placed in him, at least for the time being, are indicated by his being given command over the Muslim vanguard. Baybars was ordered to move ahead in order to collect intelligence about the Mongols. Upon reaching Gaza, he found a Mongol forward force (*ṭalīʿa*), which fled upon seeing the Muslim army.[75] Rashīd al-Dīn writes that the Mongol advance force (*yazak*) was under an officer named Baydar (= Baydarā); on learning of the approach of the "Egyptians," Baydar sent to Ketbugha, then in Baalbek, who ordered him to stand fast until his arrival. This was to no avail, because Qutuz himself attacked Baydar and pursued him to the ʿĀṣī River (*ab-i ʿāṣī*).[76] Baybars's commanding of the Muslim force would understandably have remained unknown to Rashīd al-Dīn. The exact nature of the encounter at Gaza cannot be resolved one way or the other. As for the information about the River ʿĀṣī, this would seem to refer in general to the eventual arrival of Muslim troops in the area of ʿAyn Jālūt, because Wādī or Nahr al-ʿĀṣī is a small riverbed that joins Nahr Jālūt (now Naḥal Ḥarōd) just north of Baysān (Beth Shean), after flowing in from the southwest.[77]

Qutuz soon reached Gaza with the bulk of the army and after a stopover of one day moved up the coast to Acre.[78] Faced with a large army in their

[74] The opportunity presented to the Mamluks was thus understood by both pro-Mongol and Mamluk writers: Bar Hebraeus, 437 (cited at the beginning of this chapter; = Ibn al-ʿIbrī, 489); Rashīd al-Dīn, ed. ʿAlīzādah, 72; Ibn al-Furāt, MS. Vatican, fol. 224a; ʿAynī, fol. 80a.

[75] Ibn al-Furāt, MS. Vatican, fol. 245a; cf. Maqrīzī, 1:430.

[76] Rashīd al-Dīn, ed. Quatremère, 346–7; cf. ed. ʿAlīzādah, 3:73–4.

[77] F-M. Abel, *Géographie de la Palestine* (Paris, 1933), vol 1, Map no. IV (Basse-Galilée); C.R. Conder and H.H. Kitchener, *The Survey of Western Palestine: Memoirs of the Topography, Orography, Hydrography and Archaeology*, vol. 2 (London, 1882), 80, describes ʿAyn al-ʿĀṣī as the source for this stream. Krawulsky, *Īrān*, 591, confuses this ʿĀṣī with its better known namesake to the north, the Orontes in European languages, which originates near Baalbek.

[78] Ibn al-Furāt, MS. Vatican, fol. 245a (= ed. Lyons, 1:51); Maqrīzī, 1:430.

immediate vicinity, the Frankish leaders had no choice but to make a decision regarding the Mongols and the newly arrived Mamluks. They chose to remain neutral, with a tilt towards the closer Mamluks which expressed itself by the sending out of supplies to the Muslim camp. While there was little love lost between the Franks and Mamluks, Dr. Jackson has convincingly shown that the Franks were so apprehensive of the Mongols that they felt obliged to adopt such a policy. Certainly the bellicose letters and activities of the Mongols in Syria, including the sacking of Sidon, in the previous months would have done little to commend themselves to the Latin Christians. The leaders of Acre may have seen the possibility of the Mamluks saving them from the Mongols, at little cost to themselves. But to safeguard themselves in the case of a Mongol victory (a distinct possibility), they officially maintained their neutrality.[79] At this point, Bohemond VI's unreserved support for the Mongols was probably looked upon with disfavor by the leaders of Acre. The papal legate there was certainly displeased: he excommunicated Bohemond early in 1260.[80]

At Acre, Qutuz again took the opportunity to whip up the enthusiasm of the amirs, whose fear must have been increasing as the battle drew closer. Qutuz's speech contains two main motifs: the amirs must fight to protect their families and property (and by implication, the power they enjoyed in Egypt), and the need to defend Islam against the infidels. The speech was effective: the amirs wept and swore to each other to drive the Mongols out of the country. While still at Acre, Qutuz sent Baybars ahead again with the vanguard (*ṭalīʿa* or *shālīsh*) and followed with the main part of the army.[81]

The battle

Ketbugha was in the Biqāʿ Valley when he received word that the Mamluks had entered Syria and were making their way north. He gathered his troops who were scattered over the country, probably for both garrison and grazing purposes, and headed south.[82] Although a later writer speaks of Ketbugha's complacency at this time,[83] earlier Mamluk sources report that initially Ketbugha contemplated a withdrawal from Syria, as he was unsure of the wisdom of confronting the reinforced Egyptian army.[84] The apparent reasons

79 Jackson, "Crisis," *passim*; see also the comments in J. Richard, "The Mongols and the Franks," *Journal of Asian History* 3 (1969):51–2; Thorau, *Baybars*, 69–70, 76.

80 J. Richard, "Le début des relations entre la papauté et les Mongols de Perse," *JA* 237 (1949):293; B. Roberg, "Die Tartaren auf dem 2. Konzil von Lyon 1274," *Annuarium Historiae Conciliorum* 5 (1973):272.

81 Ibn al-Furāt, MS. Vatican, fol. 245b (cf. Maqrīzī, 1:430); Ibn al-Dawādārī, 8:49; Dhahabī, MS. Laud 305, fol. 254a; *Ḥusn*, 30.

82 Yūnīnī, 1:360, 365; Ibn al-Dawādārī, 8:49; Kutubī, 20:226; Rashīd al-Dīn, ed. Quatremère, 3:346–7 (cf. ed. ʿAlīzādah, 73–4); Ibn al-Furāt, MS. Vatican, fol. 246a; Maqrīzī, 1:430. For details of Ketbugha's movement south, see Amitai-Preiss, "ʿAyn Jālūt," 122–3.

83 ʿAynī, fol. 80a.

84 Yūnīnī, 1:360; Dhahabī, MS. Laud 305, fol. 254a; Kutubī, 20:226 (all three versions repeat the same report); Ibn Kathīr, 13:227.

behind Ketbugha's hesitation were the relatively small number of soldiers at his disposal and his awareness of the strength of Qutuz's force. As has been seen, Ketbugha appears to have been left with about 10–12,000 troops. These, however, were not all Mongol horsemen, but included contingents from Georgia and Lesser Armenia; Smpad writes that the latter numbered 500 men.[85] These numbers were supplemented somewhat by local troops, formerly serving the Syrian Ayyūbids, as well as two Ayyūbid princes with their contingents: al-Ashraf Mūsā and al-Saʿīd Ḥasan.[86]

Moving south, Ketbugha took up position near ʿAyn Jālūt. There is little doubt that the Mongols were the first to arrive at the site and take up position: Baybars upon reaching a nearby hill found the Mongols camped (*nāzilin*) there.[87] This would cast doubts on the suggestion made by some scholars that the Mamluks arrived at the location first and set up an ambush.[88] ʿAyn Jālūt ("Goliath's Spring") is an all-year spring at the foot of the northwest corner of Mt. Gilboa, about 15 km north-northwest of Baysān, just west of the modern village of Gidʿōna. Today the spring is known as ʿAyn or Maʿyan Ḥarōd.[89] For the Mongols, this was a logical place to await the Mamluks. Along the northern foot of the Gilboa runs Wādī or Nahr Jālūt, which would have provided watering for the horses, and the adjacent valley offered both pasturage and good conditions for cavalry warfare. Other advantages are evident. The Mongols could exploit the proximity of the Gilboa to anchor their flank. It also offered an excellent vantage point, as did the nearby Hill of Moreh (Givʿat ha-Mōreh).[90]

Meanwhile, the Mamluks had departed from Acre. Baybars had been sent ahead with the vanguard, and the main body under Qutuz followed. At some point Baybars's force came into contact with Mongol troops and skirmishing commenced. There are reports that the vanguard under Baybars defeated their Mongol counterparts, but the exact nature and size of the latter is unknown. Meanwhile, Baybars sent word to Qutuz that contact with the enemy had been established.[91] The skirmishing must have been fairly wide-ranging, with Baybars alternately advancing and retreating. The claim by some sources, however, that Baybars actually enticed the Mongols to ʿAyn Jālūt,[92] can be

[85] Kirakos, tr. Dulaurier, 498; Smpad, tr. Dédéyan, 106. For another indication that first-rate Mongol troops did not constitute all of Ketbugha's force, see Amitai-Preiss, "ʿAyn Jālūt," 128–9.

[86] Ibn Shaddād, *Ta'rīkh*, 335–6; Amitai-Preiss, "ʿAyn Jālūt," 125–6, for a discussion of the Syrian troops serving Ketbugha.

[87] Dhahabī, MS. Laud 305, fol. 254a; *Rawḍ*, 64; *Tuḥfa*, 43.

[88] Thorau, "ʿAyn Jālūt," 236–9, and P. Herde, "Taktiken muslimischer Heere von ersten Kreuzzug bis ʿAyn Djālūt (1260) und ihre Einwirkung auf die Schlacht bei Tagliacozzo (1268)," in W. Fischer and J. Schneider (eds.), *Das Heilige Land in Mittelalter* (Neustadt an der Aisch, 1982), 86.

[89] For this location in the Arabic sources and the identification of the medieval ʿAyn Jālūt with the biblical Maʿyan Ḥarōd, see Amitai-Preiss, "ʿAyn Jālūt," 132 nn. 59–60.

[90] See Smith, "ʿAyn Jālūt," 326; Amitai-Preiss, "ʿAyn Jālūt," 132–3.

[91] Ṣafadī, *Wāfī*, 10:332; Ibn al-Furāt, MS. Vatican, fol. 245b; cf. Maqrīzī, 1:430.

[92] Yūnīnī 1:366; Ibn al-Dawādārī, 8:49; Ibn al-Furāt, fol. 245b; Maqrīzī, 1:430. It is clear that these reports have a common source; cf. Thorau, "ʿAyn Jālūt," 238.

rejected, since – as has been seen – contemporary writers report that the Mongols were already there.

Having arrived at the scene, Baybars had gone up a hill (apparently either the Gilboa or the Hill of Moreh) and seen that the Mongols had already reached the spring below. They also noticed him and started up towards him. Realizing his perilous position, Baybars beat a hasty retreat back down, but not before sending word to Qutuz, who was one day's march away. Having succeeded in escaping the Mongol encirclement of the hill, Baybars withdrew, and was eventually joined by Qutuz with the main body of the Mamluk army.[93]

The battle was joined at the dawn of Friday, 25 Ramaḍān/3 September.[94] It appears that the Mamluk army rode in from the northwest (the direction of Acre) along the Jezreel Valley. The Mamluks encountered the Mongol army somewhere in the plain to the north and north-western vicinity of ʿAyn Jālūt, where the latter had already taken up position. That the battle was near the spring, but not actually at it, is hinted at by Ibn al-Furāt, who writes in one place that Qutuz initially took up position across from ʿAyn Jālūt.[95] It would seem that the armies were drawn up more or less from north to south, and since they each numbered ten thousand or more men, their lines must have been fairly wide-spread.[96]

The battle initially did not go well for the Mamluks. The Mongols responded to the Mamluk approach by attacking them. The extent of their attack is unknown but it must have at least included the Mongol Right, since the Mamluk Left was defeated and disintegrated. Qutuz was able to rally his troops and launch a counter-attack which shook the Mongols. The Mongols attacked a second time, and again the Mamluks were close to defeat. But Qutuz was not disconcerted, and he again rallied his troops – if the reports are to be believed – with several cries of "Oh Islam! (*wā-islāmāh*) *Yā Allāh*, help your servant Qutuz against the Mongols." He then launched a frontal attack, which led to a Mamluk victory. It was probably at around this time that Ketbugha was killed, leading to the final disintegration of the Mongol army.[97]

93 Dhahabī, MS. Laud 305, fol. 254a; *Rawḍ*, 64.

94 Smpad, tr. Dédéyan, 106; Ṣārim al-Dīn Özbeg, in Ibn al-Furāt, fol. 247a (= Levi della Vida, "L'Invasione," 366); whence Maqrīzī, 1:430. For the time of the battle, see Amitai-Preiss, "ʿAyn Jālūt," 133–6; cf. Herde, "Taktiken," 86, and Thorau, *Baybars*, 77 and 86 n. 21.

95 Ibn al-Furāt, MS. Vatican, fols. 245b–246a.

96 For a detailed discussion of the position of the two armies, see Amitai-Preiss, "ʿAyn Jālūt," 134–8.

97 This is a summary of a detailed reconstruction of the battle presented in Amitai-Preiss, "ʿAyn Jālūt," 138–43, based on the conflation of the following sources: Ibn al-ʿAmīd, 174–5; Abū Shāma, 207; Ibn Wāṣil, MS. 1703, fol. 160a–b; Ibn al-Furāt, fols. 247a–248a (citing Ṣārim al-Dīn Özbeg [= Levi della Vida, "L'Invasione," 366], Ibn Duqmaq, Ibn ʿAbd al-Ẓāhir and unnamed eyewitnesses); Maqrīzī, 1:431 (who incorrectly summarizes Ibn al-Furāt); Yūnīnī, 1:361; 2:35; Ibn al-Dawādārī, 8:50, 57; Kutubī, 20:227; Ibn Kathīr, 13:225, 227; Nuwayrī, MS. 2m, fol. 132a; Qirtay, fol. 66b; Ibn Taghrī Birdī, *al-Nujūm al-zāhira* (rpt., Cairo, n.d.), 7:79; ʿAynī, fol. 76b. Another source which has since became available to me is Ibn Duqmaq, 268–9. A completely different account is provided in Rashīd al-Dīn, ed. ʿAlīzādah, 74–5; but see Amitai-Preiss, "ʿAyn Jālūt," 138–9; Thorau, "ʿAyn Jālūt," 237; Humphreys, *Saladin*, 470 n. 75.

Plate 1. Battle of ʿAyn Jālūt: Jezreel Valley, as seen from the hill on which was found the village of Zarʿīn: (a) facing east (ʿAyn Jālūt is behind the ridge marked with an arrow); (b) facing north (Hill of Moreh is in the background) (photographs: Habie Schwarz)

One contributing factor to the Mamluk victory was the timely desertion of al-Ashraf Mūsā, who was in the Mongol Left with his troops at the beginning of the fighting.[98]

After this defeat, the Mongols seem to have split up and fled in different directions. One group went up an unidentified nearby hill and attempted to make a stand. They were pursued by a force under Baybars which captured and killed most of them. Those who managed to escape were caught and slaughtered by local villagers.[99] Rashīd al-Dīn reports that some Mongol survivors sought refuge by hiding in fields of reeds in the area. This may be a reference to reed beds in either the Wādī Jālūt area or the environs of the Jordan River. These fugitives met their end, however, when the fields were set on fire by the Mamluks.[100] Al-Maqrīzī writes that at this stage the Mongols regrouped at Baysān and launched a counter-attack, which almost defeated the Mamluks until Qutuz was able to reorganize and launch the attack which decided the day.[101] This report, however, is an incorrect summary of a larger account of events as told by Ibn al-Furāt. The latter author only writes of two rounds of the same battle near ʿAyn Jālūt; there was no second battle at Baysān, as al-Maqrīzī would have us believe.[102]

The number of Mongol dead must have been large: the *MS de Rothelin* gives the figure of 1500.[103] Al-ʿAynī writes that most of the Mongols were killed in the battle.[104] Ṣārim al-Dīn Özbeg's claim that the entire Mongol army perished is surely exaggerated.[105] No figures for Mamluk casualties are given. The Mongol survivors fled north; among them was Baydar, formally commander of the Mongol advance guard at Gaza, who must have joined Ketbugha just before the battle.[106] The historian Hetʿum writes that the Mongol survivors found refuge with the King Hetʿum of Lesser Armenia.[107] The Mongol authorities in Damascus, along with several of their local cronies (al-Zayn al-Ḥāfiẓī is specifically mentioned), quickly left the city, although they were harried by local villagers, robbed and a number were killed.[108] The same happened in Hama and Aleppo.[109] Ketbugha's camp, probably still in the Biqāʿ, was captured along with his family.[110] Ibn al-ʿAmīd writes that a number of Mongol women were captured, without mentioning specifically

98 Nuwayrī, MS. 2m, fol. 131b; Ibn Wāṣil, MS. 1703, fol. 161a; Abū 'l-Fidā', 3:214; Yūnīnī, 1:377; 2:312–13; Ibn al-Dawādārī, 8:57; Amitai-Preiss, "ʿAyn Jālūt," 139–40.

99 Ibn Wāṣil, MS. 1703, fol. 160b; Yūnīnī, 1:361; 2:35; Kutubī, 20:227; Ibn Taghrī Birdī, 7:79; *Rawḍ*, 64–5.

100 Rashīd al-Dīn, ed. ʿAlīzādah, 3:74–5.

101 Maqrīzī, 1:431.

102 Ibn al-Furāt, MS. Vatican, fols. 247b–248a; see Amitai-Preiss, "ʿAyn Jālūt," 142–3, for further discussion of this.

103 In *RHC, Occ.*, 2:638.

104 ʿAynī, fol. 76a.

105 Cited in Ibn al-Furāt, fol. 248a (= Levi della Vida, "L'Invasione," 366).

106 Ibn al-ʿAmīd, 174; Ibn al-Ṣuqāʿī, 50; cf. Qirtay, fol. 66b, who writes that Baydarā was killed in the battle; as the next chapter shows, he survived.

107 Hetʿum, 175.

108 Ibn al-ʿAmīd, 174; Abū Shāma, 207; Yūnīnī, 1:366; Ibn al-Dawādārī, 8:51; Nuwayrī, MS. 2m, fol. 132b; Ibn al-Furāt, MS. Vatican, fol. 250a.

109 Ibn Wāṣil, MS. 1703, fol. 162b; Abū 'l-Fidā', 3:215; Ṣārim al-Dīn, cited in Ibn al-Furāt, MS. Vatican, fol. 247b (= Levi della Vida, "L'Invasione," 366); cf. Rashīd al-Dīn, ed. Quatremère, 352 (cf. ed. ʿAlīzādah, 3:76 and n. 6), who writes that the Mongol officials were massacred everywhere but in Damascus.

110 Rashīd al-Dīn, ed. ʿAlīzādah, 3:76–7.

where. It seems, then, that at least some Mongol soldiers had their families with them.[111]

Qutuz dispatched a force under Baybars after the routed Mongols. Baybars chased them up through northern Syria, at Homs catching up with a group of them, along with their women and children, and dealing them another beating. There are also reports that Baybars met a fresh contingent of Mongols there, numbering 2000 troopers, which had been sent by Hülegü to reinforce Ketbugha.[112] Ibn ʿAbd al-Ẓāhir writes that Baybars reached as far as Ḥārim and Afāmiya, where the Mongol reinforcements were defeated.[113] Other writers state that Baybars reached as far as Aleppo before turning back to join the main Mamluk army, now camped at Damascus.[114]

At least to some extent the Mamluk victory can undoubtedly be attributed to the decisive leadership of two men, Qutuz and Baybars, particularly the former. As was seen above, it was Qutuz who dragged the recalcitrant amirs out of Egypt, and right up to the battle he constantly harangued them about the holy war and the need to drive out the Mongols. At the battle itself, he showed himself to be a cool-headed commander, and – if the reports are to be credited with some truth – he personally led the charge that decided the battle. Qutuz also had the insight to make his peace with Baybars, in spite of the longstanding feud between them and the apprehension he must have had about the future (justified by events). He delegated to Baybars the important responsibility during the campaign of commanding the vanguard and later put him in charge of the mopping up operations. Baybars's exact role during the battle proper is not known, although the sources mention his personal bravery in the fighting.[115] This is more than just panegyrics from a later period, although certainly Ibn ʿAbd al-Ẓāhir's account is greatly exaggerated: according to him Baybars won the battle almost single-handedly.[116] With regard to Baybars's bravery, at least, the Arabic sources are supported by the Frankish *Gestes des Chiprois*.[117] The courage of other Mamluk officers is also noted in the sources.[118]

Other reasons for the Mamluk victory were the timely desertion of al-Ashraf and his troops and the relatively larger size of the Mamluk army, composed to a large degree of highly trained mounted archers, who were ignited by a sense of mission and "no choice but to win" attitude that had been successfully instilled by Qutuz. Emphasis must be placed on the similarity of fighting methods of the Mamluks and Mongols: only an army composed of masses of mounted archers had a chance of standing up to and defeating the

[111] Ibn al-ʿAmīd, 175; Ibn Taghrī Birdī, 7:82.

[112] Abū Shāma, 209; *Zubda*, fol. 38b–39a; *Tuḥfa*, 44; Ibn al-Dawādārī, 8:59–60; Ibn Kathīr, 13:221; Yūnīnī, 1:366; Kutubī, 20:228; Ibn al-Furāt, MS. Vatican, fol. 251a; ʿAynī, fol. 76a.

[113] *Rawḍ*, 65.

[114] Ibn Wāṣil, MS. 1703, fols. 160b–161a; Dhahabī, MS. Laud 305, fol. 254a.

[115] Nuwayrī, MS. 2m, fol. 132a; Ibn al-Furāt, MS. Vatican, fol. 247b; Maqrīzī, 1:431.

[116] *Rawḍ*, 63–6.

[117] In *RHC, Ar*, 2:753, cited in Thorau, "ʿAyn Jālūt," 240 n. 24.

[118] Ibn Kathīr, 13:221, reports the valor of al-Manṣūr of Hama (see also Ibn Wāṣil, MS. 1703, fol. 161a) and Aqtay al-Mustaʿrib, the *atabeg*, but does not mention Baybars.

Mongols. The reason for the similar fighting techniques of the two armies was the common origin of their troops – the Eurasian steppe, a fact discerned by several writers from the Mamluk Sultanate.[119] As Professor Ayalon has written: "In the battle of ʿAyn Jālūt, which had been fought out between the people of the same race, the infidels of yesterday had defeated the Muslims of to-morrow."[120]

In the aftermath of victory

After the fighting, Qutuz dealt with those Syrian Ayyūbid princes who had participated in the battle. Al-Manṣūr Muḥammad of Hama, who had been on the Mamluk side since the Mongol invasion, was rewarded by receiving his kingdom again, to which was added Maʿarrat al-Nuʿmān and Baʿrīn.[121] Al-Ashraf Mūsā, although he had earlier served the Mongols and had come on to the battlefield with them, had helped the Muslim cause by his timely desertion. His past actions were forgiven and he was confirmed in his old principality of Homs (returned to him by the Mongols).[122] It was obvious, however, that in both cases the continued rule of these two princes was dependent directly on their new Mamluk masters. A third Ayyūbid, al-Saʿīd Ḥasan, ruler of Banias and al-Ṣubayba, was less fortunate. His overly exuberant partisanship of the Mongols had compromised him in Qutuz's eyes. Other explanations offered by the sources are his refusal to respond to Qutuz's secret messages before the battle (as al-Ashraf is recorded to have done), his fierce fighting during the battle and even his conversion to Christianity (this last accusation was probably mere slander). In spite of his request for a pardon, Qutuz had him summarily beheaded.[123]

Qutuz thereupon moved ahead to Damascus, reaching it on 30 Ramaḍān/8 September. Previously he had sent word to Damascus of the Mamluk victory, and later sent an amir to reestablish order. This officer put an end to the depredations against Christians, who were now paying the price of seven months of relative religious freedom. The local Muslims had found it a terrible

[119] See especially Abū Shāma, 208 (quoted by Yūnīnī, 1:367), who is cited at the beginning of this book; ʿUmarī, ed. Lech, 70–1, and as summarized by Ayalon, "Yāsa," pt. C1, 122–3; Ibn Khaldūn, ʿ*Ibar*, 5:371; D. Ayalon, "The European Asiatic Steppe: A Major Reservoir of Power for the Islamic World," *Proceedings of 25th Congress of Orientalists – Moscow, 1960* (Moscow, 1963), 2:49. For general lauding of the role played by the Turkish Mamluks at ʿAyn Jālūt, see also: Qirtay, fol. 68b; *Tuḥfa*, 44; *Zubda*, fol. 39a; Ibn al-Furāt, MS. Vatican, fol. 249a; Ibn Wāṣil, MS. 1702, fol. 359a–b; Ṣārim al-Dīn, in Ibn al-Furāt, MS. Vatican, fol. 247b; ʿAynī, fol. 76a. Some of these writers single out the role of the Baḥriyya in particular. Cf. Ibn al-Dawādārī's anti-Baḥrī remark, 8:60.

[120] Ayalon, "The European Asiatic Steppe," 49.

[121] Ibn Wāṣil, MS. 1703, fol. 161a; Ibn Kathīr, 13:221.

[122] Ibn Wāṣil, MS. 1703, fol. 161a; Dhahabī, MS. Laud 305, fol. 254a–b; Ibn al-Furāt, MS. Vatican, fol. 251a; Maqrīzī, 1:433; Ibn al-Ṣuqāʿī, 129.

[123] Ibn Wāṣil, MS. 1703, fol. 161a; Abū Shāma, 207 (see MS. Br. Lib. Or. 1539, fol. 119b, for additional details); Ibn al-ʿAmīd, 175; Yūnīnī, 2:16–7; Nuwayrī, MS. 2m, fol. 132a; Ibn al-Dawādārī, 8:51–2; Ibn Kathīr, 13:225; ʿAynī, fol. 80a.

affront that the Christians were accorded equal status to them; the Christians for their part had exacerbated the situation by their assertive and even arrogant behavior towards the Muslims. With their Mongol protectors gone, churches were burnt, the stores and houses of Christians were looted and they were physically assaulted. In the general excitement, Jewish property was also attacked until it was remembered that the Jews had not offended the Muslims. In addition, Mongol sympathizers among the population were attacked and killed by angry mobs.[124]

Upon his entrance into Damascus, Qutuz completed his arrangements for the rule of Syria. Local collaborators were punished. Ḥusayn al-Kurdī, who had been instrumental in the capture of al-Nāṣir Yūsuf, was executed.[125] Sanjar al-Ḥalabī was named governor of Damascus.[126] Qutuz appointed as governor of Aleppo a refugee prince from the Jazīra, al-Saʿīd (previously called al-Muẓaffar) ʿAlā' al-Dīn b. Badr al-Dīn Lu'lu', whose father had been the ruler of Mosul (607–57/1211–59) and had submitted to the Mongols. ʿAlā' al-Dīn had been left the rulership over Sinjār by his father, but was found in Syria at this time, because earlier he had sent there to ask for assistance from al-Nāṣir Yūsuf against the Mongols. When the Syrian army went to Egypt, ʿAlā' al-Dīn joined them and returned to Syria with the Mamluks in 658/1260. Qutuz had named him governor so he could correspond with his brothers, the rulers of Mosul and Jazīrat Ibn ʿUmar who had succeeded their deceased father (d. 1259), and thus would receive information about the Mongols.[127] In addition, possibly Qutuz hoped that he would act as a counterweight to the amirs of the ʿAzīziyya and Nāṣiriyya factions in Aleppo.

In spite of these appointments, Qutuz's control over much of Syria proper, let alone the border areas, was weak or even non-existent. There were Crusader possessions along the coast and in the north, and Bohemond VI of Antioch held decidedly pro-Mongol sympathies. During the Mongol occupation, he had received territories from Hülegü and had seized many districts on his borders.[128] In northern Syria, an independent Ismāʿīlī entity had survived the Mongol conquest, Hülegü's declaration to Louis IX notwithstanding. During the Mongol occupation, the King of Lesser Armenia had gained control of several castles in the northern part of the province of Aleppo.[129]

In Aleppo itself, there were powerful groups of amirs whose loyalty was not

[124] Ibn al-ʿAmīd, 175–6; Abū Shāma, 208; Ibn Wāṣil, MS. 1703, fol. 161b; Yūnīnī, 1:361–2; Ibn al-Furāt, MS. Vatican, fols. 250a–251a; Maqrīzī, 1:432. See Ghāzī b. al-Wāsiṭī, 407–10 for a contemporary account of Christian behavior in Damascus during the Mongol occupation.

[125] Ibn al-ʿAmīd, 176; Abū 'l-Fidā', 3:214–15; Dhahabī, MS. Laud 305, fols. 254b; ʿAynī, fol. 76b–77a (cites Ibn Kathīr), who also tells of how al-Manṣūr punished collaborators when he returned to Hama.

[126] Ibn al-ʿAmīd, 176; Dhahabī, MS. Laud 305, fol. 254b; Ibn Wāṣil, fol. 162b.

[127] Ibn al-ʿAmīd, 176; Ibn Wāṣil, MS. 1703, fol. 162b; Yūnīnī, 1:370; Dhahabī, MS. Laud 305, fol. 255a; Ibn al-Furāt, MS. Vatican, fol. 251a–b; Maqrīzī, 1:433; Abū 'l-Fidā', 3:216; ʿAynī, fol. 77a. D. Patton, *Badr al-Dīn Lu'lu'* (Seattle, 1991), 50–61, gives a good reconstruction of Lu'lu''s relations with the Mongols; cf. *ibid.*, 71, for ʿAlā' al-Dīn's arrival in Syria.

[128] *Rawḍ*, 300; Nuwayrī, MS. 2m, fols. 240a, 245b; Hetʿum, 2:171; Cahen, *Syrie*, 706–7.

[129] Hetʿum, 171; Cahen, *Syrie*, 75; Canard, "Arménie," 222.

a foregone conclusion. Likewise, several of the amirs appointed to governorships might have been looking for the first opportunity to throw off Egyptian sovereignty. The situation on both sides of the Euphrates was unclear, as was the extent of Mongol control over Iraq. Qutuz's hand, however, was greatly strengthened by the submission of Sharaf al-Dīn ʿĪsā b. Muhannā of the Āl Faḍl, the leading family among the bedouin (*al-ʿarab* or *al-ʿurbān*) of northern Syria. Qutuz in turn appointed ʿĪsā commander of the bedouin (*amīr al-ʿarab*) and gave him as an *iqṭāʿ* Salamiyya, hitherto part of the province of Hama.[130] As will be seen in the subsequent chapter, this understanding with ʿĪsā was of major importance in securing the Euphrates frontier, along with the general security of northern Syria. ʿĪsā b. Muhannā is not mentioned at all during the campaign that ended at ʿAyn Jālūt, and he came to Damascus only after Qutuz's victory became known.[131] Evidently, he had wanted to remain neutral until a clear winner emerged.

Qutuz was not to savor his victory for long. He cancelled a proposed trip to Aleppo and cut short his stay in Syria, because of the widening rift between him and Baybars. The Mamluk sources attribute this to Qutuz's refusal to fulfill his promise to Baybars to appoint him governor of Aleppo, although their animosity had a long history and it had only been papered over in the face of an imminent Mongol threat. With the danger temporarily removed, the tension returned. Qutuz set off for Egypt with his army. In the desert between al-ʿArīsh and Ṣāliḥiyya, he was murdered by a conspiracy of amirs, which included Baybars and was probably under his leadership. The exact circumstances of Qutuz's assassination and the subsequent events are still unclear, but the final result was that Baybars was proclaimed sultan.[132] Thus was inaugurated the period in which Mamluk power was consolidated and the foundations were laid for their successful struggle against the Īlkhānids.

The Mamluk victory at ʿAyn Jālūt was hailed by the Mamluk writers (see above) because Islam had been saved, the Mongols had been stopped and the myth of their invincibility had been destroyed.[133] In addition, the Mongol presence in Syria had been eliminated, and as a side effect the Mamluks were able to occupy most of non-Crusader Syria. In retrospect, however, we can see that this was merely an interim victory. The Mongol army at ʿAyn Jālūt was only a small part of the total Mongol forces, and it was only a question of time before the Mongol offensive was to be renewed.[134] Yet, for various reasons,

[130] Ibn Wāṣil, MS. 1703, fol. 161a; Ibn Kathīr, 13:221; Maqrīzī, 1:433; Ṣafadī, *Aʿyān al-ʿaṣr*, MS. Aya Sofya 2963, fol. 144a–b. See ch. 3 below. [131] Yūnīnī, 1:485.

[132] See Irwin, *Middle East*, 34, 37–8; Khowaiter, *Baibars*, 24–6; Thorau, *Baybars*, 79–85; Holt, "Three Biographies," 21–3, 26.

[133] Nuwayrī (MS. 2m, fol. 135a) and Yūnīnī (1:380; 2:28) mention that this was the first victory of anyone over the Mongols since that of the Khwārazm-shāh (i.e. Jalāl al-Dīn) at Parwān in 619/1221. On the latter battle, see Boyle, "Īl-Khāns," 318–19; Barthold, *Turkestan*, 441–2.

[134] See D. Ayalon, "Studies on the Transfer of the ʿAbbāsid Caliphate from Baġdād to Cairo," *Arabica* 7 (1960):59; *idem*, "Ḥimṣ, Battle of," *EI*², 3:402; Spuler, *Iran*, 52–3; Irwin, *Middle East*, 34; Morgan, *Mongols*, 156; Lewis, "ʿAyn Djālūt," 786; S. ʿĀshūr, *al-ʿAṣr al-mamālīkī fī miṣr wa'l-shām* (Cairo, 1965), 34–7. Cf. F.Ḥ. ʿĀshūr, *al-ʿAlāqāt*, 55–6.

no serious Mongol attempt to reconquer Syria and to exact revenge on the Mamluks was made for twenty-one years. This period was utilized by the Mamluks, and Baybars's important role can already be mentioned, in preparing themselves for the real test. It is to this interim but decisive period that we now turn.

CHAPTER 3

The formulation of anti-Īlkhānid policy

This country was very far from that land which those infidels had conquered, but [then] it became their neighbor. And thus, the people [of this country] had to fight [the infidels] and resist them. In order to do so, they had to obtain two things: a large army and a brave sultan [to lead them]. Without this, it is impossible to fight these infidels with all their conquests over the many lands, and their numerous men and armies.

Ibn al-Nafīs[1]

Syria at the commencement of Baybars's rule

Upon his accession to the Sultanate, Baybars was confronted with a deteriorating situation in Syria. Qutuz's governor in Damascus, Sanjar al-Ḥalabī, refused to accept the new order, rebelled and declared himself sultan of Syria. To the north, the senior amirs of Aleppo had quickly become disenchanted with Qutuz's appointee as governor, overthrown him and elected as ruler one of their own, whose loyalty to the sultan in Cairo was uncertain. As for the Mongols, just a few months after their defeat at ʿAyn Jālūt, they dispatched a large raiding party into northern Syria to reconnoiter and generally cause trouble. The Franks on the coast did not sit still, but also took advantage of the general disarray and launched an attack in early 1261. In addition, there existed several independent, and not necessarily friendly, political entities in Syria: the Ismāʿīlīs, the "emirate" of Ṣahyūn, and al-Mughīth ʿUmar's principality at Karak. Finally, the situation along the frontier between "Mamluk" Syria and "Mongol" Iraq was in a state of flux, and without an aggressive policy on Baybars's part large areas might be lost to the Mongols by default. Baybars emerged from this inauspicious situation as the undisputed ruler of Muslim Syria, which he united firmly with Egypt. In this, he was served both by his own talents, and by the willingness of the majority of the Syrian military factions to rally behind a strong Egyptian regime in the face of the incessant Mongol danger.[2]

[1] M. Meyerhof and J. Schacht (ed. and tr.), *The Theologus Autodidactus of Ibn al-Nafīs* (Oxford, 1968), 43 of Arabic.

[2] Parts of the first two sections of this chapter appeared in Amitai-Preiss, "Aftermath," *passim.*

The most immediate threat to Baybars's rule in Syria was the rebellion of Sanjar al-Ḥalabī in Damascus, who gave himself the royal title of al-Malik al-Mujāhid. Sanjar's ultimate intentions are not clear and it is possible that he saw himself playing a subservient role to the Egyptian sultan, similar to the earlier Ayyūbid model. Baybars, however, was not in the mood for power sharing, and was able to establish his authority in central Syria. Sanjar was soon forced to flee, but after a short imprisonment he was rehabilitated and given a succession of responsible posts.[3] It is important to note that during the short period of his rebellion, Sanjar wrote to al-Manṣūr Muḥammad, the Ayyūbid prince of Hama, and Lachin al-Jūkandār, the new strongman in Aleppo, to join him. Both answered that they would follow the ruler of Egypt, whoever he might be.[4] It would seem that after their experiences of the previous few months, neither ruler thought that an independent Syrian regime could guarantee the country against the Mongols in the event of another offensive.

Soon after Sanjar al-Ḥalabī had declared his independence, Qutuz's governor in Aleppo, al-Saʿīd ʿAlā' al-Dīn b. Lu'lu', was overthrown by the local Nāṣirī and ʿAzīzī amirs. Their probable initial displeasure at having an outsider placed over them was intensified by al-Saʿīd's avarice and heavy-handed policy towards the local population. The amirs were also extremely dissatisfied by what they felt was al-Saʿīd's unprofessional response to calls for aid against Mongol raids at al-Bīra and Manbij: against their advice, small forces were dispatched and were subsequently defeated. When news reached them of Sanjar's rebellion in Damascus, the amirs met, decided to arrest al-Saʿīd and to pick one of themselves to rule, in imitation of Sanjar. Their choice fell on Ḥusām al-Dīn Lachin al-Jūkandār al-ʿAzīzī.[5] Perhaps, they had intended to carve out for themselves a separate or semi-independent "mamluk" state in northern Syria, although their above-mentioned answer to Sanjar al-Ḥalabī suggests that they were realistic enough to seek a strong guardian to the south; Sanjar perhaps did not seem to them powerful enough.

Whatever were the exact plans of the Aleppan amirs, they were cut short by the arrival of a large Mongol force a few days later (26 Dhū 'l-ḥijja 658/2 December 1260).[6] Unwilling to meet the Mongols alone, Lachin and the rest of the Aleppan army left the city and moved south to Hama. There they joined forces with al-Manṣūr. The combined forces then moved down to Homs, where al-Ashraf Mūsā came out with his army to join them. The decision was reached to stay put and meet the oncoming Mongols.[7]

It is reported in Mamluk sources that this Mongol force was under the

[3] Holt, *Crusades*, 91–2; Irwin, *Middle East*, 45; Khowaiter, *Baibars*, 28–9; Thorau, *Baybars*, 94–5. [4] Ibn Wāṣil, MS. 1703, fol. 164a; Yūnīnī, 1:375; Ibn al-Dawādārī, 8:65.

[5] Yūnīnī, 1:374–5, 2:3–6; Kutubī, 20:231; Ibn Wāṣil, MS. 1703, fols. 164b–166a; Abū 'l-Fidā', 3:217–18; Ibn al-Furāt, MS. Vatican, fols. 257b–258a; Ibn al-Dawādārī, 8:64–5; Thorau, *Baybars*, 95–6; Patton, *Lu'lu'*, 73.

[6] Yūnīnī, 1:375; Ibn al-Dawādārī, 8:65, writes that the Mongols arrived on 16 Dhū 'l-ḥijja.

[7] Ibn Wāṣil, MS. 1703, fol. 166a–b; Yūnīnī, 1:375; 2:115 (citing Ibn Wāṣil by name).

leadership of Baydarā (i.e. Baydar), who had been one of Ketbugha's officers in Syria several months earlier and had escaped to the Jazīra after ʿAyn Jālūt.[8] It is implied that this raid was the initiative of the Mongols on the other side of the Euphrates, and not undertaken at the express orders of Hülegü.[9] The Mongols found Aleppo abandoned by its army. Leaving behind *shaḥnas*, they continued on south, bypassing Hama. On Friday, 5 Muḥarram 659/11 December 1260, they arrived at Homs and met the combined forces of Aleppo, Hama and Homs near the grave of Khālid b. al-Walīd. It is unclear how far the actual battle was from this tomb, located about 1500 meters to the north of the citadel. The land to the northeast of the grave is a gentle slope that rises from west to east, and from the map at least seems suitable for cavalry warfare (see map 8). The Mongols numbered some 6000 horsemen, while the Muslim force was significantly smaller, about 1400 men. The Mongols organized themselves into eight squadrons (*aṭlāb*, plural of *ṭulb*), the first one containing 1000 men, and the others, whose numbers are not given, arranged behind it. Al-Ashraf seems to have had overall command over the Muslim troops. He kept them in one *ṭulb*; he himself was in the center, al-Manṣūr was in the Right, and the Aleppan amirs were in the Left. Al-Yūnīnī writes that birds were seen flapping in the faces of the Mongols, who were also discomforted by the fog and the sun. The Muslims launched a concerted attack and in the end were victorious. Baydarā and the rest of the Mongols fled the battlefield, pursued by the Muslims. Of undoubtable importance to the Muslim victory was the timely appearance of Zāmil b. ʿAlī, an important bedouin leader in north Syria, in the rear of the Mongols with a large group of his men. In this battle, large numbers of Mongols were killed and taken captive.[10] Among the captives was a Mongol youth named Ketbugha who was enrolled in the mamluks of the amir Qalawun, and was later to become sultan in his own right (694–6/1294–6).[11]

The pro-Mongol sources tell the story of this expedition completely differently. Rashīd al-Dīn and Ibn al-Fuwaṭī name the commander of the force as Ilge (written Ilkā) Noyan,[12] while Bar Hebraeus calls him Köke-Ilge

[8] Yūnīnī, 1:375; Ibn al-Furāt, MS. Vatican, fol. 262a.

[9] For the reasons behind this raid, see Abū Shāma, 211; Yūnīnī, 2:89; Dhahabī, MS. Laud 305, fol. 255b; Ibn al-Furāt, MS. Vatican, fol. 262a; Amitai-Preiss, "Aftermath," 2.

[10] Yūnīnī, 1:434–5, 2:89–90, 115. Similar, but less detailed accounts are found in Ibn Wāṣil, MS. 1703, fols. 166b–167b; Ibn al-Dawādārī, 8:68; Dhahabī, MS. Laud 305, fol. 255b; Mufaḍḍal, 71–5; Ibn al-Furāt, MS. Vatican, fol. 262a; Maqrīzī, 1:442; Ibn Kathīr, 13:230 (cf. *ibid.*, 240, where he reports that Baydarā was killed in the battle); see also Abū Shāma, 211. For a more detailed discussion, see Amitai-Preiss, "Aftermath," 3–4.

[11] Ibn Kathīr, 13:338–9; Ṣafadī, *Aʿyān al-ʿaṣr*, MS. Aya Sofya 2967, fol. 47a; Ibn Taghrī Birdī, 8:55. But cf. Nuwayrī, MS. 2m, fol. 132a; Ibn al-Ṣuqāʿī, 131, who say he was captured at ʿAyn Jālūt.

[12] Rashīd al-Dīn, ed. ʿAlīzādah, 3:76 (cf. ed. Quatremère, 358); Ibn al-Fuwaṭī, 344–50. Ilge Noyan is mentioned at Abagha's accession to the throne, ca. 1265; Rashīd al-Dīn, ed. ʿAlīzādah, 3:100. On this figure, the ancestor of the future Jalayir rulers of Azerbaijan, see the introduction to Ahrī, *Ta'rīkh-i shaykh uways*, ed. and tr. J.B. van Loon (The Hague, 1954), 6–7.

(written Kukālakay).[13] According to the first two writers, Hülegü himself ordered the expedition. These sources report little more than the arrival of the Mongol troops in northern Syria, the advance to Homs (in Bar Hebraeus; Ibn al-Fuwaṭī writes that they reached Damascus!), the subsequent mishandling of the local population at Aleppo (Bar Hebraeus), and the withdrawal to Rūm of the Mongols upon hearing of Baybars's arrival (Rashīd al-Dīn). These accounts are not very credible, not least because they fail to mention the Mongol defeat at Homs. Rashīd al-Dīn, it would seem, conflated the text about the reinforcements sent by Hülegü ca. September 1260, which were defeated by Baybars,[14] with that on the raid into northern Syria at the end of the year.

In spite of the relatively small size of the forces involved in this battle, the Muslim victory was a significant one. It strengthened the feeling generated by the victory at ʿAyn Jālūt that the Mongols were not invincible. In fact, Mamluk writers of a later generation claimed that the first battle of Homs was an even greater victory than the one at ʿAyn Jālūt, because whereas at the latter battle the Muslims had a numerical advantage, at Homs the Muslims were in a clear minority.[15] While this victory was achieved by the Ayyūbids of northern Syria, and not by the Mamluks of Egypt, it should be remembered that most probably a large portion of these Syrian forces was composed of mamluk units of the Ayyūbid princes and amirs. Thus, the first battle of Homs represents yet another vindication of the mamluk system in the face of the Mongol danger.

Al-Ashraf and al-Manṣūr returned to their respective cities. In Hama, when news of the Muslim victory reached the inhabitants, a number of Mongol sympathizers were attacked and one was killed. It is reported that these sympathizers wanted to dig a tunnel to let the Mongols into the city. Baybars was so impressed by al-Ashraf's role in the battle that he returned Tall Bāshir to his appanage.[16] The amirs from the ʿAzīziyya and Nāṣiriyya, not wanting to take their chances alone against the surviving Mongols who had fled north, made their way to Egypt where they were well received by Baybars and integrated into the Mamluk army in Syria.[17] As for the Mongols, they first made their way to nearby Salamiyya, where they regrouped. Moving north, they passed by Hama, seeing that it could not be taken. Evidently, al-Manṣūr

[13] Bar Hebraeus, 439–40 (= Ibn al-ʿIbrī, 492). Ibn al-Furāt, MS. Vatican, fol. 262b, reports that Kukalaqā Noyan was one of the Mongol commanders at this battle. Köke-Ilge is earlier recorded as one of the two commanders of the Right Wing of Hülegü's army early in the campaign against the Ismāʿīlīs; Rashīd al-Dīn, ed. ʿAlīzādah, 3:32.

[14] See above, ch. 2, p. 44.

[15] Mufaḍḍal, 75; Ibn al-Dawādārī, 8:68; ʿAynī, fol. 79a. According to Ibn Wāṣil, MS. 1703, fols. 166b–167a (hence, Yūnīnī, 2:115), citing Mubāriz al-Dīn, the *ustādār* ("major-domo") of al-Manṣūr, there were more Mongol heroes or elite troops (*bahāduriyya al-mughul*) at this battle than at ʿAyn Jālūt; see Amitai-Preiss, "ʿAyn Jālūt," 128–9, for a full discussion of this evidence. For the translation of *bahādur*, see ch. 5, p. 108.

[16] Ibn Wāṣil, MS. 1703, fol. 167b; Yūnīnī, 2:115–17, 313.

[17] Ibn Wāṣil, MS. 1703, fols. 167b–168a; Kutubī, 20:249; Yūnīnī, 2:91. In his obituary (he died later in AH 659), Lachin al-Jūkandār is lauded for his bravery in the battle; Yūnīnī, 2:300.

was already inside with his troops. They then returned to Aleppo, drove out all the inhabitants, massacred some of them and permitted the rest to return to the city. Thereupon they kept the city blockaded, causing great hardship, and withdrew after four months, when word of the advance of a Mamluk force reached them.[18]

If there were any doubts in Baybars's mind about Mongol intentions towards Syria they would have been dispelled by this Mongol raid. It must have been clear to him that at some point the Mongols would return to Syria en masse, to avenge their loss at ʿAyn Jālūt and reclaim the country for themselves. Subsequent Mongol raids and belligerent letters from the Īlkhāns would only strengthen this initial perception of Mongol intents. Rather than waiting quietly for the Mongols to return, and thus inviting them to raid and invade by his passivity, Baybars turned to meet this challenge: he strengthened his regime internally, giving it an ideological linchpin; Syria was firmly integrated into his kingdom; he devoted himself to preparing a war machine that could meet anything the Mongols or their allies could throw at him; he developed an active defense, carrying the war into the enemy camp; and he embarked on an active foreign policy designed to weaken and even immobilize his Mongol enemy.

The Franks at Acre perhaps hoped to take advantage of the general confusion by launching an attack of their own. In Rabīʿ I 659/February 1261, some 900 knights and sergeants, 1500 Turcopolos (light cavalry) and 3000 infantrymen set out to attack a group of Türkmen on the Golan. Their would-be victims were warned, however, and the Frankish force was severely beaten. This was essentially the end of the Frankish hopes to exploit the unsettled situation in Syria, and for the time being the Franks were to adopt a defensive posture.[19] But this did not prevent them from meddling in Mamluk–Mongol affairs. Already the next month, when Baybars sent off a force under Fakhr al-Dīn Altunba al-Ḥimṣī and Ḥusām al-Dīn Lachin al-Jūkandār (the above-mentioned leader of the Aleppan amirs) to deal with the Mongols still encamped at Aleppo, the Franks of Acre reportedly wrote to the Mongols to notify them of the approaching Mamluk army. Forewarned, the Mongols withdrew to the east at the beginning of Jumādā I 659/April 1261.[20] It is unclear whether this notification was the policy of the leaders of Acre, or the private initiative of one or more individuals.

In order to be free to consolidate his hold over Muslim Syria and pursue the war with the Mongols, Baybars had to come to some type of understanding

18 Ibn Wāṣil, MS. 1703, fols. 167a, 168a; Abū 'l-Fidā', 3:219; Yūnīnī, 1:435–6, 2:117–18; Ibn al-Dawādārī, 8:68–9; Mufaḍḍal, 76–7.

19 Abū Shāma, 212; Dhahabī, MS. Laud 305, fol. 256b; Ibn al-Furāt, MS. Vatican, fols. 285b–286a (= ed. Lyons, 1:59); Jackson, "Crisis," 509 and n. 4; Riley-Smith's comments in Ibn al-Furāt, ed. Lyons, 2:195–6.

20 Yūnīnī, 1:439–40, 2:93; Ibn al-Dawādārī, 8:71–2; Mufaḍḍal, 79–80.

with the Franks of Acre. At this early date it appears that he had little interest in confronting them. On the other hand, the attack against the Türkmen could not go unpunished, and he had to show that he was a force to be reckoned with. Thus, when the Sultan moved into Syria in Shawwāl 659/September 1261 together with the newly appointed ʿAbbāsid Caliph (see below), raids were launched against Frankish possessions. A treaty was soon concluded, although the Sultan was unable to achieve the terms that he would have liked, and had to settle for what was essentially a renewal of the agreement between al-Nāṣir Yūsuf and the Franks. The need for a secure rear and unhindered communications, along with the problems caused by a famine in Syria (and the necessity to ship food through the Syrian ports), made Baybars adopt a more conciliatory stance at this time than he would usually later take.[21]

Towards the Franks of Antioch, however, Baybars chose a different tack. Under Bohemond VI the northern Franks maintained their unequivocal pro-Mongol alliance after ʿAyn Jālūt. In the city there was found a Mongol *shaḥna*, who had held a census and collected a tax of one dinar per person.[22] In late 659/1261, a force under Balaban al-Rashīdī and Sunqur al-Rūmī, raided the country on its way to the Euphrates to provide support for the new Caliph's offensive into Iraq. This was followed in mid-660/1262 by another raid, again led by Sunqur, together with the princes of Homs and Hama, which looted Antioch's port at al-Suwaydiyya (Port Saint-Simeon).[23] During the second raid, the attackers withdrew upon the advance of a Mongol force which had been called in by the Armenians to the north.[24] The purpose of these raids, which continued with regularity until the city was taken in 666/1268, would have been to weaken Antioch's military capability, to punish it for having cooperated with the Mongols in the recent past and to dissuade its ruler from such cooperation in the future. This last goal, however, was not immediately achieved. Apparently later in 660/1262, foot soldiers from Antioch joined an Armenian expedition to al-Fūʿa in north Syria. This combined force was subsequently defeated by an army sent from Aleppo. Many captives were taken and sent to Egypt.[25] Bohemond VI had yet to learn that it was not worth provoking Baybars.

Along the Euphrates the situation was less clear-cut than in the north, where Baybars faced the hostile states of Antioch and Lesser Armenia. In the

[21] *Rawḍ*, 117–19; Ibn al-Furāt, MS. Vatican, fols. 276b–277b (= ed. Lyons, 1:52–4); Maqrīzī, 1:463–4; Thorau, *Baybars*, 142–4.

[22] Ibn al-Dawādārī, 8:127; Mufaḍḍal, 171; Ibn al-Furāt, MS. Vienna, fol. 140a–b (= ed. Lyons, 1:154); Cahen, *Syrie*, 706.

[23] Ibn al-Furāt, MS. Vatican, fol. 276a; MS. Vienna, fol. 5a (= ed. Lyons, 1:60), citing Ibn Duqmaq; Maqrīzī, 1:463, 472; Runciman, *Crusades*, 3:316; Prawer, *Histoire*, 2:440; Thorau, *Baybars*, 142; Canard, "Arménie," 222–3.

[24] *Gestes des Chiprois*, in *RHC, Ar*, 2:755; Canard, "Arménie," 222–3; Thorau, *Baybars*, 142; Riley-Smith, in Ibn al-Furāt, ed. Lyons, 2:196.

[25] Yūnīnī, 1:496; Ibn al-Dawādārī, 8:90; Ibn Kathīr, 13:234; Ibn al-Furāt, MS. Vienna, fol. 7b. This raid must have been the source of the Armenian prisoners mentioned by Canard, "Arménie," 223, citing Maqrīzī, 1:476, who imprecisely renders Ibn al-Furāt's account.

aftermath of Hülegü's withdrawal with most of his army to Azerbaijan and the subsequent expulsion of the Mongols from Syria, various Mongol possessions on the east bank of the Euphrates were all but abandoned. The extremely strategic fortress of al-Bīra, captured by Hülegü on his way into Syria in 658, was repossessed by a governor of al-Saʿīd, during the latter's short tenure in Aleppo, and soon subjected to a Mongol attack.[26] Ḥarrān was also bereft of any effective Mongol control, as attested to by the ease with which the Syrian freebooter Aqqush al-Barlī al-ʿAzīzī gained control of it later in 659/1261.[27] Other towns in the western Jazīra – al-Raqqa, al-Ruhā (Edessa) and Qalʿat Jaʿbar – were left by the Mongols in an all-but-destroyed state.[28] The existence of this no man's land on his eastern marches represented a clear challenge to Baybars and helps explain his subsequent policy towards this area.

Mention should be made of Baybars's relations with the small independent "principalities" in Muslim Syria: Karak and Shawbak ruled by the Ayyūbid al-Mughīth ʿUmar; Ṣahyūn (Saone) and Balāṭunus (Mansio Platanus), controlled since the Mongol invasion of 658/1260 by the amir Muẓaffar (or ʿIzz) al-Dīn ʿUthmān; and, the Ismāʿīlī "state" centered in several forts in north Syria – Maṣyāf, al-Kahf and others. In the decade after his accession, Baybars brought all these entities under his control, in fact, if not in name. Karak was taken in 661/1263, when its prince was tricked into leaving the safety of the fort and meeting Baybars at Mt. Tabor.[29] The Sultan's influence over Ṣahyūn and Balāṭunus had been felt as early as 660/1261–2. His suzerainty over the castles was recognized in 667/1269, and in 671/1272 he took direct control over them.[30] The subjugation of the Syrian Ismāʿīlīs was a more complicated process. Baybars began exerting influence on them in 664/1266. By 668/1270, he had them under his control, although final subjugation was not achieved until 671/1273 with the occupation of al-Kahf.[31] Over time, then, Baybars had succeeded in uniting all of Muslim Syria, thereby enabling him to better face both his Mongol and Frankish enemies. Conversely, this preoccupation with these external enemies probably slowed down the speed with which Baybars could consolidate Muslim Syria.

Baybars's domestic situation was also far from secure. Soon after he gained the throne, he faced a riot in Cairo of black slaves, stable boys and squires, who revolted in the name of the Shiʿa. This unrest was put down without difficulty.[32] More dangerous was an attempt to organize a conspiracy in 659/1260–2 among the Muʿizziya, Qutuz's *khushdāshiyya* (mamluks of the same

[26] Ibn Shaddād, *Aʿlāq*, 3:122. [27] *Ibid.*, 3:60–2; Yūnīnī, 2:104–5, 108.
[28] Ibn Shaddād, *Aʿlāq*, 3:82, 98–9, 119.
[29] See ch. 6, p. 153; Amitai-Preiss, "Karak," forthcoming.
[30] Yūnīnī, 2:407; 3:25–6; Ibn al-Furāt, MS. Vienna, fols. 3b, 102a (= ed. Lyons, 1:115), 158a–b; 213b–214a; Maqrīzī, 1:470, 546, 579, 605–6; Ibn Taghrī Birdī, 7:139; Thorau, *Baybars*, 197–8 and n. 61.
[31] Thorau, *Baybars*, 164–5, 169, 176, 201–3; 208; *idem*, "Die Burgen der Assassinen in Syrien und ihre Einnahme durch Sultan Baibars," *Die Welt des Orients* 18 (1987):152–8.
[32] Ibn al-Furāt, MS. Vatican, fol. 258a; Maqrīzī, 1:440; Irwin, *Middle East*, 44.

patron). This too was quickly resolved,[33] but it shows that the military society in Egypt was not of one mind over Baybars's sultanate, and the danger from without was not always enough to stifle dissatisfaction from within. In spite of the efforts which Baybars made to unite the disparate elements of the military society against their Crusader and Mongol enemies and his attempts to portray himself as the leader of the holy war, throughout his reign he would have to keep a watchful eye on possible enemies at home.[34]

The reestablishment of the ʿAbbāsid Caliphate in Cairo

To put his rule on a sounder footing, Baybars exploited the arrival of scions of the ʿAbbāsid family to revive the Caliphate, which had been in abeyance since the Mongol conquest of Baghdad in early 656/1258. While Baybars's position was far from unstable, it is clear why he would adopt any means to strengthen it: since its inception in 1250, the Mamluk regime had suffered from a problem of legitimacy *vis-à-vis* the Ayyūbids, and Baybars himself may have felt that, since he was a regicide, his position needed some bolstering. The quickness with which the first pretender was sworn into office indicates the importance which Baybars attributed to restoring the Caliphal institution.[35] The Caliph's subsequent bestowal of governmental powers on Baybars, a point which surely must have been understood by all parties involved beforehand, greatly enhanced the Sultan's claims to rule. The significance attributed to this legitimization is seen in Baybars's widespread use of the formula *qasīm amīr al-mu'minīn* ("associate of the commander of the faithful") on his coins and inscriptions.[36]

On 9 Rajab 659/9 June 1261, Aḥmad b. al-Imām al-Ẓāhir arrived in Cairo accompanied by a group of bedouins. When Hülegü had taken Baghdad, he freed this Aḥmad from the Caliph's prison. Aḥmad fled to the Arabs of Iraq, and eventually made his way to Syria and was sent on to Egypt. Four days after his arrival, the Sultan held a public council to ascertain his genealogy, with all the senior amirs, officials and religious dignitaries of the capital present. The correctness of his claim accepted, the new Caliph took the title of al-Mustanṣir, and all those present, led by the chief qadi and Baybars, proceeded to swear the oath of loyalty (*bayʿa*) to him. Several weeks later, the Caliph's investiture diploma (*taqlīd*) to Baybars as sultan was read out in public, calling on him to wage *jihād*, and granting him rights as ruler not only of the territories then controlled by the Mamluk Sultanate, but also of those

33 Ibn al-Furāt, MS. Vatican, fols. 266b–267a; Maqrīzī, I:447.

34 See the comments in Thorau, *Baybars*, 93–4, who also mentions the previous two incidents, and *ibid.*, 229–32, when later conspiracies are discussed.

35 P.M. Holt, "Some Observations on the ʿAbbāsid Caliphate of Cairo," *BSOAS* 47 (1984):501–2. In general, see *ibid.*, 501–3; *idem, Crusades*, 92–3; Ayalon, "Transfer," *Arabica* 7 (1960):41–59; Thorau, *Baybars*, 110–19.

36 P. Balog, *The Coinage of the Mamlūk Sultans of Egypt and Syria* (New York, 1964), 87–106; numerous inscriptions in *RCEA*, 12:128–226.

lands then under the yoke of the infidel (the Franks, and especially the Mongols), which would be liberated.[37] Baybars was to make much use of this *jihādī* motif throughout his reign, and it frequently appears in inscriptions and his many letters.[38]

Preparations were soon begun to dispatch al-Mustanṣir with a small army to recapture Baghdad. Ibn ʿAbd al-Ẓāhir tells of how Baybars assigned several amirs along with 2700 horsemen and assorted bedouin irregulars to go with the Caliph, although it is questionable whether even a force of this size was actually contemplated. The Sultan also gave him a personal entourage of 100 mamluks. In early Shawwāl 659/September 1261, the Sultan and the Caliph left Cairo for Syria. After marching at a leisurely pace, they reached Damascus. Al-Mustanṣir set off with his small force, numbering only 300 horsemen according to Ibn al-Furāt (and whence al-Maqrīzī) on 13 Dhū 'l-qaʿda/11 October. The amirs Balaban al-Rashīdī and Aqqush al-Rūmī were sent to the Euphrates via northern Syria, with orders to be ready to advance into Iraq in case the Caliph were to need their help.[39]

Al-Mustanṣir rode into Iraq accompanied by the three sons of the recently deceased Badr al-Dīn Lu'lu'. One of them, al-Saʿīd ʿAlā' al-Dīn, has already been mentioned above, as the short-term governor of Aleppo. He had been languishing in captivity in a castle in northern Syria when his two brothers made their way to the Sultanate from Mongol-occupied Jazīra. The more important of the brothers was al-Ṣāliḥ Rukn al-Dīn Ismāʿīl, who had inherited his father's lordship over Mosul, and who hitherto had shown himself to be a loyal vassal to the Mongols.[40] By Rajab/June 659, however, al-Ṣāliḥ's fear of the Mongols overcame him and he left Mosul for the Mamluk Sultanate. He was soon joined in Egypt by al-Mujāhid Sayf al-Dīn Isḥāq, lord of Jazīrat Ibn ʿUmar. Baybars received them well, and granted their request to release their brother, al-Saʿīd, from prison. They also asked that they would return to their countries along with an army to help them. The latter request was denied, but Baybars gave permission for them to go, and so they joined the Caliph on the first stage of his journey.[41]

The first stop of the Caliph al-Mustanṣir was al-Raḥba, where he was joined

[37] *Rawḍ*, 99–101; Ibn al-Furāt, MS. Vatican, fols. 267b–269a; Maqrīzī, 1:448–50, 453–7; Yūnīnī, 1:441–500; 2:94–104. Cf. Holt, *Crusades*, 93; Khowaiter, *Baibars*, 35–6; Thorau, *Baybars*, 112.

[38] See, e.g., the use of the expression *mubīd al-faranj wa'l-tatār* in inscriptions: *RCEA*, 12:128–9 (no. 4593), 142–3 (no. 4613), 193 (no. 4690), etc. The *jihādī* motif appears in many of Baybars's letters: e.g. to Berke Khan (661/1262; *Rawḍ*, 139–40); the amirs in Egypt (670/1271; *Rawḍ*, 395), the ruler of Yemen (667/1269; *Rawḍ*, 356); and to the Īlkhān himself (667/1269; Yūnīnī, 2:407).

[39] *Rawḍ*, 110–12; Ibn al-Furāt, MS. Vatican, fols. 273b–274b; Maqrīzī, 1:459–62; Yūnīnī 1:449–50, 454, 2:104, 109; Ibn al-Dawādārī, 8:79–80.

[40] See above, ch. 2, p. 46. For al-Ṣāliḥ's earlier serving of Hülegü, see Ibn al-ʿIbrī, 488 (cf. Bar Hebraeus, 437); Ibn Wāṣil, MS. 1703, fol. 128a.

[41] Ibn Shaddād, *Ta'rīkh*, 231–2; *idem*, *Aʿlāq*, 3:208; Ibn al-Ṣuqāʿī, 3–4; Yūnīnī, 1:452–3, 2:106–8; Ibn al-Dawādārī, 8:81; *Rawḍ*, 114–16; Ibn al-Furāt, MS. Vatican, fol. 274a–b; Maqrīzī, 1:460–1; cf. Rashīd al-Dīn, ed. ʿAlīzādah, 3:83.

by 400 horsemen from the Āl Faḍl bedouins. At this point, al-Ṣāliḥ Ismāʿīl and his brothers left him to head for their own countries. With his small army, al-Mustanṣir made his way south to ʿĀna, where he met another claimant to the Caliphate, al-Ḥākim Aḥmad b. al-Ḥasan, who had been recognized as Caliph by the Syrian freebooter, Aqqush al-Barlī. Al-Ḥākim commanded some 600 Türkmen horsemen, but these were enticed to cross over to al-Mustanṣir, so al-Ḥākim had little choice but to give up his claim and join his cousin's campaign. Al-Mustanṣir then received the submission of the city of ʿĀna itself, followed by that of al-Ḥadītha, further south along the Euphrates.[42]

Word of the Caliph's advance soon reached the Mongol authorities in Baghdad: Qara Bugha, the Mongol army commander in Iraq, and ʿAlī Bahādur al-Khwārazmī, the *shaḥna* of Baghdad. Qara Bugha set out with 5000 Mongols, entered Anbār on the Euphrates unexpectedly and massacred its population. The remainder of the Mongol army was brought up by ʿAlī Bahādur. At this time, the Caliph advanced to Hīt, on the west bank of the Euphrates, which he took by force (29 Dhū 'l-ḥijja 659/25 November 1261). Continuing south, the Caliph spent the night of 3 Muḥarram 660/28 November 1261 across from al-Anbār, on the west bank of the Euphrates. That same night Qara Bugha crossed the river with his troops. In the morning, the two armies faced each other. The Mongol commander set aside the Muslims in the army of Baghdad, evidently troops from pre-Mongol days, fearing that their loyalty to the Caliph would prevail in the battle.

The Caliph arranged his modest army into twelve squadrons (*aṭlāb*), putting the bedouins and Türkmen on the right and left respectively. He placed himself with the rest of his forces in the center. The Muslims attacked, driving the Mongols under ʿAlī Bahādur back. Thereupon, the Mongols sprung an ambush, and the bedouins and Türkmen promptly fled. The center was cut to pieces, and most of its soldiers were killed. As for al-Mustanṣir, his fate is unknown, but most sources claim that he escaped from the battle, and thereupon disappeared. His kinsman, the future Caliph al-Ḥākim, escaped and made his way back to Syria, as did a small group of Muslim amirs and troops. One of the soldiers reported that the Caliph had a mere 400 soldiers, compared to 6000 for the Mongols.[43]

These were fairly uneven odds, and this fact has troubled writers, medieval and modern alike. How was it that Baybars could send the recently recognized Caliph to an almost certain death in Mongol-occupied Iraq? Ibn ʿAbd al-

[42] Yūnīnī, 1:454–5; 2:109–10; *Rawḍ*, 112; Ibn al-Ṣuqāʿī, 3; Ibn al-Furāt, MS. Vatican, fols. 275b–276a (whence Maqrīzī, 1:462); Ibn al-Dawādārī, 8:82. The last three sources have a slightly different account.

[43] Ibn al-Dawādārī, 8:83–4; Ibn al-Ṣuqāʿī, 2–3; Maqrīzī, 1:467; Yūnīnī, 1:455–7; 2:110–12; Ibn Duqmaq, 184–5; Abū Shāma, 215. Baybars al-Manṣūrī (*Zubda*, fol. 49a [whence ʿAynī, fol. 85a]; *Tuḥfa*, 48) gives different names for the Mongol commanders. See also Bar Hebraeus, 442–3 (= Ibn al-ʿIbrī, 496). In spite of his *nisba* (adjective derived from place, name, etc.), ʿAlī Bahādur may be identified with a Mongol known as Asatu Bahādur; Boyle, "Death," 160 n. 5.

Ẓāhir, Baybars's secretary and official biographer, thought it politic to dodge the question, dwelling instead on Baybars's generosity to al-Mustanṣir, and mentioning laconically the latter's carelessness in not guarding himself, as well as his irresponsibility in not calling for the amirs who were waiting for his summons at the Euphrates.[44] Ibn ᶜAbd al-Ẓāhir's nephew, Shāfiᶜ b. ᶜAlī, unfettered by the subject of his biography no longer being alive and writing at a time when it perhaps was fashionable to be a little iconoclastic about Baybars, is more critical. He is amazed that since Iraq had been conquered by such a powerful and numerous enemy as the Mongols, Baybars would have sent such a pitiful force. Even the entire Egyptian and Syrian armies, with their infantry and bedouin auxiliaries, would not have been enough to deal with such an enemy![45]

Ibn al-Furāt, and in his wake al-Maqrīzī, offer another explanation for Baybars's action: originally, Baybars had planned to send 10,000 horsemen with al-Mustanṣir, a sizeable force by any standard. But one of the Mosuli princes (who is unnamed in the source) came to him and convinced him to change his mind, saying that once the Caliph regained Baghdad, he would remove Baybars from the Sultanate. Baybars was convinced and sent only 300 horsemen instead.[46] The latter number is convincing and tallies with the figure found above. It is difficult to accept the rest of this story. Ibn al-Furāt, although a late writer, is usually accurate and often cites his source. In this case, however, there is no indication from where he derived this story, and its veracity is suspect for several reasons. First, it seems unlikely that Baybars would have contemplated at this early stage dispatching such a large force, which would have represented a sizeable chunk of the troops at his disposal, especially as he was still in the first stages of organizing his army. Second, it is difficult to see what exactly worried Baybars about al-Mustanṣir, who had given the Sultan complete power to rule in his name. Third, Baybars subsequently showed himself capable of keeping a Caliph (al-Ḥākim) in the background. Fourth, even taking Baybars's known cynicism and sense of *Realpolitik* into account, it is still hard to believe that he would deliberately send the Caliph on a suicide mission. Finally, one wonders how al-Mustanṣir would agree to embark on such an ill-fated campaign.[47]

The reason must be sought elsewhere. Professor Holt has suggested that given the political realites of the Jazīra and Iraq, as they were perceived by the leadership of the Mamluk kingdom, there was a certain logic to sending off the Caliph.[48] As we have seen above, the situation on the eastern bank of the

[44] *Rawḍ*, 112. On the tendentiousness of this author as a biographer of Baybars, and the relative impartiality of his nephew Shāfiᶜ b. ᶜAlī, see Holt, "Three Biographies," *passim*; *idem*, "Observations," 502. [45] *Ḥusn*, 46; see Holt, as cited in previous note.

[46] Ibn al-Furāt, MS. Vatican, fol. 275b; Maqrīzī, 1:462.

[47] Cf. Thorau, *Baybars*, 114–16, who also rejects this information in Maqrīzī (he does not mention Ibn al-Furāt), and suggests that Baybars cynically sent the Caliph to a sure death in Iraq, in order to get rid of a potentially troublesome figure who might be unwilling to accept his role as Baybars's puppet. [48] Holt, "Observations," 502. See also Patton, *Lu'lu'*, 76.

Euphrates was not completely clear, and what was known indicated a definite lack of a substantial Mongol presence. One author, Baybars al-Manṣūrī, writing some sixty years later, reports that when the Caliph crossed the Euphrates he believed the Mongols had vacated Iraq.[49] Aqqush al-Barlī's relatively unhindered wanderings on the Mongol side of the border may show that there might have been something to this belief. In addition, the Mamluks and their clients had bested Mongol forces, albeit of modest size, twice in the past year. Perhaps, then, a certain amount of post-victory exuberance might have clouded the judgement of Baybars or the Caliph. It is not impossible that Baybars saw the dispatch of the Caliph, along with the three Mosuli princes, as a way of expanding Mamluk influence to the east, at little cost to himself. Perhaps, there was hope that the Caliph would serve as a rallying point to the disparate Muslim military elements which were floating around Iraq (some of whom in the coming months would begin to seek refuge in the Sultanate), along with local bedouin tribes. The Mongols were aware of that possibility, and thus did not include now local elements in their service to take part in the battle against the Caliph. Conceivably al-Mustanṣir himself initiated the campaign into Iraq, that is, he was not sent by Baybars, but went of his own volition, with Baybars's blessing and modest support, because he thought he had a reasonable chance of success.

Further north, the sons of Badr al-Dīn Lu'lu' were on their way into the Jazīra. After separating from the Caliph at al-Raḥba, al-Ṣāliḥ and his brothers made their way unopposed to Sinjār. Al-Saʿīd and al-Mujāhid remained there, while al-Ṣāliḥ continued on to Mosul. The former two only stayed for a short time in Sinjār. When news reached them of the Caliph's defeat, they returned to Syria; Baybars received them well and gave them large *iqṭāʿāt*. Al-Ṣāliḥ himself entered Mosul without encountering any Mongol forces, which had withdrawn upon the approach of al-Ṣāliḥ's small army (600–700 horsemen). But at the beginning of 660 (which started on 26 November 1261), Mosul was put under siege by a Mongol force commanded by Samdaghu (Ṣandaghūn in the Arabic sources). The siege continued until Shaʿbān of the same year (July-August 1262), and the garrison and local population suffered greatly. The city was taken after al-Ṣāliḥ himself surrendered, subsequently suffering a cruel death.[50]

During the siege, al-Ṣāliḥ had sent for assistance to Aqqush al-Barlī, then based at the fortress of al-Bīra and Ḥarrān. Aqqush had originally been a mamluk of al-Nāṣir Yūsuf's father; after fighting on the Muslim side at ʿAyn Jālūt, Quṭuz rewarded him with a governorship over part of Palestine. In the

[49] *Zubda*, fol. 49a (whence ʿAynī, fol. 85a); *Tuḥfa*, 48.

[50] Bar Hebraeus 442 (= Ibn al-ʿIbrī, 495–6); Ibn al-Ṣuqāʿī, 4–5; Ibn Shaddād, *Aʿlāq*, 3:208–11; Rashīd al-Dīn, ed. ʿAlīzādah, 3:84–6; Ibn al-Fuwaṭī, 345–7; Abū Shāma, 219; Ibn Kathīr, 13:234; Yūnīnī, 1:492–5; 2:156–9; Ibn al-Furāt, MS. Vienna, fol. 7a–b; Maqrīzī, 1:475; a different version is found in *Zubda*, fol. 49b (cf. shorter version in *Tuḥfa*, 48–9); Patton, *Lu'lu'*, 77–81.

aftermath of Sanjar al-Ḥalabī's revolt and the repulsion of the second Mongol invasion of Syria, Aqqush fell foul of Baybars. He fled north with some of his supporters and gained control of Aleppo for a short while, but was dislodged from the city in Shaʿbān 659/July 1261 by a Mamluk force. Al-Barlī, however, recaptured the city soon after, when the Mamluk army withdrew to the south. Again Baybars sent an army to gain control of Aleppo, which was accomplished in Dhū 'l-qaʿda 659/October 1261. Al-Barlī and his troops moved to the northeast and captured al-Bīra.[51]

From al-Bīra, al-Barlī moved to Ḥarrān, and took nearby Qalʿat al-Qarādī from its Mongol governors. He also reached as far as Āmid in his meanderings through the Jazīra. It was in Ḥarrān, probably some time in spring 660/1262, that he received the call for assistance from Mosul. Al-Barlī did not hesitate in responding, in spite of the relatively small army under his command (the Arabic sources give him 1200 or 1400 troops compared to the 10,000 the Mongols had). The Mamluk writers tell of how the Mongols under Samdaghu thought of withdrawing upon learning of al-Barlī's approach. However, al-Zayn al-Ḥāfiẓī, the former official of al-Nāṣir Yūsuf now openly serving the Mongols, was found in the Mongol camp at Mosul, having been sent to check up on the siege. He convinced the Mongols to go forth to meet the Syrians on the way, citing their small numbers. The Mongols, thus emboldened, set out, and met al-Barlī's force near Sinjār on 14 Jumādā II 660/7 May 1262. The Muslims were completely defeated; al-Barlī himself was wounded but escaped with a small part of his army. He then returned to al-Bīra, whereupon Hülegü wrote to him inviting him to submit and offering al-Bīra to him as an *iqṭāʿ*. But al-Barlī spurned the offer, and instead wrote to Baybars asking to submit. He set out for Cairo, and was well received in Dhū 'l-ḥijja 660/October 1262, although he was arrested less than a year later. It is from the time of al-Barlī's submission that al-Bīra came under the Sultan's control.[52]

During these events in northern Syria and the Jazīra, the other pretender to the Caliphate, al-Ḥākim Aḥmad b. al-Ḥasan, made his way to Egypt, arriving in Rabīʿ II 660/March 1262. Aḥmad, the great great grandson of the Caliph al-Mustarshid (512–29/1118–35), had escaped Baghdad following the Mongol conquest in 656/1258. After hiding out with the Khafāja bedouins, he came to

[51] Holt, *Crusades*, 92; Thorau, *Baybars*, 97–8; Khowaiter, *Baibars*, 30–1. On al-Barlī's early history, see: Abū 'l-Fidā', 3:216; ʿAynī, fol. 77a. For details of his adventures in north Syria, see: Ibn Wāṣil, MS. 1703, fols. 168a–170a; Yūnīnī, 1:440; 2:104–8, 119–22, 152; Maqrīzī, 1:463–6. The *nisba* al-Barlī would seem to be derived from the name of the Qipchaq tribe Ölberli. It appears that the first syllable of the tribal name was assimilated in the Arabic: al-Ölberli > al-Barlī. On the correct vocalization of this tribal name, see P. Golden, "Cumanica II: The Ölberli (Ölperli): The Fortunes and Misfortunes of an Inner Asian Nomadic Clan," *AEMA* 6 (1986 [1988]):13–14; cf. Weil, *Geschichte*, 1:17, n. 17; Ibn Wāṣil, MS. 1703, fols. 168a–170a: al-Burlī. I am grateful to Prof. Golden for elucidating this matter in a letter of 13 October 1992.

[52] Holt, Thorau and Khowaiter, as cited in the previous note; Patton, *Lu'lu'*, 79; Ibn al-Furāt, MS. Vienna, fols. 4a, 7b; Maqrīzī, 1:471; Ibn Shaddād, *Aʿlāq*, 3:62, 209–11; *Rawḍ*, 133–5; Yūnīnī, 1:492–5, 2:152–3, 157–8; Rashīd al-Dīn, ed. ʿAlīzādah, 3:85.

Syria, coming under the protection of ʿĪsā b. Muhannā, a leader of the Āl Faḍl bedouin. Al-Nāṣir Yūsuf heard of Aḥmad and invited him to join him. Hülegü's arrival in Syria in early 658/1260 prevented Aḥmad from taking up this invitation. Qutuz subsequently found out about him, promised to raise him to the Caliphate, and even performed the *bayʿa* to him via a surrogate. However, Qutuz's assassination put an end to these plans.[53] Qutuz, like Baybars, had perceived the advantages to be had from re-establishing the ʿAbbāsid Caliphate under his protection.

Probably before news had reached him of this event, Aḥmad, who had taken the Caliphal title of al-Ḥākim bi-amr Allāh, together with some of the Āl Faḍl, launched a raid into Iraq, "conquering" (in reality, they probably just passed by, and no opposition was offered) ʿĀna, al-Ḥadītha, Hīt and al-Anbār. At the end of Dhū 'l-ḥijja 658/mid-December 1260, a battle was fought with a Mongol road patrol (*qaraghul*) at al-Fallūja in the environs of Baghdad, and the Mongols were severely beaten; al-Yūnīnī says that 1500 Mongol horsemen were killed (!) while only six Muslims were lost, figures which are difficult to accept. In any event, some kind of Muslim victory seems to have taken place, and news of this may have contributed to the decision of Baybars and al-Mustanṣir to send the latter on his ill-fated campaign the next year. After this initial success, however, the local Mongol commander, Qara Bugha, who later defeated al-Mustanṣir, came up with a large force, and al-Ḥākim withdrew to Syria.[54]

Al-Ḥākim was in contact with Taybars al-Wazīrī, governor of Damascus, who sent him on to Cairo. But al-Ḥākim's hopes to have the new Sultan recognize his claim were dashed when Baybars raised al-Mustanṣir, who beat him to Cairo and Caliphate by only three days. Fearing he would be arrested, al-Ḥākim turned around and made his way to Aleppo, where he was recognized as Caliph by Aqqush al-Barlī, as part of the latter's attempt to establish himself as an independent ruler in northern Syria. Al-Barlī gave him a force of several hundred Türkmen horsemen and sent him off across the Euphrates. At Ḥārran, al-Ḥākim was recognized as Caliph by its inhabitants, including the Banū Taymiyya clan. In ʿĀna, as mentioned above, al-Ḥākim ran into al-Mustanṣir, and joined up with him, temporarily giving up his claim to the Caliphal title.[55]

As previously described, that campaign ended in the complete defeat of the ʿAbbāsid "army." Al-Ḥākim made his way to Syria, from where he was sent for by Baybars. He arrived in Cairo on 27 Rabīʿ II 660/22 March 1262, and was met by the Sultan, who had him comfortably installed in the Cairo citadel and then essentially ignored him for over half a year. Baybars was in no hurry now

[53] Ṣafadī, *Wāfī*, 6:317–18; Holt, "Observations," 502. See also: Yūnīnī, 1:484–5; Mufaḍḍal, 92–4; Ibn al-Dawādārī, 8:87.

[54] Ṣafadī, *Wāfī*, 6:318; Yūnīnī, 1:485–6; Dhahabī, MS. Laud 305, fol. 257b. Cf. Holt, "Observations," 502.

[55] Ṣafadī, *Wāfī*, 6:318; Yūnīnī, 1:454, 486; Dhahabī, MS. Laud 305, fol. 257b.

to raise a candidate to the Caliphate, for he already had Caliphal recognition from al-Mustanṣir. Only on 2 Muḥarram 661/16 November 1262 was a public council held to verify his genealogy and swear the *bayᶜa* to him. Baybars did not even bother to have a Caliphal *taqlīd* drawn up for him this time, although the next day in the *khuṭba* (Friday sermon), al-Ḥākim praised the Sultan and called for *jihād*.[56] Thereupon, the Caliph was kept in semi-seclusion, although he did play a ceremonial role on occasion, as in the early negotiations between Baybars and the rulers of the Mongol Golden Horde in south Russia (see chapter 4).

The expeditions of Al-Mustanṣir and the sons of Badr al-Dīn Lu'lu' were not the only ones to be sent over the Euphrates at this time. There was also Sayf al-Dīn Mankalān b. ᶜAlī al-Hakkārī, the ruler of Jūlamark (Chölemerik),[57] who arrived in the Sultanate in 660/1261–2, with his son and many Kurdish amirs. Sayf al-Dīn was well received and given the option of remaining in the Sultanate or accepting the lordship of Irbil. This town was, of course, in Mongol-controlled territory. Its lord, however, had also come around this time as a *wāfidī* (refugee) to Baybars, so, in a sense, the position was open. Sayf al-Dīn took the offer of Irbil, and set off with his son and a number of (presumably Kurdish) amirs. After scoring some initial success against the Mongols, Sayf al-Dīn was killed. His son, however, continued fighting the Mongols, and eventually they were compelled to come to terms with him; he remained probably up in the mountains of Kurdistan.[58] That the Mongols eventually had to acquiesce to his presence, shows the difficulty they had controlling those areas.

A similar instance concerned Shihāb al-Dīn Abū Bakr b. al-Shāyib, a *wāfidī* of unknown provenance. After treating him well, Baybars sent him to "the East." Word arrived from him in Shaᶜbān 660 (29 September-28 October 1262) claiming that he had gained control over "the Jazīra" and had sworn its inhabitants to the Sultan.[59] Nothing else was ever heard of him, so he was probably soon disposed of by the Mongols. Yet even when they failed, Baybars had much to gain from these expeditions. At no great cost and risk to himself, the Sultan could cause trouble to the Mongols. Given the numerous instances from AH 660 of these expeditions, it seems that for a time Baybars adopted a strategy of dispatching small expeditions over the Euphrates, led by figures from that region who had fled the Mongols. This strategy may have had its origins in a perceived weakness of the Mongols in the area east of the Euphrates River.

[56] Holt, "Observations," 502–3; Ṣafadī, *Wāfī*, 6:318; *Rawḍ*, 141–4; Yūnīnī, 1:483–4, 530, 2:153, 186–7 (writes that *bayᶜa* was taken on 9 Muḥarram); Ibn al-Dawādārī, 8:86 (same date); Ibn Kathīr, 13:337–8; Abū Shāma, 221 (gives 8 Muḥarram).

[57] This is the former name of Hakkâri, the name of the capital of the vilayet of Hakkâri; T.A. Sinclair, *Eastern Turkey* (London, 1987–90), 1:252. My thanks to Prof. M.A. Cook who first suggested to me the identification of this location.

[58] Ibn Shaddād, *Ta'rīkh*, 332–3; *Rawḍ*, 87–8.

[59] *Rawḍ*, 88.

The nomads of Syria

Of crucial importance in both the war against the Īlkhānids and the integration of Syria into the Mamluk Sultanate was Baybars's finding a *modus vivendi* with the bedouin tribes of the Syrian desert. These tribes, known as *al-ᶜarab* or *al-ᶜurbān*, were important for several reasons: their control of the sensitive frontier with Īlkhānid Iraq, including "the roads leading abroad through the fords and bridges of the Euphrates";[60] their contribution to the communications network in Syria, particularly in the northeast; the raids they launched across the border into Mongol-controlled territory; the not insubstantial military power they possessed, which found use as auxiliaries to the regular Mamluk armies; their service as scouts and sources of intelligence; and finally, their ability to cause the Sultan trouble, not the least by deserting to the Mongols over the Euphrates when they felt pressured by the Sultan or dissatisfied with his policies towards them. In a sense, the patronage provided by the Sultan to the bedouins can be seen as a kind of protection payment, and thus the Sultan bought their cooperation and forestalled any troublemaking on their part.[61]

Most powerful of these bedouins were the Āl Faḍl, of the Rabīᶜa branch of the Ṭayy tribe. The Āl Faḍl controlled the country between Hama and the Euphrates, and from Qalᶜat Jaᶜbar in the north to al-Raḥba in the south. During Baybars's time, they were led by Sharaf al-Dīn ᶜĪsā b. Muhannā b. Mānīᶜ b. Ḥadītha (sometimes written Ḥadhīfa; d. 684/1285–6); this particular branch was also known as the Āl Muhannā, after ᶜĪsā's father. The Rabīᶜa had already risen to prominence in the time of Zengi (521–41/1127–46), and they continued gaining in importance during the Ayyūbid period, through the patronage of various princes.[62] Throughout the last decade of the Ayyūbid rule in Syria, the *amīr al-ᶜarab* (leader of the bedouins in Syria), was Abū Bakr b. ᶜAlī b. Ḥadītha, a cousin of ᶜĪsā b. Muhannā. Al-ᶜUmarī tells the story that when Baybars had fled to Syria with the Baḥriyya early in the 1250s, he had sought refuge and protection from the father of this chief, but was refused, while ᶜĪsā b. Muhannā helped him. Thus, when Baybars became sultan several years later, he removed Abū Bakr from the *imra* (the rank of *amīr*), and

60 Ayalon, "Yāsa," pt. C1, 148–9.

61 For general discussions of these tribes in the Mamluk period, see: D. Ayalon, "The Auxiliary Forces of the Mamluk Sultanate," *Der Islam* 65 (1988):23–31; *idem*, "Yasa," pt. C1, 148–9; M.A. Hiyari, "The Origins and Development of the Amīrate of the Arabs during the Seventh/Thirteenth and Eighth/Fourteenth Centuries," *BSOAS* 38 (1975):509–24; A.S. Tritton, "Tribes of Syria in the Fourteenth and Fifteenth Centuries," *BSOAS* 12 (1948):567–73; M. Gaudefroy-Demombynes, *La Syrie a l'époque des Mamelouks* (Paris, 1923), 183–201; A.N. Poliak, *Feudalism in Egypt, Syria, Palestine, and the Lebanon, 1250–1900* (London, 1939), 9–11.

62 Maqrīzī, 1:247 and n.; ᶜUmarī, *Masālik al-abṣār . . . : qabā'il al-ᶜarab . . .* , ed. D. Krawulsky (Beirut, 1985), 116; Qalqashandī, 1:324–5, 4, 203, 7:184–5; Ibn Khaldūn, *ᶜIbar*, 5:436–8; Ṣafadī, *Aᶜyān*, MS. Aya Sofya 2963, fols. 144a–b; *idem*, *Wāfī*, MS. Br. Lib. Add. 23359, fols. 30b–31a; Hiyari, "Amīrate," 511–16; Tritton, "Tribes," 566.

replaced him with ʿĪsā.[63] The problem with this story, however, is that many other sources report that ʿĪsā had already received his appointment as *amīr al-ʿarab* from Qutuz in the aftermath of ʿAyn Jālūt, although it appears that ʿĪsā b. Muhannā and his bedouin followers did not actually participate in the battle.[64] It would seem, then, that ʿĪsā's rise to prominence and leadership within the Āl Faḍl preceded the sultanate of Baybars, who solely approved a previous appointment. Other sources only write that Baybars sent a *manshūr* (diploma) in 659/1260–1 confirming ʿĪsā in his position and his *iqṭāʿāt*. Possibly, at this time he might even have added to ʿĪsā's appanage.[65] This is not to say, however, that one of the major factors in Baybars's decision might not have been the hospitable treatment he had received from ʿĪsā several years earlier.

The title *amīr al-ʿarab/ʿurbān* was officially bestowed by the Sultan, and its holder played an important role in the Mamluk scheme of government in Syria. Even before the Mamluks gained control of Syria, there was an interaction between the rise of indigenous bedouin leadership and political patronage from the central government, a development which was refined under the early Mamluk sultans and reached its peak in the third reign of al-Nāṣir Muḥammad b. Qalawun (709–41/ 1309–40).[66] The Sultan would place his support behind a family or individual which had proven its power. The patronage they thereby enjoyed, which included official titles, gifts and – most important of all – *iqṭāʿāt*, would strengthen their hand among their nomadic followers. For example, Ibn Khaldūn writes that as a result of the Mamluk patronage of the Āl Faḍl, the latter gained predominance over the Āl Mirā, and overran their winter camping ground. The Āl Faḍl became so powerful that they lived near inhabited areas and only rarely had to seek pasturage in the desert (*barriyya*).[67] Similar patronage, albeit on a smaller scale, was spread among the *amīr al-ʿarab*'s family and other tribal leaders throughout Syria. The relationship of the *amīr* with other tribal leaders is not always clear. There is an indication that the term *amīr al-ʿarab* was also applied to the bedouin leaders in the southern Syrian desert.[68]

In the fall of 659/1261, the Sultan rode to Syria for the first time; with him was the Caliph al-Mustanṣir, soon to go off to Iraq. Once he was settled in Damascus, Baybars met with unspecified bedouin chiefs (*umarāʾ al-ʿurbān*), honored them and gave them some type of grants or allowances (*arzāq*;

[63] ʿUmarī, ed. Krawulsky, 117–18; whence, probably, Ṣafadī, as cited in previous note.

[64] See ch. 2, p. 47.

[65] *Rawḍ*, 98; Nuwayrī, MS. 2m, fol. 147a; Baybars, *Zubda*, fol. 51a (whence, ʿAynī, fol. 81a). Maqrīzī, 1:541, has the Sultan appointing him in AH 663, but this must be a mistake. Ibn Shaddād, *Taʾrīkh*, 291, adds Sarmīn to ʿĪsā's *iqṭāʿ*.

[66] See D. Ayalon, "The System of Payment in Mamlūk Military Aristocracy," *JESHO* 1 (1958):264–8; Tritton, "Tribes," 569.

[67] Ibn Khaldūn, *ʿIbar*, 6:6, who uses the expression *al-tulūl waʾl-qurā*, which seems to be hilly grazing lands and agricultural lands, as opposed to the *barriyya*. For Ibn Khaldūn's use of *tulūl*, see *The Muqaddimah*, tr. F. Rosenthal, 2nd ed. (Princeton, 1967), 1:251 n. 9.

[68] Yūnīnī, 4:36; see ch. 8, pp. 182, 185.

possibly the intention is to *iqṭāʿāt*, as understood by al-Maqrīzī). In exchange, he entrusted them with the guarding of the country up to the borders of Iraq.[69] It is unclear whether or not ʿĪsā b. Muhannā was present in this group, although if this were the case we should have expected it to be mentioned. On the other hand, the demand that they guard the country up to Iraq indicates that the group was not just made up of the local bedouin, such as the Āl ʿAlī, who lived in the environs of Damascus,[70] and the Āl Mirā from the Golan and the Ḥawrān,[71] but also included chiefs from Āl Faḍl to the north. In any event, Ibn ʿAbd al-Ẓāhir reports that in 660/1261–2, ʿĪsā came with his cousin Zāmil b. ʿAlī, evidently to Cairo, to show their loyalty to the Sultan, who received them well.[72]

Not all Syrian tribes accepted Baybars's authority without question. One such tribe was the Zubayd, which was concentrated around Damascus and to the south. In 659/1261, perhaps after the meeting with the bedouin chiefs, the Sultan heard that they had been causing trouble. Specifically they had made agreements with the Franks on the coast and shown them the weak spots (*ʿawrāt*) in the Muslim positions. Baybars secretly sent out a force to chastise them, and many of them were killed.[73] To the north of Syria, it is reported in 661/1262–3, 1000 horsemen of the Banū Kilāb joined the Armenian King in a raid against ʿAyn Tāb.[74] There is no record that the Mamluks reacted in any way to this cooperation with their enemy. The next time this tribe is mentioned in the sources is in 675/1277, when Baybars returned triumphantly from Rūm and the amirs of the Banū Kilāb came to him near Ḥārim to profess loyalty.[75] Evidently, this tribe, or at least part of it, sat beyond the effective reach of the Sultan, and only a massive Mamluk presence in their neighborhood could bring them to go openly through the motions of submission. On the other hand, the successive Mamluk raids against Lesser Armenia might have convinced them to desist from cooperating with the latter in raids against northern Syria, and hence we hear no more of such activities.

By the end of 661/1263, Baybars had succeeded in integrating the majority of the Syrian nomads into the Mamluk governing scheme. According to Ibn

[69] *Rawḍ*, 119; hence: Nuwayrī, MS. 2m, fol. 150a; *Zubda*, fol. 51a, who conflates this event with the sending of the *manshūr* to ʿĪsā b. Muhannā; Ibn al-Furāt, MS. Vatican, fol. 277b; Maqrīzī, 1:465, who also ties this in with ʿĪsā's appointment.

[70] ʿUmarī, ed. Krawulsky, 136–7; Qalqashandī, 4:210; 7:187. This tribe was the southern neighbor of Āl Faḍl, of which they were originally a subgroup. Their former leader, Abū Bakr b. ʿAlī, had been *amīr al-ʿarab* before ʿĪsā b. Muhannā; see above.

[71] ʿUmarī, ed. Krawulsky, 137–9; Qalqashandī, 4:208–9; 7:187. For problems Baybars had with their leader, Aḥmad b. Ḥujjā (or Ḥijā), in AH 664 and 667, see: *Rawḍ*, 265–6; Ibn al-Furāt, MS. Vienna, fols. 107b–108a, 159a–b; Maqrīzī, 1:580. [72] *Rawḍ*, 88. On Zāmil see below.

[73] *Rawḍ*, 120; Nuwayrī, MS. 2m, fol. 151a; Ibn al-Furāt, MS. Vatican, fol. 277a–b (= ed. Lyons, 1:54); Maqrīzī, 1:464–5; ʿUmarī, ed. Krawulsky, p. 139. According to Ibn Khaldūn, *ʿIbar*, 6:6, part of Zubayd was an ally of Āl Faḍl and lived in the Ḥawrān and to the south. Qalqashandī, 4:209, says they lived in the Ḥawrān and were subservient to Āl Mirā.

[74] *Zubda*, fol. 63b; Nuwayrī, MS. 2m, fol. 225b; Ibn al-Furāt, MS. Vienna, fol. 42a. Qalqashandī, 4:205, mentions that some of Banū Kilāb followed Āl Faḍl.

[75] Nuwayrī, MS. 2m, fol. 263a.

ᶜAbd al-Ẓāhir, early that year, on his way into Syria, he met with unspecified Türkmen chiefs in Gaza and arranged their affairs. He then met with the chiefs of the ᶜĀyid/ᶜĀyidh (or ᶜĀbid), Jarm and Thaᶜlaba tribes from Palestine.[76] The Sultan entrusted them with the country, and ordered the payment of a special nomad tax (*ᶜidād*), and they were also to help maintain the postal system based on horse relays (*barīd*) and provide horses at the Sultan's order.[77] Ibn ᶜAbd al-Raḥīm, the continuator to Ibn Wāṣil, provides an interesting version of this meeting, which contains both parallels and variants to the report in Ibn ᶜAbd al-Ẓāhir's *Rawḍ*, the ultimate source of other writers: "Baybars had the chiefs of the *ᶜurbān* brought to him and he entrusted them with the country. He appointed for them a *dīwān* (office) and *mushidd* (military inspector), and bestowed upon them much favor [so that] they would attack the accursed Hülegü, King of the Mongols, sometimes with the sword and sometimes with stratagems."[78] There seems to be some confusion here. The passage is in the parallel position to Ibn ᶜAbd al-Ẓāhir's text, which the continuator generally follows. The author, however, has conflated other information. It is unrealistic that Baybars would expect the nomads of southern Palestine to wage war against the Mongols: this is probably taken from another meeting with bedouin leaders to the north, perhaps the one to which reference has already been made. Still, the information about a special government department for "bedouin affairs," while perhaps out of place, is of great interest.

Baybars did have problems with certain bedouin leaders. Most troublesome was Nūr al-Dīn Zāmil b. ᶜAlī b. Ḥadītha, whose brother Abū Bakr had been replaced by ᶜĪsā b. Muhannā as *amīr al-ᶜarab*. Zāmil, with a bedouin following, had joined up with the Ayyūbid rulers of Hama and Homs to defeat the Mongols at Homs in Muḥarram 659/December 1260 (see above). Later that year, however, Zāmil fled to Aqqush al-Barlī, who was then at Aleppo, thus expressing his dissatisfaction with the emerging order, bedouin and perhaps otherwise, in Syria.[79] By 660/1261–2, he seems to have made his peace with Baybars, as he is reported to have gone to him with ᶜĪsā b.Muhannā to profess his loyalty.[80] He is next encountered s.a. 663/1264–5, where his adventures are told at length: because of the conflict (*fitna*) he had early in the decade with ᶜĪsā b. Muhannā, Zāmil had been arrested and imprisoned. Eventually, Zāmil was released and his *imra* and *iqṭāᶜ* were given back to him. Upon returning to his country, however, he began wreaking havoc. The sources single out that he captured the Sultan's agents (*quṣṣād*),[81] who were on their way to the ruler of

[76] Jarm was found from Gaza to Hebron; Qalqashandī, 7:189. Thaᶜlaba inhabited an area stretching from the borders of Egypt up to Kharrūba (near Acre); Qalqashandī, 4:212; Gaudefroy-Demombynes, *Syrie*, 197. The exact abode of the ᶜĀyid is not clearly indicated in the sources.

[77] *Rawḍ*, 149; Nuwayrī, MS. 2m, fol. 162b; Ibn al-Furāt, MS. Vienna, fol. 13a; Maqrīzī, 1:481. On the ᶜ*idād*, see E. Quatremère, *Histoire des sultans mamlouks de l'Égypte* (Paris, 1837–45), 1/1:189 n. 69.

[78] Ibn ᶜAbd al-Raḥīm, in Ibn Wāṣil, MS. 1702, fols. 412b–413a.

[79] Ibn al-Dawādārī, 8:72; Yūnīnī, 1:440.

[80] See above, p. 66.

[81] On the *quṣṣād*, see ch. 6, pp. 140–1.

Shīrāz, with whom Baybars was in secret contact. Zāmil took the letters they were carrying and sent them to Hülegü. He himself then went to the Khan, encouraged him to attack the Mamluks, and was granted an *iqṭāᶜ* in Iraq. He wintered in the Ḥijāz, raiding and killing pilgrims on the way to the *ḥajj*. Eventually tiring of his exile, Zāmil wrote to the Sultan, asking for a pardon. The Sultan, who in the meanwhile had given Zāmil's *imra* and *iqṭāᶜ* to his brother Abū Bakr, agreed to this, but only on the condition that Zāmil came at an appointed time. Zāmil arrived but was thrown into prison, and remained in captivity until his death in 670/1271–2.[82]

Zāmil was not the only bedouin chief to conceive of the idea to flee across the Euphrates and seek refuge with the Mongols. At one point, ca. 670/1271–2, even ᶜĪsā b. Muhannā felt sufficiently alienated from the Sultan as to contemplate such a move. The ostensible reason was that the Sultan held a number of the bedouin chiefs' sons as hostages. This in itself indicates that for some unknown reason relations had already deteriorated. ᶜĪsā must also have been angered by Baybars's sequestering of one half of his *iqṭāᶜ* in 668/1269–70, including the town of Salamiyya and other places. Upon hearing of ᶜĪsā's plan to desert, Baybars knew he had to act carefully or else he would drive him into the hands of the enemy. He secretly rode to Hama with a small entourage and surprised a gathering of tribal chiefs, whose fears he allayed. Then the Sultan wrote to ᶜĪsā himself and called on him to come. When ᶜĪsā appeared, Baybars asked him if what the bedouins said about him was true (that he was planning to leave Syria). Upon being answered in the affirmative, Baybars honored him, returned his *iqṭāᶜ* to its original size and released the hostages.[83]

This time, a potential crisis, which would have threatened the stability of the Syrian frontier, was averted. The knowledge that the bedouin chiefs could always flee to the Mongol enemy was a definite bargaining card to the chief's advantage. The care with which Baybars reacted to ᶜĪsā's plans shows the prominent place he occupied in the Sultan's mind. From the point of view of the Mongols, what they had to gain from such desertion is clear: intelligence, weakening of the frontier defenses of the Mamluks, and elements which could be sent back across the border to disrupt and raid. In the following decades ᶜĪsā and his son Muhannā repeated their threat to desert to the Mongols, which was finally realized by the latter in the third reign of al-Nāṣir Muḥammad b. Qalawun. Only with the formal Mamluk–Īlkhānid peace of 1323 was the danger of desertions finally more or less neutralized, as the bedouins could no longer play both sides against each other.[84]

[82] Nuwayrī, MS. 2m, fol. 174a–b; Ibn al-Furāt, MS. Vienna, fol. 76a–b; Maqrīzī, 1:535–6; Abū 'l-Fidā', 4:3, who writes that the arrest might have taken place in 664/1265–6; Ibn Shaddād, *Ta'rīkh*, 334; Muqrī, *Nathr al-jumān*, MS. Chester Beatty Arabic 4113, fol. 232b, for his obituary. Cf. the similarities and differences in the story of ᶜAmr b. Makhlūl, another chief of the Āl Faḍl, who also fled to the Mongols (AH 671 or 672) and subsequently returned; *Rawḍ*, 433; *Zubda*, fol. 81a; Yūnīnī, 3:7; Ibn Shaddād, *Ta'rīkh*, 61, 334; Abū 'l-Fidā', 4:8.

[83] *Rawḍ*, 390–3, hence: Nuwayrī, MS. 2m, fols. 200b–201a; Ibn al-Furāt, MS. Vienna, fols. 200b–201a [sic]; Maqrīzī, 1:597–9, with some divergence from the previous source.

[84] This is discussed in R. Amitai, "From Holy War to Reconciliation" [Hebrew] (MA thesis, Hebrew Univ. of Jerusalem, 1984), 67–8.

Beside the above-mentioned functions of guarding the border area and assisting with the postal system, the Syrian bedouins made an important contribution in the struggle with the Īlkhānids, as will be seen in chapter 5. Their military potential must have been fairly substantial, although there are no contemporary estimates of their total numbers. Had these estimates existed they would have to have been used with a great deal of caution, not the least because of the general problem of counting a nomadic population. Numbers are provided by the somewhat later writer Khalīl al-Ẓāhirī (d. 872/1468), who attributed to the Āl Faḍl 24,000 horsemen.[85] These figures should not be applied here, not even as a rough indication of the general size of the nomadic fighting population of Syria in the second half of the thirteenth century, because of the distance of this writer from the period with which we are dealing, the idealized picture he tries to paint of forces available to the Mamluk sultan, and the more general problem of statistics in medieval Muslim historiography.[86] On the other hand, the chronicles and other sources cite figures for the forces led by various chiefs in sundry battles and raids, and generally these forces numbered several thousand horsemen at the most.[87]

This discussion would not be complete without mention of the other nomads of Syria, the Türkmen tribes, who, although less prominent than the indigenous bedouin population, played an important role.[88] Since Seljuq times, Muslim Turkish tribes, known as Türkmen, had been present to some degree in Syria, and their population increased in the aftermath of the Mongol invasions.[89] In 659/1261, a group of Türkmen, who had fled there from the Mongols at some unknown date, were found on the Golan Heights. Mention has already been made of how this particular group successfully resisted an attack by the Franks of Acre, but having incurred the anger of Baybars, then moved on to Rūm.[90] Some time in the subsequent year (660/1261–2), another group of Türkmen fled Rūm for Syria, after suffering attacks and massacres from the Mongol commander there.[91] Much later, in 673/1274–5, Baybars, then raiding in Lesser Armenia, met with Türkmen and bedouins who came to profess loyalty, and brought them back with him to Syria.[92] In his biography of Baybars, Ibn Shaddād claims that a total of 40,000 Türkmen households (*bayt*) fled to Syria during Baybars's reign.[93] While this figure may be

[85] Al-Ẓāhirī, *Kitāb zubdat kashf al-mamālik*, ed. P. Ravaisse (Paris, 1894), 105.

[86] On the rather idealized figures that Ẓāhirī gives for the Mamluk army at his time, see D. Ayalon, "Studies on the Structure of the Mamlūk Army," pt. 3, *BSOAS* 16 (1954):71–4. On the problem of medieval statistics, see: *idem*, "Regarding Population Estimates in the Countries of Medieval Islam," *JESHO* 28 (1985):1–19.

[87] See below, in chs. 5, 7 and 8.

[88] This subject is discussed in general by Ayalon, "Auxiliary Forces," 15–21.

[89] See R. Irwin, "The Supply of Money and the Direction of Trade in Thirteenth-Century Syria," in P.W. Edbury and D.M. Metcalf (eds.), *Coinage in the Latin East* (Oxford, 1980), 73–4.

[90] See above, n. 19.

[91] Yūnīnī, 1:512; 2:162; C. Cahen, "Quelques textes négligés concernant les turcomans du Rūm au moment de l'invasion mongole," *Byzantion* 14 (1939):135.

[92] *Rawḍ*, 434; Nuwayrī, MS. 2m, fol. 253b; Ibn al-Furāt, *Ta'rīkh [al-duwal wa'l-mulūk]*, vol. 7, ed. Q. Zurayk (Beirut, 1942):31.

[93] Ibn Shaddād, *Ta'rīkh*, 335.

exaggerated, it does give some idea of the magnitude of the Türkmen influx from Mongol-controlled territory in these early years.

The Türkmen were well received and many were settled along the Syrian coast, from Gaza up to the borders of Lesser Armenia. *Iqṭāᶜāt* were distributed among their chiefs, many of whom were made amirs.[94] Early in 661 (which began 15 November 1262), Baybars met with Türkmen chiefs at Gaza and arranged their affairs. The actual abode of these Türkmen is unspecified, but it would seem to have been somewhere in the vicinity, because immediately afterwards the Sultan met with bedouin chiefs from the Gaza area.[95] In any event, al-ᶜUmarī records Türkmen as being part of the army of Gaza in his time, and al-Qalqashandī (d. 821/1418) reproduces a document listing them, along with bedouins and Kurds, as auxiliary troops to the army of that town.[96] Türkmen were settled in the neighborhood of Qārā in 664/1266, after Baybars took the fortress from the Franks.[97] That same year unspecified Türkmen raided Haifa.[98] The most notable mention of Türkmen in Baybars's reign is in 666/1268, when, after the conquest of Jaffa, the Sultan settled Türkmen along the coast to guard it, presumably against a Frankish attack. Since these troops were given the recently conquered lands, outside of an initial outlay of horses and equipment, Baybars was able to increase his army without any additional expense, a point emphasized in the source.[99] These may have been the Türkmen that Prince Edward of England ran into on his raid to Qāqūn in AD 1271.[100] Such settlement of Türkmen was not limited to Baybars's period. A later example is from 706/1306–7, when the governor of Damascus settled 300 Türkmen on the coast between Beirut and Antioch and gave them *iqṭāᶜāt*, so that they would patrol the shorelands and roads.[101]

It is difficult to gauge the exact contribution of the Türkmen to the Mamluk war effort against the Mongols. While they are mentioned several times in connection with the efforts of al-Mustanṣir and al-Ḥākim to reestablish the Caliphate in Iraq, in the subsequent years they are rarely found in the reports of the war with the Īlkhānids and their allies. The inescapable conclusion is that in comparison with the Syrian bedouins the Syrian Türkmen played only a minor role in the conflict with the Mongols. This may be more than a coincidence. Perhaps Baybars was not sure of their dependability and feared their connections with their kinsmen to the north. He might have thought it best to keep them away from the frontier and direct their military capabilities against the other enemy of the Sultanate, the Franks. The ongoing conquest of

[94] *Ibid.*; see also Ayalon, "Auxiliary Forces," 15. For the names of the Türkmen tribes of Syria, albeit of a later date, see Qalqashandī, 7:190, 282; Ẓāhirī, 105. [95] See above, nn. 76–7.

[96] ᶜUmarī, ed. Sayyid, 143; Qalqashandī, 12:218 (cited in Poliak, *Feudalism*, 9).

[97] Yūnīnī, 2:345; Mufaḍḍal, 155.

[98] *Rawḍ*, 267; Ibn al-Furāt, MS. Vienna, fol. 108b (= ed. Lyons, 1:125).

[99] *Rawḍ*, 294; Ibn al-Furāt, MS. Vienna, fol. 128b; Maqrīzī, 1:565; Thorau, *Baybars*, 188.

[100] *Eracles*, in *RHC, Occ*, 2:461.

[101] Ṣāliḥ b. Yaḥyā, *Ta'rīkh Bayrūt*, ed. L. Cheikho (Beirut, 1927), 33, 42; cited by Poliak, *Feudalism*, 9.

the coast, where the Türkmen could be settled and fulfill an important military role, would have facilitated such a policy.

The organization of the military machine

In the long run, Baybars's diplomatic maneuvers, discussed in the next chapter, would have had little effect were it not for the intense military preparations which he initiated. The victory at ʿAyn Jālūt and the subsequent pressure put on the Īlkhānids by the Golden Horde and other quarters granted the Mamluks the respite to prepare themselves for the next test of strength. Yet, although they were preoccupied elsewhere, the Īlkhānids sought to maintain the initiative at least on their border with the Mamluks. The success the Mamluks achieved there, along with the eventual victory at the second battle of Homs (680/1281), shows that Babyars had realized his aim of creating a military machine which could stand up to the Mongol danger.[102]

First and foremost, the army of Egypt was greatly enlarged during Baybars's reign. Al-Yūnīnī states that the Egyptian army reached 40,000 horsemen during this period, compared to 10,000 in the reigns of al-Kāmil Muḥammad (615–35/1218–38) and al-Ṣāliḥ Ayyūb (637–47/1240–9).[103] Elsewhere, the same author writes that the Egyptian army numbered 30,000 horsemen under Baybars.[104] While these numbers should be used with some caution, they do reflect the tremendous growth of the Mamluk army, at least in Egypt, in these years.

Besides the forces of the defunct Ayyūbid principalities and of his Mamluk predecessors, which Baybars inherited and which formed the initial bases of his armies, throughout his reign there was a more or less steady stream of horsemen from Mongol-controlled territory. These military refugees, called *wāfidiyya* and *musta'minūn/musta'mina*, may be divided into two groups: actual Mongol tribesmen; and indigenous Muslim military elements, including mamluks, who were escaping Mongol control. In both cases, they represented the influx of top-notch cavalrymen into the Sultanate, saving the Sultan the expense and time of training them, although they henceforth had to be provided for. In most cases, these horsemen were integrated into the personal units of the amirs and the non-mamluk *ḥalqa* formation; the latter was of clear secondary status compared to the royal mamluks, but due to the high quality of its troops then, still had a high military value.[105] Ibn Shaddād reports that both the Mongol *wāfidiyya* and the Muslim military refugees from

[102] See the comments in Ayalon, "Yāsa," pt. C1, 128–9.

[103] Yūnīnī, 3:261–2; also in Kutubī, MS. Köprülü 1121, fol. 71b; Ṣafadī, *Wāfī*, 10:342–3; Ibn Taghrī Birdī, 7:197. Cf. Ibn Wāṣil, *Mufarrij al-kurūb*, 4, ed. Ḥ.M. Rabīʿ (Cairo, 1972), 209 (cited in Thorau, "ʿAyn Jālūt," 237), who writes that al-Kāmil had 12,000 cavalrymen in Egypt. [104] Yūnīnī, 3:255.

[105] On the *wāfidiyya*, see: Ayalon, "Wafidiya," 91–104. On the *ḥalqa*, see: *idem*, "Studies on the Structure of the Mamlūk Army," pt. 2, *BSOAS* 15 (1953):448–59. On the role of non-mamluks in the units of the amirs, see *ibid.*, 472–3.

Iraq who fled to the Sultanate during Baybars's reign each numbered 3000 horsemen, and this does not include Rūmī amirs (and their entourages), military elements from the Jazīra, Türkmen and Iraqi bedouins, who also sought refuge.[106]

Even more significant, both militarily and in terms of Mamluk society, was Baybars's policy on buying mamluks. Al-Yūnīnī credits him with purchasing 4000 personal mamluks.[107] However, al-Ẓāhirī attributes 16,000 mamluks to him.[108] The late date of al-Ẓāhirī's work and unique nature of this evidence, whose source is unclear, leads to the acceptance of the smaller figure. On the other hand, perhaps al-Ẓāhirī's figure represents not only the mamluks that Baybars himself purchased, but all those who may have been previously mamluks of earlier sultans and of defunct and dead amirs, and had been integrated into the royal mamluks.[109] Al-Yūnīnī's figure is substantially larger than the number of mamluks bought by Baybars's patron, al-Ṣāliḥ Ayyūb, who is said to have established mamluk units totaling about 1000.[110] The royal mamluks, the most important component being those mamluks bought and raised by Baybars himself, were the backbone of the Mamluk army and their large numbers embody the efforts he devoted to creating a military machine to repulse the enemies of his kingdom. Baybars was not alone in purchasing and raising mamluks: the various amirs all received *iqṭāʿāt* in order to finance the upkeep of personal units, which were to a large extent composed of mamluks whom they had to purchase and train. Although there is no explicit evidence to this effect, it seems clear that in the atmosphere of *jihād* and military preparations, and under the influence if not overt encouragement of the Sultan, the amirs were also busy buying young mamluks, and thus contributing to the general increase in size of the Mamluk army.

There is little information on the size of the Syrian armies in this period. It can only be assumed that here too there was some degree of expansion, influenced both by the growth of the Egyptian army and the extra revenues generated from recently conquered Frankish possessions. One sign that the Syrian army grew is that at some point Baybars ordered the army of Hama to be expanded from 600 to 800 horsemen.[111] Indications of how important Baybars considered the Syrian army are found in the following examples: in

106 Ibn Shaddād, *Ta'rīkh*, 331, 337 (whence Yūnīnī, 3:256; Ibn Kathīr, 13:276). Both Mongol and non-Mongol *wāfidiyya* will be discussed in further detail in ch. 5.

107 Yūnīnī, 3:250; also Kutubī, MS. Köprülü, fol. 71a. See Ayalon, "Studies on the Structure," pt. 1, 223; R.S. Humphreys, "Emergence of the Mamluk Army," 159–60; Smith, "ʿAyn Jālūt," 321 n. 42.

108 Ẓāhirī, 116. Maqrīzī, 1:638, writes that Baybars had a personal army (*ʿaskar*) of 12,000, split equally between Cairo, Damascus and Aleppo, an assertion which may be rejected, given that we know that the royal mamluks were permanently stationed in Cairo; Ayalon, "Studies on the Structure," pt. 1, 205.

109 On these components of the royal mamluks, see Ayalon, "Studies on the Structure," pt. 1, 204–22.

110 The exact numbers vary in the sources and could possibly be somewhat higher. See Levanoni, "The Mamluks' Ascent to Power," 124–5.

111 Mufaḍḍal, 202–3.

662/1264, the Sultan sent a senior amir to inspect the armies and fortresses of Syria.[112] The same year, the Sultan intervened in the military affairs of the semi-autonomous principality of Hama, whose lord – al-Manṣūr – was not running things to his satisfaction.[113] Baybars also conducted inspection tours of Syria to check its military readiness, as in 667/1269 and 670/1271.[114] In addition to the regular Syrian armies, mention has been made above of the bedouin and Türkmen auxiliaries. There is no evidence, at least in the period under discussion, of large-scale contingents of volunteers joining the Mamluks on their campaigns against the Mongols.[115]

Care was not only devoted to the size of the army, but also to its quality. Baybars placed great emphasis on *furūsiyya* (horsemanship) and other military training. He had built two hippodromes in Cairo: al-Maydān al-Ẓāhirī and Maydān al-Qabaq. The latter was especially important. Built in 666/1267, it was the main center for *furūsiyya* exercises of the Sultan's army. When the Sultan was in Egypt, he would visit this *maydān* every day, training until the evening prayer. Because of the enthusiasm he generated, almost all the amirs and mamluks devoted themselves to training with the lance and bow. Since the general zeal led to the overcrowding of the hippodrome, participation had to be regulated. "Such fervour and enthusiasm were, indeed, peculiar to Baybars' reign and were much weaker under his successors, even though Sultan Qalawun and his sons Khalīl and Muḥammad, sought to uphold Baybars' tradition."[116] Besides this general description of the Sultan's participation and encouragement of *furūsiyya* training, interspersed in the chronicles are specific examples of instances of his partaking in this activity, even while on campaign in Syria.[117]

Over the years Baybars held inspections (*ʿurūḍ*, pl. of *ʿarḍ*) of his troops, thus verifying their readiness.[118] The Sultan personally conducted these inspections, which would take place in one of the *maydāns* in Cairo. He would often attempt to complete them in one day, in order to make sure that no one was passing around equipment. Failure to show up for inspection could result in execution: in 674/1275–6 five *ḥalqa* soldiers were hanged in Cairo for being

[112] *Rawḍ*, 194; Nuwayrī, MS. 2m, fol. 168a; Ibn al-Furāt, MS. Vienna, fol. 42b; Maqrīzī, 1:510.

[113] Nuwayrī, MS. 2m, fol. 166b; Ibn al-Furāt, MS. Vienna, fol. 37a–b; Maqrīzī, 1:503.

[114] AH 667: *Rawḍ*, 342; Ibn al-Furāt, MS. Vienna, fol. 154b; Maqrīzī, 1:574. AH 670: *Rawḍ*, 395; Ibn al-Furāt, MS. Vienna, fol. 205b; Maqrīzī, 1:602.

[115] Cf. Irwin, *Middle East*, 50.

[116] D. Ayalon, "Notes on the Furūsiyya Exercises and Games in the Mamlūk Sultanate," *Scripta Hierosolymitana* 9 (1961):38–39, 44, 47. See below, ch. 10, for a further discussion on the training which the mamluks underwent.

[117] AH 667: *Rawḍ*, 338; Ibn al-Furāt, MS. Vienna, fol. 149b; Maqrīzī, 1:573. AH 669: Maqrīzī, 595–6. AH 670: Ibn al-Furāt, MS. Vienna, fols. 204a, 205b; Maqrīzī, 1:601, 602. AH 671: Maqrīzī, 1:605. AH 672: Ibn al-Furāt, 7:6–7; Maqrīzī, 1:611–12. Qalawun, at the beginning of his reign, also went to the *maydān* to participate in these exercises: Maqrīzī, 1:669.

[118] AH 661: Ibn al-Furāt, MS. Vienna, fol. 35b; Maqrīzī, 1:501; Nuwayrī, MS. 2m, fol. 169b; *ibid.*, fol. 166a, also reports that that year the Sultan reviewed his troops every Monday and Thursday. AH 662: Ibn al-Furāt, MS. Vienna, fols. 45b, 50b, 53a–54b; Maqrīzī, 1:512, 517. AH 673: Nuwayrī, MS. 2m, fol. 253a; Ibn al-Furāt, 7:28. AH 675: Ibn al-Furāt, 7:68; Maqrīzī, 1:626.

absent from a review in Homs.[119] The *ᶜarḍ* was an important institution in the military life of medieval Islam, and enabled the ruler or commander to keep up the pressure on his subordinates, be they officers or soldiers.[120] Baybars made effective use of this long established institution.

Brief mention should be made of the ostensible adoption by Baybars of the *yasa* (< Mongolian *jasagh*), the Mongol legal code theoretically promulgated by Chinggis Khan.[121] Professor Ayalon has studied this question at length and has shown that Ibn Taghrī Birdī's evidence that Baybars adopted various Mongol customs and usages of Chinggis Khan, including his laws (*aḥkām*), is highly doubtful, not least because this information is not substantiated by any contemporary author, including the Sultan's biographers. If anything, Ibn ᶜAbd al-Ẓāhir cites a letter in which Baybars expressed explicit contempt for the *yasa*.[122]

Early on in his reign, Baybars organized his *barīd* ("pony express") system to expedite rapid communications between Egypt and Syria, and different points within the latter country. The need for such a system is clear. When not on campaign, the majority of the Mamluk army was concentrated in Cairo, while the Mongols could launch a raid or even an offensive at any time into Syria. In addition, the danger of a Frankish attack could not be discounted altogether. Finally, since the Sultan spent much of his time in Syria, he needed rapid communications with his capital, in case of either subversion against his rule, or a Frankish attack against the Egyptian coast. J. Sauvaget doubted that the inspiration for the postal service was the caliphal *barīd*, since this had been out of service since Seljuq times at the latest. Instead, he suggested that Baybars's source was the postal system of horse relays of the Mongols, the *yām* (< Mongolian *jam*).[123] This is not as far-fetched as might initially sound, because there was some limited Mongol influence on the Mamluk Sultanate.[124] Considering the significance of having a rapid form of communications, there is no reason why Baybars would not have adopted a successful Mongol administrative practice.

Whatever the ultimate inspiration for the *barīd*, Baybars established it in 659/1260–1. Under normal conditions messages could be sent from Egypt to Damascus in four days, and in times of particular urgency this was even

[119] Kutubī, MS. Köprülü, fol. 42a.

[120] See C.E. Bosworth, "Recruitment, Muster and Review in Medieval Islamic Armies," in V.J. Parry and M.E. Yapp (eds.), *War, Technology and Society in the Middle East* (London, 1975), 59–77, esp. 72ff.

[121] On the *yasa*, see Ratchnevsky, *Genghis Khan*, 187–96; the four sections of Ayalon, "Yāsa"; D.O. Morgan, "The 'Great *Yāsa* of Chingiz Khān' and Mongol Law in the Īlkhānate," *BSOAS* 49 (1986):163–76.

[122] Ayalon, "Yāsa," pt. C2, 127–31; see Ibn Taghrī Birdī, 6:268–9, 7:182–6. On this letter see ch. 5, p. 124.

[123] J. Sauvaget, *La poste aux chevaux dans l'empire des Mamelouks* (Paris, 1941), 10–13. See also: D. Ayalon, "On One of the Works of Jean Sauvaget," *IOS* 1 (1971):298–302; *idem*, "Yāsa," pt. C1, 131–2; Gaudefroy-Demombynes, *Syrie*, 239–48; Thorau, *Baybars*, 103–5. For the *yām*, see Morgan, *Mongols*, 103–7.

[124] See Ayalon, "Yāsa," pt. C1, 130–6.

shortened to three. Among the termini of the *barīd* were the frontier fortresses of al-Bīra and al-Raḥba, and routes connected all the major cities of Syria. The *barīd* should not be understood as a postal system in the modern sense, open to all citizens. Rather it was normally restricted for use by the Sultan, and although it was used for day-to-day matters of government, its main purpose was the conveying of military messages. The employment of members of the *khāṣṣakiyya*, the Sultan's select entourage, as postal couriers shows the great importance Baybars attached to this system.[125] The role of the Syrian bedouins in helping to maintain and man the *barīd* system has already been mentioned.

Even the *barīd*, however, was not fast enough for the Sultan. In order to relay the news from the Euphrates of an impending Mongol raid or invasion, a series of watchposts (*manāwir*) was established. Urgent news was passed from station to station via bonfires at night and smoke signals during the day. These posts, which were manned all the time, stretched in two lines from al-Bīra and al-Raḥba on the Euphrates to Damascus, and from there in a single line to Gaza, from where the alert was relayed on to Cairo via pigeon-post or *barīd*. Thus, if there was news at the northeastern border in the morning, by night it would have reached the Citadel in Cairo.[126] The pigeon-post service, again starting at al-Raḥba and al-Bīra, was also put on a firm footing in the early Mamluk period. This had existed in a precarious manner in Ayyūbid times, but under the Mamluks it was transformed into a regular institution.[127] Although the initiator of these two institutions is unspecified in the sources, they can probably be attributed to Baybars, whose efforts against the Mongols provide a logical background to these developments.[128]

In order to improve communications and facilitate the movement of troops, roads and bridges in Syria were improved and rebuilt. Outstanding examples include the bridge at Dāmiya over the Jordan (664/1266),[129] the bridge at Lydda (671/1273),[130] and guard towers on the roads to Tadmur and al-Raḥba.[131]

125 *Rawḍ*, 95; Ibn al-Furāt, MS. Vatican, fol. 266a; Maqrīzī, 1:446–7. Also Yūnīnī, 3:255; *Rawḍ*, 395–6. For the administration of this system, see: Sauvaget, *Poste*, 16–36, 42–77; Ayalon, "Sauvaget," 298–302.

126 ʿUmarī, *al-Taʿrīf fī al-muṣṭalaḥ al-sharīf* (Cairo, 1312/1894–5), 199–201; Qalqashandī, 1:127–8, who writes that fires were used as signals as far as Bilbīs in Egypt; Sauvaget, *Poste*, 39–41. The efficiency of smoke and fire signals, at least in the Byzantine Empire and Lesser Armenia, has been questioned; R.W. Edwards, *The Fortifications of Armenian Cilicia* (Washington, D.C., 1987), 42 n. 19. Bonfires were used in the Ayyūbid period to convey messages from Muslim spies in Acre to Damascus; Sibṭ ibn al-Jawzī, *Mir'at al-zamān*, vol. 8 (Hyderabad, 1370/1951):646–7. 127 Sauvaget, *Poste*, 36–9; Gaudefroy-Demombynes, *Syrie*, 250–4.

128 Sauvaget, *Poste*, 41.

129 Nuwayrī, MS. 2m, fol. 179a–b; Thorau, *Baybars*, 166.

130 Ibn al-Furāt, 7:6; *RCEA*, 12:174–5 (s.a. 671). R. Ellenblum ("The Crusader Road from Lod to Jerusalem" [Hebrew], in Y. Ben-Arieh *et al.* (eds.), *Historical–Geographical Studies in the Settlement of Eretz Israel* [Jerusalem, 1988], 215–18) shows that Baybars only rebuilt an earlier Frankish bridge. 131 Ṣafadī, *Wāfī*, 10:342.

Baybars's fortification policy is summed up in the following statement found in the proclamation released after the conquest of Caesarea in 663/1265:

> One part [of the Muslim armies] uproots Frankish fortresses, and destroys [their] castles, while [another] part rebuilds what the Mongols destroyed in the east and increases the height of their ramparts [compared with what they were].[132]

With his usual vigor, Baybars continued the Ayyūbid policy of destroying the fortifications and cities along the Syrian coast as they were conquered from the Franks. The rationale for this was the knowledge that the coastline could not be adequately garrisoned, and it was feared that if the Franks attacked from the sea, over which they had undisputed control, these cities could thus be easily recaptured and function as a bridgehead for a new Crusading effort.[133] Yet at the same time, the Sultan devoted much attention and resources to the fortresses further inland. These included Qāqūn, to the east of the coastal plain in Palestine, which was rebuilt in 664/1265–6 and served as a regional center in lieu of the destroyed cities of Caesaria and Arsūf, as well as a watchpost on the coastal plain.[134] Baybars also had Safad completely repaired after the heavy damage it had suffered in the siege to take it (664/1266).[135] Other important Frankish castles which were taken and then repaired were Shaqīf Tīrūn (Cave de Tyron), Ḥiṣn al-Akrād (Crac des Chevaliers) and Ḥiṣn ʿAkkār (Gibelacar).[136]

Baybars had also repaired early in his reign many of the fortifications which had been destroyed or damaged by the Mongols during their short occupation of Syria: the forts of al-Ṣalt, ʿAjlūn, Ṣarkhad, Bosra, Shayzar, al-Ṣubayba and Shumaymish (near Homs), along with the citadels of Damascus, Baalbek and Homs.[137] Interestingly enough, the citadel of Aleppo was not rebuilt until the 1290s.[138] When Karak was taken in 661/1263 from al-Mughīth ʿUmar, Baybars had it regarrisoned and maintained in a state of readiness.[139]

The purpose of these fortresses was manifold. All were to function as fortified regional centers, and symbols of Mamluk authority over the country. The splitting up of power in Syria among various fortified centers was also a preventative measure against would-be rebellious Mamluk officers or gover-

[132] Ibn al-Furāt, MS. Vienna, fol. 73b: Maqrīzī, 1:531; Ibn al-Dawādārī, 8:109; translation from D. Ayalon, "The Mamluks and Naval Power: A Phase of the Struggle between Islam and Christian Europe," *Proceedings of the Israel Academy of Sciences and Humanities* 1, no. 8 (1967):12. [133] Ayalon, "The Mamluks and Naval Power," 7–9.

[134] *Rawḍ*, 275; Ṣafadī, *Wāfī*, 10:341. Cf. Ibn al-Furāt, MS. Vienna, fol. 117a (= ed. Lyons, 1:127; see Riley-Smith's comments, 2:218); Maqrīzī, 1:557, who both put this event in AH 666.

[135] Holt, *Crusades*, 95–6. Baybars himself took part in these repairs; *Rawḍ*, 280–1, 285; Ibn Shaddād, *Aʿlāq*, 2, pt. 2: 150–1; T. T. al-Ṭarāwina, *Mamlakat ṣafad fī ʿahd al-mamālīk* (Beirut, 1402/1982), 52–3. [136] Thorau, *Baybars*, 188–9, 205–6.

[137] *Rawḍ*, 93; Nuwayrī, MS. 2m, fol. 142b; Ibn al-Furāt, MS. Vatican, fol. 266a; Maqrīzī, 1:446.

[138] Ibn al-Shiḥna, *al-Durr al-muntakhab fī ta'rīkh mamlakat ḥalab* (Beirut, 1909), 54–5, 57–8; trans. in J. Sauvaget (tr.), *"Les Perles Choisies" d'Ibn ach-Chihna* (Beirut, 1933), 46, 48.

[139] Ibn al-Furāt, MS. Vienna, fol. 26a; Maqrīzī, 1:492. In 673/1274, Baybars inspected Karak and nearby Shawbak; Ibn al-Furāt, 7:22; Maqrīzī, 1:614.

nors.[140] Some, such as Qāqūn and Safad, were clearly intended to contain the Franks still on the coast and any that would come from over the sea. Many, while having an anti-Frankish purpose, could also act as centers of resistance if the Mongols were to reconquer all or part of the country. This actually seems to have happened in the Mongol occupation of 699/1299–1300.[141]

There were two forts whose main purpose was to act as bulwarks against Mongol aggression: al-Bīra and al-Raḥba. Guarding the fords over the Euphrates, these forts were both subjected to many attacks throughout the entire history of the Mongol–Mamluk war. In 658/1260, al-Bīra had been occupied by the Mongols, who destroyed its walls and towers to some degree. Al-Bīra was subsequently abandoned by the Mongols after ʿAyn Jālūt, when it was taken over by a representative of al-Saʿīd ʿAlāʾ al-Dīn, governor of Aleppo. Later that year, it was subjected to an unsuccessful Mongol attack, and the following year Aqqush al-Barlī took it over. In 660/1262, Baybars finally gained control over it when Aqqush submitted to him following his defeat by the Mongols at Sinjār, and it was subsequently repaired.[142] Al-Raḥba's fate in 658/1260 is unclear. The fact that it does not seem to be mentioned in this year by the sources may indicate that the Mongols never conquered it. It seems that it came under the authority of the Ayyūbid ruler of Homs, because at al-Ashraf Mūsā's death in 662/1264, it is reported that only then did it come under the Sultan's direct control.[143] The importance of these two forts cannot be exaggerated. Besides guarding the Mamluk frontier, they acted as watchposts and termini to the various systems of rapid communication discussed above, and thus could alert the Sultan of Mongol raids or impending invasions. In addition, they served as the staging posts for the many Mamluk raids into Mongol-controlled territory, thus facilitating the carrying of the border war over into the enemy camp.[144]

140 D. Ayalon, "Egypt as a Dominant Factor in Syria and Palestine during the Islamic Period," in A. Cohen and G. Baer (eds.), *Egypt and Palestine* (Jerusalem and N.Y., 1984), 34–5.

141 Amitai, "Mongol Raids," 244.

142 Ibn Shaddād, *Aʿlāq*, 3:120–3; Ibn Wāṣil, MS. 1703, fol. 165a; Yūnīnī, 2:119; *Zubda*, fol. 36a; ʿAynī, fol. 81b; Ṣafadī, *Wāfī* 10:342. See also above, p. 61.

143 *Rawḍ*, 280; Ibn al-Furāt, MS. Vienna, fol. 39a; Maqrīzī, 1:505.

144 See, e.g.: Yūnīnī, 3:132–3. These forts are discussed at greater length in ch. 9.

CHAPTER 4

The search for a second front

... Between our older and younger brothers, there was conflict. Because of this we could not ride towards you.

Abagha, in a letter to Baybars, 667/1268[1]

Early on in the war, both the Mamluk Sultans and the Īlkhāns began to devote considerable efforts to diplomatic activities with various third parties. Both sides hoped that this would lead to the opening of a second front against their enemy, bringing about its weakening and neutralization, if not its defeat. It is true that Mamluk–Golden Horde relations as well as Īlkhānid–Frankish contacts have been well studied by modern scholars. Considering the importance of this subject for the history of Mamluk–Īlkhānid war, however, it is impossible to dispense with a discussion on this topic. It may also prove useful to re-examine the diplomatic relations within the context of the Mamluk–Īlkhānid war.

The beginnings of the Mamluk–Golden Horde entente[2]

The relationship between Baybars and Berke Khan, ruler of the Golden Horde, originated in their mutual understanding that they shared a common enemy in Hülegü. Berke's conflict with Hülegü arose from the latter's occupation of the area south of the Caucasian mountains. It appears that prior to Hülegü's arrival the Jochids had enjoyed some type of vague sovereignty over all of Mongol Iran, which had now been denied them. The studies of Professor Ayalon[3] and Dr. Jackson[4] have shown that this question of

[1] *Rawḍ*, 340–1; see ch. 5, p. 121.
[2] Besides the studies cited in the following notes, see S. Zakirov, *Diplomaticheskie Otnosheniia Zolotoi Ordy s Egipetom (XIII-XIV vv.)* (Moscow, 1966).
[3] Ayalon, "Yāsa," pt. B, 174–6.
[4] Jackson, "Dissolution," 208–35; cf. Morgan, *Mongols*, 148–9. See above, ch. 1, pp. 13, 29.

sovereignty,[5] along with the related matter of the control of revenues,[6] were the fundamental reasons behind the Īlkhānid–Golden Horde war.[7]

Other causes contributed to the escalation of tension which led to open conflict. Hülegü himself significantly contributed to the deterioration of relations by the execution of three Jochid princes who were leading contingents in his army.[8] Tensions were also exacerbated by Berke's and Hülegü's support for Arigh-böke and Qubilai respectively for the succession to the Qa'anate.[9] Some authors stress Hülegü's execution of the Caliph as arousing Berke, a convert to Islam, to action.[10]

Open warfare between Berke and Hülegü may have erupted as early as the winter of 660/1261–2,[11] although it appears that the war was carried out at a leisurely pace. Berke sent an army under Prince Noghai, who went through the Darband Pass (the "Iron Gate," on the eastern flank of the Caucasian mountains, next to the Caspian Sea), and took up position in the region of Shirvān. Hülegü himself left his *ordo* at Ala Tagh on 2 Shawwāl 660/20 August 1262. His advanced forces defeated Noghai on 29 Dhū 'l-ḥijja/14 November, who retreated into the Darband. Hülegü's forces advanced and defeated Noghai again, who withdrew back into the Qipchaq Steppe on 1 Ṣafar 661/15 December 1262. Under the command, probably nominal, of Abagha, Hülegü's son and future successor, the Īlkhānid force advanced into the Steppe,

5 See especially the important evidence of ʿUmarī, ed. Lech, 15; discussed in Ayalon, "Yāsa," pt. B, 174–5, and Jackson, "Dissolution," 209. Cf. ʿUmarī, ed. Lech, 78–9, where the Jochid claims to northwest Iran are presented in a more ambiguous manner. Marco Polo, *The Travels* (Harmondsworth, 1958; rpt., 1986), 335, writes that the conflict was over boundaries.

6 Ibn Shaddād cited in Yūnīnī, 1:497–8, 2:161–2; Ibn al-Dawādārī, 7:92–3; Mufaḍḍal, 102–3; Ibn Kathīr, 13:234. Also Ibn Wāṣil, in W. de Tiesenhausen, *Recueil de matériaux relatifs à l'histoire de l'Horde d'Or*, vol. 1 (St. Petersburg, 1884), 70–1; Qirtay, fol. 79a. This evidence is discussed in Ayalon, "Yāsa," pt. B, 174; Jackson, "Dissolution," 226–7. Some type of revenues may have continued flowing for several decades from Iran to the Golden Horde, because we hear that the Īlkhān Ghazan (694–703/1295–1304) finally put a stop to this early in his reign; Ṣafadī, *Aʿyān*, MS. Aya Sofya 2968, fol. 4b; MS. Emanet Hazinesi (Topkapı Sarayı) 1216, fol. 129a. See also ʿUmarī, ed. Lech, 78–9.

7 See B.G. Lippard, "The Mongols and Byzantium, 1243–1341," Ph.D. diss., Indiana Univ. (Bloomington, 1983), 188–90, where most of the reasons listed above and below are also mentioned.

8 Rashīd al-Dīn, *Djami el-Tévarikh*, vol. 2, ed. E. Blochet (Leiden, 1911), 138–9; trans. in J.A. Boyle, tr., *The Successors of Genghis Khan* (London-New York, 1971), 122–3; Rashīd al-Dīn, ed. ʿAlīzādah, 3:77; Grigor, 337–41; Kirakos, tr. Dulaurier, 504–5; cf. Ibn Shaddād, as cited in the previous note. See Jackson, "Dissolution," 232–3; Boyle, "Īl-Khāns," 353.

9 Abū Shāma, 220; cited in Yūnīnī, 1:497; Ibn al-Dawādārī, 8:91; Mufaḍḍal, 101–2. For Berke's support of Arigh Böke, see: ʿAynī, fol. 80a. Berke struck coins in Arigh Böke's name; Spuler, *Iran*, 55 n. 94. On Hülegü's support for Qubilai, which initially may not have been unequivocal, see Jackson, "Dissolution," 234.

10 Yūnīnī, 2:365; similar wording in Ṣafadī, *Wāfī*, 10:118. Rashīd al-Dīn (ed. ʿAlīzādah, 3:87) adds this as a secondary reason for the estrangement between the two cousins. See also Jūzjānī, *Ṭabaqāt-i nāṣirī*, ed. ʿA. Ḥabībī (Kabul, 1964–5), 2:198; trans. in H.G. Raverty, *Ṭabaḳāt-i-nāṣirī* (London, 1881), 2:1257; Vardan, tr. Thomson, 221. On Berke's conversion, see J. Richard, "La conversion de Berke et les débuts de l'islamisation de la Horde d'Or," *REI* 35 (1967):173–84.

11 For this date, see Jackson, "Dissolution," 233–4 and n. 210.

crossed the Terek River, and came upon Berke's deserted but well stocked winter encampment (*qıshlaq*). For three days the Īlkhānid troops indulged in merriment, until they were surprised by Berke's forces and completely routed (1 Rabī^c I 661/14 January 1263). Retreating across the frozen Terek, Abagha's forces suffered another disaster, when the ice broke under their weight and many troops were drowned. Abagha himself escaped, and his surviving soldiers were pursued to the southern end of the Darband by Berke, who then returned to his own country.[12]

Of great interest are Berke's words, as reported by Ibn Wāṣil and later sources, upon surveying the carnage on the battlefield after Hülegü's army had been defeated. Bemoaning the large number of Mongol dead, he cursed Hülegü and said: "Mongols are killed by Mongol swords. If we were united, then we would have conquered all of the world."[13] A contemporary Mamluk author, at least, believed that in spite of his emerging understanding with Baybars against Hülegü, Berke had not totally given up the traditional Mongol ideal of world conquest. Only political realities, about which he complains here, forced him to abjure this idea. Perhaps his renouncing of his plans to launch a renewed attack on eastern Europe, due to this conflict with Hülegü,[14] lay behind this speech, or the record of it in Mamluk sources.

Rashīd al-Dīn writes that the following year there was a rumor that Noghai was intending to invade through the Darband. However, when this general learnt that Hülegü now enjoyed the recognition of Qubilai, he abandoned his plans. This same author also reports that Hülegü ordered the preparation of another army to avenge this defeat. These plans, however, were not realized before Hülegü's death (Rabī^c II 663/February 1265), and it was only in the beginning of Abagha's reign that the war was to be continued.[15]

While the sources indicate the sundry causes that led Berke to send his army into the Caucasus, they are silent about the exact goals that he had in mind for his campaign. We can only assume that he intended that Jochid lordship over northern Iran would be recognized and that the flow of disrupted revenues would be restarted.

News of the incipient conflict began to reach the Sultanate some time in 660/

12 Rashīd al-Dīn, ed. ʿAlīzādah, 3:87–9 (summarized in Boyle, "Īl-Khāns," 353–4); Mustawfī, 59. A slightly different version is found in the lost part of Ibn Shaddād's biography of Baybars, cited in Yūnīnī, 1:535–6; 2:196; cf. shorter versions in Ibn Kathīr, 13:239; Dhahabī, *Ta'rīkh*, MS. Laud 279, fol. 2a. A very different account of the events leading up to this battle, which was supposedly initiated by Hülegü at the instigation of a disgruntled Jochid princess, is found in Nuwayrī, 27:329–30 (= *Tuḥfa*, 37); 27:357–9. The credibility of Nuwayrī's account is undermined by the writer's assertion that it took place in 653/1255–6, i.e. before Hülegü had even reached this part of Iran! Cf. the versions in Kirakos, tr. Dulaurier, 503–6; Marco Polo, tr. Latham, 335–9, who both claim that Hülegü's troops actually won this battle. They must have confused the final outcome with Hülegü's earlier victory; see also P. Pelliot, *Notes on Marco Polo*, vol. 1 (Paris, 1959–63), 94–5.

13 Ibn Wāṣil, in Tiesenhausen, 72; Ibn Kathīr, 13:239; Qirtay, fol. 80b. Cf. the version of this speech reported by Ibn Shaddād, cited in Yūnīnī, 1:535; translated and analyzed by Ayalon, "Yāsa," pt. B, 171 and nn. 2–3.

14 Jackson, "Dissolution," 236.

15 Rashīd al-Dīn, ed. ʿAlīzādah, 3:89–90.

1262, evidently before mid-Ramaḍān/3 August.[16] This information, together with knowledge of Berke's adherence to Islam, must have been the inspiration for Baybars's first letter to Berke, sent via a merchant (or merchants) from the Alan country. In this message, Baybars harps upon Berke's Islam, encouraging him to fight Hülegü. As a Muslim, Berke must wage the *jihād* against the infidels, even if they are his kinsmen, just as the Prophet Muḥammad fought the Quraysh. The letter continues that news has come that Hülegü had become a Christian and ends by describing Baybars's own *jihād*.[17]

More precise information on this conflict was brought by a group of 200 Mongol refugees (*wāfidiyya*), who fled to the Mamluk Sultanate and reached Egypt in Dhū 'l-ḥijja 660/November 1262.[18] These had been part of the Jochid expeditionary force sent to Hülegü years before.[19] Even prior to the open conflict, Hülegü had begun to massacre these troops.[20] At some point Berke had ordered these soldiers to return to him, and barring that, to make their way to Baybars's kingdom.[21] This was the first band of Mongol *wāfidiyya* to reach the Sultanate, although it was the only known one to have originated from Jochid troops.

Baybars responded to the news brought by these *wāfidiyya* by dispatching ambassadors to Berke, who set out in Muḥarram 661/November-December 1262, carrying a letter from Baybars. As in his first letter, Berke was urged to wage *jihād* and Hülegü was vilified. The power of the Sultan and his army was described, and finally mention was made of the arrival of a group of Berke's followers and of how they had been well received. No less important was the verbal message which Baybars gave to the envoys, in which the soundness (*ṣalāh*) of Islam was expressed, along with the state and numbers of the Sultan's army, his attention to the holy war and his affection for Berke. The

16 Abū Shāma, 219; hence Yūnīnī, 1:487.

17 *Rawḍ*, 88–9; Dhahabī, MS. Laud 305, fol. 258b. Later sources write that this first letter was sent in 659/1260–1: *Zubda*, fol. 51a–b; Ibn al-Furāt, MS. Vatican, fol. 278a; Maqrīzī, 1:465; ʿAynī, fol. 81a. But as Jackson, "Dissolution," 237 n. 231, has stated, Baybars al-Manṣūrī's text (and by extension the others) is taken from Ibn ʿAbd al-Ẓāhir's *Rawḍ*, and therefore AH 660 is the correct date. On the Alans, a people living in the Caucasus mountains, see Pelliot, *Notes on Marco Polo*, 1:16–17.

18 *Rawḍ*, 137; cf. Thorau, *Baybars*, 130 n. 30.

19 In 656/1258–9, a contingent from Berke's army participated in Hülegü's campaign to take Baghdad; Ibn Wāṣil, MS. 1703, fol. 128a; Rashīd al-Dīn, ed. ʿAlīzādah, 3:55–6. It is possible that elements of this contingent took part in Hülegü's campaign in Syria two years later. On the other hand, there is no evidence that this contingent was ordered to defect to the Mamluks before ʿAyn Jālūt, and thus contribute to Qutuz's defeat of Ketbugha, as suggested by D. Sinor ("The Mongols and Western Europe," in K.M. Setton, ed., *A History of the Crusades* [Madison, 1975], 528) and I. de Rachewiltz (*Papal Envoys to the Great Khans* [London, 1971], 149). Only in late 660/1262 did the first group of Jochid refugees arrive in Egypt.

20 Jackson, "Dissolution," 232–3, citing Grigor, 339.

21 *Rawḍ*, 137; cf. Abū Shāma, 220, that these soldiers of Hülegü were a remnant of Hülegü's army defeated by Berke. Jackson, "Dissolution," 237 n. 230, is right in ascribing to the *Rawḍ* of Ibn ʿAbd al-Ẓāhir, with his connections to Baybars, more authority in this case. In addition, there would have been little logic for Hülegü's troops to flee to Baybars. For the various later writers who derive their accounts from these two authors, see Jackson, as cited here; Ayalon, "Yāsa," pt. C1, 141–2; *idem*, "Wafidiya," 98.

embassy set out, and in Constantinople ran into envoys of Berke on their way to Baybars. One of the Mamluk envoys was forced to return to Egypt due to illness, but the embassy continued on its way.[22] Eventually, it reached the Khan's *ordo*, was brought before Berke and handed over Baybars's letter, which was translated into Turkish for the Khan's benefit. All those present were delighted with the letter. Berke prepared an answer, and dispatched these envoys with his own. They arrived back in Egypt on 10 Dhū 'l-qaʿda 662/4 September 1264 (see below).[23]

Berke's first envoys had arrived in Egypt on 11 Rajab 661/22 May 1263 along with the Mamluk envoy who had become sick in Constantinople. They were accompanied by a retinue, and envoys from the Byzantine Emperor Michael Palaeologus and Genoa. When the Sultan returned from an expedition in Syria, he received Berke's letter. According to Ibn ʿAbd al-Ẓāhir, Berke requested assistance against Hülegü, who had contravened the *yasa* (which may be translated here as either "a decree" or "the law") of Chinggis Khan and the law of his people (*wa-sharīʿat ahlihi*), and had killed human beings. Berke added that he and his four brothers had become Muslims, and that he was ready to exact revenge for the murdered Caliph and the Muslim nation (*umma*). Getting down to specifics, Berke requested that Baybars dispatch an army towards the Euphrates to hold the roads against Hülegü.[24] In another version of this letter, transmitted by al-Yūnīnī and others, there is no mention of the *yasa*, but only of the Islamic basis for the enmity between Berke and Hülegü: Baybars is called upon to launch an attack from his direction, as Berke will from his, thereby trapping Hülegü in the middle; each ruler will keep whatever he has conquered.[25] Ibn ʿAbd al-Ẓāhir's position at court, however, leads to the conclusion that the reference to the *yasa* must have been in the original letter.

Berke's letter is important for several reasons. First, as Professor Ayalon has written, the initial argument given to Baybars to justify Berke's war with Hülegü was the latter's breaking of the *yasa* and it appears that "Islam is only a secondary factor in the rift."[26] It is not clear to what *yasa* is exactly referring here, but it has been suggested that the intention is to the contravening of a

[22] *Rawḍ*, 139–40; *Zubda*, fol. 60a–b (who seemingly conflates this and Berke's subsequent mission; see p. 84 below); Ibn al-Furāt, fols. 7a, 11b–12a; Maqrīzī, 1:474–5, 479–80; Yūnīnī, 2:189–90, 418; Thorau, *Baybars*, 124, 259.

[23] *Rawḍ*, 214–18; Nuwayrī, MS. 2m, fols. 170b–171b; Ibn al-Furāt, MS. Vienna, fols. 51b–53a (whence summary in Maqrīzī, 1:517); Yūnīnī, 1:540–2; Ibn al-Dawādārī, 8:99–101. The last two sources, while containing some misleading information (Ibn al-Dawādārī mistakenly writes that the meeting with Berke was in AH 667; both have placed this report after the story of Aqqush al-Masʿūdī's mission later this year), both contain material not found in *Rawḍ*, although the two cite Ibn ʿAbd al-Ẓāhir by name. For the dating of Baybars's embassy and its mission, see Thorau, *Baybars*, 125, 259–60.

[24] *Rawḍ*, 170–1; summarized in Nuwayrī, MS. 2m, fol. 165a–b; Ibn al-Furāt, MS. Vienna, fol. 30a. See Ayalon, "Yāsa," pt. B, 167–72, for a translation and analysis of this passage. On the dating of Berke's first mission, see Thorau, *Baybars*, 125, and 131 n. 35.

[25] Yūnīnī, 1:533–4; 2:194–5; Mufaḍḍal, 110–11; Ibn al-Dawādārī, 8:97. A third version is found in Qirtay, fol. 79a. [26] Ayalon, "Yāsa," pt. B, 176–7.

specific decree, namely Hülegü's not sending his share of spoils and occupying territory that Berke thought was his.[27] Secondly, this letter is the first serious attempt to move this budding alliance from the level of mere expressions of goodwill and vague encouragement to one of common strategy against their mutual enemy. As will be seen, however, neither this nor later attempts in that direction were to bear any tangible fruits. Finally, the letter indicates a major change in the way of thinking among at least some of the Mongol leadership. In Dr. Jackson's words: "It signifies the first occasion on which a Mongol prince was prepared to collaborate with an independent external power against fellow Mongols; and in this vital sense – remembering the claims to worldwide dominion that the Mongols had hitherto expressed – it may be said to signify the dissolution of their empire."[28]

The factor of Islam, however, should not be completely discounted. If nothing else, it helped smooth the way for the rapprochement with Baybars. It may also have soothed some of the qualms the Mongols of the Golden Horde could have had about fighting their kinsmen to the south. Finally, the conviction of Berke and others in their new faith does not necessarily have to be doubted and it may well have contributed to the fervor with which they pursued the war against the Īlkhānids. Yet, it must be remembered that for the Golden Horde, the questions of sovereignty and revenues were the main underlying causes for both the Jochid–Īlkhānid war and the alliance between the Mamluks and the Golden Horde, as testified by the above letter and subsequent developments under the non-Muslim rulers of the Golden Horde.

As would be expected, Berke's envoys were well received, and Baybars prepared an embassy in return, along with a whole series of splendid gifts and a letter. Before being sent back, Berke's envoys heard a *khuṭba* delivered by the Caliph al-Ḥākim and later met with him. The Caliph encouraged them about the *jihād* and sent with them an oral message for Berke. Ibn ʿAbd al-Ẓāhir himself wrote the Sultan's letter, which contained the already standard exhortations to wage the *jihād*, incitements against Hülegü and boasts about the strength of the Sultan's army. This author adds that both Baybars and Fāris al-Dīn Aqtay al-Mustaʿrib, the *atabeg*, made additions to the letter.[29] On the other hand, a second, more "business-like" response is found in other, slightly later sources. Here Baybars expresses his agreement to Berke's suggestion of launching a joint attack. Thereupon there follows a somewhat problematic phrase, that "the letter contained [Baybars's expression] of submission and loyalty" (*al-dukhūl fī 'l-īliyya wa-'l-ṭāʿa*).[30] It is difficult to conceive of Baybars submitting to Berke; certainly the latter did not call for it and no additional similar statements or corroborating evidence have come to light. Thus, the phrase can only be understood in a more general sense as

[27] Jackson, "Dissolution," 235.

[28] *Ibid.*, 237–8; see also the remarks of Spuler, *Mongol Period*, 23–4.

[29] *Rawḍ*, 171–2; Ibn al-Furāt, MS. Vienna, fols. 31a–b; Maqrīzī, I:497–8; Thorau, *Baybars*, 125–6. [30] Yūnīnī, 1:537, 2:197; Mufaḍḍal, 112.

agreement with Berke, perhaps couched in such terms that would be more appealing in his eyes, by the use of the Arabized form of a Mongol expression, *īl* (⟨ *el*) which had come to mean "to be submitted" but originally meant "to be in peace."[31] It is clear that Baybars sought ways to tighten his ties with Berke, as shown by the repeated references to Islamic themes in his letters. In the same vein, before the return of the envoys, Baybars ordered that Berke's name be mentioned after his name in the *khuṭba* in Mecca, Medina and Jerusalem and that he be prayed for at this time.[32]

Baybars's envoys, the amir Fāris al-Dīn Aqqush al-Masᶜūdī and ᶜImād al-Dīn ᶜAbd al-Raḥmān al-Hāshimī, set off on 17 Ramaḍān 661/26 July 1263. Having reached Constantinople, their trip was unexpectedly brought to a halt. Envoys from Hülegü were also at Michael's court, and so as not to antagonize the Īlkhān, the Emperor did not permit the Mamluk envoys to continue on their way. Al-Hāshimī returned to Egypt after fifteen months, but Aqqush al-Masᶜūdī was to languish a total of two years before he could complete his mission. This was only after Aqqush interceded on Michael's behalf with the Jochid general Noghai, who had invaded Thrace with a large army and was threatening Constantinople itself. Al-Masᶜūdī convinced Noghai that since the Emperor was at peace with Baybars, the army of Berke, who was also the Sultan's ally, should desist from attacking him. This brought about the desired effect, and as a reward al-Masᶜūdī was able to continue on to Berke's court. He returned to Egypt in 665/1267.[33]

In Jumādā I 662/March 1264, Baybars sent another mission to Berke; its members were not named, and it is not mentioned again in the sources.[34] Several months later, as mentioned above, a second embassy from Berke arrived in Egypt on 10 Dhū 'l-qaᶜda 662/4 September 1264, along with Baybars's first envoy. They also brought with them a refugee scion of the branch of the Ayyūbids which had ruled Mayyāfāriqīn, who provided an eye-witness account of the battle between Hülegü and Berke. The Mongol envoys delivered Berke's letter, which stressed the Islamic basis of his war with Hülegü, and also contained a list of Mongol nobles who had converted to Islam.[35]

[31] On this original meaning, see Erdal, "Titel," forthcoming.

[32] *Rawḍ*, 173–4; Ibn al-Furāt, MS. Vienna, fol. 32a–b; cf. the version in Maqrīzī, 1:498, where Cairo and Fustat have been added to these cities. Prof. Ayalon ("Yāsa," pt. C1, 136–40) has conclusively shown that this evidence could not be used as proof that the Mamluks were in some type of vassaldom to the Golden Horde, as suggested by A. Poliak, "Le caractère colonial de l'état mamelouk dans ses rapports avec la Horde d'Or," *REI* 9 (1935):231–45; *idem*, "The Influence of Chingiz Khan's Yāsa on the Mamlūk State," *BSOAS* 10 (1942):862–72. See also Ayalon, "Wafidiya," 95–6; *idem*, "Yāsa," pt. C1, 143–5.

[33] *Rawḍ*, 174; Ibn al-Dawādārī, 8:97–8; Yūnīnī, 1:537–9, 2:196–9, 362; Mufaḍḍal, 112–15. See the detailed discussion in M. Canard, "Un traité entre Byzance et l'Egypte au XIIIe siècle et les relations diplomatiques de Michel VIII Paléologue avec les sultans mamlûks Baibars et Qalâ'ûn," in *Mélanges Gaudefroy-Demombynes* (Cairo, 1937), 213–17; Thorau, *Baybars*, 127.

[34] *Rawḍ*, 194; Ibn al-Furāt, MS. Vienna, fol. 43a; Maqrīzī, 1:511.

[35] Abū Shāma, 232; Ibn Kathīr, 13:242; Nuwayrī, MS. 2m, fol. 177b; Yūnīnī, 2:323; *Rawḍ*, 213; Ibn al-Furāt, MS. Vienna, fol. 54b; Maqrīzī, 1:519; ᶜAynī, fol. 88b. The contents of Berke's letter are found in *Zubda*, fols. 59b–60a (= Tiesenhausen, 77–8), but the chronology seems to be confused there.

There is no record of a subsequent mission from the Golden Horde for several years, and likewise it appears that between 663/1265 and 665/1266–7, Baybars did not dispatch any embassies. Only when news reached him of Berke's death in 665/1267 and Möngke Temür's subsequent accession to the throne was another embassy sent in Ṣafar 666/October-November 1267. Since Möngke Temür was not a Muslim, Baybars had no reason to harp on the previously used Islamic themes. Instead, he consoled him about the death of his great-uncle Berke and encouraged him to fight Hülegü.[36]

At this point there is some confusion regarding various missions. In 667/1268–9, an envoy came from Michael Palaeologus saying that with news of Berke's death he had sent on the mission that he had previously delayed in Constantinople. The chronology is strange, since Berke had already been dead for about two years. It is also unclear which Mamluk mission is being referred to here. Perhaps this was the mission sent in 666/1267, mentioned above, since no other Mamluk mission is noted. Upon receiving this envoy from the Emperor, Baybars sent off Berke's ambassadors who had been waiting in Cairo, so Baybars must have been aware that Michael had again blocked the route to the Golden Horde. Yet, had he known this, why did he send the mission in 666/1267? It is also unclear when this mission from the Golden Horde had originally arrived in the Sultanate. This confusion must be left unresolved. In any case, the Sultan sent back a letter with these envoys, inciting Möngke Temür to fight Hülegü's family. In addition, he stressed the size of his army. Finally, he told him of the peace between himself and the Byzantine Emperor, encouraging the Khan to do the same.[37]

It would seem that this second blockage did not greatly affect Mamluk–Golden Horde relations. By this time neither leader had any real reason to keep sending off envoys who had little more to do except deliver messages of mutual goodwill and vague encouragement. In fact, it would seem that this early contact and the resulting understanding were limited to two spheres. First, Berke and his successors permitted the export of young mamluks to the Sultanate. Without this constant influx of mamluks, the majority of whom came from the territory under the control of the Golden Horde, the military strength of the Sultanate would have eventually withered, and Baybars would not have been able to successfully withstand the Īlkhānids.[38] For the Mamluks, the maintenance of an open Bosphorus was of the greatest

[36] *Rawḍ*, 288; Nuwayrī, 27:362; Ibn al-Furāt, MS. Vienna, fols. 125b, 147b; Maqrīzī, 1:563; cf. Thorau, *Baybars*, 235.

[37] *Rawḍ*, 334–5; Ibn al-Furāt, MS. Vienna, fols. 149b–150a; cf. Qirtay, fol. 94a (s.a. 668). These envoys of the Golden Horde may be the envoys of Möngke Temür who passed through Syria in 667/1268–9; *Ḥusn*, 143.

[38] On the slave trade and its importance, see A. Ehrenkreutz, "Strategic Implications of the Slave Trade between Genoa and Mamluk Egypt in the Second Half of the Thirteenth Century," in A.L. Udovitch (ed.), *The Islamic Middle East, 700–1900* (Princeton, 1981), 335–43, esp. 341 and nn. 14–15; S.Y. Labib, *Handelsgeschichte Ägyptens in Spätmittelalter* (Wiesbaden, 1965), 327–8. For the importance of mamluks from the Golden Horde, see Ayalon, "Yāsa," pt. C1, 126–7.

importance, because the Īlkhāns exercised control over the alternative land routes through eastern Anatolia and Iran.[39]

While Michael at times put a crimp on communications between Berke and Baybars, it would seem that the slave trade between their two countries continued. These years witnessed an unparalleled growth of the military strength of the Mamluk Sultanate, and an interruption of the main source of military manpower could well have been reflected in the sources. Such a negative argument is far from conclusive, but taken together with the strong commercial interests of the Genoese merchants, allies of Michael Palaeologus and main purveyors of young mamluks, until shown differently, it can be assumed that this trade continued in some form even in times of diplomatic crisis.[40]

The second sphere of understanding revolved around Baybars's and Berke's discovery that they had a mutual enemy in Hülegü and his followers. Beyond this, little else of substance was attained; certainly, no workable strategy was agreed upon.[41] Thus, once Berke's intentions *vis-à-vis* the slave trade and the war with Hülegü were ascertained (and vice versa, Baybars's attitude towards Hülegü), there was little need continually to send envoys, particularly when Michael Palaeologus's attitude towards their passage was not a certainty. Perhaps then, part of the interruption in the movement of envoys was because both Baybars and Berke had decided to stop sending them so frequently. Later, when news of Berke's death reached Baybars, another embassy was organized to make sure that the "alliance" would continue in its previous form.[42]

The continuing Īlkhānid–Golden Horde war

The Jochid–Īlkhānid conflict *per se* had little to do with the Mamluk–Golden Horde alliance. There is little doubt that the war would have broken out whether or not Berke and Baybars had reached an understanding, although the knowledge that the Mamluks were fighting their enemy may have led the leading elements of the Khans of the Golden Horde to pursue this struggle

[39] At the same time, the possibility of some mamluk trade via Anatolia, even at this early date, should not be totally discounted; see below, ch. 9.

[40] See the comments in Ayalon, "Yāsa," pt. C1, 126–7. Genoese relations with Michael had its ups and downs, and from 1264 to 1267 they were even expelled from Constantinople itself; see D.J. Geanakoplos, *Emperor Michael Palaeologus and the West* (Cambridge, MA, 1959), 168–71; 204–9. There is no indication of how this rupture affected the Genoese trade in mamluks to Egypt.

[41] The one incident in which Baybars tried actively to exploit the Īlkhānid–Golden Horde rift was in 663/1264–5, when he received news of the renewal of the war followed upon Hülegü's death. Baybars thought of invading Iraq, but he was unable to bring his plans to fruition, because his troops were split up among their *iqṭāʿāt*; Yūnīnī, 2:322. Ibn al-Dawādārī, 8:114, tells the same story, but gives the fear of a Frankish attack against Syria as the reason that he did not exploit this opportunity.

[42] Some possible explanations for this stoppage are offered by Khowaiter, *Baibars*, 49; Canard, "Un traité," 219.

with greater vigor. For the Mamluks, however, this ongoing conflict was of crucial importance, because the Īlkhānids were unable to concentrate all of their military strength against them. The knowledge that the Mongols of Iran were preoccupied elsewhere raised the morale of the Mamluks, and provided them with the interlude to organize their resistance, time which Baybars put to good use. The Mongols of Iran were aware of the impact of this conflict: Rashīd al-Dīn writes that after the defeat of Ketbugha, Hülegü had resolved to send another army to avenge his defeat, but because of Möngke's death and then the conflict with his relatives (i.e., the Jochids) he was unable to execute this plan for the time being.[43] A second example is Abagha's letter to Baybars from 667/1268, cited at the beginning of this chapter.

War with the Golden Horde erupted again in 663/1265, when Berke sought to exploit what he probably perceived as instability following Hülegü's death and Abagha's accession. He sent an army under Noghai, which, however, was defeated by an Īlkhānid army under Yoshmut, Abagha's brother, south of the Caucasian mountains some time in the summer of 663/1265. Subsequently, probably over a year later, Abagha himself advanced with the bulk of his army and encountered Berke just north of the Kur River. Abagha recrossed the river, and after two weeks of skirmishing Berke moved towards Tiflis (Tbilisi) to attempt a crossing, but died on the way, apparently early in AD 1267. His disheartened army dispersed, thus ending this round of the war. Before returning south, Abagha had a palisade (*sibe*) built along the southern bank, and stationed a garrison there.[44]

The next foreign threat to the Īlkhāns was from the direction of the Chaghatai Khanate in Central Asia.[45] Already in 667/1268–9, its Khan, Baraq, had succeeded in rousing his kinsman Tegüder, who since Hülegü's time had commanded a Chaghatayid contingent in Iran. Tegüder sought to rejoin Baraq, by fleeing with his troops via the Darband Pass, but he was pursued by a force loyal to Abagha, was defeated and surrendered.[46] Baraq himself advanced across the Oxus River in the spring of 668/1270, with the connivance – at least initially – of both Möngke Temür and Qaidu, the Ögedeiyid ruler of Central Asia. Abagha personally led his army eastward to

[43] Rashīd al-Dīn, ed. ʿAlīzādah, 3:77.

[44] Boyle, "Īl-Khāns," 356; Rashīd al-Dīn, ed. ʿAlīzādah, 3:103–4; Mustawfī, 591 (the battle took place in AH 664). The Mamluk sources are somewhat confused: Nuwayrī, 27:361; Ibn al-Dawādārī, 7:114; Ibn Kathīr, 13:245; Ibn al-Furāt, MS. Vienna, fol. 91b–92a; ʿAynī, fol. 94a; all these write that Noghai was victorious. On the other hand, s.a. 665, Yūnīnī, 2:363, gives a report that approximately corresponds to that found in the Persian sources (except that he wrote that this happened in Möngke Temür's reign and not Berke's); see also Ibn Kathīr, 13:249 (shorter version); Qirtay, fol. 89a. For the date of Berke's death, see B. Spuler, *Die Goldene Horde* (Wiesbaden, 1965), 51.

[45] For Hülegü's relations with the Chaghatayids earlier in the decade, see Jackson, "Dissolution," 234–5.

[46] Boyle, "Īl-Khāns," 357; Rashīd al-Dīn, ed. ʿAlīzādah, 3:111–13; Grigor, 375–7. Interesting details are provided by some Mamluk sources, which generally corroborate the pro-Īlkhānid writers: Ibn al-Furāt, 7:9; Ibn al-Dawādārī, 8:140–1; Yūnīnī, 2:410–11. Some authors (*Zubda*, fols. 81b–82a; whence ʿAynī, fol. 106a) tell this story differently and place it in 672/1273–4.

repulse him. Near Herat, on 30 Dhū 'l-qaʿda 668/22 July 1270, the two armies met and Baraq was completely defeated; he himself escaped with just a small part of his army.[47] Throughout the remainder of Abagha's reign, the eastern borders of his kingdom remained secure.[48]

While Baybars was at Ascalon in Ṣafar 669/October 1270, news reached him that the nephew of Berke had defeated Abagha in battle. The sources must be referring here to Möngke Temür, as was understood by Ibn Kathīr, who inserted this name in his version. The Sultan was quite happy to receive this news,[49] but his delight was gratuitous, because none of the Persian or other pro-Mongol sources mention this battle. The conclusion, then, must be that this news was only an inaccurate echo of the campaigns in Khurasān of the previous year.

In the decade after ʿAyn Jālūt, the Īlkhāns were confronted three times by serious threats from the outside (1262–3, 1265 and 1270) along with the incident with Tegüder (1268–9) and the general problems associated with the accession of a new khan and his consolidation of power. Thus, it is not surprising that during this decade neither Hülegü nor Abagha was able to make any serious attempts to invade Syria, and that they had to content themselves with raids over the frontier and diplomatic contact with the European leaders. With relative calmness finally achieved on the northwestern and northeastern borders, Abagha was able to turn his attention to the Mamluks and he launched a number of large-scale raids against the border. But for reasons unclear to us, he did not exploit this lull in the conflict with his northern neighbors to mount a major offensive. Later in the 1270s he was unable to profit from the instability in the Mamluk Sultanate in the years after Baybars's death (676/1277), because of an invasion by the Negüderi/Qaraunas Mongols into Fārs and Kirmān in 677/1278–9,[50] and a flare-up in the conflict with the Golden Horde (678/1279–80).[51] Only at the beginning of the

[47] Rashīd al-Dīn, ed. ʿAlīzādah, 3:105–30; summarized in Boyle, "Īl-Khāns," 357–60. Also Ibn al-Fuwaṭī, 357 (s.a. 665); Mustawfī, 591. Similar, detailed accounts are found in Ibn al-Dawādārī, 13:148–50; Yūnīnī, 2:434–6; Mufaḍḍal, 178–83; Ibn al-Furāt, MS. Vienna, fols. 184b–185a. Cf. *Zubda*, fol. 77a (whence ʿAynī, fol. 104a, where this battle is reported s.a. 670). Ibn al-Furāt, MS. Vienna, fol. 147b, mentions this conflict as also happening in AH 667; hence, it seems, ʿAynī, fol. 100a. A detailed comparison of Persian and Arabic sources is found in M. Pumpian-Biran, "The Battle of Herat (668/1270)" [Hebrew], unpublished M.A. seminar paper, Hebrew Univ. of Jerusalem, 1991.

[48] On the reawakening of tension on the Chaghatayid front in the 1280s, see P. Jackson, s.v. "Chaghatayid Dynasty," *EIr*, 5:344; Rashīd al-Dīn, ed. ʿAlīzādah, 3:207; cf. Boyle, "Īl-Khāns," 360. [49] Yūnīnī, 2:443; Ibn Kathīr, 13:258; Ibn Taghrī Birdī, 13:149.

[50] Boyle, "Īl-Khāns," 362–3; J. Aubin, "L'ethnogénèse des Qaraunas," *Turcica* 1 (1969):84–6. Waṣṣāf, 203 (cited in Aubin, 86), states that the Negüderis also attacked the Persian Gulf area in winter 680/1281–2. As early as 670/1272, the Negüderis raided Kirmān; Aubin, 83. On the Negüderis/Qaraunas, see Aubin, 65–94; Morgan, *Mongols*, 95–6. Jackson, "Dissolution," 239–44; Pelliot, *Notes on Marco Polo*, 1:183–96.

[51] Mustawfī, 592 (s.a. 678), writes that an invading army came over the Khazar Plain and was defeated by the Īlkhānid army led by Abagha's brother, Mengü Temür. Ibn al-Dawādārī, 7:239, and Mufaḍḍal, 321, report that news of two Golden Horde victories arrived in Egypt (s.a. 679).

subsequent decade was Abagha able to give his full attention to the Mamluks.

The quiet on the Golden Horde–Īlkhānid border belied the continuing desire of the Jochids to regain the territory they claimed as theirs. It is true that Abagha, in the above-cited letter sent to Baybars in 667/1268, asserted that all the Mongols were now united after a period of disunity. The implication here was that differences had been settled with the Golden Horde. There is some *prima facie* evidence for some type of accord. Rashīd al-Dīn writes that the Golden Horde was forced to make peace with Abagha in the aftermath of Berke's death. This author adds that the state of peace lasted until 687/1288 with the invasion by the Golden Horde.[52] Rashīd al-Dīn ignores the above-mentioned hostilities on the border some ten years earlier. Elsewhere, Rashīd al-Dīn describes the mission Möngke Temür sent to Abagha after the latter crushed Baraq's invasion, congratulating him on his victory, although Möngke Temur appears to have been involved in the dispatch of Baraq.[53] In a statement delivered by an Īlkhānid mission to the second Council of Lyon in AD 1274, it was claimed that Abagha was now at peace with some of his (apparently Mongol) neighbors after having defeated them in battle.[54]

There thus appears to have been an agreement of some kind,[55] but it seems to have been merely an attempt to play for time on Möngke Temür's part, because in the subsequent years several embassies were sent from the Golden Horde to Egypt, some with the explicit intent of getting Baybars to launch a joint campaign against the Īlkhānids. Thus in 670/1272, Baybars sent a letter to Abagha in which he claimed that Möngke Temür had written him to call for a joint attack against the Īlkhān.[56] It might be claimed that this was mere bluster on Baybars's part. But at the beginning of Muḥarram 669/August 1270, a letter had arrived from the Jochid general Noghai, announcing his conversion to Islam, and reporting that he had heard of how Baybars pursued the *jihād*. He continued: "We are with you like the finger tips of the hand. We will agree with whomever agrees with you and oppose those whom oppose you." Baybars answered by congratulating Noghai on his becoming a Muslim and following Berke's example, especially in fighting the holy war. He added that he would attack from the west and the Golden Horde from the north, until the unbelievers were defeated.[57] This answer must have been sent with Noghai's envoys, since there is no record of Baybars sending his own envoys.

In 670/1272, envoys of Möngke Temür were captured in the Mediterranean Sea by pirates from either Marseilles or Pisa, along with a translator

[52] Rashīd al-Dīn, ed. Blochet, 2:140; tr. Boyle, 124. This information is repeated in Naṭanzī, 74.

[53] Rashīd al-Dīn, ed. ʿAlīzādah, 3:139.

[54] The passage is found in the letter reproduced in Roberg, "Tartaren," 300, and discussed on *ibid.*, 282. I am grateful to Dr. R. Ellenblum for his assistance in the translation of this text.

[55] G. Vernadsky, *The Mongols and Russia* (rpt. 1966 of New Haven, 1953), 165; Khowaiter, *Baibars*, 56; Thorau, *Baybars*, 178, all attribute too much importance to the treaty; cf. Spuler, *Die Goldene Horde*, 53–4, who correctly states that this conclusion of peace had little long-term importance.

[56] *Rawḍ*, 399–400.

[57] *Rawḍ*, 371–3; *Zubda*, fols. 74b–75b; Ibn al-Furāt, MS. Vienna, fol. 187a–b; Maqrīzī, 1:590.

previously sent by Baybars to the Golden Horde. These prisoners were interned in Acre. The Sultan, who was afraid that they would be sent to Abagha, quickly forced the rulers of Acre to release them. They brought letters in Arabic and Persian to Baybars in which the Khan said he was the enemy of Baybars's enemy and he loved the Sultan as had Berke.[58] An alternative version to this letter stated that the Khan repeated an earlier offer by Berke giving the Sultan possession of whatever Īlkhānid territory he conquered and asking for help in exterminating Hülegü's progeny.[59] Be this as it may, the Sultan did not respond to this latter request, but rather reported to the Khan about the recent arrival of ambassadors from Abagha, who had called upon him to submit, and of the fresh Mamluk victory over the Mongols at al-Bīra. He sent them off with his envoys in Shaᶜbān 671/February-March 1273, along with an expensive gift.[60]

Baybars next sent off an envoy with a gift to Möngke Temür around Rajab 674/beginning of 1275.[61] In 675/1277, before setting off to invade Seljuq Rūm, Baybars received unspecified Mongol envoys. The warm welcome they received leads to the conclusion that they were from the Golden Horde and not from Abagha.[62] Mention is made of another mission from the Golden Horde, which arrived in Cairo in Rabīᶜ II 676/August 1277, after Baybars's death.[63] There is no further record of contact with the Golden Horde until after Qalawun's accession in 678/1280, when he wrote to Möngke Temür and Noghai to announce his accession and to encourage them to continue to fight the infidels. His envoys found that the Khan had just died and gave his successor, Töde Möngke, the letter and gifts.[64]

Golden Horde–Mamluk relations as they developed under Baybars were of crucial importance because they made possible the continuation of the trade in young mamluks. No less significant was the hope that the Golden Horde would put pressure on the Īlkhānids, who would thus be deflected from attacking Syria.[65] In reality, the war between the Golden Horde and the Īlkhānids prevented the latter from devoting all their power against the Mamluks. On the other hand, as Professor Ayalon commented, the importance of the alliance between the Mamluks and the Golden Horde should not be exaggerated. The Golden Horde was far away, and the long journey there, part of which was through Byzantine territory, made constant contact between the two countries "tenuous and difficult."[66] Most tellingly, in spite of occasional efforts by the khans, no common strategy was ever developed

[58] *Rawḍ*, 400; *Zubda*, fol. 77a; Ibn al-Furāt, MS. Vienna, fols. 204b–205a (= ed. Lyons, 1:200).
[59] Ibn Shaddād, *Ta'rīkh*, 35–6; Yūnīnī, 2:472–3; Mufaḍḍal, 207–8. See also Thorau, *Baybars*, 221.
[60] *Rawḍ*, 404, 411; Ibn Kathīr, 13:264; Ibn al-Furāt, MS. Vienna, fols. 213b, 217a; Maqrīzī, 1:607. [61] Ibn al-Furāt, 7:44; Maqrīzī, 1:621.
[62] Ibn Kathīr, 13:271; Ibn Taghrī Birdī, 7:166. [63] Yūnīnī, 3:235.
[64] Nuwayrī, 27:364–5; *Faḍl*, fol. 27a; *Zubda*, fol. 124a; fol. 137a–b.
[65] See the comments to this effect in Ibn Khaldūn, *ᶜIbar*, 5:430–1.
[66] Ayalon, "Yāsa," pt. C1, 129.

against the Mongols of Iran. In addition, we have attempted to show that the Jochid–Īlkhānid conflict developed without Mamluk interference. In short, given the relatively limited scope of this alliance, perhaps the term understanding would be preferable to describe these relations.

The role of the Byzantine Empire

It is impossible to study early Mamluk–Golden Horde relations without taking into account the critical role played by the Byzantine Empire, which was reestablished in Constantinople by Michael Palaeologus (1259–82) in 1261.[67] Controlling the Bosphorus as he did, it is clear that without a sympathetic attitude on his part communications between Baybars and Berke, let alone the continuation of the vital slave trade from the Qipchaq Steppe to Egypt, would become difficult, as the alternative land route was now controlled by the Īlkhānids. At the same time, Michael had as neighbors the warring Mongol states of the Golden Horde and the Īlkhānids, and if he tilted too close to one, he was likely to incur the wrath of the other. Michael was thus forced to walk a very narrow path, a task which he managed to do with some success.

In 660/1261–2, Michael Palaeologus sent to Baybars an expression of his goodwill and support.[68] Baybars in turn dispatched an envoy, the amir Fāris al-Dīn Aqqush al-Masʿūdī, with a gift of captured Mongols from ʿAyn Jālūt, and the Melkite Patriarch of Egypt, who had been requested by Michael. It was probably during this mission, which returned to Egypt in Shaʿbān 660/ July 1262, that a treaty was agreed upon giving Baybars free passage through the Bosphorus for slaves and envoys.[69] Michael's motivation for initiating this contact must have been a desire to establish as many allies as possible in order to strengthen his hand before what he considered as the likelihood of a Latin attempt to regain Constantinople.

Baybars's understanding with Michael, however, was short-lived, because the latter prevented the second Mamluk embassy to Berke (led by Aqqush al-Masʿūdī who had departed Cairo in Ramaḍān 661/July 1263) from leaving Byzantine territory. As mentioned above, when these envoys reached the

[67] As the Byzantine role has been studied in detail by Canard, "Un traité," 209–23; and Holt, *Crusades*, 159–63, in the following paragraphs, I will briefly survey the important points. See also G. Ostrogorsky, *History of the Byzantine State*, tr. J. Hussey (New Brunswick, NJ, 1957), 396, 404, 407–8; Sinor, "Western Europe," 529–31; Geanakoplos, *Emperor*, 290–3 and n. 59; Thorau, *Baybars*, 121–8; Ehrenkreutz, "Slave Trade," 341 and nn. 14–15; J.J. Saunders, "The Mongol Defeat at Ain Jālūt and the Restoration of the Greek Empire," in *idem*, *Muslims and Mongols* (Christchurch, NZ, 1977), 67–76.

[68] Thorau, *Baybars*, 122, suggests that this was an answer to an earlier mission sent by Baybars.

[69] Canard, "Un traité," 211–12, who mentions the treaty, which is reported only by the Greek historians; Holt, *Crusades*, 159; *Rawḍ*, 88, 129; Ibn al-Furāt, MS. Vienna, fol. 4a; Maqrīzī, 1:471–2; *Zubda*, fol. 51a, but s.a. 659 (whence, ʿAynī, fol. 84a). According to Pachymeres (cited in Thorau, *Baybars*, 122), Michael's first mission to Baybars, sent after his conquest of Constantinople, requested the Melkite Patriarch would be sent and granted the Sultan freedom of passage through the Bosphorus.

Emperor, they found that ambassadors from Hülegü were also at his court. Actually, as early as the fall of 1261, Michael had drawn up a secret treaty of friendship with Hülegü, one of the provisions of which was that the exiled Seljuq ʿIzz al-Dīn Kaykāwūs would be kept at his court.[70] One motive for this treaty would have been the common desire to pacify the Anatolian border.[71] The Emperor himself explained to the Mamluk envoys that the reason he detained them was that his country was close to Hülegü, and he was afraid that if Hülegü were to hear that he had helped the envoys of Baybars, he would suspect that the state of peace (*ṣulḥ*) between Michael and Hülegü was over; thus Hülegü would attack Michael's country. Baybars's response, on being notified in Ramaḍān 662/July 1264 about his envoys' delay, was to convene a gathering of Orthodox prelates in Egypt and have Michael excommunicated for breaking an oath. Thereupon he sent off a strongly worded message to the Emperor, to which he added that if the reason for the detention of his envoys was the war between the Byzantines and the Golden Horde, he would send to the latter to mediate peace, which he subsequently did. Ibn ʿAbd al-Ẓāhir writes that upon receiving this message Michael sent al-Masʿūdī on his way, a doubtful assertion, since only after two full years of waiting was this envoy permitted to go.[72]

For several years there is no record of any communications between Michael Palaeologus and Baybars, and for that matter between Berke and Baybars, although Aqqush al-Masʿūdī returned home after finally completing his mission, and must have passed through Constantinople on his way back to Egypt, probably in 665/1266. It is clear that during this time relations had not returned to the heights they had reached earlier in the decade, because in 667/1268–9, when Michael finally sent an envoy, the message he carried contained an announcement that he was discontinuing his chilly attitude which he had hitherto adopted and was returning to the earlier state of peace (*ṣulḥ*). He also sent on envoys of Baybars, whom he had detained until Berke's death that year. The fact that Berke died in 665/1266–7 raises some questions (discussed above). In his letter, Michael also tried to mediate between Baybars and Abagha, an offer which was spurned by the Sultan. Baybars was also unwilling to swear an oath suggested by Michael, which contained a provision that Baybars was to be a friend to Michael's friend, as this could be understood to be Abagha. On the other hand, Baybars expressed his willingness to mediate between the Emperor and Möngke Temür.[73] M. Canard suggested that Michael's rapprochement with Baybars was occasioned by his fear of Charles of Anjou, who had conquered Naples and Sicily in 1266 and the following year

[70] Spuler, *Iran*, 58–9; Geanakoplos, *Emperor*, 81. Knowledge of this treaty is based on Greek sources. [71] Lippard, "Byzantium," 198.

[72] Canard, "Un traité," 213–15; *Rawḍ*, 202–3; Yūnīnī, 1:537–9, 2:197–8; Mufaḍḍal, 112–14; Ibn al-Dawādārī, 8:97–8 (last three sources s.a. 661); Ibn al-Furāt, MS. Vienna, fols. 46b–47b (cites Ibn Shaddād, by name); Maqrīzī, 1:514.

[73] Canard, "Un traité," 219; *Rawḍ*, 334–5; Ibn al-Furāt, MS. Vienna, fols. 149b–150a; *Ḥusn*, 143; cf. Thorau, *Baybars*, 195.

formed a coalition against the Byzantine Empire with the intention of conquering Constantinople.[74]

The chill in Byzantine–Mamluk relations may have been related to Michael's developing closer contacts with the Īlkhāns. In 1265, he had sent an illegitimate daughter to marry Hülegü. But she arrived after Hülegü's death and instead was wedded to his son and successor Abagha.[75] As will be seen in the next section, there is some evidence in 1267–8 of a Mongol–Byzantine alliance against the Mamluks, which was to receive aid from James I, King of Aragon. Dr. Geanakoplos has suggested that Michael's motives may have been to forestall James's joining of an anti-Byzantine entente led by Charles of Anjou.[76] Although this possible Īlkhānid–Byzantine–Aragonese alliance slightly pre-dates Michael's renewed overtures to Baybars, it is difficult to know with certainty what Michael's plans were exactly. In any event, nothing was to come of all the anti-Mamluk diplomatic activity, and eventually Byzantine–Mamluk relations were to return to a relatively even keel.[77]

In light of the above discussion, we might question the suggestion made by J.J. Saunders, who wrote that "by 1266 something like a Mamluk–Qipchaq–Byzantine alliance against the Il-khans and the Latins existed." Later, he adds that "the expulsion of Baldwin II from and the entry of Michael Palaeologus into Constantinople greatly facilitated Baybars's defence of Egypt against the Il-khans," since this enabled Baybars's communication with the Golden Horde.[78] These statements are contradicted by the evidence presented above; if anything, the Byzantine Empire was more closely allied with the Persian Mongols than with their cousins in the Qipchaq Steppe. It can certainly be seen that Michael was doing his best to play both sides. There is also the whole question of the Latin role in these relations. In the next section it will be shown that, at this stage at least, the Latin–Īlkhānid alliance was much less unequivocal than Saunders would have us believe. In addition, one group of "Latins," the Genoese, were certainly instrumental in maintaining the Golden Horde–Mamluk connection alive. Finally, we might indulge in speculation over what might have happened had the Latins managed to maintain their grip on Constantinople. Perhaps the healthy commercial instincts of the Venetians, the major backers of the Latin rulers in Constantinople, might have led to a sympathetic view towards the Mamluk–Jochid connection even if Michael

[74] Canard, "Un traité," 220; see also Spuler, *Goldene Horde*, 55. For the diplomatic struggle between Michael and Charles, see Geanakoplos, *Emperor*, 189–371; S. Runciman, *The Sicilian Vespers* (Harmondsworth, 1960), 152–312.

[75] Spuler, *Iran*, 59–61; Canard, "Un traité," 214; Bar Hebraeus, 445 (= Ibn al-ʿIbrī, 497); Vardan, tr. Thomson, 222; Kirakos, tr. Dulaurier, 508; Rashīd al-Dīn, ed. ʿAlīzādah, 3:97 and n. 27; cited by J.A. Boyle, "The Il-Khans of Persia and the Princes of Europe," *CAJ* 20 (1976):25, who notes that Rashīd al-Dīn makes no other mention of relations between the Īlkhānids and the Byzantines. [76] Geanakoplos, *Emperor*, 220.

[77] There is, however, information on offers made in 1274 and 1276 by Michael to assist the Western Christians against the Mamluks; see Geanakoplos, *Emperor*, 287–91.

[78] Saunders, "Mongol Defeat," 75, 76 and *passim*; a similar approach is adopted in Lippard, "Byzantium," 233–4.

Palaeologus had not succeeded in reestablishing the Greek Empire on the Bosphorus.

Throughout the remainder of Baybars's reign, relations with Michael Palaeologus recede into the background. Only twice are Byzantine envoys mentioned coming to Baybars, in 671/1272–3 and 674/1275–6. In the former case, at least, Baybars sent the envoys back with his own embassy.[79] In the second half of his reign, the comings and goings of Genoese ships bringing fresh shipments of Turkish slaves from the Qipchaq Steppe, along with the occasional envoy to or from its Khan, must have become such accepted practice that the sending of additional envoys to the Byzantine Emperor became superfluous. Only at the beginning of Qalawun's reign in 678/1279 do we see a rekindling of serious diplomatic activity between these two kingdoms.[80]

The Īlkhāns and the Franks

The traditional Mongol attitude to the Latin Christians, be they in Europe or the Levant, was identical to that shown to the Muslim princes: submit unconditionally or face destruction.[81] This stance, however, began to change, albeit gradually, in the aftermath of ʿAyn Jālūt, and henceforth the Īlkhāns condescended to make advances to the Pope and European princes. This change was initiated by Hülegü, who surely desired to avenge the defeat at ʿAyn Jālūt and continue the Mongol conquest to the southwest. Yet, because of the ongoing war with Berke and the setbacks he there suffered, Hülegü was unable to commit a large proportion of his forces to Syria. It would appear that the Īlkhān must have felt that to effectively pursue his war against the Mamluks he had no choice but to turn to the West, with an offer of an alliance against their mutual enemy.

Some of the responsibilty for Hülegü's decision to write to the West may be laid at the feet of a Dominican named David of Ashby. Late in AD 1259 or early in 1260, he had been the head of an embassy sent to Hülegü by Thomas Agni, then the papal legate at Acre. Presumably, the purpose of this mission had been to dissuade the Mongol ruler from attacking the Frankish possessions. David, who evidently remained for several years at the Mongol court, was well received, witnessed at least part of the Mongol campaign against Aleppo, and had Christian slaves freed. The presence of a respected clergyman

[79] *Rawḍ*, 404, 411; Ibn al-Furāt, MS. Vienna, fols. 213a, 217a; 7:44; Maqrīzī, 1:607, 621. Ostrogorsky, *Byzantine State*, 408, writes that after 1272, "the exchange of embassies between Byzantium and Egypt grew more and more frequent," but this does not seem warranted by the Mamluk sources. [80] See Holt, *Crusades*, 162–31; Irwin, *Middle East*, 69.

[81] For general discussions on Mongol–European relations before ʿAyn Jālūt, see K-E. Lupprian, *Die Beziehungen der Päpste zu islamischen und mongolischen Herrschern im 13. Jahrhundert anhand ihres Briefwechsels* (Vatican, 1981), 47–63; Sinor, "Western Europe," 518–26; de Rachewiltz, *Papal Envoys*, 76–143; Boyle, "Princes of Europe," 25–40; Jackson and Morgan, introduction to William of Rubruck, tr. Jackson, 25–39.

at Hülegü's court, at a time of some soul-searching and strategic rethinking, may have contributed to the Mongol leader's final decision to turn to the West.[82]

In AD 1262, Hülegü sent an embassy to the West. It is clear from an extant letter from Hülegü to Louis IX that one of the embassy's goals was to reach the French King. The envoys, however, never fulfilled their mission, since upon reaching Sicily they were ordered to return by its ruler, Manfred, then at odds with the Pope. Hülegü's letter mentions one John the Hungarian. This John is named in Urban IV's letter to Hülegü, evidently from AD 1263 (see below), as the source of the information that Hülegü was about to convert to Christianity, as well as his appeal for assistance against the Muslims. It might well be, then, that John the Hungarian had been a member of Hülegü's mission, and perhaps managed to slip past Manfred's officials and make his way to the Pope's court, reporting the general tenor of Hülegü's message. Hülegü's letter, which seemingly did not reach its destination, urged Louis's forces to take up a defensive position along the (Syrian and Egyptian) coasts using naval vessels, so when the Mongols attacked the Egyptians would have no refuge.[83]

An appeal of this type from a Mongol prince was still somewhat of a novelty in AD 1262. But it did not mean that the Mongols were ready yet to give up the ideological underpinnings of their empire. P. Meyvaert has written of this letter, that despite its friendly tone, it "can be seen as an impressive instance of the Mongolian perspective on the world . . . Louis IX was not exempt from the duty of obeying a divine order. Behind the request for military help one discerns the threat that if this help is not forthcoming, the French king will one day also experience the fate meted out to the disobedient." Hülegü further strengthens his plea by providing an account of the divine revelation given to Chinggis Khan and recites his and other Mongol conquests.[84]

Whether or not John the Hungarian was a member of Hülegü's mission of 1262, he is credited by Urban IV with bringing news to the papal court of Hülegü's request for aid and his inclination towards baptism. In reponse to this information, the Pope sent off, evidently in AD 1263, the short letter, *Exultavit cor nostrum*, in which he expressed his joy at Hülegü turning towards

[82] Most of our information on David's activities is derived from the letter published by Roberg, "Tartaren," 298–302; see the discussion in *ibid.*, 273–6. See also C. Brunel, "David d'Ashby auteur méconnu des Faits des Tartares," *Romania* 79 (1958):43–5; J. Richard, "Une ambassade mongole à Paris en 1262," *Journal des Savants*, 1979, 299–300; *idem*, "Debut," 295–7; Boyle, "Princes of Europe," 28–9. David must have been with the Mongols for several years after 1260, at least until the early days of Abagha's reign, and then he returned to Palestine. Subsequently, he would have been the chaplain to Thomas Agni, now Patriarch of Jerusalem (see Brunel, 44 n. 2; Jackson, "Crisis," 505 n. 1). In 1273–4, David was sent back to the west as representative of the Patriarch and King Hugh III of Jerusalem and Cyprus, together with Abagha's ambassadors. I am grateful to Dr. Jackson for helping me clarify David's career.

[83] Roberg, "Tartaren," 300; Boyle, "Princes of Europe," 28–9; Meyvaert, "Letter," *passim*; Richard, "Ambassade," 298–301, suggests that the mission and letter actually made it to Louis; but cf. Morgan, *Mongols*, 183; Meyvaert, "Letter," 247; Jackson, "Crisis," 236 n. 228.

[84] Meyvaert, "Letter," 249.

Christianity, and his desire for a missionary to instruct and execute his baptism. With his baptism effected, Christendom would help Hülegü in his struggle against the Saracens, including the dispatch of soldiers. The Pope concluded by telling Hülegü that he had instructed the Patriarch of Jerusalem to make inquiries of his intentions, as John had not provided any authorization of these.[85]

While Hülegü may have had pro-Christian sympathies, his real intentions towards embracing the Christian faith are unknown.[86] There is no mention of such in the letter to Louis IX. This claim may have been wishful thinking on John's part, or a deliberate ploy by him, with or without Hülegü's connivance, in order to cultivate support among the Latins. As will be seen below, this is not the last time that Christian envoys of the Īlkhāns were to convey such information in the West.

Nothing concrete came of this letter. While, perhaps, the European Christian leaders were now willing to see the Mongols in a less negative light and to consider them as partners in the anti-Muslim struggle,[87] this did not bring about a willingness to undertake a concerted joint effort. Evidently, the reality of the intra-European struggle, especially between the papacy and its supporters against the House of Hohenstaufen, prevented a new crusade. It is also possible that the Pope did not want to commit himself until he had received a more official message from the Īlkhān. It seems, however, that Urban's insistence on baptism before any assistance could be offered was just an excuse not to give a substantial reply to Hülegü's interesting offer. There were no additional diplomatic contacts between Hülegü and Latin Christendom.

By late 1266, Abagha must have felt secure enough on the throne to initiate diplomatic contacts with the West, in the hope that this would lead to military cooperation which would help decide the war against the Mamluks. Abagha's repeated missions show the great importance he attached to this idea. In late 1266 or early 1267, the Īlkhān sent a mission with letters to the West. Abagha's envoys reached both Pope Clement IV and King James I of Aragon, arriving at the latter's court in the early months of 1267 and bringing convincing assertions of Abagha's friendship and assistance. James, in turn, sent James Alaric to Abagha as an envoy. On his way eastward, James met the Pope, who commissioned him to act as his envoy as well. Clement also gave an answer to Abagha's now lost letter, whose general contents can be reconstructed from the reply: Abagha had suggested that the Western forces should join with his and Michael Palaeologus's armies, in order to trap the Mamluks between them. He then enquired about which route the western armies would take to

[85] Lupprian, *Beziehungen*, 216–19 (no. 41); partial translation in D'Ohsson, *Histoire*, 3:410–12. See also Boyle, "Princes of Europe," 28–9.

[86] See, e.g., Vardan, tr. Thomson, 220; Rashīd al-Dīn, ed. Quatremère, 94. It would seem from Vardan, tr. Thomson, 222, that he never became a Christian.

[87] Richard, "Debut," 297.

Palestine.[88] In his reply, dated 20 August 1267, Clement first expressed his consternation that Abagha's letter was in Mongolian, and there was no one at his court who could translate it for him. The envoy, however, was able to give a rendition of it. The Pope proceeded to express his joy that Abagha had seen the true faith,[89] and at reports that the Kings of France and Navarre, followed by a great number of nobles and soldiers, had taken the cross and been joined by many lords from other countries. The Pope added, however, that he did not yet know the route they intended to follow, but would send word to Abagha when he learnt this.[90]

Encouraged by this seemingly positive response, Abagha wrote another letter in the summer of 1268 and dispatched it with James Alaric and two of his own envoys. In it, he confirmed that he had received the Pope's letter and explained that he had written his previous letter in Mongolian because his Latin scribe was not present. Abagha had sent his brother Hegei [= Ejei] with an army to help the Christians; Hegei would hurry to join up with the Christian army promised by the Pope. Together with the King of Aragon [James I] and the Byzantine Emperor, they would destroy the Egyptians. To negotiate this joint campaign, Abagha sent the custodian of the Church at his court, Salomon Arkaoun [=*erke'un*, "oriental Christian"], and a certain Nekpei (Negübei?).[91]

James Alaric, accompanied by envoys of Abagha and Michael Palaeologus, met with the Pope. Subsequently, he made his way to King James, to whom he delivered a letter from the Īlkhān. James himself recorded the contents of this missive in his diary: if James were to come to Ayās or another port, in order to recover the Holy Land, Abagha would provide supplies and other assistance.[92] James's nascent plans for a crusade thus received a boost, and he went about fervently making preparations for his departure. In September 1269, he set out with a large flotilla, but soon after leaving port most of the force was scattered by a sudden storm, and was compelled to turn back.[93] Only James's

88 R. Röhricht, "Der Kreuzzug des Königs Jacob I. von Aragonien (1269)," *Mittheilungen des Instituts für Oesterreichische Geschichtsforshung* 11 (1890):372–95; Boyle, "Princes of Europe," 29.

89 Actually, Abagha was probably a shamanist with strong Buddhist sympathies; see P. Jackson, "Abagha," *EIr*, 1:63.

90 Lupprian, *Beziehungen*, 220–2 (no. 42); trans. in D'Ohsson, *Histoire*, 3:540–2; Boyle, "Princes of Europe," 29.

91 Lupprian, *Beziehungen*, 71, 223–5 (no. 43; summary on p. 223); Boyle, "Princes of Europe," 29–30, who in n. 20 notes (following Rashīd al-Dīn, ed. ʿAlīzādah, 3:11) that Ejei died in 1265, ten days after Hülegü. But Ejei was active in Seljuq Rūm, ca. 669–670/1271; see below, ch. 7, pp. 161–2. He was also found in the consultations after Abagha's death in 1282; Rashīd al-Dīn, ed. ʿAlīzādah, 3:168.

92 *The Chronicle of James I of Aragon*, tr. J. Forster and P. de Gayngos (London, 1883), 599–600; Röhricht, "Jacob I.," 374.

93 Röhricht, "Jacob I.," 373–8; Geanakoplos, *Emperor*, 220; Boyle, "Princes of Europe," 30; J. Abel-Remusat, "Mémoires sur les relations politiques des princes crétiens, et particulièrement, des rois de France, avec les empereurs mongols," *Mémoires de l'Institut Royal de France*, 7 (1824):341–2. The Mamluk sources have some knowledge of these relations, and report the destruction of the Aragonese flotilla; *Rawḍ*, 361–2. Nuwayrī, MS. 2m, fol. 247a–b

two bastard sons, accompanied by a small body of troops, eventually made their way to Acre. Their impact on developments there was minimal, and they returned soon afterwards without having achieved anything.[94]

In the summer of 1270, Louis IX finally launched the crusade about which Pope Clement IV had written to Abagha in 1267. Yet, instead of taking the forces at his disposal to Syria or Egypt, and attempting to realize the potential of a joint campaign with the Mongols, Louis attacked Tunis. Louis's exact motives and the fate of his crusade are not our subject here.[95] What would have happened had he taken his army and landed on Mamluk soil remains only speculation. The chances are, however, that he would have fought Baybars alone. No matter how interested Abagha was in an anti-Mamluk alliance, at this time he was personally involved in a fierce war with Baraq in Khurasān.[96] The Mamluk sources report that Baybars received word that Louis had set out to invade his territory, and made the necessary arrangements. Subsequently, he learnt that the French King had gone to Tunis instead and died there. Unlike James's would-be crusade, the Mamluk sources have no information that Louis's expedition had been preceded by negotiations with the Mongols.[97]

The Mamluks were more aware of the contacts the following year between Edward of England and the Mongols. Edward and his men arrived in Acre in the spring of 1271, having been with Louis IX in Tunis. Upon reaching the Holy Land, Edward sent an embassy to Abagha.[98] The Īlkhān sent back the following reply: "After talking over the matter, we have on our account resolved to send to your aid Cemakar [= Samaghar][99] at the head of a mighty force; thus, when you discuss among yourselves the other plans involving the afore-mentioned Cemakar be sure to make explicit arrangements as to the exact month and day on which you will engage the enemy."[100]

(s.a. 667/1268–9); Ibn al-Furāt, MS. Vienna, fol. 179a (= ed. Lyons, 1:173); cf. Maqrīzī, 1:584. See R. Amitai-Preiss, "Mamluk Perceptions of the Mongol–Frankish Rapprochement," *MHR* 7 (1992):53–4.

[94] Röhricht, "Jacob I.," 378; Prawer, *Histoire*, 2:494–6; Grousset, *Croisades*, 3:649–51; Thorau, *Baybars*, 199–201; cf. Runciman, *Crusades*, 3:331.

[95] See Prawer, *Histoire*, 2:496–9; Runciman, *Sicilian Vespers*, 157–61; cf. R.S. Lopez, "Fulfillment and Diversion in the Eight Crusades," in B.Z. Kedar *et al.* (eds.), *Outremer* (Jerusalem, 1982), 25–6.

[96] See above, pp. 87–8.

[97] Ibn al-Furāt, MS. Vienna, fol. 184a (= ed. Lyons, 1:177–8; cf. shortened version in Maqrīzī, 1:587–8); Yūnīnī, 2:455–6; *Tuḥfa*, 69. Information on this expedition is mistakenly repeated s.a. 661 by Ibn al-Furāt, MS. Vienna, fol. 36b; hence Maqrīzī, 1:502. See the fuller discussion in Amitai-Preiss, "Mamluk Perceptions," 54–5.

[98] R. Röhricht, "La croisade du Prince Édouard d'Angleterre (1270–1274)," in "Études sur les derniers temps du royaume de Jérusalem," *AOL* 1 (1881):622–7; L. Lockhart, "The Relations between Edward I and Edward II of England and the Mongol Il-Khans of Persia," *Iran* 6 (1968):23–4; Riley-Smith, in Ibn al-Furāt, ed. Lyons, 2:242–3; Grousset, *Croisades*, 3:659–60.

[99] Samaghar was the Mongol commander in Rūm at this time. The Mamluk sources name him as leading the Mongol force into northern Syria this year. See ch. 7, p. 160.

[100] Röhricht, "Études," 623 n. 35, citing *Liber de Antiquis Legibus*, ed. T. Stapleton (London, 1846), 143; translation from Sinor, "Mongol Strategy," 244.

The result of these contacts was that in mid-Rabīᶜ I 670/ca. 20 October 1271, a Mongol corps under Samaghar and the Pervāne raided north Syria, advance elements reaching as far south as the environs of Ḥārim and Afāmiya. Baybars, already in Syria, quickly organized his forces, sent for reinforcements from Egypt, and began to move north. Probably alerted by his intelligence service, the Sultan had gained advance warning that both the Mongols and the Christians were planning attacks. It was thought, however, that the latter would attack Safad. The Mongol forces, nonplussed by the approaching Mamluk army, withdrew, ending any prospect of Mongol–Frankish cooperation at this time. On 12 Rabīᶜ II/17 November, Baybars entered Aleppo.[101]

About two weeks later, while Baybars was still at Aleppo, he received word that Edward had raided Qāqūn. Even before Baybars could return south, Edward was chased back to Acre by Mamluk amirs stationed in Palestine. Edward, it would appear, was merely taking advantage of what appeared to him as a momentary tactical advantage, Baybars's preoccupation elsewhere. Ibn ᶜAbd al-Ẓāhir reported that Edward's attack on Qāqūn was in agreement with the Mongols, but in reality there was no effective coordination between Edward and Abagha, and the latter's above quoted letter occasioned no effective response by the Christian leaders. Edward's "crusade" brought about no change in the balance of power in Syria, even in the short run. After surviving a severe wound sustained during an assassination attempt inspired by Baybars, he returned to England in September 1272.[102]

In 1277, envoys of Abagha delivered a message to Edward, now King of England, apologizing for not providing sufficient aid (in 1270); no explanation, however, was offered. For what it is worth, the message implies that in the future Abagha would be more forthcoming.[103] While the reason for Abagha's failure to mount a serious campaign in 1270 remains a mystery,[104] it is clear that he had missed a real (and perhaps the only) opportunity for a joint campaign with the Franks.

After a hiatus of three years, Abagha again tried to establish contact with the West. News had reached him of an impending council of Christian leaders. Abagha thus sent a delegation to call for a concerted effort against the common enemy. In May 1274, a council of Church and lay leaders was

[101] *Rawḍ*, 395; Ibn al-Furāt, MS. Vienna, fol. 202a; Maqrīzī, 1:599–600. See ch. 5, p. 125, for this raid.

[102] *Rawḍ*, 396–7; Ibn al-Furāt, MS. Vienna, fol. 202b–203a (= ed. Lyons, 1:197; see Riley-Smith's detailed remark in *ibid.*, 2:243); Maqrīzī, 1:600. See Amitai-Preiss, "Mamluk Perceptions," 55–6; Thorau, *Baybars*, 221–2; Runciman, *Crusades*, 3:337–8; Prawer, *Histoire*, 2:499–505.

[103] Grousset, *Croisades*, 3:693; Röhricht, "Prince Edouard," 626 n. 57. On the mission see below.

[104] Both Lockhart, "Relations," 24 and Boyle, "Princes of Europe," 30–1, write that Abagha was unable to send a larger force to aid Edward because he was preoccupied on the Chaghatayid front. This suggestion, however, is mistaken: the war with Baraq was in 1270, while Edward arrived in Syria in 1271.

convened in Lyon by Pope Gregory X, who was greatly concerned about the fate of the Holy Land. The Council was called to discuss Church reform, the union of the Latin and Greek Churches and a crusade to the East. In the end, decisions were taken only on the second topic, although in the long run nothing was to come of these.[105]

The Mongol delegation included Abagha's translator, the Dominican Richard, and numbered sixteen in all. It was accompanied by David of Ashby, who had been at the Īlkhānid court for several years, had evidently returned to Palestine, and had now come to the Council as an envoy of the Patriarch of Jerusalem (Thomas Agni) and the King of Jerusalem (Hugh III).[106] The Mongol delegation was introduced to the Council at the beginning of July. The original letter, which they brought from Abagha, has not come down to us, but there exists a memorandum written by Richard for the edification of the Council participants. It begins with an account of Mongol–Christian relations, in which are described David of Ashby's mission ca. 1260, Hülegü's attempt to send envoys to the West and the Īlkhāns' concern for the Christians in their realm. It then tells of Abagha's wish for peace and an alliance with the Latins. Previously, Abagha could not set out against the Mamluks, who were the adversaries of the Christians, because he was threatened by other enemies around him (that is, other Mongol states). He had, however, been victorious, and then made peace with his former enemies. Abagha had been in the midst of preparations against the Egyptians[107] when he heard of the Council and decided to inform it of his plans.[108]

Gregory's answer, dated 13 March 1275, was couched in general terms. After the reading of his letter to the Council and the hearing of the envoys, the Pope had prayed that Abagha would be shown the way to the true faith. The Pope would send envoys before the setting out of a crusading army, as early as the situation would allow. These envoys would bring Abagha a full answer (to the proposals made in his letter of the previous year), and would speak of spiritual matters of interest to the Īlkhān and his family.[109] This response was not due to Gregory's lack of enthusiasm for a crusade. From the beginning of his papacy, he had been concerned with the Holy Land and the possibility of organizing a new crusade. Even if the crusading spirit was not on the wane, it could not be translated into an effective plan of action for a campaign to the Levant, not least because the various European rulers had their own pressing interests and problems. Gregory's death in 1276 brought to a formal end these

[105] For the second Council of Lyon, see: S. Schein, *Fideles Crucis* (Oxford, 1991), 22–50; Runciman, *Crusades*, 3:341; *idem*, *Sicilian Vespers*, 166–86; Roberg, "Tartaren," 283–6.

[106] See above, p. 95, n. 82; also: Brunel, "David," 39–46, esp. 44. David prepared a memorandum for the Council, *Faits des Tartares*, but the MS of his tract was lost in a fire in Turin in 1904; see also de Rachewiltz, *Papal Envoys*, 153.

[107] In August 1273, Baybars heard of an impending Mongol campaign into Syria, although this offensive never materialized; see ch. 5, pp. 132–3.

[108] Roberg, "Tartaren," 298–302 (see discussion in 289–94); Lupprian, *Beziehungen*, 226–32 (no. 44). [109] Lupprian, *Beziehungen*, 75, 231–2 (no. 45).

incipient crusading efforts, and with it the hope for Christian–Mongol cooperation in Abagha's reign.[110]

After the Council, David of Ashby continued on to England and delivered Abagha's message to Edward I. Edward wrote back at the beginning of 1275, first noting Abagha's affection for the Christian religion and the resolution that he had "taken to bring help to the Christians and the Holy Land against the enemies of Christianity." He prayed that the Pope would execute his plan for the crusade. But, he himself would be unable to say when he could arrive in the Holy Land, because the Pope had yet to order an expedition. As soon as Edward gained some more certain information about this crusade, he would inform Abagha.[111] Edward was clearly hiding here behind formalities, and it is doubtful whether he harbored any desire to return to the Holy Land, especially after his experiences there at the beginning of the decade.

At the end of 1276 or beginning of 1277, two new envoys – John and James Vassalli – arrived in Rome, during the papacy of John XXI. They brought a letter, now lost, calling on the Christians to launch a campaign to the Holy Land, and promising free passage, logistical help and Abagha's personal intervention if such an expedition were to set out. No less important in Christian eyes, the envoys reported that Abagha's uncle, Qubilai Qa'an, had converted and had requested missionaries for instruction. Thereupon these two envoys continued on to both the courts of Philip III of France and Edward I of England, conveying the same message. To Edward they brought an additional missive offering apologies for Abagha's inability to effectively intervene in Syria in 1270 (see above).[112]

This entreaty engendered no political or military response. In his answer, the Pope – now Nicholas III – echoed Abagha's offer for aid, but made no further comment. As for the news of Qubilai's conversion, the Pope was beside himself with joy. He wrote that he would send five friars to administer the baptism to those Mongols who requested it; they were then to continue on to Qubilai. Abagha was then requested to receive them well, to protect and provide for them and to listen to what they had to say.[113] The Pope also sent a letter for Qubilai with these friars, in which he congratulated him on his conversion and enjoined him to receive the friars well.[114] For the time being, at least, the diplomatic activity of the papacy with the Īlkhāns was reduced to a policy of religious propaganda.[115]

[110] Schein, *Fideles Crucis*, 44–50; Runciman, *Sicilian Vespers*, 168, 186–90; Lopez, "Fulfillment," 20; Grousset, *Croisades*, 3:693.

[111] Abel-Remusat, "Mémoires," 7:345; D'Ohsson, *Histoire*, 3:543–4; Lockhart, "Relations," 24; Boyle, "Princes of Europe," 30–1.

[112] Abel-Remusat, "Mémoires," 7:345–50; D'Ohsson, *Histoire*, 3:544–6; Roberg, "Tartaren," 296 n. 311; Lupprian, *Beziehungen*, 75, 233; Lockhart, *Relations*, 24–5; Boyle, "Princes of Europe," 31; Grousset, *Croisades*, 3:693. It is unclear if there were two separate missions to England, one in 1276 and the other in 1277, or if these are different accounts of the same mission. The latter possibility seems more likely.

[113] Lupprian, *Beziehungen*, 76; 233–6 (no. 46); trans. in D'Ohsson, *Histoire*, 3:546–8.

[114] Lupprian, *Beziehungen*, 76, 237–41 (no. 47).

[115] De Rachewiltz, *Papal Envoys*, 154–7.

An interesting addendum to this episode is a safe conduct pass issued by Abagha for his territory (in Mongolian), and dated November 1279. The pass was made out for one Baracirgun, who can be identified with Gerhard of Prato (frère Gerard), and other Church officials. Gerhard was one of the five friars mentioned by name in the above letter to Abagha, who had been sent as missionaries to both Abagha and Qubilai.[116] It is clear that Nicholas's envoys reached as far as Iran, although whether they went any further is unclear.[117] This is the last record of any contact between Abagha and the Latin West.

Although the main Īlkhānid diplomatic effort in opening a second front was directed towards the rulers of Latin Europe, the Mongols also had contact with the Franks of the Levant. There is ample evidence in the Mamluk sources that Baybars was aware of these relations. Thus, after the Mongol withdrawal from al-Bīra in 663/1265, Baybars complained to the Castellan of Jaffa about the Frankish leaders: "This people have committed many offences against me, such as their writing to the Mongols to attack my territories."[118] Frankish-Īlkhānid relations were affected by the arrival of European crusaders, as in 668/1269, when the remnants of the Aragonese crusade reached Acre, and "the Franks of the coast made common cause with the Mongols to attack Muslim territory."[119]

Some idea of the Mamluk apprehension of a joint European–Mongol attack may be seen in the following passage by Qirtay al-Khaznadārī, who reported s.a. 670/1271–2 that Baybars had heard of an impending crusade called by the Pope. Qirtay writes: "[Baybars] was frightened for himself, for Egypt, for Syria and for his armies. He said to himself, 'If the Franks come to me by way of Alexandria, Damietta and Acre, I am afraid that the Mongols will attack me from the East. My position will be too weak to deal with these two parties.'"[120] Baybars thereupon sent an envoy to the King of England (Edward), and won over his friendship. The English King subsequently refused to participate in the crusade, which thus does not get off the ground.[121] While this particular passage is surely apocryphal,[122] it does provide an indication of Baybars's fear, or at least the perception of this fear by a writer in the next generation, of having to deal with a war on two fronts. It is well

[116] A. Mostaert and F.W. Cleaves, "Trois documents mongols des archives secrètes vaticanes," *HJAS* 15 (1952):430–45; Lupprian, *Beziehungen*, 242–3 (no. 48).

[117] Lupprian, *Beziehungen*, 76; de Rachewiltz, *Papal Envoys*, 157.

[118] *Ḥusn*, 87–8; trans. in P.M. Holt, "Some Observations on Shāfiʿ b. ʿAlī's Biography of Baybars," *JSS* 29 (1984):127, who writes that the Castellan was presumably John d'Ibelin, Count of Jaffa. The continuation of this passage shows that Baybars is referring to the Frankish princes of Syria and not those of Europe.

[119] *Rawḍ*, 361–2; Ibn al-Furāt, MS. Vienna, fol. 179a–b (= ed. Lyons, 1:172); Maqrīzī, 1:584 (abridged version); ʿAynī, fol. 100a. See ch. 5, p. 124, for this Mongol raid.

[120] Qirtay, fol. 98a; see fols. 96a–97b for the Pope's call for a crusade, as a result of the defeat of Baybars's navy at Cyprus in 670/1271.

[121] *Ibid.*, fols. 98a–99a.

[122] R. Irwin, "The Image of the Byzantine and the Frank in Arab Popular Literature," *MHR* 4 (1989):237–40; Amitai-Preiss, "Mamluk Perceptions," 63–4.

possible that Mamluk aggression towards the Franks of Outremer was at least partly motivated by this apprehension.[123]

Throughout this period, the Italian cities of Venice and Genoa played a certain, if ambivalent, role in the war between the Mamluks and the Īlkhānids. Genoa exercised effective control of the important trade in young mamluks from the territory of the Golden Horde, via the Bosphorus to Egypt.[124] Genoese embassies are known to have come to the Sultan's court in 661/1263, 663/1265 and 674/1275,[125] and doubtless the Genoese traded regularly with the merchants of the Sultanate.[126] At the same time, at least from the 1270s onwards, the Genoese also traded inside Īlkhānid territory, and subsequently individual Genoese were highly favored in the Īlkhān's court.[127] Merchants from Venice, Genoa's bitter rival, found fertile ground for their activities in the Īlkhānid state, and as early as 1264 there is an example of a Venetian trading in Tabrīz.[128] This did not prevent them from engaging in trade with the Mamluks.[129] In fact, the Italian trading cities do not seem to have been too troubled by the Mamluks systematically taking apart the crusader states of the Levant, nor were the Mamluks overly perturbed by the Italian support of these states and their commercial links with the Īlkhānids. In the interest of trade and profit, other considerations were put aside. This explains why later Church interdictions against trade with the Mamluks, especially of strategic goods, were generally ignored by the Italians.[130]

In *The Sicilian Vespers*, Sir Steven Runciman has written: "The Mongol alliance [with the West] was particularly advocated by the Genoese, who had a practical monopoly of the Mongol trade in the Black Sea and in northern Syria. It was therefore opposed by the Venetians, and by Charles [of Anjou], who also had no wish to see Genoa enriched."[131] While there is no questioning the point that Charles had little interest in an alliance with the Īlkhānids, it must be admitted that Runciman has confused the issue here. He does not distinguish between the Mongols of the Golden Horde and those ruled by the dynasty of Hülegü. It does not necessarily follow that because the Genoese enjoyed a predominant role in trade with the former, that they would have advocated an anti-Mamluk alliance between the West and the Īlkhānids, as understood here. In fact, from the Genoese point of view, such an alliance would have been quite detrimental to their very profitable position as middlemen in the Golden Horde–Mamluk slave trade.

[123] This point is further developed in Amitai-Preiss, "Mamluk Perceptions," 62-5.
[124] See above, pp. 85–6.
[125] *Rawḍ*, 171; Ibn al-Furāt, MS. Vienna, fol. 30a; 7:44; Maqrīzī, 1:495 (addition by editor from Ibn Wāṣil), 1:621; *Ḥusn*, 101; Thorau, *Baybars*, 163; Irwin, "Supply of Money," 77, 83.
[126] E. Ashtor, *Levant Trade in the Later Middle Ages* (Princeton, 1983), 10–11.
[127] *Ibid.*, 57; L. Petech, "Les marchands italiens dans l'empire mongol," *JA* 250 (1962):560–1.
[128] Petech, "Marchands," 560. [129] Ashtor, *Levant Trade*, 9–10.
[130] *Ibid.*, 17–18; Canard, "Un traité," 210 n. 1. [131] *Sicilian Vespers*, 201.

A number of observations can be made about the nature of Īlkhānid–European relations during the reigns of Hülegü and Abagha. First, throughout this period, the Īlkhāns were presented in Europe as having inclinations towards Christianity (usually of an unspecified variety), if not being on the verge of undergoing baptism. This, however, is not evident from the extant Mongol letters, where we only find expressions of the Īlkhāns' friendliness to Christianity and Christians, be they in their kingdom or elsewhere, and the desire for an alliance with the Christian West against the Muslims. Rather, it seems that this information, or more accurately disinformation, was conveyed verbally by the envoys themselves. Whether this was because of orders from the Īlkhān or the envoys' own initiative (or both) is difficult to say, but the recurrence of this disinformation indicates that there were at least some guidelines from above. The obvious intent of such a ploy was to increase sympathy among the Western leaders for the Mongols and their proposal for a joint campaign against the Mamluks. As we have seen, such a device had no real impact.

Second, a change in attitude can be discerned among both the Mongols and the papacy towards each other. In his 1262 letter to Louis IX, Hülegü adopted a fairly haughty tone, in which he essentially ordered the French King to join him in a joint military operation against the Muṣlim enemy. We see here the traditional Mongol approach to diplomatic relations at work, albeit perhaps in a more moderate form than before. Abagha adopted a different tack and turned to the various European rulers, be they popes or kings, as equals. The final dissolution of the united Mongol empire, successive Īlkhānid defeats and Mamluk success in the border war may have brought him to eschew the supercilious approach, at least in his diplomatic dealings with the West. At the same time, the papacy was also adopting a more flexible approach. Urban IV had conditioned Western assistance to the Mongols on their becoming Christians. Later popes, at least during the period under discussion here, dropped this demand, limiting themselves to attempts to convince Abagha of the advantages, spiritual and otherwise, to be gained if he were to convert. Perhaps the popes had arrived at a more realistic understanding of the religious inclinations of the Īlkhān, or, in some cases, were so desirous of an alliance that they became less fastidious.[132]

Why did these diplomatic contacts not bear fruit? First, Īlkhānid–European negotiations suffered from the vast distances that envoys had to travel. The long duration of each mission clearly made difficult the coordination of a common strategy, let alone the planning of a joint campaign, against the Mamluks. This "objective" condition, however, does not free the European rulers, including popes, of the responsibility for the failure of these exchanges.

[132] De Rachewitz, *Papal Envoys*, 153–4, makes this point about Gregory X's response to Abagha after the Council of Lyon. See also Roberg, "Tartaren," 279–80.

The European princes were unable or unwilling to heed the repeated Mongol calls for a joint campaign of some sort. Of course, there was no *a priori* reason why any ruler had to be interested in a crusade or the fate of Outremer. But the actions of most of these rulers (Charles of Anjou being the apparent exception) demonstrate that many of them did evince such an interest, at least during one stage of their lives. The one time a large multi-national crusading force did set out, under Louis IX in 1270, its strength was dissipated at Tunis. It must be remembered, however, that during that particular year Abagha was in no position to extend much help, had it actually reached the Levant.

Yet, Abagha must bear a certain amount of blame himself. In 1271, he sent only a large raiding party at Edward of England's request, even though the war in Khurasān had been concluded the previous year. A larger Mongol army, with clear objectives, could well have caused Baybars much worry, particularly with the Franks, still a sizeable force and reinforced by a small but not insignificant contingent under Edward, found in his rear. This was the closest Abagha came to realizing his goal of a common campaign and he essentially let the chance go by. Abagha's behavior that year is inexplicable, especially in view of his subsequent requests for an alliance against the Mamluks.

Be that as it may, the fact is that throughout his reign Abagha sent at least four embassies to the West. Each visited more than one court, including that of the Pope, and carried a letter calling for a joint anti-Muslim campaign. This phenomenon, perhaps more than any other, indicates the importance which Abagha attributed to the war with the Mamluks, and the extent to which he wanted to extend his sway into Syria and perhaps beyond. Most of his successors shared these goals, and in order to realize them they attempted, like him, to interest the Christian West in a common venture. They were all equally unsuccessful in achieving this goal.

CHAPTER 5

Military and diplomatic skirmishing

The people were reassured that the Sultan did not neglect an act, [but rather] carried it out, and he did not abandon his servants. The hearts of the castle defenders were calmed at this, and they said: "The Sultan moves quickly to our aid, and his armies reach the besieging enemy before news [of his approaching armies] comes."

Ibn ʿAbd al-Ẓāhir[1]

The origin of the border war

Already in the first years after the battle of ʿAyn Jālūt, some of the major motifs of the Mamluk–Īlkhānid "cold war" can be discerned: first, and most important, were the raids and other forms of intervention over the border by both sides. Second was the role of the Armenians, active allies of the Mongols, and the subsequent retribution that Baybars exacted from them. Third was the arrival in Syria of Mongol refugees, or *wāfidiyya*, from Hülegü's army, the first group of which arrived in late 660/1261. These *wāfidiyya* included both Mongol and indigenous Muslim military elements from Īlkhānid territory, and all were integrated into the Mamluk army. Finally, mention should be made of the role of the Syrian Franks, already discussed in the previous chapter. Throughout his reign, Baybars embarked on a systematic campaign against the Franks whenever lulls in the more pressing war with the Mongols permitted him to do so.

In this chapter, the ongoing, but usually limited, hostilities during the period 1262–77 between the Mamluks on the one hand, and the Īlkhānids and their allies the Armenians on the other, will be presented in a straightforward, chronological narrative. The intention here is to give a sense of the relative continuity of the border war. The topics of *wāfidiyya* and the occasional diplomatic *démarches* are also integrated into this narrative. Baybars's relations with the Franks are dealt with in a most cursory manner, only in as much as they impinge on the topic of this chapter, and also to give a sense of the Sultan's activities when he was not busy fighting the Īlkhānids and their associates. The large amount of material on the "secret war" between Baybars

[1] *Rawḍ*, 227.

and the Īlkhānids warrants a separate chapter. It should be remembered that this on-going skirmishing between the Mamluks and Mongols took place in the context of Baybars strengthening his army, the consolidation of Mamluk power throughout Syria, and his relations with the Khans of the Golden Horde, subjects dealt with in the previous two chapters.

For several years, the Mongols did not launch another raid of the same magnitude as the one which they had sent into Syria under Baydar in AH 658–9. Evidently, Hülegü and Abagha were too preoccupied with their struggle against the Jochids to devote much attention or forces to adventures against Baybars; instead they were content to have the Armenians initiate several incursions into north Syria, along with several small-scale raids or probes of their own along the border.

Towards the end of 660/fall of 1262, Baybars received information that Hülegü had gathered a large army. The source of this information was Baybars's agents in the Mongol camp. These agents were not able, however, to inform the Sultan where this army was heading. In retrospect, this was most probably the army that Hülegü was preparing to send in order to stop the invasion of the Golden Horde into the Darband Pass.[2] Baybars, however, did not have the advantage of historical hindsight, and made frenzied preparations to meet what he thought was a new Mongol invasion of Syria. He ordered scouts from his personal retinue (*al-khawāṣṣ*) to ride with lightly armed Turks (*min al-turk al-khifāf*),[3] and many remounts up to the borders of Iraq to obtain information. These scouts even managed to capture some Mongols, but no additional information was obtained.[4] A unit of Syrian troops, to be accompanied by bedouin chieftains (*umarā' al-ᶜurbān*), was ordered to follow the scouts. As the news worsened, Baybars ordered preparations to be made for the evacuation of the civilian population in Syria, along with measures to be taken against those known for their pro-Mongol sympathies. A large group of Syrian refugees made it safely to Egypt.

Baybars also sent orders to Aleppo that the grasslands (*al-aᶜshāb*) on the expected path of Hülegü's troops be burnt. One group of "burners" reached as far as the environs of Amid in Diyār Bakr, while another made it to the area around Akhlāṭ. It was reported that the plains were burnt for an area equal to the distance covered in ten days riding. A second group of scouts was sent out with bedouins. As an added precaution, travel on the roads was prevented.[5]

[2] See ch. 4, p. 79.

[3] Alternatively, this expression might mean that these "Turks" (alluding to either mamluks or Türkmen) were unencumbered by heavy baggage.

[4] One wonders what kind of Mongols (*al-tatār*) these were exactly, since they were also Muslims. Perhaps they were Muslim troops who had been inducted into the Mongol army. Or perhaps we have an early example of the Islamization of Mongols. In any case, the Mamluk scouts let them go.

[5] Abū Shāma, 219; *Rawḍ*, 135–6. The latter report is cited in Ibn Wāṣil, MS. 1702, fol. 405a–b (with additional details); Nuwayrī, MS. 2m, fol. 156a–b; Ibn al-Furāt, MS. Vienna, fol. 6b; Maqrīzī, 1:473 (much shorter version).

Baybars had ordered the extensive burning of the grasslands because he knew that this would seriously hamper any Mongol offensive. The Mongols did not bring fodder with them for their horses, but rather lived off the land.[6]

In the end, it turned out that these measures were unnecessary, because this Mongol offensive did not take place. Rather, the Mongol armies went off in another direction, to the front with the Golden Horde. It was important, however, to examine Baybars's reaction to the news in some detail, because it demonstrates that he expected another invasion at any time. It also shows that he was willing and capable of taking decisive action to frustrate Mongol plans.

One group of Mamluk scouts did bring back news that some 200 Mongols and their families were seeking refuge with the Sultan. This was the first group of *wāfidiyya*, part of a Jochid contingent in Hülegü's army, which was mentioned in chapter 4. Their arrival had two important effects. First, the news they brought of the conflict between Berke and Hülegü compelled Baybars to increase his efforts to reach an understanding with Berke. Second, the news of the good reception which Baybars gave these first *wāfidiyya* reached the Mongols and propelled other groups to desert to the Sultanate.[7]

The next *wāfidī* group arrived at the end of the following year (661/1263). They numbered over 1300 horsemen, presumably accompanied by their families. Our main source for this information, Ibn ʿAbd al-Ẓāhir, states that they were composed of Mongols and Bahādurīs (*min al-mughul wa'l-bahādur-iyya*). The use of *mughul* instead of the generally found *tatar* would seem to indicate that these were "true" Mongols, and not Turks or other soldiers who served the Mongols, all of whom seem to be lumped under the rubric of *tatar*.[8] *Bahāduriyya* appears to be an Arabized plural of the Mongol word for brave, warrior, or hero (*ba'atur* < *baghatur*, pl. *ba'atud*).[9] More specifically, it was used as a technical term for the elite shock troops of the Mongol imperial guard.[10] Whether *bahāduriyya* refers here exactly to troops of this unit is unclear, but the combination of this term with *mughul* indicates that this was a fairly elite group of refugees. The importance of this group is seen by its leader, Geremün Agha, who – according to Ibn ʿAbd al-Ẓāhir – "had conquered all of

6 For the operatives who lit the fields, see ch. 9, pp. 205–6. For a discussion of Mongol logistical problems, see ch. 10, pp. 225–9.

7 *Rawḍ*, 137–8; Nuwayrī, MS. 2m, fols. 156b–157a; Ibn al-Furāt, MS. Vienna, fols. 6a–7b. For the reception of these and later *wāfidiyya*, see Ayalon, "Wafidiya," 90–4, 98–9.

8 "It has been suggested on philological grounds that in the context of the Mongol Empire, 'Tatar' carried the implication of 'people who have become (politically) Mongol.'" Morgan, *Mongols*, 57, citing O. Pritsak, "Two Migratory Movements in the Eurasian Steppe in the 9th-11th Centuries," in *Proceedings of the 26th International Congress of Orientalists, New Delhi 1964*, 2 (1968):159. This is perhaps speculative, but my impression is that this distinction is confirmed by much of the usage of the terms in some of the Arabic sources. A detailed discussion of this topic is beyond the scope of the present study, but mention is made whenever the term *al-mughul* appears instead of the more usual *al-tatar/tatār*.

9 Hsiao, "Military Establishment," 218 n. 59.

10 *Ibid.*, 36; Allsen, *Mongol Imperialism*, 21–2 and n. 14.

the land of the Turks." Shāfiʿ b. ʿAlī describes him as a *tümen* commander in Hülegü's army; while al-Yūnīnī writes *sub anno* AH 659 that he had been Mongol commander of the Jazīra.[11] Unlike the *wāfidiyya* of the previous year, the original impetus for this group's desertion is unclear.[12]

Not only groups of Mongols fled to the Sultanate. Indigenous Muslim military elements who had joined the Mongols, either voluntarily or under coercion, also left their new masters and sought refuge in the west. It would seem that Baybars's successes convinced them that the unending conquests of the Mongols were not a foregone conclusion, and by fleeing they stood a chance of survival under a non-Mongol, and Muslim, regime. Several important individuals came with their entourages in 660/1261–2, including the lord of Irbil. All were well received and given ranks in the Mamluk army.[13] Also this year (Rajab/June 1262), a group of mamluks of the late Caliph al-Mustaʿṣim arrived in the Sultanate. They were led by Sayf al-Dīn Salār, who was first given a commission in Syria and then was made an amir of 40 (the second highest rank in the Mamluk army) in Egypt. As a result of the good treatment he received, he wrote to his cohorts who had remained in Iraq and the Khafāja bedouin there to tell them of this.[14] In Rajab 662/May 1264, a group of soldiers arrived from Shīrāz. They were accompanied by Khafāja bedouin from Iraq. All were well received; the Shīrāzis were integrated into the army and the Khafāja Arabs were sent back to their country.[15] At the end of this year, the unnamed Mongol *shaḥna* in Takrīt arrived in the Sultanate.[16]

Perhaps the most prominent of the non-Mongol *wāfidīs* was Jalāl al-Dīn Yashkar, the son of the Mujāhid al-Dīn Aybeg, the Caliph al-Mustaʿṣim's Lesser Dawādār, who had been killed by Hülegü in 656/1258.[17] Jalāl al-Dīn, however, had survived his father, and had clearly earned the trust of the

[11] *Rawḍ*, 178–81; Nuwayrī, MS. 2m, fols. 165b–166a; Ibn al-Furāt, MS. Vienna, fol. 34a–b (citing *Naẓm al-sulūk* of Shāfiʿ b. ʿAlī); Maqrīzī, 1:500–1; *Faḍl*, fol. 4a; Yūnīnī, 2:112. This wave of *wāfidiyya* came in three contingents, and it seems that the number of 1300 is the total for all three. Cf. Yūnīnī, 1:534; 2:195, who has this group come in two contingents in Rajab of this year (May-June 1263).

[12] Cf. *Zubda*, fol. 61a–b (whence, ʿAynī, fol. 89a), who writes that a large group of 1000 *musta'minūn* (= *wāfidiyya*) came under Geremün; these had been followers of Berke, and had fled from Hülegü. Baybars al-Manṣūrī has seemingly conflated this present group of refugees with the one of the previous year, which he does not mention.

[13] Ibn Shaddād, *Ta'rīkh*, 332–3; *Rawḍ*, 87–8. Ibn Shaddād also gives information of other non-Mongol military *wāfidiyya* from Kurdistan and the Jazīra, but no date of their arrival is known.

[14] Ibn al-Furāt, MS. Vienna, fol. 2a (citing Shāfiʿ's *Naẓm*); Maqrīzī, 1:468; Nuwayrī, MS. 2m, fol. 153a–b; see below, in ch. 6, p. 150. This Salār might be identical with Sharaf al-Dīn Salār al-Mustanṣirī, who had served the Mongols as *shaḥna* at al-Hilla, before coming to the Sultanate with 300 horsemen; Ibn Shaddād, *Ta'rīkh*, 330. For mamluks from Mārdīn and Mayyāfāriqīn, whose date of arrival in the Sultanate is not known, see Ibn Shaddād, *Ta'rīkh*, 338; also *Zubda*, fol. 34b; Nuwayrī, 27:383–4.

[15] *Rawḍ*, 198; Nuwayrī, MS. 2m, fols. 168b–169a; *Zubda*, fol. 64a–b; Ibn al-Furāt, MS. Vienna, fols. 44a–45a; Maqrīzī, 1:512. For Baybars's relations with Shīrāz, see ch. 6, pp. 145–6.

[16] *Rawḍ*, 219; Ibn al-Furāt, MS. Vienna, fol. 55b; Maqrīzī, 1:520. It is unknown if this *shaḥna* was himself a Mongol.

[17] For the Lesser Dawādār, see Boyle, "Īl-Khāns," 346–8.

Mongols. Around 662/1263–4, Hülegü ordered him to Baghdad, so that he could gather the many former soldiers of the Caliph who were scattered and hiding throughout Iraq. Rashīd al-Dīn, in a singular mention of the desertion of a Mongol supporter to the Mamluks, says that Jalāl al-Dīn had suggested this action to Hülegü, so that these troops could participate in the struggle with Berke. Since they were of Qipchaq origin, they would be of particular use in this war. On the other hand, Ibn ʿAbd al-Ẓāhir states that Hülegü's aim was that Jalāl al-Dīn gather these troops, in the name of the war against Berke, so that they could be exterminated. According to the former source, Jalāl al-Dīn betrayed his trust by fleeing, while the latter writer states that he understood what Hülegü's true intentions were, so he decided to desert with these soldiers. On his way, they were assisted by the Khafāja bedouin of Iraq.[18]

When news of Jalāl al-Dīn's approach reached Baybars, then in Cairo, in Shawwāl 662/July-August 1264, he was wary because of their large numbers, diverse origins and unclear intentions. He thus ordered that an army be sent out to meet them as a precaution.[19] The Sultan, having received assurances of Jalāl al-Dīn's friendly intentions, had him brought to Cairo, which he reached at the beginning of 663/October-November 1264. His entourage of 150 mamluks (some of whom had belonged to his father) were put into the army, while Jalāl al-Dīn was made an amir of 40.[20] His warm reception, however, was short-lived. Evidently at the end of 664/1266, information reached Baybars that the Mongols had been sending secret envoys (*quṣṣād*) to Jalāl al-Dīn, who was then arrested. Horses and camels were found in his possession, which indicated (at least to Baybars) that he was preparing to flee. Suspicions had first been aroused when Jalāl al-Dīn had requested to maintain secret communications with his mother and sister, still in Mongol territory. His eventual fate is unknown, although chances are it was not a happy one.[21] Why Jalāl al-Dīn went to such trouble to flee to the Mamluks, only to plan a return to the Mongols remains a mystery. It indicated, perhaps, a great disappointment with life in the Sultanate. He may possibly have expected a higher commission than an amirate of 40, the standard rank given to prominent *wāfidīs* at that time.

While Hülegü was preoccupied with his war with Berke, King Hetʿum of Lesser Armenia embarked on a number of campaigns into north Syria. Armenian forces, at times accompanied by Mongolian troops or soldiers from Antioch, raided in 660/662, the beginning of Ṣafar 661/end of December 1262, and twice in 662/1263–4. In all of these attempts, Hetʿum's forces were

[18] Rashīd al-Dīn, ed. ʿAlīzādah, 3:92–3, who writes that he attacked the Khafāja; *Rawḍ*, 209–10 (whence Ibn al-Furāt, MS. Vienna, fol. 50a–b), 220; cf. Ibn al-Fuwaṭī, 350–3, who tells a different story. [19] *Rawḍ*, 203; Ibn al-Furāt, MS. fol. 48a; Maqrīzī, 1:515–16.

[20] *Rawḍ*, 209–10, 220; *Zubda*, fol. 67a; Ibn al-Furāt, MS. Vienna, fol. 37b (whence Maqrīzī, 1:503–4; this passage is not based on *Rawḍ*, and is placed at the beginning of AH 662), 50a–b; Ibn Shaddād, *Ta'rīkh*, 331; cf. ʿUmarī, ed. Lech, 18–19, who reports that Jalāl al-Dīn died before he reached Egypt.

[21] *Rawḍ*, 273, who here gives Jalāl al-Dīn's private name as K-J-Q-N (?).

unsuccessful. They were either defeated by local Syrian troops, neutralized by harsh weather or withdrew upon the approach of large Mamluk forces.[22]

The frequency of these forays, the size of the forces involved and the care which the Armenian King devoted to their organization indicate that their primary aim was more than just gaining booty. It appears, rather, that Hetᶜum hoped to take advantage of both the perceived unsettled conditions in northern Syria and the support of the Mongols, in order to widen the area under his control. This, however, was a serious strategic mistake on his part. He evidently did not expect that he would encounter serious resistance from the Muslims. Nor did he calculate that Baybars would react so strongly, and later wreak such a furious revenge. Finally, any hope he entertained of substantial assistance from the Mongols remained unfulfilled, and he was essentially left alone to face the consequences of his adventures. Probably the main effect of the raids was to whet Baybars's desire to invade Lesser Armenia, in order to seek revenge for anti-Muslim activities, to dissuade its king from further behavior of this sort, and to weaken his capability of aiding the Mongols or acting independently.[23]

First Mongol and Mamluk initiatives

The first serious Mongol probe along the border was an attack on the border fortress of al-Bīra, located on the eastern bank of the Euphrates River. As has been mentioned in chapter 3 (and will be discussed further in chapter 9), this fort, along with al-Raḥba further to the south (but on the west bank of the river), played an essential role in the emerging Mamluk stategy *vis-à-vis* the Mongols. There are two early indications of the important role that al-Bīra was to play. In Jumādā II 662/March-April 1264, Baybars sent an amir, Sayf al-Dīn Balaban al-Zaynī, to inspect the readiness of the armies and castles of Syria. The only fort which is mentioned by name is al-Bīra: orders were carried by this amir to Damascus that a large amount of money be sent to this fort, for the allocations (*nafaqāt*), presumably to the garrison.[24] Perhaps this distribution is connected to the second piece of information. In Ramaḍān/June-July of the same year, a report from al-Bīra reached the Sultan in Cairo that a force had raided up to Qalᶜat al-Rūm.[25] This was the first of many Mamluk raids into Mongol territory, and it is significant that it set out from al-Bīra.

In the winter of 663/1264–5, the Īlkhānid Mongols turned their attention to the west for the first time since the battle of Homs in 659/1261. Perhaps the timing was not coincidental, and this campaign could get under way because there was a lull in the war with the Golden Horde. Around the beginning of Rabīᶜ I 663/late December 1264, Baybars, who was hunting in the Egyptian

[22] These raids are discussed in detail in Amitai-Preiss, "Aftermath," 10–12; see also Canard, "Arménie," 224; Thorau, *Baybars*, 150–1. [23] See Ibn Kathīr, 13:247; ᶜAynī, fol. 95a.

[24] *Rawḍ*, 194; Ibn al-Furāt, MS. Vienna, fol. 42b; Maqrīzī, 1:510.

[25] *Rawḍ*, 201; Ibn al-Furāt, MS. Vienna, fol. 46a–b.

countryside, received news that the Mongols were heading for al-Bīra. Ibn ʿAbd al-Ẓāhir adds that (unspecified) Franks had informed the Mongols that the Mamluk army was split up throughout the country for the (annual) grazing of the horses. Baybars realized the gravity of the situation and immediately returned to Cairo, but not before sending an order with Bilig al-Khaznadār to Damascus, to dispatch a force of 4000 light cavalry (*min al-ʿaskar al-khafīf*; evidently the intention is to a force not weighed down by heavy baggage) to al-Bīra from the Syrian armies. Arriving in Cairo, the Sultan at once sent a force under ʿIzz al-Dīn Ughan (or Ighan) Samm al-Mawt and three other senior amirs, who together with amirs (evidently of lower rank) and *ḥalqa* troops set out "in light order" (*bi'l-tawajjuh jarā'id*) on 4 Rabīʿ I 663/25 December 1264.[26] The next day, another force of 4000 horsemen under Jamāl al-Dīn Aqqush al-Muḥammadī and Jamāl al-Dīn Aydoghdi al-Ḥājibī left for Syria. Orders were sent to al-Manṣūr of Hama and the governor of Aleppo to join this force, along with all the amirs of Syria (i.e. Damascus). ʿĪsā b. Muhannā, *amīr al-ʿurbān*, was ordered to cross the desert in order to raid Ḥarrān, seemingly as a diversion.

Throughout the next month, the Sultan busied himself with preparing the main part of the army; this included calling in the scattered horses and troops. Baybars set out on 7 Rabīʿ II 663/27 January 1265, reaching Gaza 13 days later. There he received an update that the Mongols had built seventeen mangonels (*manjānīq*s) at al-Bīra, indicating that this was no mere raid, but a serious effort to take the fort. Baybars kept this disquieting news from all but two of his most trusted amirs (Sunqur al-Rūmī and Qalawun) and wrote to Ughan to encourage him to make haste. At this point, however, it does not seem that Baybars was in much of a hurry; he even took time off to hunt. Probably he wanted to keep an eye on the Franks on the coast and see how things would develop at al-Bīra. At Yabnā (Yavneh, Ibelin), near Jaffa, he received news on 26 Rabīʿ II/15 February that the Mongol forces had fled upon seeing the Mamluk reinforcements. This information, which arrived by pigeon-post at Damascus and from there via the *barīd*, took four days to reach the Sultan.

The Mongol force, a *tümen* led by Durbai, had made a determined effort to take the fort. The defenders, including the female inhabitants, withstood the siege and bombardment, and fought back with determination. When the Mongols filled the moat with wood, the defenders dug a tunnel and set the wood on fire. The Mongols made attempts to scale the walls by shooting pegs, with ropes attached, but these were thrown off. The resolution of the defenders paid off when the Mamluk army appeared and the Mongols fled in disarray, leaving behind their siege equipment.[27] When news of the Mongol retreat

[26] Maqrīzī, 1:523, adds that there was a total of 4000 riders, a sentence not found in either *Rawḍ* or Ibn al-Furāt.

[27] There are several groups of accounts. The first is based on *Rawḍ*, 221–5; whence Nuwayrī, MS. 2m, fol. 226a–b; Ibn al-Furāt, MS. Vienna, fols. 62a–64a; Maqrīzī, 1:523–5. The report in *Ḥusn*, 87, is independent: according to him, Baybars reached Baysān before he received the news of the Mongol withdrawal. A different, shorter account, but with some additional

Plate 2. Al-Bīra (Birecik), ca. 1930 (from P. Deschamps, *Les Châteaux des croisés en Terre-Sainte*, vol. I: *Le Crac des Chevaliers, Album* [Paris, 1934], pl. VII [original photograph: Abbé G. Bretocq; reproduction: Zev Radovan]

reached King Het'um, who was leading a force to al-Bīra as he had been ordered, he turned around and returned to his country.[28] Professor Cahen has suggested that an additional reason for the withdrawal was the arrival of news of Hülegü's death.[29] This could well be, although the sources are silent on this point.

Baybars, having received the news of the Mongol retreat, now ordered the expeditionary force to assist in the repair of al-Bīra. Supplies and armaments were sent from all over Syria, and it was ordered that the fort would have enough provisions for ten years. Mangonels were sent, and the garrison was put in order. The defenders and inhabitants were rewarded for their tenacity. During the repair work, a group of Mongols attacked, but were beaten back, sustaining many casualties.[30]

information, is found in Yūnīnī, 2:318; Mufaḍḍal, 131–2; Kutubī, 20:318; Dhahabī, *Ta'rīkh al-islām*, MS. Bodleian Laud Or. 279, fol. 3a; Ibn al-Dawādārī, 8:107; the lost part of Ibn Shaddād's biography may well be the original source for this last group of accounts. A fourth version, seemingly derived from *Rawḍ*, but containing interesting information about the attacking force, is in *Zubda*, fols. 68b–69a; whence 'Aynī, fol. 92a.

28 Smpad, tr. Der Nersessian, 163, who also reports that the raid was led by Durba[i]. This is the only mention of the raid in any of the pro-Mongol sources.

29 Cahen, *Syrie*, 712. Hülegü died on 19 Rabī' II 663/8 February 1265 (Spuler, *Iran*, 59 and n. 121). If the news of the Mongol withdrawal took four days to reach Baybars on 26 Rabī' II (i.e., the news was sent on the 22nd of the month), then it is possible that the Mongols at al-Bīra would have heard of the death of their ruler.

30 *Rawḍ*, 226–8; Nuwayrī, MS. 2m, fols. 226b–227a; Ibn al-Furāt, MS. Vienna, fols. 64a–65a; Maqrīzī, 1:525. The Mongols who attacked during the repair work were a group of "Mongol Tatars" (*firqa min al-tatār al-mughul*), indicating perhaps that they were "authentic" Mongols and not allies or subject troops.

Ibn ᶜAbd al-Ẓāhir wrote that the minds of the garrisons of the castles (*ahl al-qilāᶜ*; possibly the reference is to the inhabitants as well) were put at ease as a result of Baybars's quick and effective response to the Mongol attack and his subsequent repair of al-Bīra's fortifications.[31] This desire to show the officers, soldiers and even the civilians in the frontier forts and towns that they would not be abandoned may be another reason why Baybars had reacted with such forcefulness to the initial news of the Mongol attack.

While the repair work was under way, an additional force was sent to help the expeditionary army already at al-Bīra. Upon the completion of this work, this new force was to go to Tall Bāshir and from there to raid Lesser Armenia. There are no details of this raid, except that a letter arrived from its commanders saying that their mission had been completed. This might be the Mamluk force referred to by Smpad, which apparently reached the Qara Su River near Antioch around Easter 1265, before turning back in the face of a large Armenian force.[32] The main force, under Ughan and Aqqush al-Muḥammadī, returned to Cairo in early Ramaḍān 663/June 1265.[33]

Baybars was now in Palestine with a large part, perhaps most, of his army. The danger from the Mongols had been averted for the time being. The Sultan now turned his attention to the Franks.[34] In just over two months (late February to late April 1265), his armies conquered Caesarea, Haifa and Arsūf, and raided ᶜAthlīth (Chastel Pelerin) and Acre. The fortifications and harbors of all the conquered cities were destroyed, to prevent their re-use in the future by the Franks.[35] It was in this campaign that Baybars established the pattern for his future relations with the Franks. There was now no doubt that they were on the defensive, and Baybars enjoyed the initiative. In periods between dealing with the Mongols and their allies or when the danger from their quarter seemed minimal, Baybars turned his attention to the Franks, systematically reducing their power and territory.

Upon returning to Cairo, Baybars received envoys from Hetᶜum. This was probably in early Shawwāl 663/mid-July 1265. According to al-Yūnīnī and other Syrian writers, these envoys informed the Sultan that Hülegü had died, Abagha had succeeded him to the throne and Berke had attacked and defeated the new Khan. The last part of the statement appears to be both an anachronism and incorrect: only in the summer of this year did fighting break out between Berke's and Abagha's armies, and Berke's army was eventually worsted in this round. In any event, so the story goes, Baybars wanted to exploit the opportunity to invade Iraq, but was unable to do so because the

[31] *Rawḍ*, 227 (partially cited at opening of this chapter); discussed in Thorau, *Baybars*, 157.

[32] *Rawḍ*, 228; Ibn al-Furāt, MS. Vienna, fol. 65a; Smpad, tr. Der Nersessian, 163 (cited also in Canard, "Arménie," 225).

[33] Ibn al-Furāt, MS. Vienna, fol. 77a; Maqrīzī, 1:537.

[34] On Baybars's relations with the Franks before AH 663, see Runciman, *Crusades*, 3:315–18; Prawer, *Histoire*, 2:440–60; Thorau, *Baybars*, 142–50.

[35] See Thorau, *Baybars*, 160–2; Runciman, *Crusades*, 3:318–19; Prawer, *Histoire*, 2:460–70. On Baybars's policy of destroying coastal fortifications as he captured them, see ch. 3, p. 76.

army was split among the *iqṭāʿāt*.[36] It is difficult to imagine, however, that Baybars entertained real intentions of invading Iraq at this time. This would have overextended his forces and left his kingdom exposed, with a still strong Frankish presence in his rear. In addition, it would seem that had Baybars truly wanted to invade Iraq he would have done so. Just seven months before, he had been able to gather his army which was scattered throughout the country. Besides, during his entire reign Baybars showed himself capable of achieving difficult feats, if he thought the results were worth the trouble. So, assuming the sources are correct in conveying Baybars's true intentions, it would seem that this was just wishful thinking, which could be conveniently dismissed with the excuse of the army being split up in the countryside.

In Ramaḍān of this year (June-July 1265), a Mamluk force was able to retake Qarqīsiyā, a fort on the Khābūr River not far from al-Raḥba. At some point before, Baybars had sent an amir to the fort, who remained there for a while but left upon the approach of a Mongol force. This shows the uncertain and fluid nature of the situation in the border region in these early years. Then the local commanders of Qarqīsiyā, evidently not Mongols themselves, made contact with the governor in al-Raḥba and asked to submit. Some joint plan against the Mongol garrison was probably agreed upon. A force, composed of horsemen and "archers" (*uqjiyya*) set out from al-Raḥba, and entered the city at daybreak through the gate which had been opened for them. They killed both the Mongols and the Georgians in the city, and captured eighty renegades (*al-murtadda*), evidently Muslims who served the Mongols.[37] The following year, the Sultan ordered a bridge to be built at al-Raḥba, perhaps so that communications with Qarqīsiyā could be more easily maintained. In the long run, however, the fort remained beyond Mamluk reach: Ibn Shaddād reports that it was [again] in Mongol hands at the time of the writing of his *al-Aʿlāq al-khaṭīra*, in 679/1280–1.[38]

The border with the Mongols remained quiet throughout the winter of 664/1265–6. The following spring, Baybars was making preparations for his next campaign, once more against the Franks. The Egyptian army set out in early Shaʿbān 664/May 1266, and together with Syrian units launched a series of devastating raids against the Frankish possessions throughout Syria. In Ramaḍān/June, Baybars arrived at Safad. The Templar fort fell after a siege that lasted over a month, and the garrison was massacred.[39] Baybars now turned his attention to Lesser Armenia, and sent the first of many large-scale Mamluk raids against that country.

[36] Yūnīnī, 2:322; Dhahabī, MS. Laud 279, fol. 3b; Kutubī, 20:320–1; Mufaḍḍal, 145; Ibn Kathīr, 13:245; ʿAynī, fol. 94a. Cf. Ibn al-Dawādārī, 8:114, who writes that Baybars wished to attack but was afraid of a Frankish attack; see ch. 4, p. 86n.

[37] *Ḥusn*, 101–2; Ibn al-Furāt, MS. Vienna, fol. 77b (similar to *Ḥusn*, but with additions); Maqrīzī, 1:537; *Tuḥfa*, 55; Yūnīnī, 4:108; cf. Thorau, *Baybars*, 165. [38] *Aʿlāq*, 3:153.

[39] For the siege and the events preceding it, see: Runciman, *Crusades*, 3:320–1; Prawer, *Histoire*, 2:470–5; Thorau, *Baybars*, 166–71.

After the failures of 662/1263–4, King Hetʿum justly feared Baybars's retribution and sought to placate him. In 663/1264–5, Armenian envoys arrived in Egypt and asked the Sultan for peace. These may be the same envoys mentioned above who had brought news of Hülegü's death. In spite of the valuable presents they brought with them, Baybars did not agree to their request.[40] The following year, after the conquest of Safad, Baybars received another Armenian mission there. According to the Mamluk sources, the Sultan did not accept either the gift or the letter they brought with them.[41]

Bar Hebraeus and the Armenian writers tell the story of these "negotiations" differently. According to the former, in 1266, it was Baybars himself who first wrote to Hetʿum, calling on him to submit and pay the *jizya*.[42] In addition, Baybars demanded that Hetʿum permit the free trade of horses, mules, wheat, barley and iron from Cilicia. The Armenian King was unable to comply because of his fear of the Mongols.[43] Smpad writes that Hetʿum opened the negotiations. Baybars sent envoys, who made demands – including the cession of fortresses – with which the Armenian King could not comply, both out of fear of the Mongols and his refusal to come under the authority of the Sultan.[44] Vardan reports that Baybars demanded the fortresses in northern Syria which the Armenians had seized during the Mongol occupation of 658/1260. Hetʿum, however, refused to comply, because he feared the Mongols.[45]

It is difficult to reconcile all of these various reports. It would seem that the Mamluk writers suppressed, perhaps deliberately, knowledge of Baybars's dispatch of envoys. This embassy might have been in 663/1264–5, after the first Armenian mission, although the pro-Mongol sources place this *sub anno* 1266 (i.e. AH 664). With the second Armenian mission of 664/1266, it would seem that Baybars had already set his mind on sending a raid into Cilicia and saw no point in receiving the embassy. It appears that from the beginning Baybars had laid down conditions that Hetʿum could not meet.

Baybars did not wait long to execute his plans. Having taken some measures to repair Safad, Baybars went to Damascus. There, he ordered an army, according to Ibn ʿAbd al-Ẓāhir, under al-Manṣūr of Hama (who held the

40 *Ḥusn*, 102.

41 Yūnīnī, 2:343; Dhahabī, MS. Laud 279, fol. 14b; Ibn Taghrī Birdī, 7:139. Cf. Thorau, *Baybars*, 163.

42 The poll-tax paid by non-Muslims to the Muslim state, symbolizing here the formal submission of the Armenians to the Sultan.

43 Bar Hebraeus, 445; Ibn al-ʿIbrī, 498 (the passages are not identical). Labib, *Handelsgeschichte*, 66–7, saw the latter passage as evidence of Mamluk–Cilician trade in these items, and of how the Mamluks were willing to wage war to protect this trade. All this passage shows, however, is that the Mamluks were interested in trading these commodities. Recent research by C. Otten-Froux ("L'Aïas dans le dernier tiers du XIIIe siècle d'àpres les notaires génois," *AAS* 22 [1988]:166–7) shows that wood, iron and tin were imported into Egypt, albeit in the next decade. For more on the Cilician–Mamluk trade, see ch. 9.

44 Smpad, tr. Der Nersessian, 164; Canard, "Arménie," 228.

45 Vardan, tr. Thomson, 223.

overall command), Qalawun and Ughan to proceed to Cilicia. Ibn Shaddād writes that the force was under the nominal command of al-Manṣūr, but the real officer in charge was Aq Sunqur al-Fāriqānī. The army left Damascus on 5 Dhū 'l-qaʿda 664/12 August 1266. Advancing by way of al-Darbassāk (Trapesac) and Nikopolis (Islahiye), they entered the Amanus Gate, a pass in the Amanus mountains called in the Arabic sources simply al-Darband (from the word "defile" in Persian).[46] Shāfiʿ b. ʿAlī remarks that when al-Manṣūr entered the country, Hetʿum sent to express his submission, but al-Manṣūr paid no attention to this and imprisoned his envoys. In the pass they encountered an Armenian force which had taken up position in the fortifications in the hills above the road. Hetʿum himself was not with his army, which he had left under the command of his brother, who had with him two of the king's sons. The Muslims charged up the slopes, and after hard fighting, defeated the Armenians, who fled. Hetʿum's brother was killed, as was one of his sons. The other son, his heir Leon (Layfūn in the Arabic sources), was captured. Cilicia now lay unprotected before the raiders.[47]

There is some disagreement about the whereabouts of Hetʿum. Ibn ʿAbd al-Ẓāhir writes that prior to the attack he had abdicated in favor of his son Leon, and had retired to a monastery. The Armenian sources make no mention of this, and say that he was off trying to get help from the Mongols.[48] The latter version is strengthed by Bar Hebraeus's account: Hetʿum had gone to the Mongol commander "Nafjī", stationed in Seljuq territory, to ask for help. This officer claimed he could not aid them of his own volition, but only upon Abagha's express orders. Eventually, some type of order must have arrived, because both Bar Hebraeus and Grigor mention the eventual dispatch of a Mongol force, although it was too late to make any difference.[49]

The Mamluk army marched unopposed into the country, killing, burning and taking captives as it went. From al-Darband, they continued on to the region of Tall Ḥamdūn (Til Hamdoun, now Toprakkale), and from there to Ḥamūṣ, which was burnt. Then they crossed the Jayḥān (Pyramus) River, and took up position at al-ʿAmūdayn (Adamodana), a great fortress belonging to

46 On this and other passes through the Amanus mountains, see Edwards, *Fortifications*, 39–40, 216–21, and the maps in C. Mutafian, *La Cilicie au carrefour des empires* (Paris, 1988), vol. 2, esp. map no. 14.

47 *Rawḍ*, 263, 269–70; hence Ibn al-Furāt, MS. Vienna, fols. 105 a–b, 109b; Maqrīzī, 1:549, 551–2; *Ḥusn*, 115. Cf. Yūnīnī, 2:343–4, who writes that the Armenians abandoned the forts when the Mamluks appeared; similar accounts in Kutubī, 20:337; Ibn al-Dawādārī, 8:118; Ibn Taghrī Birdī, 7:140. See also Ibn Shaddād, *Aʿlāq*, ed. Eddé, 321; Abū 'l-Fidā', 4:3; *Tuḥfa*, 58, where the author gives an eye-witness account of the fighting (he seems to have conflated his version with that in *Rawḍ*). Two Armenian sources (Smpad, tr. Der Nersessian, 164–5; Grigor, 357) describe this encounter and how the Armenians fled, leaving behind the princes to their fate. Jean Dardel, "Chronique d'Arménie," *RHC, Ar*, 2:12 has the Armenians fleeing after fighting; Hetʿum, 177, only briefly mentions the whole incident. For a detailed discussion, see Canard, "Arménie," 229–31.

48 See the relevant references in the previous note.

49 Bar Hebraeus, 445–6 (= Ibn al-ʿIbrī, 498); Grigor, 357; Thorau, *Baybars*, 174. According to Ibn Shaddād, *Ta'rīkh*, 156, one Nabjī was a Mongol commander in Rūm, ca. AH 675.

the Teutonic Knights. Although the garrison surrendered, they were massacred and the women and children were taken into slavery. Interestingly enough, a group of Mongols was in the fortress when it was taken. Sīs, the capital of the kingdom, was the next target. The Mamluk army entered it on 22 Dhū 'l-qaʿda/29 August, and commenced looting and destruction, but was unable to take the citadel. The Mamluk forces split up: Ughan went in the direction of the Seljuk border, while Qalawun raided al-Maṣṣīṣa (Mamistra or Mopsuestria), Adhana (Adana), Ayās (Lajasso) and Ṭarsūs (Tarse). A Templar fortress, al-Tīna (Canamella; on the coast east of Ayās), was also destroyed. Al-Manṣūr remained in Sīs. Thereupon, the army was reunited and laden with a tremendous amount of booty, set back for Syria. It was met by the Sultan near Afāmiya around the middle of Dhū 'l-ḥijja/ca. 20 September.[50]

Diplomatic maneuvers

The capture of Leon led to a series of interesting diplomatic exchanges between Baybars and Hetʿum. The Armenian king was evidently quite distraught by the capture of his son and heir, let alone the death and destruction in his kingdom. Sometime around the beginning of Rabīʿ I 665/ca. December 1266, an Armenian envoy arrived in Cairo to discuss Leon's return. In contrast to the cold reception which the Armenian envoys had received the previous year, Baybars was now willing to act magnanimously. Hetʿum was granted a respite from hostilities for a year.[51]

In Shaʿbān/October 1267, a second Armenian mission met at least twice with Baybars in Syria.[52] It was probably then that Hetʿum initially offered both money and several castles in return for Leon. Baybars, however, demanded more. He wanted both the forts taken during the Mongol occupation of 658/1260 and also the return of his *khushdāsh*, Sunqur al-Ashqar, who was in Mongol captivity. Sunqur had been taken prisoner by Hülegü after the conquest of Aleppo, along with several other Baḥrī mamluks, and taken back with him when he withdrew from Syria.[53] Baybars now thought he had an opportunity to get his friend back, and made the return of Leon conditional upon Hetʿum's obtaining Sunqur from the Mongols. Hetʿum promised he

[50] *Rawḍ*, 270–1; Nuwayrī, MS. 2m, fols. 235b–236a; Ibn al-Furāt, MS. Vienna, fols. 109b–110a, who adds the information about al-Tīna (see also ed. Lyons, 1:126, and Riley-Smith's comments, 2:217); Maqrīzī, 1:552; Yūnīnī, 2:334; *Tuḥfa*, 58; Thorau, *Baybars*, 174–5; Canard, "Arménie," 231–2. The Armenian sources recount the inhabitants' suffering: Grigor, 357–9; Vardan, tr. Thomson, 223; Smpad, tr. Dédéyan, 118; "Table chronologique de Hethoum," *RHC, Ar*, 1:487. There are also accounts of the raid in Bar Hebraeus, 446 (= Ibn al-ʿIbrī, 498–9); Ibn al-Fuwaṭī, 355 (with mistakes). For the locations in Cilicia, see the Gazetteer in Boase, *Cilician Kingdom*, 146–85.

[51] *Rawḍ*, 272; Ibn al-Furāt, MS. Vienna, fol. 114a; Maqrīzī, 1:555; cf. Thorau, *Baybars*, 176.

[52] *Rawḍ*, 281–2; Nuwayrī, MS. 2m, fol. 237b; Ibn al-Furāt, MS. Vienna, fols. 118b, 119a (= ed. Lyons, 1:129–30); Maqrīzī, 1:558–9.

[53] Sunqur and the other Baḥrīs had been languishing in al-Naṣir Yusuf's prison when the Mongols took Aleppo; *Zubda*, fols. 29b, 37a.

would try and asked for a year's grace to go to Abagha's *ordo* to arrange for this.

At some point, Baybars received word from Hetʿum that he had permission to exchange Sunqur for Leon, and Armenian envoys then came bringing a letter from Sunqur. But Hetʿum had now changed his mind about returning the fortresses, thinking that Baybars would be satisfied with Sunqur's return only. The Sultan, however, said he would call the deal off unless he received the fortresses as originally promised. This evidently all happened around the time of the conquest of Antioch (4 Ramaḍān 666/19 May 1268), as Baybars is said to have been at this city at the time, and the subsequent agreement was written up in Ramaḍān 666. Hetʿum saw he had no choice but to assent to Baybars's demands. Perhaps the proximity of Baybars to his kingdom made him fear another Mamluk raid. The final agreement was that six forts would be handed over to the Muslims: Bahasnā (Behesni), al-Darbassāk, Barzamān (written Marzamān), Raʿbān (Raban), al-Zarb (?) and Shīḥ al-Ḥadīd (Sheh).[54] The forts were to be returned with the monies and other supplies that were in them on their capture in 658/1260. Sunqur al-Ashqar would be exchanged for Leon, and other Armenian prisoners were to be returned. Mamluk envoys were sent to swear Hetʿum on this treaty. Armenian hostages arrived until Baybars could gain possession of the fortresses which were subsequently returned. Meanwhile, Leon was brought from Cairo to Syria. Throughout his captivity, he had been well treated and had even hunted with Baybars. Leon was also sworn on the treaty and then sent north (11 Shawwāl 666/24 June 1268). Sunqur and Leon were exchanged across a river near al-Darbassāk, and the Sultan's representatives took over the designated forts.[55]

Baybars was overjoyed at having Sunqur al-Ashqar back, made him a senior amir and part of his inner circle. Al-Yūnīnī reports that Sunqur prevailed on Baybars not to take possession of Bahasnā. Before his return, Hetʿum had requested him to intercede with Baybars regarding this fortress. Dr. Thorau is probably correct in suggesting that this request was based on Hetʿum's fear that his lines of communication (let alone trade) with the Īlkhānid state would be cut, and Bahasnā was needed to keep these open.[56]

Ibn ʿAbd al-Ẓāhir implies that Hetʿum had no trouble convincing Abagha to release Sunqur al-Ashqar. Ibn al-Fuwaṭī, in his concise recountings of the episode, explicitly says the same.[57] Other sources, however, say that the

[54] On these locations, see the Gazetteer cited in n. 50; Thorau, *Baybars*, 212, n. 37. The location of al-Zarb (in Nuwayrī and Ibn al-Furāt [see next note]: *r-w-b*; Ibn Shaddād [*Aʿlāq*, ed. Eddé, 376]: al-Zūb) is unclear, but would seem to be near Marzabān; see Cahen, *Syrie*, 718 ("adh-Dhoub").

[55] *Rawḍ*, 327–9; Nuwayrī, MS. 2m, fols. 188b–189a; Ibn al-Furāt, MS. Vienna, fols. 143a–144b; Maqrīzī, 1:568–70; Yūnīnī, 2:384–5; Thorau, *Baybars*, 193.

[56] *Rawḍ*, 330; Ibn Shaddād, *Aʿlāq*, ed. Eddé, 375; Yūnīnī, 2:385–6; Abū 'l-Fidā', 4:5; Thorau, *Baybars*, 193.

[57] Ibn al-Fuwaṭī, 355–6. The latter version contains many mistakes: the King, and not the son, is called Leon, and this exchange is placed *s.a.* AH 664.

Armenian King had some difficulty obtaining Sunqur. Smpad writes how initially Sunqur could not be found, and that it took some time for him to be located.[58]

A particularly interesting story is told by al-Yūnīnī and other fourteenth-century Syrian writers. Upon receiving Baybars's demand to obtain Sunqur al-Ashqar's release, Hetʿum went to Abagha, secretly taking with him one of the Mamluk envoys, the Baḥrī amir ʿAlam al-Dīn Sulṭān, who was disguised as an Armenian. At the *ordo*, ʿAlam al-Dīn met with Sunqur, who feared a trick. Sunqur was eventually convinced that ʿAlam al-Dīn was really a representative from Baybars, and he agreed to flee from the *ordo*; he was given Armenian clothes and left with Hetʿum. Upon reaching Cilicia, ʿAlam al-Dīn went to Baybars and reported to him what had happened. This led to the exchange of Leon and Sunqur, as described above.[59] It is difficult, however, to accept this story, intriguing as it is. First, there is the problem of reconciling it with the Armenian sources. Secondly, it is hard to accept that Hetʿum, so dependent on Mongol goodwill, would have dared to abscond with a prisoner at the Mongol court, and expect that Abagha would blithely accept this *fait accompli* when he discovered Sunqur's absence.

Sunqur al-Ashqar, who left behind him a Mongol wife and several children,[60] was to play an important role in the events of the coming years, and we will meet him again. Leon, upon his return, went with his father to Abagha, and was recognized as Hetʿum's successor. After their return to Cilicia, Hetʿum abdicated and retired to a monastery, leaving Leon to become king. Hetʿum died in 669/1270, and Leon wrote to announce this to Baybars. Mamluk raids into Cilicia were to begin again in 1271.[61]

The successful conclusion of the negotiations led to a period of parleying between Baybars and Abagha. This, however, was not the first diplomatic contact between the two rulers. As early as 664/1265–6, Abagha had sent his first mission to Baybars, then in Syria. According to Ibn al-Furāt, the envoys brought with them a present and called for peace (*ṣulḥ*). If earlier and subsequent Mongol missions are any indication, this "peace" meant submission to Abagha. Baybars left the Mongol envoys in Damascus, and their fate is not clear.[62]

Early in 667/1268, Hetʿum, still the King of Lesser Armenia, wrote to Baybars, offering to act as an intermediary, both to make peace (*ṣulḥ*) and to intercede on behalf of Sunqur al-Ashqar's children, who had remained with

[58] Grigor, 369–71; Smpad, tr. Dédéyan, 120. Bar Hebraeus, 447 (= Ibn al-ʿIbrī, 499–500), who writes that Abagha promised that Sunqur would be brought from another place; in 1268, he came from Samarqand [!] and was sent to Hetʿum.

[59] Yūnīnī, 2:384–5; Kutubī, 20:361–2; Dhahabī, MS. Laud 279, fol. 6b; Ibn al-Ṣuqāʿī, 85–6. See also *Tuḥfa*, 64. [60] Ibn al-Ṣuqāʿī, 85; see also *Rawḍ*, 339.

[61] Der Nersessian, "Kingdom," 654; Canard, "Arménie," 237.

[62] Ibn al-Furāt, MS. Vienna, fol. 110b; Maqrīzī, 1:553. A somewhat different version is found in Qirtay, fols. 87a–88a.

the Mongols. The Sultan wrote to him that he could deal with the matter of the children, but there was no mention of anything else. The motive of Hetᶜum, whose position had become even weaker with the conquest of Antioch in 666/1268, is obvious enough: he hoped to forestall another Mamluk raid by bringing about an end to hostilities between them and his patrons, the Mongols. Hetᶜum's desperation may have led him to overstep his instructions, in the hope that some kind of negotiations would lead to the end of the conflict. He must have misled Abagha about Baybars's message, because the Īlkhān's response was to call on the Sultan to submit to the Mongols.

Abagha sent, via Cilicia, an official envoy to the Sultan. An amir from Aleppo was ordered to go to Cilicia and bring the envoy to Damascus. The envoy was to be kept in isolation so he could not speak to anyone. Baybars was evidently apprehensive of the corrupting influence of this envoy or of his ability to gather intelligence. The Sultan himself set out with a small entourage from Cairo in Jumādā I 667/January-February 1269.[63] He met the Mongol envoy – or rather envoys as it turned out – in Damascus, who first delivered a truculent verbal message to Baybars:

> When the King Abagha set out from the East, he conquered all the world. Whoever opposed him was killed. If you go up to the sky or down into the ground, you will not be saved from us. The best policy [*maṣlaḥa*] is that you will make peace [*ṣulḥ*] between us. You are a mamluk who was bought in Sīwās. How do you rebel against the kings of the earth?[64]

Thereupon a letter was handed over, which had been written in Baghdad on 20 Rabīᶜ II 667/29 December 1268. This message left no doubts regarding Abagha's intentions *vis-à-vis* the Mamluks: Abagha understood that the Mamluks wanted to submit (*yaṣīrū īl*) and to admit that it was only Qutuz who had killed the Mongol envoys (in 658/1260). He also knew that they wanted the return of the Qipchaqs (i.e. Baḥrīs) still with him. Previously, there had been a conflict between the Mongols, and this was the reason why he had been unable to ride against the Mamluks. But now, all are agreed that the command and regulation (*farmān wa-yāsāh*) of the Qa'an should not be changed.[65] Abagha thought highly of the Sultan's willingness to submit, and restated that Baybars was not responsible for Qutuz's crimes. If Baybars was true to what

[63] *Rawḍ*, 339; Ibn al-Furāt, MS. Vienna, fol. 152b. These negotiations and the letters which were exchanged are discussed in detail in R. Amitai-Preiss, "An Exchange of Letters in Arabic between Abaγa Īlkhān and Sultan Baybars (AH 667/AD 1268–9)," *CAJ*, 38 (1994): 11–33.

[64] Yūnīnī, 2:407; Dhahabī, MS. Laud 279, fol. 7a; Kutubī, 20:378; Ibn Kathīr, 13:254; Ibn al-Dawādārī, 8:139–40; Ibn Taghrī Birdī, 7:144–5; Maqrīzī, 1:573–4. It is possible to see this message (*risāla*) as a second version of the next letter, but in Amitai-Preiss, "Exchange of Letters," 32, this possibility is discussed and rejected. With the exception of Maqrīzī, these sources tell that the Mongols' envoys were called Majd al-Dīn Dawlat Khān ibn Jāqir and Sayf al-Dīn Saᶜīd Turjumān, names which are also given by sources for the Mongol envoys of 670/1272 (see below); different names are given in the text of the letter.

[65] It should be mentioned that Abagha's claim of newly founded Mongol unity was perhaps only wishful thinking on his part; see above, ch. 4, p. 89.

he said, suitable respresentatives (for example, from among his sons or senior amirs) should be sent so they would hear the order and regulations (*yarligh wa-yāsāt*) of the Qa'an; these envoys would then be sent back. Upon the acceptance of such an agreement, the Baḥrīs would be released. On the other hand, if Baybars were not true to his word and refused to submit, then God would know of this (the warning is implicit). The letter concludes with the name of the two envoys with whom it was sent: Bīk Ṭūt (= Bektüt) and Abū 'l-Gharīb. Here the source contradicts itself, because previously it stated that only one envoy arrived.[66]

Baybars's reply, according to Ibn ʿAbd al-Ẓāhir, begins with a disclaimer that the Armenian King had no right to deal with any other matter except that concerning Sunqur al-Ashqar's children. In any event, his intercession led to no discernible results. The question of the murder of the Mongol envoys by Qutuz is skirted by claiming that Abagha's envoys would be returned safely. Then comes a particularly important passage: "How can agreement be achieved [between us]? The *yasa* [here, it would seem, referring to a law code, evidently to the *Sharīʿa*] that we have today is greater than the *yasa* of Chinggis Khan. Allah has given us rule over 40 kings."[67] As for Mongol claims of world domination, Abagha is reminded of Ketbugha's defeat (at ʿAyn Jālūt). If Abagha had done what he had told Sunqur al-Ashqar he would do and sent one of his brothers, sons or great amirs, then Baybars would have done the same, as Abagha had requested.[68]

Another version of Baybars's response exists, in which he wrote to Abagha, calling on him to abandon the territories conquered by the Mongols in Iraq, the Jazīra and Rūm. Certain writers add that Baybars swore that he would continue fighting until he liberated all the lands of the Caliph. He then sent the envoys back.[69] Neither version had any further information on the envoys' fate.

It is clear from both Abagha's verbal and written message that for the Mongol the idea of "peace" still meant unconditional surrender, and Abagha is still talking in terms of world conquest. As is seen in the two versions of Baybars's reply, the Sultan found this unacceptable, and believed he had the power to resist. Thus, he sent a militant answer and did not bother to send his own envoys to Abagha. At this point, and for several decades to come, there was no possibility for compromise and real peace.[70]

Mongol raids across the border

The year after the unsuccessful negotiations of 667/1269, the Mongols began increasing the tension on the border and in north Syria. Abagha was surely

[66] *Rawḍ*, 339; Ibn al-Furāt, MS. Vienna, fol. 152b; ʿAynī, fol. 99a. Cf. the shorter version in *Ḥusn*, 144–5. [67] This passage is analyzed in Ayalon, "Yāsa," pt. C2, 129–30.

[68] *Rawḍ*, 341–2; Ibn al-Furāt, MS. Vienna, fols. 153b–154a; ʿAynī, fol. 99a.

[69] See the sources cited in n. 64 above, except for Maqrīzī. [70] Cf. Thorau, *Baybars*, 197.

influenced by his ongoing contacts with Western princes and there was also a lull (after 668/1270) in his conflicts with other Mongol rulers. These years also saw the increase, both in frequency and scale, of Mamluk raids across the border.

Not that the years 664–7/1265–9 were devoid of examples of Mongol–Mamluk enmity. In early spring 665/1267, Baybars, who was at Safad overseeing repairs to the fort, received word that the Mongols had attacked al-Raḥba. He rushed to Damascus and began making preparations for an expedition. Then word came that the Mongols had withdrawn and the forces there had chased after them, inflicting casualties and taking captives. It is unclear what prompted the Mongols to retreat; evidently, they had only a small force and it was beaten off by the local garrison. Baybars thereupon returned to Safad.[71]

About a year later, Baybars, then on a hunting trip in Egypt, received word that a Mongol force was heading for Aleppo. He returned to Cairo, and set out for Syria on 1 Jumādā II 666/17 February 1268. Nothing more is heard of the Mongols, and Dr. Thorau seems to be right in suggesting that this "news" of a Mongol attack was just an excuse to get out the troops and keep his real intentions *vis-à-vis* the Franks a secret.[72] In the subsequent campaign, Baybars took Jaffa (and destroyed it), Shaqīf Arnūn (Beaufort) and raided Tripoli. From there, he moved to Antioch, which he conquered on 4 Ramaḍān/19 May; its population was subjected to a terrible bloodbath. As seen above, Prince Bohemond VI, then at Tripoli, had been a firm supporter of the Mongols both before and after their invasion of Syria in 658/1260. Yet this Prince, for all his allegiance to the Mongols, was to learn that they were in no position to assist him when he was in trouble. In the aftermath of the conquest of Antioch, a number of Frankish castles in northern Syria were abandoned by their garrisons; the most important of these was the Templar fortress of Baghrās (Gaston).[73]

In 667/1268–9, raiders (*ghayyāra*) from al-Bīra and elsewhere struck in the region of Karkar (Gargar, in the northern Jazīra) and burned the town. The Mamluk troops overran Sharmūshāk, a castle between Karkar and Kakhtā, and killed its garrison. It is unclear if these were Mongols or local subject troops. Many peasants were brought back to Syria and settled in the regions of Homs, Shayzar and Antioch.[74]

71 *Rawḍ*, 280; Ibn al-Furāt, MS. Vienna, fol. 118a (= ed. Lyons, 1:128), who makes some changes; Maqrīzī, 1:558; *Ḥusn*, 120; Abū 'l-Fidā', 4:4. Cf. Yūnīnī, 2:361; Kutubī, 20:349, who write that the Mongols attacked al-Bīra at this time.

72 *Rawḍ*, 291–2; *Ḥusn*, 125; Ibn al-Furāt, MS. Vienna, fols. 126b–127a (= ed. Lyons, 1:133); Maqrīzī, 1:564; Thorau, *Baybars*, 187.

73 For these campaigns, see: Thorau, *Baybars*, pp. 187–92; Runciman, *Crusades*, 3:324–6; Prawer, *Histoire*, 2:476–85. On the Templar presence on the Cilician–Syrian border, and their fortress at Baghrās, see the articles by Lawrence and Riley-Smith in Boase, *Cilician Kingdom*, 34–83, 92–117.

74 *Rawḍ*, 351; *Tuḥfa*, 66; Ibn al-Furāt, MS. Vienna, fol. 158b; Maqrīzī, 1:579; *Ḥusn*, 146, who calls this castle Shumayṣāṭ.

At the end of this year, Baybars decided to perform the pilgrimage to Mecca, although he kept his intentions secret. This covertness is not unusual, since concealment of plans and movements was standard practice for Baybars throughout his reign.[75] In order to hide his true intentions, Baybars, then in Syria, called the *amīr al-ᶜurbān* ᶜĪsā b. Muhannā, told him that he planned to attack Iraq, and ordered him to make the necessary preparations. ᶜĪsā subsequently heard that the Sultan had gone to the Ḥijāz, having waited all this time in the expectation of taking part in an expedition and gaining booty.

While Baybars was on his way to Mecca, a group of Mongol raiders was riding to the Ḥijāz. "They intended thus to reconnoitre the roads and to loot those areas ... With [these raiders] were a group of Mongols [*al-mughul*] who did not recognize Allāh and his sanctuary ... Their aim was to spill the blood of the pilgrims in the sanctuary." When these raiders, however, heard of the Sultan's approach, they panicked and turned back. Supposedly, Baybars already knew of their plan even before he set out for the Ḥijāz, and was hoping for the opportunity to combine the commandments of holy war and pilgrimage.[76] This might well be, because – as will be seen in chapter 6 – the Sultan operated an effective intelligence network among the Mongols. In addition, it would seem to be more than coincidental that he set out in the same year the Mongols were planning a raid on Mecca during the pilgrimage season.

All of these raids were relatively modest affairs. The Mongol raid of 668/1269 was, however, a more serious matter. Shāfiᶜ b. ᶜAlī writes that due to his intelligence operatives Baybars knew in advance of an impending attack on the fringes of his kingdom around this time. In the fall of that year, Baybars, then near Alexandria, received word that the Mongols had coordinated plans with the Franks of the coast, and had raided Sājūr near Aleppo, looting livestock from the local bedouin. This was soon after the arrival of the remnants of the Aragonese crusade at Acre at the end of October 1269. The Mongols were led by Samaghar, the Mongol commander in Rūm. The Sultan returned to the capital, and sent out Aydegin al-Bunduqdār[77] with an advance force to wait at the border of Syria. He himself set out with a small force on 21 Rabīᶜ I/18 November and arrived in Damascus on 7 Rabīᶜ II/4 December, after a particularly difficult march due to poor weather. At Damascus, he heard that the Mongols had withdrawn when they heard of his approach.[78]

The following year (669/1270–1), there are no recorded Mongol–Mamluk incidents. Learning that Louis IX of France had taken his crusade to Tunis

[75] See the comments in Khowaiter, *Baibars*, 38–9.

[76] *Rawḍ*, 354–8; Ibn al-Furāt, MS. Vienna, fols. 160a, 175b; cf. Maqrīzī, 1:580–2, who does not mention Mongol raiders; *Ḥusn*, 146, writes that these were Mongols and Tatars (*min al-mughul wa'l-tatār*) from Baghdad.

[77] This amir had the distinction of being Baybars's first patron (*ustādh*), before al-Ṣāliḥ Ayyūb gained possession of him; Thorau, *Baybars*, 28–9.

[78] *Ḥusn*, 150; *Rawḍ*, 361–2; Nuwayrī, MS. 2m, fol. 194b; Ibn al-Furāt, MS. Vienna, fol. 179a–b (= ed. Lyons, 1:172); Maqrīzī, 1:584; ᶜAynī, fol. 100a; Thorau, *Baybars*, 200–1. On the Aragonese crusade, see ch. 4, pp. 96–8.

and died there, Baybars felt free to apply himself to his ongoing project of conquering Frankish castles and cities. In short order, he took Ṣāfīthā/Ṣāfītā (Chastel Blanc, of the Templars), Ḥiṣn al-Akrād (Crac des Chevaliers, of the Hospitallers), Ḥiṣn ᶜAkkār (Gibelacar, also of the Hospitallers) and al-Qurayn (Montfort, headquarters of the Teutonic Knights), plus several minor fortified points, thus dealing a blow to all three military orders. The Sultan had planned to attack Tripoli, but he then received news of the arrival of Prince Edward of England at Acre in the spring of 669/1271, at the head of a body of troops. He thought it wise to conclude a truce with Bohemond VI, Count of Tripoli and now titular Prince of Antioch. He was also nonplussed by the arrival of Hugh of Lusignan, King of Cyprus, at Acre at the head of a large force. In order to divert him back to Cyprus, Baybars sent out a flotilla to attack Limassol. This attack, however, was a total failure and most of the ships ran aground off the coast of Cyprus and their crews were captured.[79]

Samaghar, together with the Pervāne, Muᶜīn al-Dīn Sulaymān (the strong-man in Seljuq Rūm), returned to north Syria in mid-Rabīᶜ I 670/ca. 20 October 1271. This attack, initiated at Abagha's express order, was to some degree coordinated with the Franks of Acre. Soon after his arrival, Edward had sent envoys to Abagha, who wrote back promising to send Samaghar at the head of a "mighty force." In reality, this force seems to have been relatively modest in size. Initial reports spoke of how the Mongols had raided ᶜAyn Tāb and were on their way to ᶜAmuq al-Ḥārim. Baybars, who was in Damascus, having just completed an inspection tour in north Syria, responded immediately. He seems to have had advance knowledge of some type of Mongol offensive, as well as Frankish preparations for war. He first wrote to Egypt and ordered Baysari to come to Syria with 3000 troops. Baybars waited until Baysari arrived on 4 Rabīᶜ II/9 November, and set out from Damascus with the forces at his disposal. Meanwhile, the Mongols raided Ḥārim and al-Rūj (to the west of Aleppo), killing many people. Al-Yūnīnī and others write that the total Mongol force numbered 10,000 Mongols (*al-mughul*) and Rūmīs. At Marᶜash, Samaghar and the Pervāne halted with the majority of their army, and sent ahead a force of 1500 elite troops (*min aᶜyānihim* or *min akābir al-mughul*) to reconnoiter and raid. After reaching ᶜAyn Tāb, the advance force went to Qasṭūn, in the region of al-Rūj. Between Antioch and Ḥārim, they fell upon a group of Türkmen and devastated them.

At Hama, Baybars met up with al-Manṣūr and the Aleppan army which had fallen back upon the approach of the Mongols. Baybars had ordered the flight of the population of north and central Syria, including Damascus, in order to encourage the Mongols to penetrate further into the country, so he could better deal with them. From Hama, he dispatched forces in different directions to put pressure on the Mongols and act as diversions. One, led by Shams al-Dīn Aq Sunqur al-Fāriqānī and including a group of bedouin, went to

[79] Thorau, *Baybars*, 203–9; Runciman, *Crusades*, 3:333–5; Prawer, *Histoire*, 2:487–503.

Mar^cash. They did not succeed in getting there in time to make contact with the main Mongol army. The second force, under Taybars al-Wazīrī and ᶜĪsā b. Muhannā, crossed the Euphrates and raided Ḥarrān and al-Ruhā (Edessa). Meanwhile, the Sultan continued north. He sent out scouts (*kashshāfa*) and "burners" (*munawwirūn*). The latter term probably refers to the operatives whose job it was to burn grasslands.[80] At some point, the Mongols, aware of the approach of a large Mamluk force, withdrew from Syria. Baybars continued on to Aleppo, reaching it on 18 Rabīᶜ 670/23 November 1271.[81] Thus ended the one real attempt to launch a concerted Mongol–Frankish campaign against the Mamluks.

Meanwhile, the force under Taybars and ᶜĪsā had reached Ḥarrān. Because of its exposed position, and the depredations perpetrated on the city by bedouins loyal to Baybars, much of the population had already fled Ḥarrān in the preceding years, to both the Jazīra and Syria.[82] The Mongol garrison there was quite modest, some sixty troops. They set out on hearing of the approach of the Mamluk force, and first encountered ᶜĪsā's bedouins. Thereupon Taybars's troops appeared on the scene, and the Mongols surrendered. Taybars continued on to Ḥarrān. On 26 Rabīᶜ II 670/1 December 1271, its notables came out to make their surrender. Taybars called on the Mongol *shaḥna* to submit, but he barricaded himself in one of the towers, saying that he would only surrender to the Sultan in person. Taybars left without entering the city and returned to Syria. He was followed by the notables of the city.[83] At the end of Ramaḍān (end of April 1272), a group of Mongols came to the city, destroyed the mosque, part of the walls, much of the market and many houses. Upon leaving, the Mongols forced the remaining population to go with them. Ḥarrān was left desolate and uninhabited. Ibn Shaddād writes that the Mongols had seen that they could not defend the city and thus decided that it was best left destroyed.[84]

After returning from Aleppo, Baybars planned to raid Acre, so as to punish the Franks for their activities while he was preoccupied with the Mongols in north Syria. He set out for Acre, but unusually severe weather dissuaded him, and he returned to Egypt. It was there that Baybars heard in Rajab of this year

80 See ch. 9.

81 For Edward's arrival in Acre and his contact with Abagha, see ch. 4. The above account of the Mongol raid is based on a conflation of two groups of sources. The first: *Rawḍ*, 395–7; whence, *Zubda*, fol. 76a–b; Ibn al-Furāt, MS. Vienna, fols. 202a–203a; Maqrīzī, 1:599–600. The second: Yūnīnī, 2:467–8; Mufaḍḍal, 203–4; Ibn al-Dawādārī, 8:164–5; Kutubī, 20:417–18; Dhahabī, MS. Laud 279, fol. 9b. For a Frankish account of this raid, see: "Eracles," *RHC, Occ*, 2:461.

82 Ibn Shaddād, *Aᶜlāq*, 3:62. In 667/1268–9, much of the population, including the young Ibn Taymiyya, fled to Syria; Kutubī, 20:379; Ibn Kathīr, 13:255.

83 Ibn Shaddād, *Aᶜlāq*, 3:62–3; Yūnīnī, 2:468–9; Mufaḍḍal, 205–7; Kutubī, 20:418–19; Ibn al-Dawādārī, 8:166.

84 Ibn Shaddād, *Aᶜlāq*, 3:63; *idem*, *Ta'rīkh*, 33; Yūnīnī, 2:471; Mufaḍḍal, 206–7; Ibn al-Dawādārī, 8:167–8.

(2 February-2 March 1272) of another Mongol advance towards Syria. Baybars, however, left Cairo only on 3 Shaᶜbān/5 March. In Palestine, negotiations commenced between the Sultan and the Franks, which led to the signing on 21 Ramaḍān 670/21 April 1272 of a peace treaty with the Kingdom of Jerusalem, for a period of ten years and ten months.[85] The conclusion of this treaty did not prevent Baybars from trying to assassinate Edward of England less than two months later.[86]

The Franks received relatively good terms from the Sultan, probably because he wanted to secure that front so as to be able to devote his full attention to the danger from the Mongols. For the time being, however, no more is heard of an expected Mongol raid. Instead, the Sultan received word that Mongol envoys had arrived in Damascus, and he himself reached there on 8 Shawwāl/8 May. These envoys represented Samaghar and the Pervāne, each having sent their own envoy, and their names were given as Majd al-Dīn Dawlat Khān and Saᶜd al-Dīn Saᶜīd al-Turjumān.[87] According to Ibn ᶜAbd al-Ẓāhir, Samaghar and the Pervāne sent these envoys in response to a letter which Baybars had sent them. Having delivered a verbal message, they delivered a letter, the upshot of which was their desire for peace (*ṣulḥ*) and the request that Baybars would send envoys. Ibn Shaddād relates a different message: after greeting him, Samaghar Noyan complains that since becoming his neighbor, Baybars has not sent to him on any matter. If he had done so, Samaghar would have obeyed (*muṭāwiᶜan*). Samaghar then suggested that Baybars send a letter to Abagha, and he will help the Sultan reach his goal. According to both authors, Baybars responded by dispatching two amirs, Mubāriz al-Dīn al-Ṭūrī Amīr Ṭabar ("hatchet bearer") and Fakhr al-Dīn Ayaz al-Muqrī al-Ḥājib ("chamberlain"), who set off in the middle of Shawwāl/15 May. It seems that these "Mongol" envoys had been sent on the private initiative of Samaghar and the Pervāne, and that Abagha was still in the dark regarding this *démarche*. Passing through Cilicia, the Mamluk envoys paid a visit to King Leon, and then continued on to Rūm, where they consecutively met with Samaghar and the Pervāne. Each received gifts from the Sultan. The envoys, together with the Pervāne, continued on to Abagha, to whom they gave a number of presents.

Ibn ᶜAbd al-Ẓāhir writes that Mubāriz al-Dīn told the Īlkhān: "The Sultan greets you, and says that the envoys of Möngke Temür (Khan of the Golden Horde) have come to him several times so that the Sultan should attack [Abagha's territory] from his side, and King Möngke Temür will attack from his side. Wherever the horses of the Sultan reach, that [land] is his, and wherever

85 Thorau, *Baybars*, 209–10; *Rawḍ*, 397–9; Ibn al-Furāt, MS. Vienna, fols. 203b–204a (= ed. Lyons, 1:199–200); Maqrīzī, 1:601.

86 Thorau, *Baybars*, 221–2; Riley-Smith, in Ibn al-Furāt, ed. Lyons, 2:244; cf. Runciman, *Crusades*, 3:337–8.

87 These were also the names that Yūnīnī and others gave for the Mongol envoys in AH 667; see above.

the horses of Möngke Temür reach, that is his." Abagha – so it is reported – was greatly disturbed at what he heard, and promptly left the assembly. Again, Ibn Shaddād offers a different version: Abagha asked the envoys what they wanted. They replied that Samaghar had sent to the Sultan that Abagha would be pleased if an envoy were sent to him. The Sultan sent the envoys to tell Abagha that if "you want us to be obedient [*muṭāwiʿan*] to you, and to desist from [attacking] you, then give up what you have of the Muslim lands." The Īlkhān responded to this by saying that this was not possible, and at least each ruler should keep what he had. The source adds that Abagha spoke rudely to the envoy and – not surprisingly – no agreement came about. In both versions, the envoys were allowed to return and they eventually made their way back to the Sultanate, arriving in Damascus on 15 Ṣafar 671/11 September 1272.[88]

Dr. Thorau is probably correct in preferring Ibn Shaddād's version to that of Ibn ʿAbd al-Ẓāhir, who evidently was trying to extol Baybars's power by showing that Abagha was extremely disconcerted by the Sultan's bellicose letter. Likewise, Dr. Thorau rightly judges that Baybars's provocative message – in both its versions – shows he was not really interested in successful negotiations. It is misleading, however, to speak of "Baybars's wish to strengthen his negotiating position out of fear" [it is not clear of what exactly] and to imply that now the Sultan, "having no longer anything to fear from the Christians," was not interested in making peace and wanted to provoke Abagha.[89] There is no discernible change here from Baybars's previous messages to the Īlkhānids, or his public thoughts on the subject. At this point, as before, no compromise would have been possible. Abagha had not given up the Mongol imperial ideal of manifest destiny, and the memory of the defeat of ʿAyn Jālūt was still fresh. On the other hand, publicly at least, Baybars proclaimed his desire to liberate the Caliphal lands and to return the Caliph to his capital.

At the beginning of 671/early August 1272, Baybars was in Damascus. Reports had been coming in about a Mongol attack. Meanwhile, his envoys to Abagha had yet to return. After consulting with the amirs, Baybars decided to go back to Egypt to prepare the army there for an expedition to Syria. Keeping his exact whereabouts a secret, Baybars arrived in Cairo via the *barīd* on 13 Muḥarram/10 August. The Egyptian army set out on 27 Muḥarram/24 August, and the Sultan left for Syria two days later, arriving in Damascus on 2 Ṣafar/29 August. For the time being, no more was heard of the expected Mongol offensive, but during the month of Ṣafar (which ended 25 September), news of the approaching envoys from Abagha and Rūm reached the Sultan. He sent orders that they should perform three genuflections (*yaḍribū al-jūk*), a Mongol custom showing subservience, before the governor of Aleppo and al-Manṣūr of Hama. Thereupon, these envoys were brought to Damascus.

[88] *Rawḍ*, 399–400; Nuwayrī, MS. 2m, fol. 203a; Ibn al-Furāt, MS. Vienna, fol. 204a–b; Maqrīzī, 1:602. Second version: Ibn Shaddād, *Ta'rīkh*, 34–5; Yūnīnī, 2:471–2, Dhahabī, MS. Laud, 279, fol. 10a; Kutubī, 20:421. [89] Thorau, *Baybars*, 220–1 and 243 n. 2.

Initially, they delivered a verbal message to the Mamluk amirs: "What injury comes from peace [*ṣulḥ*], and what advantage comes from hostility? [Abagha] says that the Sultan should send Sunqur al-Ashqar to act as an intermediary between us to [achieve] the peace [*ṣulḥ*]." At a subsequent meeting, however, the envoys became more demanding: "Abagha says that the Sultan or whoever follows him in rank should come to Abagha for the sake of the *ṣulḥ*." Baybars certainly had no illusions what was meant by *ṣulḥ* in Abagha's lexicon, i.e. acceptance of Mongol suzerainty. He answered, that if Abagha meant peace then he or one of his brothers should come. That was the end of negotiations. The Mongol envoys were sent back in the following month.[90]

What was the point, then, of exchanging envoys, if there was no chance of real negotiations? The answer must be that this was part of the psychological warfare waged by both sides. Each ruler was trying to intimidate his opponent. The mutual bluster must have also been designed for home consumption, at least for the military elite of both kingdoms, demonstrating the rulers' resolution and disdain for the enemy. I cannot agree with Professor Cahen that Abagha initiated these negotiations in order to seek "a peace settlement that would allow the internal re-organization of the war-devastated territories he governed."[91] It has been seen that the first initiative came from Samaghar and the Pervāne in Rūm. Secondly, Abagha's message is not at all conciliatory. Thirdly, had it been important to Abagha to devote himself to reorganization, he could have desisted from attacking Syria, thus significantly lessening tension, and perhaps achieving even a *de facto* peace. It can be admitted, however, that the possibility does exist that Abagha may have feared that an inactive policy on his part might have encouraged aggression by Baybars.

More sparring on the border

Soon after the return of the Mongol envoys, the Mongols attacked al-Bīra and put it under siege. We have three independent contemporary sources for this Mongol offensive and the Mamluk counter-attack: Ibn ʿAbd al-Ẓāhir, Ibn Shaddād and Baybars al-Manṣūrī. The last mentioned author actually participated in the campaign. There are no major disagreements between the sources, although they differ on details. In addition, Waṣṣāf has left us with an account of the battle written from a Mongol perspective, which only very roughly agrees with the Mamluk sources.

On 5 Jumādā I 671/28 November 1272,[92] Baybars received word in Damascus that the Mongols were heading for al-Bīra. Baybars set out for the north with the army, including large forces from Egypt, which had been

[90] *Rawḍ*, 403–4; *Zubda*, fols. 77b–78a; Ibn al-Furāt, MS. Vienna, fol. 213a–b; Maqrīzī, 1:605 (shorter, confused version); cf. also Nuwayrī, MS. 2m, fol. 205a; Thorau, *Baybars*, 221. On the *jūk* (< Mongolian *chuk*), see Dozy, 1:235b; note in Rashīd al-Dīn, ed. Quatremère, pp. 322–3 n. 121; *TMEN*, 3:120 (no. 1141).

[91] C. Cahen, *Pre-Ottoman Turkey*, tr. J. Jones-Williams (London, 1968), 285.

[92] On this date, see Thorau, *Baybars*, 244 n. 14.

ordered to Syria earlier in the year. One force, under Fakhr al-Dīn Altunba al-Ḥimṣī, was sent to Ḥārim, while another, commanded by Taybars al-Wazīrī and including bedouins, was dispatched in an unspecified direction; since the latter eventually rejoined the main army, he was probably sent as an advance guard towards al-Bīra. Baybars went via Hama, collecting boats there to facilitate his crossing of the Euphrates. Passing through the region of Aleppo, he sent ahead mamluks and bedouin to scout. At Manbij, they returned to him, and reported that some 3000 Mongols were on the east bank of the Euphrates. The Sultan continued on to the Euphrates, reaching it on 18 Jumādā I/11 December.

The total Mongol force was under the command of Durbai, who had commanded the earlier Mongol attack at al-Bīra in 663/1264. He himself conducted the siege of the castle. The Mongol force included a contingent from Seljuq Rūm (some 3000 troops).[93] To prosecute the siege, mangonels and other siege machines were erected. The force at the river was commanded by Chinqar, who reportedly had 5000 men. The Mongols had prepared themselves well for the arrival of Mamluk troops. First, they took up position at a difficult ford, hoping that the Mamluks would think that it was a shallow one and so attempt their crossing there. The exact position of this ford in relation to al-Bīra is not clear, although, as seen below, it was not within eyesight. In addition, the Mongols constructed a palisade (*sibe*) and positioned themselves behind it, planning to fight dismounted with bows and arrows.

The stratagem worked, and the Mamluks did cross at the more difficult ford. First, Baybars sent foot archers (*al-rajjāla al-uqjiyya*) in boats to scout out the terrain on the east bank. The Mamluk army then crossed the river. The depth of the water obliged the troops to swim, holding their horses' reins. There is some disagreement about which amirs (and their private units of mamluks) were the first into the river, and thus the first to encounter the enemy on the other side. All agree, however, that Qalawun was in the first wave.[94] The Sultan followed behind this vanguard. Once the Mamluk troops began to climb up onto the east bank, fierce hand-to-hand fighting ensued. Eventually the Mongols were defeated, in spite of their advantageous position. Chinqar himself was killed during the fighting – according to Baybars al-Manṣūrī – by Ketbugha al-Manṣūrī, the future sultan. Some 200 Mongols were captured. When the main Mongol force under Durbai at al-Bīra learned of how the Mamluks had defeated the corps at the river, it fled, abandoning the mangonels and other equipment. The Mongols had reportedly been on the verge of taking the fort. There is some disagreement in the sources about Baybars's subsequent actions, but it seems that for some reason he returned to the west bank of the Euphrates; only four days later did he recross the river and

[93] Ibn Shaddād gives a list of non-Mongol amirs, mostly Rūmīs, serving in the battle.
[94] Thorau, *Baybars*, 244 n. 15.

go to the fort. Meanwhile, Baysari had been pursuing the Mongols from the ford up to Sarūj (between al-Bīra and Ḥarrān). At the fort, its governor and defenders were rewarded by Baybars, who thereupon set back for Damascus, reaching it on 3 Jumādā II/26 December 1272.[95]

It is interesting to compare the above account with Waṣṣāf's version of the battle: after al-Bīra was put under siege by a Mongol army, its inhabitants sent calls for help by pigeon to Hama and Homs and from there to Cairo. Baybars wrote to the defenders to be firm and promised that his army would be at al-Bīra within seven days. If not, they were allowed to surrender. Baybars rode ahead of his army accompanied by only seven *ghulāms*, which can presumably be understood to mean mamluks. Riding on postal horses (*marākib-i yām*), he reached al-Bīra in four days. There he was joined by 200 horsemen from Hama. He went up a small hill on the Syrian bank of the Euphrates, and set out his banners; the people of al-Bīra were overjoyed. About twelve days later, the Egyptian army came and threw themselves into the river. Thereupon, the Mongols fled, having seen the boldness of their enemy and their own distress, even though their army was twice the size of the Sultan's force. The Egyptians then took much booty.[96] Waṣṣāf skips several important details that he should have known, such as the fighting at the ford, while inserting information in other places which contradicts the evidence in the Mamluk sources. Again, Waṣṣāf shows himself to be a less than credible source for Mamluk–Īlkhānid relations. In passing, it should be observed that this appears to be the one mention by a Persian source of an occurrence in the border war during Baybars's reign.

Had the Mongol expedition to take al-Bīra been successful, Abagha would have secured a bridgehead in Mamluk territory, and been in a better position to launch an invasion of Syria when he chose. Needless to say, he was angry at the results. When Durbai appeared, the Īlkhān rebuked and reviled him, asking him how it was that he had fled unwounded while his comrade Chinqar had been killed. Durbai was exiled and his command given to Abtai.[97]

Late in AH 671 (ca. early July 1273), Baybars ordered the governor of Aleppo, Ḥusām al-Dīn Lachin al-ʿAyntābī to attack Kaynūk. This Armenian fortress, also called Ḥadath al-Ḥamrā', was situated to the northeast of Marʿash, on the bank of the Aq Su River. It has been suggested that this location is at the present-day Başpınar, in the area of Gölbaşı in modern Turkey. The inhabi-

95 *Rawḍ*, 405–8; Ibn Shaddād, *Ta'rīkh*, 55–7; *Zubda*, fols. 78b–79a; *Tuḥfa*, 75–6; Ibn al-Furāt, MS. Vienna, fols. 214a–215b (quotes both *Rawḍ* and *Zubda*); Maqrīzī, 1:606–7; Nuwayrī, MS. 2m, fols. 251b–252a (a condensed version of *Rawḍ*); Qirtay, fol. 99a–b, gives information derived from Ibn Shaddād's account of the raid of AH 674, but places it under this year. The other Mamluk sources that I checked were based on Ibn Shaddād, e.g.: Yūnīnī, 3:2–3; Mufaḍḍal, 212–14; Ibn Taghrī Birdī, 7:158–9. Cf. Thorau, *Baybars*, 223–4; Spuler, *Iran*, 65.

96 Waṣṣāf, 87–8; cf. Āyatī, 54–5. The latter corrects the mistaken date in Waṣṣāf, who writes that this was in AH 679.

97 *Zubda*, fol. 79a; *Tuḥfa*, 76; Ibn al-Furāt, MS. Vienna, fol. 215a–b.

tants of Kaynūk were guilty of attacking both merchants and agents (*quṣṣād*) going to and from Syria. These Armenians would wear Mongol hats (*sarāqū-jāt*) in order to disguise themselves and attack caravans. Baybars had first sent to the Armenian King to force them to desist, but to no avail, so he dispatched an expedition. Lachin reached the fort on 3 Muḥarram 672/20 July 1273, and took both the town and the citadel. The men were massacred and the women and children taken into captivity. From there, Lachin continued on to "Ṭarsūs". Canard has suggested that this is not Tarse, but rather Trush, near the confluence of the Euphrates and the Gök Su, an identification which certainly makes sense from a geographical point of view. This attack did not result in the permanent occupation of Kaynūk, but it is unclear if the town was eventually resettled by Armenians or others.[98]

Bar Hebraeus may be referring to this raid, when he writes that in the summer of 1273, "robber bands from Syria," setting out from al-Bīra and ʿAyn Tāb, raided a town called "Ḳlâwdyâ" (= Qalawdhiya, on the Euphrates, some 50 km to the southeast of Malaṭya). According to him, the raid was quick and many captives were taken. The raiders hurried back to their country out of fear of the Mongols.[99]

Around this time, reports of another Mongol advance reached Baybars in Cairo. In response, the Sultan set out with several amirs on 26 Muḥarram 672/11 August 1273. While he was riding, additional news of a Mongol offensive reached him. The Sultan then sent an order that the entire Egyptian army was to set out, together – according to Ibn ʿAbd al-Ẓāhir – with the Egyptian bedouins (*ʿurbān*). This appears to be the first and only time that Egyptian nomads were explicitly called to take part in an anti-Mongol campaign. Whether they actually participated in the campaign is a different matter. Baybars must have taken quite seriously the prospect of a Mongol offensive, because he also allegedly ordered that everyone in his kingdom owning a horse was to show up, and every village in Syria was to send out horsemen (*khayyāla*) according to its capability. It is questionable, however, whether Baybars really wanted the assistance of such a ragtag force, including the bedouin of Egypt. I would hazard the guess that Ibn ʿAbd al-Ẓāhir is guilty here of some hyperbole, and what he is essentially saying is that Baybars ordered a general call-up of all the soldiers of the kingdom. In any case, we hear no more of a Mongol danger at this point. The Egyptian army reached Jaffa, where it was met by the Sultan, who had ridden on to Damascus before turning back to meet his troops.[100]

98 *Rawḍ*, 417, 432; Ibn al-Furāt, 7:2; *Ḥusn*, 152; *Zubda*, fol. 80b; Nuwayrī, MS. 2m, fol. 252a; Canard, "Arménie," 237–8 and n. 81, 243; Thorau, *Baybars*, 232–3. Ibn al-Furāt, MS. Vienna, fol. 219a (and whence Maqrīzī, 1:608) also mistakenly reports this incident s.a. 671. On the location of Kaynūk, see Sinclair, *Eastern Turkey*, 3:76–9; S. Ory, "al-Ḥadath," *EI*², 3:19–20.

99 Bar Hebraeus, 450; not in Arabic version. On Qalawdhiya, see Yāqūt, *Muʿjam al-buldān*, ed. F. Wüstenfeld (Leipzig, 1866–73), 4:167.

100 *Rawḍ*, 420–1; Ibn al-Furāt, 7:3; Maqrīzī, 1:610; Ibn Shaddād, *Ta'rīkh*, 71–2; Yūnīnī, 3:31–2; Mufaḍḍal, 217–18; Nuwayrī, MS. 2m, fol. 207b, who conflates Ibn Shaddād and Ibn ʿAbd al-Ẓāhir.

According to Ibn ᶜAbd al-Ẓāhir, later in the year there was still news of a Mongol advance of some kind. Baybars had in the meanwhile returned to Egypt. Probably to reconnoiter and act as a diversion, he ordered ᶜĪsā b. Muhannā to lead his tribesmen in a raid across the Euphrates. They reached al-Anbār, and encountered a group of Mongols there. The Mongols, however, withdrew without fighting, thinking – so we are told – that the Sultan himself was at the head of the raiders. ᶜĪsā did, however, manage to engage a group of Khafāja bedouins, and fought them for half a day, on 18 Shaᶜbān/10 March 1274. The fighting seems to have been inconclusive.[101]

In the memorandum to the second Council of Lyon in AD 1274, it was claimed that in 1273 Abagha had planned an offensive against the infidels of Egypt. Upon hearing of the impending meeting of Church leaders, he postponed this campaign in order to communicate his plans to the Council.[102] This, then, might be the reason why no more was heard of the expected Mongol invasion at this time in Mamluk sources.

The year 672/1273–4 also saw the arrival of another important non-Mongol *wāfidī* to the Sultanate: Shams al-Dīn Bahādur b. al-Malik Faraj, the lord of Shumayṣāṭ/Sumaysāṭ, whose father had been *amīr tasht* ("ewer holder") of the Khwārazm-shāh Jalāl al-Dīn. The Mongols suspected (correctly) that Bahādur was in secret contact with Baybars and arrested him. Bahādur, however, succeeded in escaping from the *ordo*. Previously, more than a thousand – so it is reported – of his mamluks and soldiers had fled to the Sultan, who had received them well. Bahādur eventually made his way to Baybars, who rewarded him with *iqṭāᶜāt* in Egypt and made him an amir of 20, and later of 40.[103]

In 673/1274–5, Baybars again turned his attention to Lesser Armenia. Cilicia had enjoyed several years of respite from Mamluk depredations, probably due more to Baybars's preoccupations with the Mongols than his treaty with the Armenian King, now Leon III. The port city of Ayās was rebuilt and became an active trading center, profiting from the conquest and subsequent decline of Antioch. It seems that trade from Īlkhānid territory and beyond no longer went to Europe via Antioch, now in Mamluk hands, but through Ayās. New privileges granted to the Genoese in 1271 only strengthened Ayās's prosperity. This same prosperity, however, also appeared to have attracted the Mamluks.[104]

According to Smpad, Baybars had set his sights on Cilicia in 1271 (= AH

101 *Rawḍ*, 426; Nuwayrī, MS. 2m, fol. 252b; Ibn al-Furāt, 7:6 (in MS. Vienna, fol. 219a, he also mentions this raid, mistakenly s.a. 671); Maqrīzī, 1:611.

102 Roberg, "Tataren," 282–3. See ch. 4.

103 Ibn Shaddād, *Ta'rīkh*, 336; *Rawḍ*, 421–3; *Ḥusn*, 153; *Zubda*, fol. 81a; Nuwayrī, MS. 2m, fol. 208a–b; Ibn al-Furāt, 7:4–5; Maqrīzī, 1:611. See also ch. 6.

104 Der Nersessian, "Kingdom," 655; Runciman, *Crusades*, 3:326. On the prosperity and trade of Ayās, see: Marco Polo, tr. Latham, 46; E. Ashtor, *A Social and Economic History of the Near East in the Middle Ages* (London, 1976), 264–5, 298–9; W. Heyd, *Histoire du commerce du Levant au moyen âge* (Leipzig, 1936, rpt. of 1885–6 ed.), 1:365–72; 2:72–80, 88–9.

669–70), when he led an army towards it. Leon, however, sent envoys and Baybars returned to Egypt. The Armenian King then went to Abagha, who promised to send 20,000 men within a few months to protect his kingdom. A number of Mongol troops then returned with Leon.[105] The Mamluk sources make no mention of this aborted raid, a fact that casts doubt on the veracity of this report. It is clear that no significant Mongol force was in Lesser Armenia when Baybars did attack in 673/1275.

Ibn ʿAbd al-Ẓāhir and Ibn Shaddād offer different reasons for Baybars's campaign to Cilicia this year. The former writes that the Armenian King had stopped sending the tribute that had been agreed upon, had broken the conditions of the agreement by rebuilding and strengthening forts, and had not sent true information as he had sworn. (None of these conditions were mentioned in the accounts of the treaty.) In addition, there was the episode of Kaynūk, which has been mentioned above. The King knew what was in store for him, and he so attempted to gain the support of the Mongols and (unnamed) Franks by deprecating the Muslims in their eyes. This information is more or less seconded by Ibn Shaddād in *al-Aʿlāq al-khaṭīra*. In his biography of Baybars, on the other hand, Ibn Shaddād states that Baybars launched his campaign because the Pervāne, fearing the Mongols, had secretly written to the Sultan and urged him to attack Cilicia. In exchange, the Pervāne promised that in the following year he would make Baybars the ruler of Rūm.[106] It would seem that the intention here was to neutralize Cilicia before attempting an offensive to Rūm, although this is not explicitly stated. There is no real contradiction between these explanations, because the Sultan could have had several reasons for attacking Lesser Armenia. He may also have wished to inflict damage on the international trade that passed from Īlkhānid territory via Lesser Armenia to the West.

As a prelude to the major campaign, a raiding force was sent out from Aleppo under its governor, Lachin al-ʿAyntābī some time in 673/1274–5. This force went on to Marʿash, raiding the countryside along the way. At Marʿash, they knocked down the gates of the faubourg (*rabaḍ*).[107] Perhaps this is the first invasion of Cilicia mentioned by Bar Hebraeus for AD 1275. According to him, the Egyptian army was put to flight by the Armenians.[108] The Mamluk sources make no mention of such a setback, if there indeed was one. On 3 Shaʿbān 673/1 February 1275 Baybars left Cairo at the head of the army, after reviewing the troops. He reached Damascus at the end of Shaʿbān and departed for the north a week later (6 March), accompanied also by the army of Damascus. On the way he was joined by al-Manṣūr of Hama and local bedouins. Leaving the heavy baggage and part of his army in the environs of

[105] Smpad, tr. Der Nersessian, 166.

[106] *Rawḍ*, p. 432; Ibn Shaddād, *Aʿlāq*, ed. Eddé, 321; *idem*, *Taʾrīkh*, 107; see also the comments in Canard, "Arménie," 238–9; Thorau, *Baybars*, 233. The Pervāne's relations with Baybars will be discussed in ch. 9.

[107] *Rawḍ*, 431; Nuwayrī, MS. 2m, fol. 252b; Ibn al-Furāt, 7:25; Maqrīzī, 1:616; Thorau, *Baybars*, 233.

[108] Bar Hebraeus, 452.

Aleppo, Baybars and his army proceeded in the direction of al-Darbassāk. A force was sent ahead to al-Nahr al-Aswad (= Qara Su) to seize the ford, which was crossed with difficulty. The main army camped between al-Darbassāk and Baghrās.[109]

While marching through north Syria, Baybars ordered Lachin al-ᶜAyntābī and ᶜĪsā b. Muhannā to advance to al-Bīra. They were to give the impression that they were the vanguard of the whole army, in order to mislead the Mongols and Armenians alike as to the true whereabouts of the Sultan and the main Mamluk force. Having reached al-Bīra, this force continued on to Ra's al-ᶜAyn in the Jazīra and looted that town. No actual fighting took place, because the Mongols stationed there withdrew. The Mamluk force then returned to Syria.[110]

Before entering the Syrian Gate (Bab Iskandarūn), just south of Alexandretta,[111] the Sultan ordered senior amirs up into the mountains, presumably to reconnoiter and drive out Armenians who were hiding there. Having traversed the pass (21 Ramaḍān/20 March), the Sultan advanced along the coast to al-Muthaqqab, and then inland to al-Maṣṣīṣa. According to Baybars al-Manṣūrī, who participated in the campaign, his patron Qalawun and Bilig al-Khaznadār were sent ahead with the vanguard. The author tells how this vanguard reached al-Maṣṣīṣa, catching its inhabitants by surprise in the morning and killing most of them. Probably around this time, a large group of both local Türkmen and bedouin came to the Sultan with their horses and livestock, to express their loyalty to him. They were sent on to Syria. Baybars entered the capital of Sīs on 29 Ramaḍān/28 March, and from there rode as far as Darband al-Sīs (Pylae Ciliciae), where he found some Mongol women and children, probably evidence of a rapidly abandoned Mongol camp. He then returned to the capital and spent the holiday of ᶜĪd al-Fitr there. Baybars was unable to take the citadel, but he razed the city, and then returned to al-Maṣṣīṣa. Meanwhile, Mamluk columns had reached Ṭarsūs (Tarse), the sea coast, Qalᶜat al-Barzīn (location not clear) and Adhana. Bar Hebraeus adds that they reached as far as Cyricus (Corycus). One column, under Baysari and *Etmish (or Aytamish ⟨ '-Y-T-M-SH) al-Saᶜdī, reached Ayās (on 25 March according to Bar Hebraeus), killing and burning; some inhabitants and Franks managed to flee to sea in boats, although a number of them drowned. Having wrought havoc in all directions, the various forces rejoined the Sultan at al-Maṣṣīṣa, bringing with them much booty and more Mongol children and womenfolk. From there, the whole Mamluk force started home, going via Tall Ḥamdūn, which they attacked. Crossing the Amanus mountains, probably at

[109] For the references, see n. 112.

[110] *Rawḍ*, 433, 436; Nuwayrī, MS. 2m, fols. 253a, 254a; Ibn al-Furāt, 7:29, 31; Maqrīzī, 1:616, 618, wrongly transcribes ᶜAyn Tāb (this was already in Mamluk hands) instead of Ra's al-ᶜAyn (see Thorau, *Baybars*, 248 n. 63).

[111] On the Syrian Gate, also called the Pass of Beylan, see Boase, *Cilician Kingdom*, 157, 182; Edwards, *Fortifications*, 30. It is conceivable that what is referred to is a second pass on the coastal road north of Alexandretta.

the Syrian Gate (20 Shawwāl/18 April), the whole army camped near Ḥārim, where the booty was redivided. On 5 Dhū 'l-ḥijja/1 June 1275, the Sultan was back in Damascus.[112]

An interesting story is told by Ibn ʿAbd al-Raḥīm, the continuator of Ibn Wāṣil. He cites the amir Fakhr al-Dīn Ayaz al-Muqrī al-Ḥājib, who had been sent in 670/1272 as an envoy to Abagha (see above). Ayaz tells of how news had reached the Sultan from Mamluk spies (*jawāsīs*) in the entourage of the Armenian King who reported that the King was with his army in the mountains near the country of the Qaraman Türkmen.[113] This would explain why, during this whole raid, Leon was not to be seen, and there were virtually no signs of concerted Armenian resistance. Evidently, Leon's trauma from the Mamluk raid of 664/1266 was so great that he did not want to risk another confrontation with the Mamluks. The one example of resistance was a joint force of Armenians and unspecified Franks; Ibn ʿAbd al-Raḥīm reports that there were 1500 of the former and 500 of the latter. According to this writer, Baybars himself fought them. Ibn ʿAbd al-Ẓāhir writes, evidently referring to the same incident, that they were defeated by the Syrian army.[114] Bar Hebraeus states that after the Mamluks left the country, the Armenian King appeared and killed all the Türkmen who also had been ravaging the country at this time.[115] We can perhaps doubt this report.

The following year, Abagha once again sent another army against al-Bīra. The command of this army was under Abtai, who had replaced Durbai after the latter's failure and ignominious retreat at the same fort in 671/1272. Abtai was joined by the Rūmi army under the Pervāne, the Mongol units in Rūm, and troops from Mārdīn, Mayyāfāriqīn, Mosul, Shahrazūr (i.e. Kurds) and Iraq. The total army under Abtai was 30,000 strong, of which half was Mongols (*al-mughul*).[116]

Baybars was in Damascus when he heard of the Mongol advance to al-Bīra, and called for the mobilization of the army. Meanwhile, he waited for more certain news. On receiving confirmation that the Mongols had reached al-Bīra on 8 Jumādā II 674/29 November 1275 and had set up mangonels there, Baybars set out (17 Jumādā II/8 December). Ibn Shaddād reports that this

112 The most detailed version is in *Rawḍ*, 432–6; *Tuḥfa*, 80–1, summarizes this but adds a short personal reminiscence; Ibn al-Furāt, 7:28–31, who cites *Rawḍ* extensively, but also Ibn Duqmaq and, it would seem, Baybars al-Manṣūrī; Maqrīzī, 1:617–18. A different, shorter version is in Ibn Shaddād, *Ta'rīkh*, 106–8; hence Yūnīnī, 3:88; Mufaḍḍal, 225–6 (with some additions); Ibn al-Dawādārī, 8:177; Kutubī, MS. Köprülü, fol. 34a–b, but also cites poetry by Ibn ʿAbd al-Ẓāhir. Also Ibn Shaddād, *Aʿlāq*, ed. Eddé, 320–1; Bar Hebraeus, 452–3. See Canard, "Arménie," 240–1; Thorau, *Baybars*, 233–4.

113 Ibn ʿAbd al-Raḥīm, in Ibn Wāṣil, MS. 1703, fol. 185b.

114 *Ibid.*; *Rawḍ*, 435. 115 Bar Hebraeus, 453.

116 Ibn al-Furāt, 7:41; Ibn Shaddād, *Ta'rīkh*, 124–5, who has Abtai holding a joint command with Tabishi; Baybars, *Tuḥfa*, 82, writes that Abtai received command over Durbai's *tümen*. According to Bar Hebraeus, 454, the Mongols had seven myriads (= *tümens*) at this siege, i.e. theoretically 70,000 men.

same day the Mongols withdrew from al-Bīra. Baybars received this news not far from Damascus, but as he was uncertain of the veracity of this information, he continued on to Homs. There, verified reports arrived, and he returned to Damascus.

One reason that the Mongols had ended their siege was the dearth of supplies. Bar Hebraeus reports that the weather was cold, there was snow, and many of the horses had died. An additional cause is offered by Ibn Shaddād: the Mongol commanders learnt that the Pervāne was in communication with Baybars, and planned to betray the Mongols upon the arrival of the Mamluk army. These commanders feared the divided loyalty of their Muslim troops, and thought to kill them, but were apprehensive that many of them would flee to al-Bīra. Certainly, strife within the army during a siege was inadvisable, with a rapidly approaching Mamluk army led by Baybars. The siege itself was not going well: the fort was well-defended and stocked, and the defenders scored some success against the Mongol mangonels and launched a night sortie. The Mongol commanders thus decided to withdraw, planning to justify this to Abagha by the lowness of supplies, disease and the poor state of their equipment, all valid reasons.[117]

The importance attributed to the border war

In chapter 9 I will attempt to summarize the nature of the Mamluk–Īlkhānid frontier region, based to a large degree on material found in this present chapter. At this point, I will limit myself to a comment on the disparity noticed in the sources. The Mamluk sources are replete with information on both the border war and diplomatic *démarches* with the Mongols. Virtually a year does not go by without the mention of some event of major or minor importance concerning the Mongol danger. These sources also provide us with important information about events occurring within the Īlkhānid state. On the other hand, the main pro-Mongol Persian sources, Rashīd al-Dīn and Waṣṣāf, are generally silent about the ongoing skirmishing, both over the frontier and in the diplomatic sphere, and have little to say about internal events within the Mamluk Sultanate. The situation is only partially rectified by the non-Persian pro-Mongol sources, such as the Armenian writers and Bar Hebraeus.

One explanation for this phenomenon might be the vast difference in the size of the corpus of Mamluk historiography compared to its pro-Mongol counterpart. Taken as a whole, the latter is much smaller than the former. However, Rashīd al-Dīn's and Waṣṣāf's chronicles, including the parts devoted to the years AH 658–75, are large and often quite detailed. The explanation for this dearth of information on the border war must be found elsewhere. I would suggest that it derived from the different degrees of

[117] Ibn Shaddād, *Ta'rīkh*, 126–8; Ibn al-Furāt, 7:41–3 (based *inter alia* on Ibn Shaddād); Maqrīzī, 1:621 (very condensed); Nuwayrī, MS. 2m, fol. 212a; Yūnīnī, 3:114–16; Bar Hebraeus, 454; Thorau, *Baybars*, 238–9. See also ch. 7.

importance that the Mamluks and Mongols attached to this ongoing simmering conflict. For the Mamluks, it was a matter of life and death to hold the Mongols. One defeat, even in a minor campaign, might have had critical results. This concern is naturally reflected in the widespread attention that the border war received in the Mamluk sources. The general success that the Mamluks scored in the border war may also have played a role in the widespread coverage that it received. For the Mongols, occupied on several distant fronts, this border war was just one of many concerns. Setbacks on the Syrian front might be annoying and embarrassing, but the fate of the kingdom was not at stake, as it possibly was in the wars with the Golden Horde and the Chaghatayids. The secondary importance of the Syrian front along with a general lack of success in the border war were probably the reasons that we hear virtually nothing of the border war in the pro-Mongol Persian sources.[118] Only with Baybars's invasion of Seljuq Rūm in 675/1277 do the Persian writers serving the Mongols turn their full attention to the enemy based across the Euphrates.

[118] Spuler, *Iran*, 13, briefly makes this latter point.

CHAPTER 6

The secret war

The Sultans of the Saracens had many spies, who desired to know all of the deeds of the Christians, not only in nearby regions, but also in remote regions.

Fidenzio de Padua[1]

In order to combat better the Mongol danger, Baybars established an intelligence service, which was based on secret operatives and informants in enemy territory. The information thus obtained was vital for the timely adoption of proper measures for the defence of the Sultanate. Baybars, however, did not stop at the mere gathering of information, but initiated assorted covert activities to weaken the Mongols, including assassination, disinformation to discredit opponents, and the cultivation of contacts with indigenous Muslim princes, officers and officials in the Īlkhānid state. This was in addition to the activities described in previous chapters which could also be placed under the rubric of "secret war," such as the raids across the border, the burning of grasslands and the dispatch of Muslim rulers to reestablish their "kingdoms" (the Caliph al-Mustanṣir, al-Ṣāliḥ of Mosul and the "lord" of Irbil). Baybars's successors continued these activities until the end of the Mamluk–Īlkhānid war in 720/1320 and even after. As is to be expected, the sultans also used espionage and subterfuge against the Franks in Syria.[2]

The Īlkhāns also tried their hand at both espionage and "dirty tricks." In general, however, their efforts were not crowned with success, at least, according to the Mamluk sources, who probably only knew of such Mongol activities when they failed or those involved were caught. We have no

[1] *Liber recuperationis Terrae Sanctae*, in G. Golubovich, *Biblioteca Bio-Bibliografica della Terra Santa et dell' Oriento Francescano* (Quaracchi, 1906–23), 2:33, cited in J.R. Alban and C.T. Allmand, "Spies and Spying in the Fourteenth Century," in C.T. Allman (ed.), *War, Literature and Politics in the Later Middle Ages* (Liverpool, 1976), 73.

[2] For preliminary and brief discussions on Mamluk espionage, see: Cahen, *Syrie*, 714; Blochet's comments in Mufaḍḍal, 719 n. 2; Khowaiter, *Baibars*, 39–42. For Mamluk espionage against the Franks and after Baybars, see: R. Amitai, "Mamluk Espionage among Mongols and Franks," *AAS* 22 (1988):173–81. Espionage during Baybars's reign is briefly discussed there. This present chapter is an expansion of that discussion.

knowledge regarding successful Mongol efforts in the secret war, if any actually existed. The pro-Mongol sources, in Persian and other languages, are silent on the subject.

Mamluk espionage

There is information regarding the use of spies by some Syrian Ayyūbids against their Frankish neighbors.[3] It is unclear, however, if these princes ran a regular, ongoing intelligence service. Yet even without Ayyūbid antecedents, it is easy to understand the nature and extent of Baybars's espionage service: confronted by the Mongol, Frankish and Armenian enemies and having set up a centralized state, Baybars was both motivated and able to establish a regular intelligence service. In a sense, Baybars was continuing in the path already established by Qutuz: after ʿAyn Jālūt, the latter had appointed al-Malik al-Saʿīd ʿAlā' al-Dīn b. Badr al-Dīn Lu'lu' as governor of Aleppo, so he could communicate with his brothers, still in the Jazīra, and thus learn about the Mongols.[4]

It is clear that Baybars ran a regular, professional intelligence service. On several occasions, Baybars is praised by his biographer, Ibn ʿAbd al-Ẓāhir, who wrote of the Sultan's concern for the gathering of information and how this led to early warnings of impending attacks (by the Mongols and Armenians) and to the uncovering of enemy spies.[5] It is legitimate to wonder if such fulsome praise is mere panegyric, of which many examples are found in *al-Rawḍ al-zāhir*. In this case, however, we can trust the author. Ibn ʿAbd al-Ẓāhir was Baybars's *kātib al-sirr* (privy secretary), and thus would have had at least some knowledge of such activities. More importantly, as will be seen, his evidence is corroborated by other sources.

The linchpin of Baybars's intelligence operation was the *quṣṣād* (sing. *qāṣid*). This term has the basic meaning of envoy or messenger, a meaning also concurrently found in the Mamluk sources. But in many cases it is clear that these sources use the word as a technical term to denote intelligence operatives employed by the Sultan to go back and forth from enemy (Mongol, Armenian and Frankish) territory. The preferred translation in such cases is secret courier or agent. A particularly enlightening passage for the meaning and function of the *quṣṣād* is found in Ibn ʿAbd al-Ẓāhir's *Rawḍ*:

> The Sultan did not cease to take interest in the affairs of the enemy. He was on guard against their tricks and resolute in all regarding them. His *quṣṣād* did not stop coming from Baghdad, Khilāṭ [= Akhlāṭ] and other places in the eastern country [*bilād al-sharq*] and Persia [*al-ʿajam*]. [The Sultan] spent on them much money, because whoever travels for this matter and plays loosely with his life, there is no choice but that he

[3] Sibṭ ibn al-Jawzī, 8:646–7; C. Marshall, *Warfare in the Latin East, 1192–1291* (Cambridge, 1992), 264–6. [4] See ch. 2, p. 46.

[5] *Rawḍ*, 192, 195, 423. For Baybars's concern for internal surveillance, see Yūnīnī, 3:255.

should take his blood money [*diya*]. Without this, who would risk his life? When Allāh showed the Sultan this good policy, the *quṣṣād* went back and forth, and they recognized [in the Mongol countries] those who could inform them of the [Mongol] secrets.[6]

The official responsible for the activities of the *quṣṣād* was the amir Sayf al-Dīn Balaban al-Dawādār al-Rūmī, a trusted personal mamluk of the Sultan. Al-Ṣafadī writes that the Sultan had him convey his secrets to the *quṣṣād*.[7] Ibn al-Ṣuqāʿī provides more details of Balaban's activities and the workings of the intelligence service: "[He] alone spoke with the *quṣṣād* who went back and forth [engaged] in the secret activities (*al-ashghāl al-sirriyya*), and he paid their salaries and grants. Their names were not written in the *dīwān* (registry) and their condition was not revealed to the military class (*al-nās*). If one came during the day, they were veiled so as not to be identified."[8]

More information on Balaban's activities is found in his obituary in al-Yūnīnī's work: this amir was party to Baybars's secrets and the administration of matters relating to *quṣṣād*, spies (*jawāsīs*) and correspondents (*mukātibūn*; see below). Except for another amir, Ḥusām al-Dīn Lachin al-Aydemürī al-Darfīl (who was replaced on his death in 672/1273–4 by ʿIzz al-Dīn Aydemür al-Dawādār al-Ẓāhirī), Balaban had no associates in these matters, neither the wazir nor the *nā'ib* (vice-sultan).[9]

It remains unclear whether or not the responsibility for the *quṣṣād* was connected to Balaban being a *dawādār* ("inkwell holder"). Already in Baybars's period, this position gained in importance, and its holder exercised a certain supervisory function over the *barīd* and chancery.[10] It is possible, however, that this double responsibility was a coincidence, and was due only to the trust Baybars put in his mamluk, who happened to be a *dawādār*. On the other hand, Balaban's second associate – Aydemür al-Ẓāhirī – was also a *dawādār*, which strengthens the suggestion that supervision of the *quṣṣād* indeed fell within the purview of the *dawādār*. It would appear that Balaban was not directly responsible for the specific missions of all the operatives. Some of this may have been in the hands of forward commanders: the governor of al-Raḥba is reported to have dispatched *quṣṣād* into enemy territory.[11]

The above use of *jawāsīs* (pl. of *jāsūs*) for Mamluk spies or secret operatives

6 *Rawḍ*, 135; whence Ibn al-Furāt, MS. Vienna, fol. 6a. 7 Ṣafadī, *Wāfī*, 10:282.
8 Ibn al-Ṣuqāʿī, 53.
9 Yūnīnī, 4:106–7; cited in Ibn Taghrī Birdī, 7:332–3. Balaban was also an expert on relations with the Franks, and conducted negotiations with Tripoli; P.M. Holt, "Mamluk-Frankish Diplomatic Relations in the Reign of Qalāwūn (678–89/1279–90)," *JRAS* 1989:281–2. He was killed at the battle of Homs in 680/1281.
10 Both Irwin, *Middle East*, 39, and P.M. Holt, *Memoirs of a Syrian Prince* (Wiesbaden, 1983), 6, suggest that espionage was among the responsibilities of the *dawādār*. ʿUmarī, ed. Sayyid, 58, only vaguely refers to the secret activities of the *dawādār* in his description of the position; see also D. Ayalon, "Dawādār," *EI*[2], 2:172. 11 Yūnīnī, 4:109; Ibn al-Furāt, 7:74.

is not common. I have found only two other unambiguous examples in the Mamluk sources for this usage.[12] The distinction between *jāsūs* and *qāṣid*, if there was one, is not clear. *Jāsūs* was sometimes applied by the Mamluk writers to Mongol agents, as will be seen below. Given the several instances of the use of *jāsūs/jawāsīs* by Mamluk writers for Mamluk agents, I must revise my earlier suggestion that this was a term of disparagement.[13]

Shāfiᶜ b. ᶜAlī's biography of Qalawun provides further confirmation of the connection of *quṣṣād* with intelligence work: in 678/1279–80, information about an impending Mongol attack is confirmed in letters from the Sultan's correspondents (*mukātibūn*, see below) and *quṣṣād akhbārihi* who were always sending information.[14] *Quṣṣād akhbārihi* can be translated as "the agents [who provided] his intelligence"; the second word may have been added in this case to emphasize that these *quṣṣād* were engaged in espionage and were not just mere couriers.

Additional proof for the application of *quṣṣād* to those engaged in spy work comes from Mongol espionage. Ibn ᶜAbd al-Ẓāhir uses the terms *jāsūs* and *qāṣid* for the same two Mongol agents in 662/1263–4.[15] As will be seen below, these agents were subsequently arrested upon their arrival in the Sultanate. These two terms were used interchangeably because in the author's mind *qāṣid* was associated with espionage.

As said before, during the period that *qāṣid/quṣṣād* was used as a technical term, it was also employed by the same sources in its simple meaning of Mamluk envoys or couriers.[16] The Mamluk writers also used *quṣṣād* for couriers sent by Hülegü to Mārdīn in 658 and 659/1259–61.[17] The term was also applied to secret couriers, although not connected to espionage, from Mamluk amirs or the Sultan.[18] Secret envoys sent to the Sultan by important personages in enemy territory were also known as *quṣṣād* (see below). In spite of the many shades of meaning for this word, it is clear from the context that, in many cases, *quṣṣād* refers specifically to Mamluk intelligence operatives, and this appears to have been the technical term by which they were known.[19]

[12] Ibn ᶜAbd al-Raḥīm, in Ibn Wāṣil, fol. 185b (s.a. 673/1274–5); *Ḥusn*, 138 (ca. 689/1290). See also: Amitai, "Espionage," n. 12.

[13] Cf. Amitai, "Espionage," 175.

[14] *Faḍl*, fol. 28b; the continuation of this passage tells of how widespread was Qalawun's intelligence service. This may be patterned on the above cited passage from *Rawḍ* cited in n. 6.

[15] *Rawḍ*, 195; whence, Ibn al-Furāt, MS. Vienna, fol. 43a.

[16] *Rawḍ*, 95, 296; Kutubī, 20:301 (= Ibn Taghrī Birdī, 7:143); *Zubda*, fols. 60a, 124a; *Tuḥfa*, 71; Maqrīzī, 1:511 (cf. Ibn al-Furāt, MS. Vienna, fol. 43a, who does not mention *quṣṣād*).

[17] Yūnīnī, 1:379, 2:112; Ibn al-Dawādārī, 8:66.

[18] *Rawḍ*, 169–70 (= Ibn al-Furāt, MS. Vienna, fol. 28b); *Zubda*, fols. 91b, 104a; *Faḍl*, fol. 36a. Qalqashandī, 1:126–7, describes *quṣṣād* in his own time as secret couriers (but not intelligence agents *per se*), particularly to foreign lands.

[19] Cf. Alban and Allmand, "Spies," 75: "To the mind of the fourteenth century [in Europe, R.A.] the distinction between the spy and the messenger was a fine one . . . it appears that the term messenger could be employed as a synonym for spy." Alban and Allmand's discussion of espionage in Western Europe has many parallels to that of the Mamluk Sultanate in the thirteenth–fourteenth centuries.

Ibn Shaddād[20] relates that one of Balaban al-Rūmī's men or followers (*aṣḥāb*) was called ʿAlā' al-Dīn ʿAlī b. ʿAbdallāh al-Baghdādī, and from the context it is clear that he was an intelligence agent, probably a *qāṣid*. The identity of the other *quṣṣād* during Baybars's and Qalawun's reigns is unknown. We do, however, have the names of several of these agents from the post-Qalawun period. None of these men were mamluks, since they did not have Turkish names, but rather Arabic-Muslim ones. This makes sense, since native Arabic or Persian speakers would attract less attention moving about in enemy territory than Turks trying to speak the local patois. It can be tentatively assumed that during the times of Baybars and Qalawun, the same kind of men served as *quṣṣād*.[21] There is, however, one indication of an Armenian *qāṣid*.[22] Perhaps those at the *ordo* (see below) may have been of steppe origin. As would be expected, *quṣṣād* on a mission were constantly in danger: their lives were threatened not only by the Mongols, but by Armenians and bedouins not loyal to the Sultan.[23]

One of the main functions of the *quṣṣād* was to relay information from the informants in enemy territory. These were known as *munāṣiḥūn*; *nuṣaḥā'*, *nāṣiḥūn* and *nuṣṣāḥ* (sing. *nāṣiḥ*); *mutanaṣṣiḥūn*; *mukātibūn* ("correspondents"); *arbāb al-akhbār* ("possessors of intelligence"); and, ʿ*uyūn* ("eyes", sing. ʿ*ayn*).[24] The terms based on the root *n-ṣ-ḥ* are by far the most common, and can be literally translated as "honest friends" or "givers of good or true advice." It is clear that these terms have positive connotations and show the appreciation with which the Mamluks held these informants. Unlike the *quṣṣād*, the informants seem to have been volunteers, local Muslims (at least those in Mongol territory), who were motivated by a religious feeling to help the Muslim Sultan against the infidel Mongols. As seen in the above cited passage of Ibn ʿAbd al-Ẓāhir, the *quṣṣād* were commissioned to take the initiative to identify those locals who could be of use and provide information.

Two examples will help to demonstrate the relationship between *quṣṣād* and *nuṣaḥā'*, etc. Both are taken from Shāfiʿ b. ʿAlī's biography of Qalawun, and relate to the events before the Mongol invasion of Syria in 680/1281:(1) "The information from the *nuṣaḥā'* was verified and the *quṣṣād* from and to [Qalawun] went back and forth"; (2) "The *mukātibūn*, by sending the *quṣṣād*,

20 Cited in Ibn al-Dawādārī, 8:92.

21 See Amitai, "Espionage," *passim*.

22 See below, p. 149.

23 Armenians at Kaynūk: *Rawḍ*, 417; see ch. 5, p. 132. Zāmil b. ʿAlī, who intercepted *quṣṣād* going to Shīrāz: see ch. 3, pp. 167–8.

24 The following also includes examples of informants in Frankish territory. *Munāṣiḥūn*: *Zubda*, fol. 110a; *Tuḥfa*, 78; Nuwayrī, MS. 2m, fol. 168a (cf. his source, *Rawḍ*, 195, who only mentions *quṣṣād*); *Faḍl*, fols. 43b–44a. *Nuṣaḥā'*: *Rawḍ*, 382; whence, Ibn al-Furāt, MS. Vienna,fol. 192b (= ed. Lyons, 1:189; cf. trans., 2:149: "advisors"); *Rawḍ*, 428; *Faḍl*, fols. 29b, 40b. *Nāṣiḥūn*: Nuwayrī, MS. 2n, fol. 20b; Ghāzī b. al-Wāsiṭī, 410. *Nuṣṣāḥ*: ʿUmarī, *Taʿrīf*, 200. *Mutanaṣṣiḥūn*: Ghāzī b. al-Wāsiṭī, 411. *Mukātibūn*: *Ḥusn*, 150; *Faḍl*, fols. 28b, 29b, 41a, 43b–44a, 48b–49a, 59b–60a. *Arbāb*: *Rawḍ*, 195. ʿ*Uyūn*: Yūnīnī, 3:299 (= Ibn al-Ṣuqāʿī, 12). These last two terms may refer to another type of Mamluk agent. On the use of all these terms after AH 680, see Amitai, "Espionage," n. 5. According to Canard, "Djāsūs," *EI*², 2:487, ʿ*Ayn* was virtually a synonym for *jāsūs*.

exerted themselves to inform us as best they could."[25] It is clear, then, that the job of the *qāṣid* was to convey the information collected by the local contacts.

The investment of resources and energy in the establishment and maintenance of an espionage system was soon to pay dividends. First, Baybars received timely warning of Mongol offensive preparations, as in 660/1262, and thus took the necessary measures to meet this challenge, until it became clear that this offensive was directed elsewhere.[26] Likewise, Qalawun was to receive critical information on Mongol plans and the strength of their forces before the Mongol invasion of Syria in 680/1281.[27] Because of the efforts devoted to intelligence gathering, Baybars gained advance information of an Armenian raid in 662/1263–4, and dispatched forces to deal with it.[28] Mamluk agents also obtained information on Mongol espionage efforts, and thus Baybars could catch the Mongol spies and their local contacts.[29] We can assume that at least some of the information on Īlkhānid–Frankish contacts and the attempts at concerted action against the Mamluks was gained through the intelligence system, be it among the Mongols or the Franks.

This is not to say that *quṣṣād* and *nuṣaḥā'* were the only ways for the Sultan to obtain information on happenings in the enemy camp. Intelligence was surely gleaned from *wāfidiyya*, Mongol and otherwise, pilgrims on the way to the *ḥajj*, scouts (*kashshāfa*), the bedouin of north Syria and Iraq, and merchants – especially from Lesser Armenia and the Frankish ports in the Levant and Europe, although those from Mongol territory should not be discounted (see chapter 9). Important as this information may have been, it was of a fortuitous nature and could not replace the intelligence gathered by the ongoing, organized activities of the *quṣṣād* service.

Besides cultivating contacts with local informants and conveying their information to the Sultan, the *quṣṣād* had an additional task of maintaining contact with indigenous, generally Muslim, lords and rulers in Īlkhānid controlled territory. There were several reasons for these contacts: to receive intelligence, to encourage the rulers to rebel and to urge them to flee with their troops to the Sulṭan. Among these lords were the ruler of Shīrāz, the Ayyūbid lord of Ḥiṣn Kayfā, the lord of Shumayṣāṭ, the King of Georgia, and the amirs of Seljuq Rūm, including the Pervāne. These contacts will be discussed below, except for Seljuq Rūm, which will be examined in chapter 8.

Baybars received important assistance in intelligence activities from the bedouins of Iraq, primarily the Khafāja tribe. The reason for this assistance may well have been Muslim solidarity against infidels, although traditional bedouin opposition to central authority (the Īlkhāns and their governors) was probably also a factor. Iraqi bedouin had been instrumental in assisting both Caliphal pretenders, al-Mustanṣir and al-Ḥākim, from escaping from Bagh-

[25] *Faḍl*, fols. 40b–41a. [26] *Rawḍ*, 135–68. For another example s.a. 668/1269, see *Ḥusn*, 150.
[27] See ch. 8, pp. 187–9.
[28] *Rawḍ*, 192. Mamluk spies (*jawāsīs*) were found in the entourage of the Armenian King in 673/1275; Ibn ʿAbd al-Raḥīm, in Ibn Wāṣil, MS. 1703, fol. 185b (s.a. 673/1274–5); ch. 5, p. 136.
[29] See below for the two examples.

dad and making their way to Syria (see chapter 3). In 660/1261–2, Baybars warmly received the chiefs (*shuyūkh*) of the Khafāja and ʿAbbāda tribes, who were located in the regions around Hīt, al-Anbār, al-Hilla and al-Kūfa. He commanded these tribes to keep an eye on the Mongols for him.[30] Not all of the Khafāja were ready to side with the Sultan. The same year, tribesmen from this tribe and the Ghāziya tribe raided Wādī al-Rabīʿa, between Homs and Qārā, and waylaid caravans. Some, at least, were caught and hanged by al-Ashraf Mūsā of Homs.[31]

While Baybars was at Gaza the following year (ca. early spring 1262), he wrote to the Khafāja (as well as the lord of Shīrāz and the chiefs of the Lur, an Iranian mountain people) and called upon them to mobilize against the Mongols. As an encouragement to them, Baybars described the defeat of Hülegü's army by Berke's forces.[32] These exhortations may not have occasioned a general uprising against the Mongols, but they perhaps helped to predispose the Iraqi bedouin to help the Mamluks in other ways. Evidently later this year, a group of Khafāja chiefs (*umarā'*) came to Baybars. He gave them a warm welcome, and sent them back with coats of honor for the chiefs (*kubarā'*) who had remained in Iraq, together with an envoy – ʿIzz al-Dīn Aydemür al-Atābakī – to the lord of Shīrāz. Letters to Shīrāz and elsewhere were also sent to encourage resistance to the Mongols.[33]

During 662/1263–4, the Khafāja appear several times. In early spring of that year (1264), a group of Khafāja bedouin came with letters from those who remained in Iraq. The bedouin told of how they had raided up to the gates of Baṣra and Baghdad. They also related news from Shīrāz, including that its lord had defeated a Mongol force which had come his way. Baybars wrote to encourage the ruler of Shīrāz. He also wrote to Aydemür al-Atābakī, who was still in Iraq, to set out for Shīrāz along with Khafāja amirs.[34] In Rajab 662 (May 1264), *wāfidiyya* from Shīrāz arrived, together with a number of Khafāja amirs. The Khafajī leader was Ḥusām al-Dīn Ḥusayn b. Milāḥ (?),[35] who was given an *iqṭāʿ* of a village in Syria. Along with another chief, he also received a commission in the Mamluk army. The Khafajīs were then sent back to their country.[36] Towards the close of this year (which ended on 4 November 1264), the Sultan ordered the Khafāja bedouins to assist the *wāfidī* Jalāl al-Dīn Yashkar, then making his way from Baghdad to Syria.[37]

30 Maqrīzī, 1:476; the parallel folio(s) in Ibn al-Furāt, MS. Vienna (between fols. 8 and 9), is missing. 31 Ibn al-Ṣuqāʿī, 135.

32 *Rawḍ*, 149; Ibn al-Furāt, MS. Vienna, fol. 13a; Maqrīzī, 1:481.

33 *Rawḍ*, 182; Nuwayrī, MS. 2m, fol. 166a; Ibn al-Furāt, MS. Vienna, fol. 35b; Maqrīzī, 1:501–2.

34 *Rawḍ*, 194; Ibn al-Furāt, MS. Vienna, fols. 42b–43a; Maqrīzī, 1:511. It would seem that the mamluk of the Atabeg Aqtay al-Mustaʿrib, who was caught by the renegade bedouin leader Zāmil b. ʿAlī (see ch. 3, pp. 67–8) can be identified with this individual. If so, it is no wonder that he did not complete his mission.

35 In another context, his name is found in Yūnīnī, 1:484, as Ḥusayn b. Fallāḥ.

36 *Rawḍ*, 198; Nuwayrī, MS. 2m, fols. 168b–169a; Ibn al-Furāt, MS. Vienna, fols. 44a–45a, who arranges differently the information from *Rawḍ*; Maqrīzī, 1:511–12; see ch. 5, pp. 67–8.

37 *Rawḍ*, 209–10; Ibn al-Furāt, MS. Vienna, fol. 50b; Maqrīzī, 1:516; see ch. 5, pp. 109–10.

The news brought by the Khafāja about events in Shīrāz roughly fits in with our knowledge of the events in that city. The Salghurid rulers had long submitted to the Mongols, and kept a modicum of independence. It would seem that the ruler of Shīrāz referred to above was Seljuq-Shāh b. Salghur-Shāh, who came to rule after his brother Muḥammad-Shāh was removed from the throne, seemingly some time in 661/1262–3. Seljuq-Shāh is known to have killed Mongol *basqaqs*, i.e. *shaḥnas*. Hülegü then sent an army whose commander sought to reconcile Seljuq-Shāh. The latter refused and was defeated in 662/1263–4. The reports brought to Baybars by the Khafāja in the spring of 1264 would fit this chronology, although they wrongly stated that the ruler of Shīrāz was victorious. The Mongol victory would have thus led to the Shīrāzī *wāfidiyya*, who arrived in Rajab 662 (May 1264).[38]

At this point, the Khafāja disappear from the chronicles. The next mention of them is in 672/1274, when the *amīr al-ᶜurbān* of the Syrian bedouin, ᶜĪsā b. Muhannā, launched a raid to al-Anbār. There he fought a group of Khafajīs. Nothing, however, came of this engagement.[39] In 675/1277, ᶜĪsā – together with the governor of Aleppo – bested a group of Khafajī tribesmen at the Euphrates.[40] It is unclear whether this was a faction of the Khafāja tribe which was never pro-Baybars, or reflected a change in the orientation of the tribe's leaders. Given the lack of evidence of Khafāja–Mamluk relations in the previous years, we can only tentatively conclude that the latter supposition is more likely. We see here that the loyalty of the Iraqi bedouin was far from a foregone conclusion. Like many of the Syrian bedouin leaders, the Khafāja chiefs alternately – or even concurrently – served both the Mamluks or Mongols, depending on what was in their best interest at a given time or which of the two powers was capable of exerting the most influence.

Only Mamluk sources have been used in the above discussion, since the pro-Mongol writers say little on the topic of Mamluk espionage in the Īlkhānid kingdom. Bar Hebraeus refers to the subject several times, albeit not always explicitly. First, in 1263 (= AH 661–2), envoys were caught from the former ruler of Jazīrat Ibn ᶜUmar, al-Mujāhid Sayf al-Dīn b. Badr al-Dīn Lu'lu', then in Syria, to its present governor. The local Mongol commander, Samdaghu, referred to these envoys as spies.[41] In September 1268 (early 667), an Egyptian lawyer (*faqīh* ?), "ᶜAlam al-Riyīsa" in Mosul was seized and put to death,[42] perhaps for spying. Around 1275 (= AH 673–4), 30 *faqīrs* (Muslim mendicants) came from Syria to Cilicia to visit the tomb of the Caliph Ma'mun at Ṭarsūs (Tarse). It was suspected that Baybars himself, in disguise, was among them. King Leon had the group arrested; the many envoys who came to gain their release only strengthened his suspicions that Baybars was among them.[43]

It may be surprising that Leon, who had become acquainted with Baybars

[38] A.K.S. Lambton, "Mongol Fiscal Administration in Persia," *SI* 65 (1987):103; cf. Spuler, *Iran*, 119–20. [39] *Rawḍ*, 426; Ibn al-Furāt, 7:6; Maqrīzī, 1:611; see ch. 5, p. 109.
[40] See ch. 7, p. 168. [41] Bar Hebraeus, 444. [42] *Ibid.*, 447. [43] *Ibid.*, 452.

during his captivity in Egypt and Syria, had difficulty ascertaining the presence of the Sultan among the *faqīrs*. It is clear from whence sprang this apocryphal aspect of the story. Baybars's mobility and secretiveness must have been well known,[44] and perhaps information of his intelligence service was beginning to filter through to Mongol controlled territory.

In a similar vein, Waṣṣāf relates how Baybars, having developed a desire to gain control of Rūm, travelled there in disguise, along with two or three associates, on a spying mission. He learnt the roads of the country and the strength of its forces. Having returned to his kingdom, he then wrote to Abagha, informing of how he had gone to Rūm and traversed it from end to end. As proof of this, he had left his ring in a shop. The Sultan then requested the Khan to send the ring back to him. Abagha wrote to the Pervāne, who obtained the ring and dispatched it to him. Thereupon, the Khan forwarded it to Baybars.[45] The fantastic nature of this story and the lack of any corroborating evidence in the Mamluk sources leads to the rejection of this account. It may indicate, however, that the Mongols had a hint of the extent to which Mamluk agents had crossed the border. What Waṣṣāf had done, intentionally or not, was to identify this phenomenon with the already legendary personality of Sultan Baybars.

One slightly later example will serve to show how the Mongols perceived Mamluk espionage. In 681/1282–3, the Īlkhān Aḥmad Tegüder (680–3/1281–4) wrote to Qalawun, and expressed his desire for peace. In his letter, he complained that a Mamluk spy (*jāsūs*), dressed as a *faqīr*, had been captured by the Mongol road patrol (*qaraghul*). Normally he would have been killed, but instead he was sent back to the Sultan, as a gesture of goodwill. Many other spies like this had been uncovered in the past, and the result was that the army had killed many *faqīrs*, having suspected them of being spies.[46] Qalawun does not deny this accusation in his answer, but only counters by accusing the Mongols with employing the same tactic (see below). It would seem then that *quṣṣād* or other Mamluk agents did cross the border and travel in Īlkhānid territory disguised as mendicants. Leon's suspicions of the *faqīr*s may well have been justified, even if Baybars was not among them.

Baybars's use of subterfuge

In order to weaken both the morale and the military capabilities of the Mongols, Baybars employed to great success artifices which today would be called "dirty tricks." These included assassination, the spreading of disinformation both to discredit opponents and to "convince" friends to desert to the Mamluks, and the cultivation of contacts among prominent figures in Īlkhānid territory. One result, perhaps not deliberate, of these activities was to strengthen the atmosphere of distrust among the Mongols of their Muslim

[44] See the comments in ch. 5, p. 174 and n. 75. [45] Waṣṣāf, 85–6.
[46] *Zubda*, fol. 132b; published as appendix to Maqrīzī, 1:979.

officials and officers. In such an atmosphere these office holders could easily be falsely accused of aiding the Mamluks.

The simplest form of subterfuge seems to have been assassination. Baybars employed assassins twice against Frankish adversaries: Philip of Montfort (successfully) and Prince Edward of England (unsuccessfully).[47] Baybars is reported to have twice used the services of assassins against personalities in the Īlkhānid kingdom. The first, interestingly enough, was against a Frank living there, and evidently it was not successful. The would-be victim was Bartholomew, the lord of Maraqiyya (Maraclea), who had fled to the Mongols after the Mamluk conquest of Ḥiṣn al-Akrād (668/1270). In a letter sent from Syria to the amirs in Egypt in 670/1271, Baybars wrote that Bartholomew had gone to the Mongols to ask for assistance, but he had sent assassins (*fidāwiyya*, i.e., the Ismāʿīlīs from Syria) after him. One of them had fallen upon Bartholomew and killed him. The truth, however, was that this character was alive and well, and returned to Syria several years later.[48]

Qirtay al-Khaznadārī relates a story s.a. 661/662–3 about three Kurds who came from Mongol territory. They managed to penetrate the Sultan's tent before they were apprehended. Because of their courage and honesty, Baybars rewarded them and sent them back across the border to murder three Mongol princes. They succeeded in their task but were then killed by the Mongols.[49] No hint of this story is found in either the Mamluk or Persian sources, and taken together with the many unbelievable details, it would seem justified to cast serious doubts on its veracity.

Baybars must have decided that a more efficient, if much more complicated, method to rid himself of obnoxious personalities on the other side was the intentional use of wrong information, disinformation in modern parlance, in order to discredit them in the eyes of the Īlkhān. Baybars first used this technique against al-Zayn al-Ḥāfiẓī (Zayn al-Dīn Sulaymān b. al-Mu'ayyad al-ʿAqrabānī), who had been the wazir of the last Ayyūbid ruler of Syria, al-Nāṣir Yūsuf. Long before Hülegü's invasion of Syria, al-Zayn had been secretly loyal to the Mongols and had acted to undermine al-Nāṣir's regime and his will to resist the Mongols. He fled with the Mongols after the defeat at ʿAyn Jālūt and became a Mongol official. Baybars had found himself at odds with him in the final months of al-Nāṣir's reign, and it was this old score to be settled rather than al-Zayn's danger as an Īlkhānid official which probably motivated Baybars to have him eliminated.[50] In 662/1263–4, Baybars started the process of discrediting al-Zayn, by sending false messages to him, in which the impression was given that he was in secret league with the Sultan. Al-Zayn himself showed these letters to Hülegü, who believed his disclaimers, and permitted him to try his hand at a similar trick among the Mamluks. Not only was that trick unsuccessful, but Baybars sent another, even more incriminat-

[47] Runciman, *Crusades*, 3:332–3, 338; Thorau, *Baybars*, 204, 222.

[48] *Rawḍ*, 395; Irwin, "County of Tripoli," 248.

[49] Qirtay, fols. 76b–78a.

[50] See above, pp. 23, 30, 43.

ing, letter with *quṣṣād*, and made sure it reached Hülegü. The Īlkhān would hear no excuses. Al-Zayn's fate was sealed, and he and his family were executed.[51]

It is reported that some ten years later (672/1273–4), Baybars used the same technique to bring about the demise of the Catholicos (*jathalīq*) in Baghdad, who had a great deal of influence with Abagha, and had been making life difficult for the local Muslims. The Sultan had composed an incriminating letter, which included *inter alia* gratitude for providing secret information about the Mongols (*akhbār al-mughul al-bāṭiniyya*). An interesting stratagem was devised to have the "secret letter" (*mulaṭṭaf*) come to Abagha's notice. An Armenian (called a *qāṣid*) was sent from al-Bīra to carry the message. At Baybars's orders, however, the governor of al-Bīra wrote to the lord of Shumayṣāṭ/Sumaysāṭ, Shams al-Dīn Bahādur. This lord had been for some time in secret communication with the Sultan and had sent information about the Mongols. Bahādur was to intercept the Armenian, and bring him and the letter to Abagha. This was done and resulted – it is implied – in the execution of the Catholicos. At some point after this, however, the Mongols began to suspect Bahādur for his pro-Mamluk activities. He was arrested and brought to the *ordo*, but managed to escape and make his way to al-Bīra. Bahādur's mamluks and entourage, supposedly numbering about 1000, had already fled to Syria, and he himself was well received by the Sultan.[52]

If we are to remain faithful to the chronology of the Mamluk sources, it might appear that the story is referring to the Nestorian Catholicos Mar Denha. He had replaced Mar Makika, who had died in 1265.[53] But Mar Denha lived until 1281, so he is not a possibility. Assuming that there is a chronological problem in the Mamluk sources, Mar Makika could be a candidate, but the pro-Mongol sources which mention him – such as Bar Hebraeus and Ibn al-Fuwaṭī – do not report that he suffered such a demise, a fact which does cast some doubt on the ultimate success of this stratagem.

Baybars was not beyond using such tactics to convince potential friends that it was in their interest to flee to the Sultanate. In 660/1261–2, the Sultan was in contact with Salār al-Baghdādī, who had been an officer in the ʿAbbāsid government and was now serving the Mongols. Salār promised Baybars that he would desert to his side, but kept postponing his setting out. The Sultan then forced his hand. He sent two *qāṣids* with a message to Salār. One of the

51 Yūnīnī, 2:334–6; Kutubī, 20:297–300; Ibn al-Dawādārī, 8:104–5, who cites Ibn Shaddād's biography of Baybars as his source; Ibn al-Ṣuqāʿī, 78–9. Another reason for al-Zayn's execution was that he had accepted a bribe during the siege of Mosul, where he had been ordered to inspect conditions in the Mongol camp.

52 *Rawḍ*, 421–3; *Tuḥfa*, 78; Nuwayrī, MS. 2m, fol. 208a–b; Ibn al-Furāt, MS. Vienna, fol. 219b; 7:4–5; see ch. 5, p. 132.

53 E.A.W. Budge, *The Monks of Ḳûblâi Khân Emperor of China* (rpt., New York, 1973 of Manchester, 1928), 58–9; J.B. Chabot, "Histoire du patriarche Mar Jabalaha III et du moine Rabban Çauma," *ROL* 1 (1893):593 n. 2; 2 (1884):301. On the *jathalīq*'s high status with the Mongols, see ʿUmarī, ed. Lech, 92; see Spuler, *Iran*, 170–9, for the condition of the Nestorians under the first Īlkhāns.

qāṣids, however, had secret orders to kill the other and leave the body in a place where the Mongols would find it and the letter. The unfortunate Salār, discovering that his secret had become known to the Mongols, had no choice but to flee. In spite of Salār's original diffidence in coming to the Sultanate, he was welcomed warmly by Baybars.[54]

Baybars's contact with a subject ruler could, of course, be discovered by the Mongols. Around 665/1266–7, the Sultan was corresponding with the Ayyūbid ruler of Ḥiṣn Kayfā, al-Malik al-Muwaḥḥid (al-Awḥad) b. al-Muʿaẓẓam Tūrānshāh b. al-Ṣāliḥ Ayyūb, encouraging him to abandon the Mongols and make his way to Syria. Under the influence of two of his eunuchs, al-Muwaḥḥid agreed. But the *quṣṣād* carrying his answer were caught by the local Mongol commander, and the letters brought to Abagha. The two eunuchs were executed, but al-Muwaḥḥid's life was spared, although he had to reside at the *ordo*; seven years later he was allowed to return to Ḥiṣn Kayfā, where he "ruled" until his death in 682/1283.[55]

Contact was also maintained with the Christian kings of Georgia, which was under Mongol domination. As early as 663/1264–5, envoys came from Georgia in response to the *quṣṣād* which Baybars had earlier sent to the princes of the small countries (*mulūk al-ṭawā'if*). These princes included one of the two kings of Georgia, David the son of Rusudani (Dāwūd b. Sūdān), known as David Narin ("the clever"). A letter came back from this prince, in which he expressed friendship for the Sultan and enmity towards the Sultan's enemies, and told of his contacts with Berke.[56] In 666/1268, Baybars's envoy (*rasūl*) returned with letters from both "the King of al-Abkhāz" and Ulu[gh] ("big") David of Tiflis, David Narin's ostensible co-sovereign. In their letters, they professed their loyalty to the Sultan and spurned the Mongols.[57] The "King of Abkhāz" must be a reference to David Narin, who had fled Tiflis to Abkhazia in the late 1250s in order to escape the Mongols.[58] The Mongols certainly had some idea of these contacts early on: at some date before Hülegü's death (663/1265), envoys (*quṣṣād*) of Baybars returning from Georgia with gifts were captured when their ship was blown off course into Tripoli, whose ruler (Bohemond VI) then sent them on to Hülegü.[59]

Nothing came of these negotiations. An indication of this is seen in 672/1273–4, when Baybars arrested a Georgian prince who had entered Palestine

[54] Nuwayrī, MS. 2m, fol. 153a–b. For Salār's arrival and reception, see ch. 5, p. 109.

[55] Nuwayrī, MS. 2m, fol. 110a–b. It is doubtful that Baybars intended to make al-Muwaḥḥid ruler of Egypt, as the source claims; this may have been a ploy to pique al-Muwaḥḥid's interest.

[56] Ibn al-Furāt, MS. Vienna, fol. 77a; ʿAynī, fol. 93b; Maqrīzī, 1:537; *Ḥusn*, 101; Thorau, *Baybars*, 163.

[57] *Rawḍ*, 299; Ibn al-Furāt, MS. Vienna, fol. 131a; Thorau, *Baybars*, 219–20. *Rawḍ* writes *abjār*, which in Ibn al-Furāt is written *abkhār*. This is al-Abkhāz (Abkhazia), a region in western Caucasia on the Black Sea; Yāqūt, 1:78; *EI*², 1:1006. On the relations of the Georgians with the Mongols, and the careers of the two Davids, see W.E.D. Allen, *A History of the Georgian People* (London, 1932), 112–18.

[58] Kirakos, *History of the Armenians*, tr. R. Bedrosian (New York, 1986), 265, 325.

[59] *Rawḍ*, 300; Ibn al-Furāt, MS. Vienna, fol. 134a (= ed. Lyons, 1:146).

incognito, so as to perform the pilgrimage to Jerusalem.[60] For all their talk, the Georgians were too firmly under Mongol domination to assert their independence. Georgian troops fought with the Mongols at the battles of Abulustayn (675/1277) and Homs (680/1281). It is doubtful whether Baybars harbored any illusions about the prospects of drawing the Georgians from the Mongol camp and their enlistment in his struggle against the Īlkhāns. But, even if the Sultan was only successful in stirring up some trouble in the Mongols' backyard, at little cost or danger to himself, he stood to profit from the cultivation of contacts with the Georgian rulers. Certainly, the Mongols, having discovered the existence of such contacts, would have been nonplussed and that much more distrustful of these "allies."

The Mongol rulers harbored a certain distrust towards the Muslim lords, officials and officers who served them. The Mongols knew that the existence of a strong Muslim state, which furthermore enjoyed the support of the Caliph, exerted a powerful attraction on this indigenous elite.[61] These suspicions were surely strengthened by the desertion of Muslim military elements from the Mongols to the Mamluks, along with revelations of the infiltration of Mamluk agents and contacts between the Sultan and various Muslim local rulers and others. Because of such an atmosphere of distrust, Baybars's stratagems of disinformation against al-Zayn al-Ḥāfiẓī and the Catholicos were successful (or at least as reported in the Mamluk sources). For all their suspicions, however, the Mongols were unable to dispense with the services of the Muslim bureaucrats and soldiers who served them, as they needed them to run their empire.

Accusations of pro-Mamluk feelings, contacts with the Sultan, or plans to flee to Syria were banded about quite frequently in the Īlkhānid kingdom. In 659/1261–2, Hülegü ostensibly suspected the Artuqid lord of Mārdīn, al-Muẓaffar Qara Arslan, of contemplating fleeing to the Mamluks. While this may have been merely an excuse for Hülegü to gain firmer control over this ruler and his city, the fact that it was given as a pretext shows that it was considered a real possibility.[62] Around this same time the Pervāne, in a letter to Hülegü, accused ʿIzz al-Dīn Kaykāwūs, one of the Seljuq co-sultans, of corresponding with Baybars; at this point, there is no evidence that ʿIzz al-Dīn had already written to Baybars.[63] For the next seventeen years, the Pervāne was often to use this tactic of accusing his enemies of secret pro-Mamluk

[60] The Sultan received word of this noble's imminent arrival because of the concern he devoted to intelligence gathering (*istiṭlāʿ al-sulṭān li'l-akhbār*); *Rawḍ*, 423; Ibn al-Furāt, 7:5; *Zubda*, fol. 81a; Brosset, *Histoire de la Géorgie*, 1:596, n. 4; Howorth, *Mongols*, 3:311. In 675/1276–7, a Georgian envoy arrived to free this nobleman; Ibn Shaddād, *Ta'rīkh*, 168–9. In 681/1282–3, another Georgian nobleman was caught in Jerusalem, again because of an intelligence tip; *Zubda*, fol. 139a; Nuwayrī, MS. 2n, fols. 23b–24b; Maqrīzī, 1:710. This may perhaps be the same incident told twice.

[61] A comment to this effect is made by Abel-Remusat, "Mémoires," 7:336.

[62] Yūnīnī, 1:457–8, 2:112–13; Ibn al-Dawādārī, 8:83.

[63] Ibn Bībī, 295 (= tr. Duda, 282); Cahen, *Pre-Ottoman Turkey*, 279. See ch. 7, pp. 158–9.

sympathies and actions. In 664/1265–6 and again in 666/1267–8, he accused the (now singular) Seljuq sultan Rukn al-Dīn Qilich Arslan of such activities, and thus obtained permission from Abagha to kill him.[64] Again, in 666/1267–8, the Pervāne and Hetᶜum of Cilicia were both at Abagha's court and accused each other of corresponding with the Sultan of Egypt.[65] The Pervāne was not beyond charging members of the Mongol royal family with pro-Baybars feelings. Twice in the early 670s (1270s), he accused Abagha's brother Ejei, who was the Mongol commander in Rūm, of secretly communicating with Baybars.[66] All of these denunciations are ironic, since during at least part of this time it was the Pervāne himself who was maintaining secret contact with Baybars, a subject that will be discussed in chapter 7.

Even trusted servants of the Mongols, such as the *ṣāḥib-dīwān* (first minister) Shams al-Dīn Muḥammad Juwaynī and his brother ᶜAlā' al-Dīn ᶜAṭā Malik (the governor of Baghdad and famous historian), were not exempt from accusations of having contacts with the Mamluks. These vicissitudes in the career of the Juwaynīs should be seen against the backdrop of intrigues among the high officials serving the Mongols. Early in Abagha's reign, ᶜAṭā Malik was accused by the *shaḥna* of Baghdad of planning to flee to Syria.[67] In 677/1278–9 and 678/80, both brothers were accused of being in league with the Mamluks. In all cases, the charges were eventually dropped.[68] Some of the Mamluk writers have an inkling of these accusations against ᶜAṭā Malik and imply that he died in prison (680/1281–2).[69] There is no indication in the Mamluk sources that either of the Juwaynīs had actually had any kind of contact with the Mamluks.

Mongol efforts at espionage

The Mongols also tried their hand at secret activities, but if we are to judge from the evidence in the Mamluk sources, their attempts were not rewarded with success. The pro-Mongol sources have no information whatsoever on Mongol espionage among the Mamluks, although occasionally they make some mention of spying between different Mongol states.[70]

The Mamluk sources often use the term *qāṣid/quṣṣād* for Mongol agents or secret couriers, employing the terminology used for Mamluk agents for their Mongol counterparts. In addition, the term *jāsūs/jawāsīs* is at times applied to Mongol agents. The mention of Mongol agents, and the knowledge that Chinggis Khan already attributed importance to intelligence gathering,[71]

64 Yūnīnī, 2:347, 388, 404–5; Kutubī, 20:364–5.

65 Yūnīnī, 2:388. Hetᶜum had been, of course, negotiating with the Sultan to get his son back; see ch. 5, pp. 118–20.

66 Yūnīnī, 3:33–4, 113.

67 Ibn al-ᶜIbrī, 498; cf. Bar Hebraeus, 497–8.

68 Rashīd al-Dīn, ed. ᶜAlīzādah, 3:156–61; cf. Boyle, "Īl-Khāns," 362; Spuler, *Iran*, 68–9. See also the two articles on the Juwaynī brothers in *EI*², 2:606–7, by W. Bartold-[J.A. Boyle] and B. Spuler.

69 Abū 'l-Fidā', 4:16; Maqrīzī, 1:705–6. *Zubda*, fols. 126b–127a, 128a, 129b, reports that the Juwaynī brothers were indeed involved in a plot to poison Abagha.

70 Mustawfī, 590–1; Rashīd al-Dīn, ed. ᶜAlīzādah, 3:89.

71 S. Jagchid and P. Hyer, *Mongolia's Culture and Society* (Boulder and Folkestone, 1979), 264.

leads to the tentative conclusion that the Īlkhāns had some type of regular intelligence service, even if there is no explicit evidence to that effect.

Īlkhānid attempts at subterfuge appear early on, and thus do not seem to have been imitations of Mamluk activities but an independently initiated policy. In 660/1262, Mongol *quṣṣād* came to al-Manṣūr of Hama, with a *farmān* (official letter or order), evidently from Hülegü, to woo him over to his side. Instead, al-Manṣūr arrested the couriers and sent them and the letter to Baybars.[72] The following year (661/1263), two Mongol spies (*jāsūsayn li'l-tatar*) were caught at Damietta, as a result of information received from Baybars's agents in the Mongol *ordo*, Lesser Armenia and Acre. These Mongol spies carried a *farmān* to Fāris al-Dīn Aqtay al-Mustaʿrib, the *atabeg*. Baybars knew, however, that this was a Mongol trick and did not doubt the loyalty of this senior amir.[73]

In 661/1263, al-Mughīth ʿUmar, the Ayyūbid ruler of Karak, who had hitherto maintained his independence, came out of his fortress and submitted to Baybars at Mt. Tabor. In spite of pledges of good conduct, al-Mughīth was arrested (and subsequently executed). This breaking of a pledge caused some murmuring among the amirs. According to Ibn ʿAbd al-Raḥīm (and whence, it would seem, al-Yūnīnī and al-Kutubī), Baybars then produced letters from al-Mughīth to the Mongols encouraging them to come to Syria, and a letter from Hülegü thanking him, recognizing his rule over the territory from Bosra to Gaza and promising him 20,000 troops to conquer Egypt. Ibn ʿAbd al-Ẓāhir, as would be expected, does not mention the amirs' doubts, but only that Baybars produced letters from the Mongols to al-Mughīth. Al-Yūnīnī and al-Kutubī question the veracity of these claims and letters, but elsewhere al-Yūnīnī gives evidence which indicates that al-Mughīth had been in contact with Hülegü for some time. As early as 659/1261, Syrian bedouins had stumbled across envoys (*quṣṣād*) going from al-Mughīth to the Mongols carrying letters stating that he was still loyal to the Mongols. At another point, the Sultan had heard of the arrival of a Mongol envoy (*rasūl*) at Karak and sent an emissary to al-Mughīth to demand that he be handed over. Eventually, al-Mughīth gave in. The Mongol envoy was brought to Baybars, and finally confessed that Hülegü had sent him.[74]

Evidently early in Baybars's reign, Aq Sunqur al-Fāriqānī was on a reconnaissance mission in the Jazīra, and caught a Mongol spy (*jāsūs*) carrying letters. This spy was presumably a secret Mongol courier with messages for contacts or sympathizers in Mamluk territory. His fate is not indicated.[75]

More evidence on Mongol spying in Hülegü's reign is related by Ghāzī b. al-Wāsiṭī, a contemporary Damascene. The information, interesting as it is, is

72 *Rawḍ*, 128; *Zubda*, fol. 3b; Ibn al-Furāt, MS. Vienna, fol. 3b; Maqrīzī, 1:471.

73 *Rawḍ*, 195.

74 *Rawḍ*, 150; Ibn ʿAbd al-Raḥīm, in Ibn Wāṣil, MS. 1702, fol. 413b; Yūnīnī, 2:107, 193–4, 299; Kutubī, 20:288–9, 309; Ibn al-Dawādārī, 8:96; Ibn al-Furāt, MS. Vienna, fols. 15a–b, 51a; Maqrīzī, 1:482. See Amitai-Preiss, "Karak," forthcoming. Cf. Thorau, *Baybars*, 134–41.

75 Yūnīnī, 3:299 (= Ibn al-Ṣuqāʿī, 12), who tells how this amir later met with Mamluk informants/agents (*ʿuyūn*) in the area.

somewhat suspect, since it was embedded in an anti-Christian polemic, and several of the author's Christian enemies are specifically mentioned. According to Ghāzī, Baybars received word from "informants of the Muslims" (*nāṣiḥū al-muslimīn*) in the Mongol countries that the Christian al-Makīn b. al-ʿAmīd, the well known historian and *kātib al-jaysh* (chief army clerk) in Damascus, was corresponding with Hülegü, on the numbers of the army in Egypt, the *ḥalqa* and the amirs. Baybars had him arrested and wanted to execute him, but because of Christian influence Ibn al-ʿAmīd was imprisoned for eleven years and eventually released.[76] Ibn al-Ṣuqāʿī tells the story of al-Makīn's arrest differently. This was in the aftermath of the arrest of the governor of Damascus, Taybars al-Wazīrī (660/1262), for improprieties connected to the *dīwān al-jaysh* (army registry office).[77]

Ghāzī relates that at some subsequent unknown date (but during Baybars's reign), it was discovered that a group of local Christians, Armenians and Georgians living in the vicinity of the Church of the Cross (*al-kanīsa al-muṣallaba* [*sic*, should be *kanīsat al-maṣlaba*]) in Jerusalem were in fact Mongol spies (*jawāsīs*). These spies sent information about the amirs, and the army and its movements. News of this was brought to the Mongols by Christian pilgrims to Jerusalem. It was ordered then that those involved be killed and that the church be turned into a mosque.[78]

This information is not found anywhere else, which is surprising given that it would seem to be such a newsworthy event. This does not mean that it must be rejected out of hand, but it does call its credibility into question. Even more important, we know that the Church of the Cross was expropriated by the powerful Sufi shaykh Khaḍir b. Abū Bakr al-Mihrānī. His motives were ostensibly religious and no mention is made of Mongol spies.[79] It seems, then, that Ghāzī may have taken real events and attached to them information about Mongol spies, in order to defame Christians generally or individually. Yet, even if Ghāzī's information is a partial fabrication, it does indirectly show that some perception of Mongol espionage evidently existed in the Mamluk Sultanate. Ghāzī's attempt to besmirch Christians in this way only makes sense if real Mongol spies and informants existed and were uncovered.

We do have information that certain individuals, not only Christians, were known for their pro-Mongol sentiments. In 660/1261–2, when rumors of a Mongol offensive reached Damascus, those men who had cooperated with the Mongols during the occupation of Damascus were rounded up and sent to Egypt.[80] In 663/1264–5, it is reported that two men were in prison for having written to the Mongols and assisted them. The Sultan, who reviewed their case in the Dār al-ʿAdl ("hall of [administrative] justice"), refused to reconsider their punishment.[81] This same year, the qāḍī of al-Bīra was hanged for writing to the ruler of Lesser Armenia offering to sell him the castle.[82]

[76] Ghāzī b. al-Wāsiṭī, 410.
[77] Ibn al-Ṣuqāʿī, 110–1. Ibn al-ʿAmīd's work is extensively cited in chapters 1–3.
[78] Ghāzī b. al-Wāsiṭī, 411–12. [79] Yūnīnī, 3:267–8. On Khaḍir, see Thorau, *Baybars*, 225–9.
[80] Abū Shāma, 219; Yūnīnī, 1:487. [81] Ḥusn, 100–1. [82] Dhahabī, MS. Laud 279, fol 3b.

During Abagha's reign, additional Mongol clandestine activities were uncovered. In 664/1266, Baybars learned that Jalāl al-Dīn Yashkar, the son of the Lesser Dawādār in pre-Mongol Baghdad, who had come over as a *wāfidī* only two years before, was in secret communication with his former masters via Mongol *quṣṣād*. At al-Bīra, one of these *quṣṣād*, a Persian named al-Qazwīnī, was caught. He was brought to the Sultan, forced to confess and hanged.[83] In 673/1274–5, the Sultan learnt that a group of amirs, mostly Mongol *wāfidīs* who had sought refuge in the Sultanate in the early 660s, were in correspondence with the Mongols. First evidence of this case was brought by a bedouin who chanced to learn of this correspondence. Then the *wālī* (governor) of Gaza caught three men, one of whom was a bedouin, carrying letters to the Mongols from these amirs. The amirs were arrested and admitted their guilt, claiming they had been inspired by the feeling that their interests had been ignored. They were subsequently executed.[84]

According to Ibn al-Dawādārī, in 675/1277, while Baybars was with his army in Rūm (see chapter 7), he announced his plans to march to Sīwās. Mongol agents, called *quṣṣād*, set off to convey this news to Abagha. By the time Abagha reached Sīwās, Baybars was back in Syria. It turned out that this had been a deliberate ploy to mislead the Īlkhān.[85] This evidence may well be a fabrication, since it does not appear in the parallel passage in Ibn Shaddād's biography of Baybars, upon which Ibn al-Dawādārī based most of the account of the expedition to Rūm. Even so, it does show that the author picked the term *quṣṣād* to designate Mongol agents.

As a final piece of evidence, slightly later than the period dealt with here, there was the exchange of letters between Qalawun and Aḥmad Tegüder, referred to above. Qalawun, answering Aḥmad's charges that the Mamluks disguised their spies as *faqīrs*, countered that the Mamluks had caught many Mongol spies (*jawāsīs*) dressed like *faqīrs*.[86] It is difficult, however, to ascertain the truth of this claim, as it was part of a polemical exchange and may have been no more than propaganda.

On the basis of the Mamluk sources, who provide virtually all our information on the Mamluk–Īlkhānid secret war, it would seem that here – as in the border war – the Mamluks bested their Mongol adversaries. This is said with the reservation that perhaps the Mongols had been more successful than the Mamluk writers knew. Mamluk success may perhaps have been due to the greater attention paid by the Sultan to his intelligence service as compared to the Mongols. As has already been suggested in chapter 5, the Mamluks seemingly took the conflict more seriously than the Mongols, as they realized that even a minor setback might have fateful implications. Likewise, the Mamluks apparently devoted more attention to the secret aspect of the war.

[83] *Rawḍ*, 273; *Ḥusn*, 117 (s.a. 665); see ch. 5, p. 110.
[84] Ibn Shaddād, *Ta'rīkh*, 104–5; Yūnīnī, 3:87–8; Nuwayrī, MS. 2m, 221a; Ibn Kathīr, 13:268.
[85] Ibn al-Dawādārī, 8:202; cf. Ibn Shaddād, *Ta'rīkh*, 177.
[86] *Zubda*, fol. 135b; in appendix to Maqrīzī, 1:983.

The Mamluks had another advantage over the Mongols because of the great deal of sympathy they enjoyed among the Muslim population in Mongol controlled territory. This sympathy was found among both the indigenous civilian inhabitants and the remnants of the pre-Mongol military class, and was exploited by Baybars and his successors. The Mongols were aware of the potentially divided loyalties of the indigenous Muslim bureaucrats and members of the local military class who served them, but could not do without their services. It is true that the Mongols were also able to find people willing to cooperate with them in the Mamluk Sultanate, either for "religious" (i.e. anti-Muslim) or material reasons, but it seems that this support did not come close to the extent of pro-Mamluk feeling in the east.

The Armenian historian Hetʿum, writing at the beginning of the fourteenth century, offers another reason for Mamluk successes in the war in general, and by implication in the secret war: the Muslims (Sarazins) kept their plans relatively secret, while the Mongols, who each year met in a council and publicly discussed their campaigns, revealed their designs.[87] What Hetʿum is essentially saying is that the Mamluks knew how to keep a secret better than the Mongols. Whether the Mongol leaders actually planned their strategy together is unclear, but it has been seen that Baybars at least knew how to keep his own counsel, and succeeded in maintaining a cloak of secrecy around his own movements and those of his army.

[87] Hetʿum, 2:251–2; cited in Howorth, *Mongols*, 579; Sinor, "Mongol Strategy," 240. On the Mongol council (*quriltai*), see *ibid.*

CHAPTER 7

Baybars's intervention in Seljuq Rūm

At that time the Sultan of Egypt entered with his power into the realm of Turkey. He killed and drove out all the Tartars that were there and took many lands and cities, because a traitor that Abagha had made head official [*chevetaine*] of Turkey, who was called Parvana, had turned and became obedient to the Sultan of Egypt, and exerted himself to drive the Tartars out of Turkey.

Het῾um[1]

Mamluk incursions over the border may have disconcerted the Īlkhāns and their local commanders and confederates, but they did not seriously endanger the integrity and security of the Īlkhānid kingdom. In 675/1277, however, Baybars mounted a major invasion of Rūm, in the course of which he defeated a Mongol army at Abulustayn (Elbistan) and occupied the Seljuq capital of Qaysāriyya (Kayseri, Caesarea). Baybars's goals are not known. Perhaps he had hoped to wrest Seljuq Rūm from the Mongols, thinking that he would find significant support from various military elements in that country. Possibly, however, his plan was more modest, and he had only launched a massive raid in order to destabilize the Mongols, test their reactions and try his own troops.

Early Mamluk interest in Seljuq Rūm

In the aftermath of the victory at Köse Dagh (641/1243), the Mongols gained control over the Seljuq kingdom in Rūm. Mongol rule, however, was indirect, and the Seljuq sultans, or rather their senior officials and officers, still ran the country, although under Mongol supervision. Actual Mongol presence in Rūm was minimal. This changed with the approach of Hülegü. Baiju (or Baichu), the Mongol commander in western Iran, who hitherto had camped in the Mughan plains, was ordered to take his troops and herds to Anatolia, in order to make room for Hülegü. This movement of Mongol troops meant two things: increased interference in Seljuq affairs, and less grazing lands available for Seljuq commanders and their soldiers.

[1] *RHC, Ar*, 2:179.

Around the time of Hülegü's arrival in northwest Iran, the Sultanate of Seljuq Rūm was divided between two brothers, ʿIzz al-Dīn Kaykāwūs and Rukn al-Dīn Qilich Arslan. Relations between the two brothers, each with his supporters among the notables of the kingdom, had never been good. Both brothers joined Hülegü for the conquest of northern Syria, including the siege of Aleppo, and returned to Rūm when Hülegü set out for the East. Open warfare broke out between them in 659/1261, when Hülegü, having suspected ʿIzz al-Dīn of secretly communicating with the Mamluks, ordered Rukn al-Dīn to move against him. Rukn al-Dīn, with Mongol support, advanced towards Konya, his brother's capital. ʿIzz al-Dīn fled first to Anṭalyā and then to Constantinople, where he was initially well received by the Emperor Michael Palaeologus.[2]

These events were not without interest for Baybars. In late 659 or very early 660/1261, he had sent envoys to ʿIzz al-Dīn. They met with this ruler at Anṭalyā, where he had retreated after being dislodged from Konya. The envoys brought with them a letter from Baybars, which sought to encourage ʿIzz al-Dīn and promised him assistance. But ʿIzz al-Dīn remained undecided about what action to adopt and the envoys returned to Egypt. His situation continued to deteriorate and he eventually fled to Constantinople.[3]

Baybars's envoys probably returned some time in the spring of 660/1262, accompanied by two envoys from ʿIzz al-Dīn, who brought with them a letter, in which ʿIzz al-Dīn asked for assistance and offered Baybars one half of his kingdom. He also sent signed, blank *iqṭāʿ* deeds for Baybars to distribute as he saw fit. The Sultan received the envoys well, and ordered the organization of an expeditionary force of an unknown size, placing it under the command of Nāṣir al-Dīn Oghulmush al-Silāḥdār al-Ṣāliḥī. For good measure, and perhaps to encourage him, this amir was granted an *iqṭāʿ* worth 300 horsemen in Rūm and/or Āmid and its environs.[4] These preparations seem to have been little more than a propaganda measure. ʿIzz al-Dīn was not in a position to distribute such largesse, and it is unlikely that Baybars entertained serious hopes of success in this endeavor. The dispatch of a Mamluk force would surely have led to the loss of valuable troops. In addition, our primary source, Ibn ʿAbd al-Ẓāhir, makes no more mention of this campaign, so it can be assumed that it never got off the ground. Baybars al-Manṣūrī writes, after citing this author, that while preparations for the expedition were underway news came of ʿIzz al-Dīn's defeat, and the plan was dropped.[5]

Soon after this mission, another letter arrived from ʿIzz al-Dīn. This told of

[2] On the period from Köse Dagh to ʿIzz al-Dīn's defeat, see: Cahen, *Pre-Ottoman Turkey*, 269–79; Holt, *Crusades*, 173–4. For the deterioration of relations and the eventual conflict between the two brothers, see: Ibn Bībī, 295; *Zubda*, fols. 51b–53b; Yūnīnī, 2:113–14; Bar Hebraeus, 442. [3] Yūnīnī, 2:160–1, where Anṭalyā is written Anṭākiya.

[4] *Rawḍ*, 125–7; Nuwayrī, MS. 2m, fols. 153b–154a; Ibn al-Furāt, MS. Vienna, fols. 2b–3b; Maqrīzī, 1:469–70. Originally, *Rawḍ* implies that ʿIzz al-Dīn's envoys arrived in Shaʿbān/July-August, but Oghulmush's commission (*tadhkira*) is dated the end of Jumādā II/mid-May.

[5] *Zubda*, fol. 54b; whence ʿAynī, fol. 86a.

how his enemy (i.e. Rukn al-Dīn and supporters) had been so disconcerted by the news of ᶜIzz al-Dīn's agreement with Baybars that they had fled. ᶜIzz al-Dīn had sent an army to besiege Konya.[6] This was mere bluster, and Baybars seems to have understood it as such. In Rajab 661/May 1263, envoys from the Golden Horde arrived at Baybars's court. Among other matters, the message that they brought from Berke called on Baybars to assist ᶜIzz al-Dīn, presumably in the latter's endeavors to regain his kingdom. The envoys from the Golden Horde were accompanied by representatives of ᶜIzz al-Dīn himself.[7] There is no record that Baybars was moved to act on this matter.

Contacts between the Pervāne and Baybars

The dominant figure in Seljuq Rūm during the period parallel to Baybars's reign was Muᶜīn al-Dīn Sulaymān b. Muhadhdhab al-Dīn ᶜAlī al-Daylamī, known usually as the Pervāne.[8] Essentially, he was the strongman of the Seljuq regime, while only nominal power was in the hands of the sultan. The Pervāne had the dual role of representing the Seljuq kingdom *vis-à-vis* the Mongols, and acting as the latter's agent in Rūm. Professor Cahen has aptly described the Pervāne as "a true dictator under the Mongol protectorate," and sums up his achievement thus:

> The period extending from the flight of ᶜIzz al-Dīn or, alternatively, from the appointment a little earlier of Muᶜīn al-Dīn Sulaymān (still known as the *pervane*) as the real head of the government under Rukn al-Dīn, until his tragic death in 1277, marks a stage in the decline of the Seljuqid State, an attempt to strike a balance – a difficult feat which, save at the end, he managed to achieve – between the desire to retain the Mongols' full confidence and the re-organization of the State in some of its traditional aspects, particularly as a Muslim State. The task was not easy but, whatever his personal ambitions, it may be thought that Muᶜīn al-Dīn succeeded in giving the inhabitants of Rūm a respite, or indeed a period of recovery, after the ordeals of recent years.[9]

An essential condition for the Pervāne's effective control was the compliance of the Seljuq Sultan. Initially, he could not have found a more cooperative candidate than Rukn al-Dīn, who – it is reported – devoted himself mainly to the pursuit of pleasure. At some point, however, the Sultan began to chafe at the Pervāne's control, and plotted his removal. The Pervāne, however, acted first. According to al-Yūnīnī, as early as 664/1265–6 and again

[6] *Rawḍ*, 128; Ibn al-Furāt, MS. Vienna, fol. 3b; cf. Maqrīzī, 1:470, who inserts Hülegü after ᶜ*adūw* (enemy). See also Holt, *Crusades*, 159–60, 174.

[7] *Rawḍ*, 171; Nuwayrī, MS. 2m, fol. 165a–b; Ibn al-Furāt, MS. Vienna, fol. 30a; Maqrīzī, 1:495. For ᶜIzz al-Dīn's fate, Canard, "Un traité," 215–16; Geanakoplos, *Emperor*, 181–2; Cahen, *Pre-Ottoman Turkey*, 279.

[8] The Persian title *pervāne*, written *barwānāh* in Arabic, literally means "butterfly," but had the additional meanings of "official letter" and "commander" or "supervisor." See: Cahen, *Pre-Ottoman Turkey*, 221–2; F. Steingass, *Persian-English Dictionary* (rpt., London, 1977), 245; cf. Boyle, "Īl-Khāns," 366.

[9] Cahen, *Pre-Ottoman Turkey*, 222, 280.

in 666/1267–8, the Pervāne calumniated the Sultan before Abagha, accusing him (falsely) of sympathy and contact with the Mamluks. The Īlkhān gave permission to have him killed. Soon afterwards, the Pervāne arranged for Rukn al-Dīn's execution by several of the Mongol officers stationed in Rūm. His successor was his son Ghiyāth al-Dīn Kaykhusraw III. Since the new sultan was a mere boy (the sources give his age from two to ten years old), there would be no question of his resisting the Pervāne's tutelage.[10]

For several years, little is heard of the Pervāne or Rūm in general, a phenomenon which Professor Cahen attributes to the relative stability in that country.[11] At the beginning of the 670s, the north Syria–Rūmī frontier began to heat up and the Pervāne and Seljuq Rūmī troops played an important role in the military activities of the Mongols, participating in Samaghar's raid into northern Syria in Rabīᶜ II 670/November 1271. Several months later (Shawwāl/May 1272), separate envoys from both Samaghar and the Pervāne arrived together in Damascus, and thus began a period of "negotiations" between Baybars and Abagha, from which nothing tangible resulted. Rūmī amirs and troops, but not the Pervāne himself, participated in the unsuccessful Mongol siege of al-Bīra in Jumādā I 671/November-December 1272.[12]

Samaghar had been the senior Mongol officer in Rūm for some time, perhaps since Baiju's execution.[13] In one place Baybars al-Manṣūrī calls him the commander of the Mongol *tümen* in Rūm.[14] Whatever the exact number of soldiers under his command, he had several missions: to maintain order and loyalty to the Mongols, to fight the often troublesome Türkmen, and to intervene in north Syria when called upon to do so.[15] The impression gained is that the Pervāne and Samaghar had found a *modus vivendi*, as no friction is noted in the sources.

The situation became more complicated with the arrival of Abagha's

[10] Yūnīnī, 2:347, 387–8, 403–6; Ibn al-Furāt, MS. Vienna, fol. 147a–b; Maqrīzī, 1:571–2; ᶜAynī, fol. 98b; Ibn Bībī, 299–303; Cahen, *Pre-Ottoman Turkey*, 284. The Mamluk sources place the execution of Rukn al-Dīn s.a. 666, while Ibn Bībī has him die in AH 664.

[11] Cahen, *Pre-Ottoman Turkey*, 284.

[12] For these campaigns and diplomatic *démarches*, see ch. 5.

[13] Baiju was executed at Hülegü's orders, probably around the same time that he was eliminating the Jochid princes in his army, some time in the period following ᶜAyn Jālūt; Jackson, "Dissolution," 217 n. 138, 233; see Nuwayrī, 27:384. Perhaps Baiju was initially succeeded by Shiremün the son of Chormaghun, but cf. Qalqashandī, 5:361–2. Another Mongol officer ca. 1260 was Alinjaq (= Alinaq ?) Noyan, who was sent with a force and was based near Aqsaray; al-Karīm Āqsarāyī, *Musāmarat al-akhbār*, ed. O. Turan (Ankara, 1944), 68. The fact that he is not heard of again in the sources at this time either indicates the modest nature or the short duration of his command; cf. J.M. Smith, Jr., "Mongol Nomadism and Middle Eastern Geography: Qīshlāqs and Tümens," in D.O. Morgan *et al.* (ed.), *The Mongol Empire and its Legacy*, forthcoming; I am grateful to Prof. Smith for kindly sending me a draft of this paper.

[14] *Tuḥfa*, 74; the equivalent passage in *Zubda*, fol. 76b (whence ᶜAynī, fol. 104a), reads that he was the governor (*nā'ib*) in Rūm. Qalqashandī, 5:361–2, calls him the son of Baiju, and gives him the title of *shaḥna*. See also Mostaert and Cleaves, "Trois documents," 436; Pelliot, *Notes on Marco Polo*, 2:824–5.

[15] Cahen, *Pre-Ottoman Turkey*, 283, who adds that the Mongol troops, from ca. 1261 onward, were stationed in almost all of Asia Minor. The basis for this last statement is not clear. See also *ibid.*, 331, on the source of the livelihood of these troops.

younger brother, Ejei, in 669/1271.[16] Ejei seems to have enjoyed some type of joint governorship with Samaghar.[17] Abagha's reasons for sending the former are unclear, but they perhaps included the desire to find an appanage for his younger brother, to get him away from the center of the empire, and to place an extra check on the power of both the Pervāne and Samaghar.[18] The presence of the additional Mongol troops who had accompanied Ejei strained the resources of the kingdom even more, and must have also grated on the Pervāne and the Rūmī amirs. Ejei had made financial demands on the Pervāne (and it seems also the state treasury). Around 670/1271, therefore, the Pervāne went to Abagha (he was accompanying Baybars's envoys),[19] and spoke to him secretly of recalling Ejei. He claimed that Ejei was planning to kill him, was aspiring to become ruler of Rūm and to place himself under the protection of Baybars. Abagha promised the Pervāne that both Ejei and Samaghar would be recalled, and that Toqa (also: Toqu, Toqai) Noyan would be sent in their place. Upon returning to Rūm, the Pervāne saw that the promised change of governors had been delayed, while Ejei's demands became even greater.[20]

This, then, was the background to the Pervāne's secret correspondence with Baybars, although it has been suggested that perhaps Baybars's victories against the Mongols were another factor that attracted the Pervāne to seek his help.[21] In 672/1274, the Pervāne sent an envoy to Baybars, who presented a request that Baybars dispatch an army against the Mongols in Rūm. The Sultan was asked to keep Ghiyāth al-Dīn as sultan and the Pervāne as his regent. Baybars's response was carefully chosen. He first demanded that a large amount of money be paid in advance for the costs of sending an army. The Sultan then added that since his horses could not negotiate the roads at this time, he would only come next year.

Baybars had not committed himself too far, but left room for further negotiations if the Pervāne had indeed been serious. But by the time the envoy returned to the Pervāne, Abagha had finally withdrawn Ejei, along with Samaghar, and replaced them by Toqa Noyan as promised. The Pervāne's position having thus improved, at this time he did not send a response back to Baybars, especially as he did not see any aid coming his way in the immediate future.[22]

16 Yūnīnī, 2:457. Ejei is mentioned in Rūm as early as 666/1267–8, when he returned with the Pervāne and Samaghar after their visit to Abagha; *ibid.*, 2:387–8. This must have been only a temporary stay. For Mongol commanders in Rūm in AH 666, see: *ibid.*, 2:404–5.

17 Ibn Shaddād, *Ta'rīkh*, 62, mentions their council (*majlis*).

18 See Cahen, *Pre-Ottoman Turkey*, 285.

19 See ch. 5, p. 127.

20 Ibn Shaddād, *Ta'rīkh*, 78–9; whence Yūnīnī, 3:33–4; cf. the confused version in Qirtay, fol. 99a. Toqa was the son of Ilge Noyan (see ch. 3, p. 51); Rashīd al-Dīn, ed. ʿAlīzādah, 3:102.

21 Cahen, *Pre-Ottoman Turkey*, 285.

22 Ibn Shaddād, *Ta'rīkh*, 79; Yūnīnī, 3:34. For the above, see also Thorau, *Baybars*, 235–6. According to ʿAynī, fol. 116a, Samaghar was reappointed governor (*nā'ib*) in Rūm after the battle of Abulustayn. There seems to be some confusion in Rashīd al-Dīn, ed. ʿAlīzādah, 3:102, who writes that after his accession, Abagha sent Toghu (= Toqa) Bitikchi ("secretary") and Tudawun to Rūm, where they took part in a battle, and were replaced by Samaghar and Kuharkai (?). The author is apparently mistaken in ascribing Toqa and Tudawun's arrival at this early date.

According to Ibn Shaddād, when Baybars came to Syria in 673/1275, the Pervāne was afraid that the Sultan might actually fulfill his promise and invade Rūm. While this no longer served his immediate purpose, the Pervāne may have wanted to keep all his options open. Thus, he sent to Baybars and told him to invade Lesser Armenia, and advised him to invade Rūm the following year with the Pervāne's assistance.[23] It would appear, however, that Baybars had planned to raid Lesser Armenia even before the arrival of the Pervāne's message.[24]

It is clear that, in spite of the personnel changes enacted at the Pervāne's request, Abagha did not have complete faith in him. Toqa Noyan had arrived with orders to conduct a fiscal survey of Rūm. Henceforth, the Pervāne and his officers were not to govern and issue orders except in Toqa's presence. The Pervāne saw that he had no choice but to submit. Toqa then conducted an inspection tour of the country and sent a great deal of revenue back to Abagha.[25]

At the end of 673/ca. late spring 1275, the Pervāne, Toqa Noyan and Sultan Ghiyāth al-Dīn were ordered to report personally before Abagha. En route, they ran into Ejei in eastern Anatolia, on his way back to Rūm to resume his command. This disconcerted the Pervāne and Toqa alike, the latter surely because he understood that Ejei's return meant the reduction of his own authority. For the time being, however, they sent presents to Ejei to mollify him. After assorted machinations at the Mongol court, the party set out to return to Rūm. At Sīwās, news was received that Ejei had struck the Pervāne's representatives (*nuwwāb*, perhaps governors), including Ḍiyā' al-Dīn ibn Khaṭīr. The Pervāne and Toqa thereupon conspired to get rid of Ejei and wrote to Abagha to this effect. Ejei, having heard of this letter, in turn sent to Abagha and accused the Pervāne and Toqa of embezzling revenues. Abagha answered his brother that he should disregard the Pervāne and kill him if he wanted. The Pervāne, however, intercepted this message, and acted quickly. He first sent presents to placate the Īlkhān, and then obtained written statements from various Rūmī notables that Ejei was out to kill him and Toqa, and planning to surrender Rūm to the Sultan of Egypt. By then, Abagha had probably had enough of these incriminations and ordered everyone involved to come to the *ordo* (Rabīᶜ I 674/August-September 1275). Ejei was removed from his position, several of his followers were killed and the Pervāne and Toqa Noyan returned to Rūm.[26]

The Pervāne, however, continued to play a double game. Soon after his return to Rūm, orders were received for both the Mongol units in Rūm and the Seljuq troops to take part in a new attack against al-Bīra. Before the expedition, the Pervāne wrote to inform Baybars, promising that when the

[23] Ibn Shaddād, *Ta'rīkh*, 107; Ibn al-Dawādārī, 8:177–8; Mufaḍḍal, 226–7.
[24] For other reasons for Baybars's raid to Lesser Armenia, see ch. 5, p. 134.
[25] Ibn Shaddād, *Ta'rīkh*, 108; Yūnīnī, 3:89; Mufaḍḍal, 227–8. Cf. Qirtay, fol. 100a; Ibn al-Dawādārī, 8:178.
[26] Ibn Shaddād, *Ta'rīkh*, 122–4; Yūnīnī, 3:112–14.

Sultan's army approached the Mongol army, he and the Rūmī amirs would turn on the latter. According to Ibn Shaddād, during the siege itself (Jumādā II 674/November-December 1275),[27] the Pervāne sent 400 troops across the Euphrates to scout and raid. His hope was that this force would be caught by the Sultan and annihilated. Instead, these soldiers captured three of the Pervāne's couriers returning from Baybars, carrying the latter's agreement to the Pervāne's plan described above. This letter was brought to the Mongol commanders, who accused the Pervāne of perfidy. The Pervāne, however, pleaded his innocence, and claimed that this was a trick of King Leon of Lesser Armenia. The Mongol leaders ostensibly accepted these excuses, although secretly they thought differently. They were, however, wary of the possible divided loyalties of the Muslim, mainly Rūmī, soldiers and amirs, and this was one of the reasons they gave up the siege. The incriminating letters were subsequently sent on to Abagha. The case against the Pervāne was growing.[28]

Some unclear points remain in the above account. If the 400 troops sent by the Pervāne were Rūmīs, why would he want them killed, and why did they hand over his couriers to the Mongol leaders? If they were Mongols, how is it that they were obeying his orders? There are no clear-cut answers to these questions. On the other hand, however, Ibn al-Furāt and al-ʿAynī, evidently following Baybars al-Manṣūrī, state that it was Abtai, the Mongol commander, who sent the 400 troops after he found out about the Pervāne's contacts with the Sultan.[29] This makes more sense than Ibn Shaddād's version.

Events leading to the invasion

The events in Rūm preceding Baybars's invasion at the end of 675/early summer 1277 come fast and furious, and are somewhat confusing. Our main source, Ibn Shaddād, provides us with a huge amount of information, although some of it is undated. He is cited by a number of fourteenth-century Syrian writers. The befuddlement is compounded by the additional evidence found in Ibn al-Furāt and al-ʿAynī, seemingly derived from some now-lost folios of Baybars al-Manṣūrī's *Zubda*, which does not completely tally with Ibn Shaddād's account. For convenience's sake, in the following discussion, the two accounts will be referred to as those of Ibn Shaddād and "Baybars al-Manṣūrī."

When the Rūmī army returned to its country after the ignominious conclusion of the siege of al-Bīra (674/1275), the Pervāne met with a group of Rūmī amirs. Ibn Shaddād writes that they adopted an anti-Mongol resolution

[27] See ch. 5, pp. 136–7.

[28] Ibn Shaddād, *Ta'rīkh*, 126–7; Nuwayrī, MS. 2m, fol. 212a; Ibn al-Furāt, 7:41–2; Kutubī, MS. Köpülü, fol. 41a; Yūnīnī, 3:115.

[29] Ibn al-Furāt, 7:42; ʿAynī, fol. 108b, citing Baybars al-Manṣūrī. This portion of *Zubda* is lost, but see *Tuḥfa*, 82.

when they realized the damage done by the discovery of the Pervāne's contact with Baybars. Incipient anti-Mongol feelings now probably came to the fore, and the amirs, together with the Pervāne, decided that they could no longer afford not to act. They agreed to write to Baybars, expressing their loyalty, and calling on him to come to Rūm to their assistance against the Mongols. These amirs were Ḥusām al-Dīn Bījār al-Bābīrī (governor of Kharpurt/Khartabirt), his son Bahā' al-Dīn Bahādur (governor of Diyār Bakr, i.e. the environs of Āmid), Sharaf al-Dīn Masʿūd b. Khaṭīr (governor of Nigde/Nakīda), his brother Ḍiyā' al-Dīn Maḥmūd, and Amīn al-Dīn Mikā'īl. When word of this plot reached other Rūmī amirs, they refused to have a part in it, perhaps out of self-interest or fear of the Mongols. Surprisingly, for all their protestations and claims of loyalty (*īliyya*) to the Mongols, they did not inform them of this "traitorous" action.

Baybars, when he received the request of the Pervāne and the others, sent back thanks, but stated that he was unable to launch a campaign at this time, due to the lack of water. At the end of "grazing season" (*al-rabīʿ*),[30] he would set out for Rūm. Besides such "objective" circumstances, the Sultan may have been waiting to receive more substantial proof of the new-found loyalty of these Rūmi amirs.

Towards the end of 674/late spring 1276, the Pervāne set off to Abagha, taking with him the sister of the Sultan Ghiyāth al-Dīn, who was to become the Īlkhān's wife. According to Ibn Shaddād, the Pervāne left after despairing of Baybars's arrival. "Baybars al-Manṣūrī" gives a different account: after receiving evidence of the Pervāne's traitorous activities during the siege of al-Bīra, Abagha had sent several times ordering the Pervāne to come and explain himself. After repeatedly putting off his visit, and excusing himself with the need to prepare the Sultan's sister for her marriage to Abagha, the Pervāne finally set off.

Different accounts are also given of subsequent events. According to "Baybars al-Manṣūrī," before setting off for Abagha, the Pervāne sent the army of Rūm (or rather only that part loyal to him) to Abulustayn, evidently to wait for Baybars. Among the amirs there were the Pervāne's son ʿAlā' al-Dīn ʿAlī, Sharaf al-Dīn b. Khaṭīr, his brother Ḍiya' al-Dīn, and Sayf al-Dīn Turantay (governor of Amāsiyya). On his way to Abagha, the Pervāne arranged for the amirs to return to Qaysāriyya, where they were to write to Abagha warning him of Baybars's imminent attack on Rūm. The amirs did as he wished, and only a small force under Sayf al-Dīn Abū Bakr Jandar Beg, the governor of the area, remained at Abulustayn. The Pervāne hoped, it would

30 Ibn Shaddād, *Ta'rīkh*, 128–9; whence, Dhahabī, MS. 279, fol. 59a; Kutubī, MS. Köprülü, fol. 41b; Ibn Kathīr, 13:269; Yūnīnī, 3:116–17. See also Khowaiter, *Baibars*, 69. The modern meaning of *rabīʿ*, "spring", is inadequate here. More appropriate is the classical sense of "season of herbage," or even fall-winter (i.e. when the rains fall and thus the herbage grows); see Lane, s.v. *r-b-ʿ*, 1:1018–19. If Baybars was to set out after spring, his troops and horses would surely have suffered from a lack of water, and the latter would have lacked pasturage.

seem, that at a time of crisis, the Īlkhān would not dare to dispense with his experience.

Ibn Shaddād, on the other hand, does not mention the presence of the amirs in Abulustayn in this context. Instead, the Pervāne sent to Bījār, lord of Kharpurt, and his son Bahādur (Professor Cahen calls them Kurds), and urged them to flee to Baybars. Bahādur had been involved in the murder of several Mongols, so he and his father had good reason to disappear. Possibly, the Pervāne also wanted them to encourage Baybars to come to Rūm. Bījār and Bahādur were preceded to the Sultanate by two Mongol officers, the brothers Sögetei (< Sh-K-T-'-Y / S-K-T-'-Y) and Ja'urchi (? < J-'-W-R-J-Y), who were also involved with Bahādur in the murder of the Mongols; in addition, Bahādur was married to their sister. All of these *wāfidiyya* arrived in Egypt in early 675/early summer 1276.[31]

Some time around this time, two raids were launched by the Mamluks into Īlkhānid territory. The first was to Dunaysir, in the territory of Mārdīn, from which the raiders returned safely after wreaking much havoc.[32] The second raid was to the Rūmī frontier. Baybars sent a detachment of 1000 troops there under Bektüt al-Atābakī, who was joined by a contingent from Aleppo. Bektüt's mission was to reconnoiter and raid (*kāshifan wa-mughīran*) and to bring messages to sympathetic Rūmī amirs. Ibn Shaddād tells us that the specific reason that the Sultan had sent this force was to make contact with Sharaf al-Dīn b. Khaṭīr, who after the Pervāne had gone to Abagha had written Baybars to encourage him to come to Rūm. At Abulustayn, Bektüt ran into the force under Sayf al-Dīn Jandar Beg. The latter had initially asked Bektüt to stay and fight with them against the Mongols. Bektüt demurred and convinced Jandar Beg and the others to return with him. Baybars, then in northern Syria, met them near Ḥārim and received them warmly.[33]

Before setting out to return to Syria, Bektüt had sent letters from Baybars to the Rūmi amirs, who were somewhere near Qaysāriyya. Sharaf al-Dīn b. Khaṭīr, Tāj al-Dīn Güyü and the others agreed that each amir would write to Baybars individually and express his loyalty to him. In these letters, they were to inform Baybars that the Pervāne had gone to Abagha and that they were on their way to Qaysāriyya, where Sultan Ghiyāth al-Dīn was located, in order to

[31] Ibn Shaddād, *Ta'rīkh*, 153–6; whence *inter alia* Ibn al-Dawādārī, 8:188–91; Yūnīnī, 2:164–5. "Baybars al-Manṣūrī": Ibn al-Furāt, 7:42–3; ʿAynī, fol. 108b. Cf. Cahen, *Pre-Ottoman Turkey*, 286–7 (his source must be Bar Hebraeus, 455), who writes that Bījār was responsible for the assassination of Sarkīs, the Armenian bishop of Erzinjan; cf. Ibn Shaddād, 169. See also Ibn al-Ṣuqāʿī, 54–5. Sögetei's daughter was eventually married to Qalawun and was the mother of the Sultan al-Nāṣir Muḥammad; Ibn al-Furāt, 7:251; Maqrīzī, 1:709.

[32] Ibn Shaddād, *Ta'rīkh*, 185–6; Yūnīnī, 3:186–7.

[33] Ibn Shaddād, *Ta'rīkh*, 154–5; Yūnīnī, 3:165–6; Ibn al-Furāt, 7:65–6 (here follows Ibn Shaddād); cf. Ibn Bībī, 311. Bektüt's mission appears to be the same episode described by Bar Hebraeus, 454, in which 1000 Egyptians joined a number of Türkmen in the summer of 1276, and fought an Armenian force at Marʿash; see Thorau, *Baybars*, 237 and n. 83. Jandar Beg's son Ḥusayn became an important amir in the Mamluk Sultanate in the early fourteenth century; Ṣafadī, *Wāfī*, 12:347–50.

draw the other amirs into the plot. Sharaf al-Dīn b. Khaṭīr also ordered that the Rūmī army should split up and attack local Mongols. The Qaramanid Türkmen, who were also in contact with Baybars, exploited the growing disorder to attack the Mongols and increase their control. Whether this was in conjuncture with the Rūmī amirs remains a moot point.[34]

Sharaf al-Dīn and his cohorts arrived at Qaysāriyya, and camped outside the city. The Sultan Ghiyāth al-Dīn was in the city, together with Muhadhdhab al-Dīn, the son of the Pervāne. Güyü and Turantay, who before had ostensibly at least agreed with Ibn Khaṭīr, were now in the city and unenthusiastic about events. When Güyü came out to meet Ibn Khaṭīr, an argument ensued, and Ibn Khaṭīr killed him and another amir. For the time being, Turantay pretended agreement with Ibn Khaṭīr. Muhadhdhab al-Dīn wanted no part in these seditious activities and was able to get away from Ibn Khaṭīr and withdraw to the family castle of Dokat. Ibn Khaṭīr, together with Turantay, and the Sultan Ghiyāth al-Dīn, rode to his castle of Nigde. From there, Ibn Khaṭīr sent his brother Ḍiyā' al-Dīn, and Turantay his son Sinān al-Dīn, to Baybars to express their loyalty.[35]

These amirs, along with their entourages and other officers, met Baybars near Homs on 13 Ṣafar 675/27 July 1276. The Sultan was not at all pleased with this unexpected development. He complained that they had acted precipitously, and that he had promised the Pervāne that he would come to Rūm at the end of this year. Most of the army was in Egypt, and Baybars was in no position to go to Rūm with the few troops then at his disposal. In spite of his displeasure, the Rūmīs were well received. Ḍiyā' al-Dīn tried to convince him to enter Rūm even with a small army, but to no avail. Baybars, however, did dispatch a small force under Balaban al-Zaynī to bring the Seljuq Sultan, Ibn Khaṭīr, Turantay and the rest of the loyal amirs to Syria. Balaban reached as far as Kaynūk (Ḥadath al-Ḥamrā'), the scene of a Mamluk raid in 671/1273,[36] when he heard of the Pervāne's return to Rūm with a large Mongol army (supposedly 30,000 men) under Tudawun. Balaban thus aborted his mission. Baybars, thinking himself unsafe in northern Syria with the small force which accompanied him, then returned to Egypt, taking the Rūmī *wāfidiyya* with him. He entered Cairo on 13 Rabīᶜ I/17 August, and began making preparations for the invasion of Rūm.[37]

[34] Ibn Shaddād, *Ta'rīkh*, 157–9; whence Mufaḍḍal, 245–7; Yūnīnī, 3:167. For the revolt of the Türkmen, see also Cahen, *Pre-Ottoman Turkey*, 288, and below.

[35] Ibn Shaddād, *Ta'rīkh*, 159–60; Yūnīnī, 3:167–9; Mufaḍḍal, 247–8. The account in Ibn Bībī, 311–13, generally agrees with Ibn Shaddād, and provides some additional details. The "Baybars al-Manṣūrī" version (Ibn al-Furāt, 7:43; ᶜAynī, fol. 108b; cf. Maqrīzī, 1:621), does not contradict the above, but is much less detailed. Cf. Khowaiter, *Baibars*, 70–1.

[36] See ch. 5, p. 131, where this place's location is discussed.

[37] Ibn Shaddād, *Ta'rīkh*, 160–1, who adds that the army was accompanied by Abagha's brother Mengü Temür; Yūnīnī, 3:169–70; Mufaḍḍal, 250–2. Ibn al-Furāt and ᶜAynī (s.a. 674, as cited in the previous note), state that Tudawun was accompanied by Toqa, and their army was composed of 30,000 "noble Mongols" (*min aᶜyān al-mughul*). In the annal for AH 675, Ibn al-Furāt (7:66–7; whence Maqrīzī, 1:625–6) and ᶜAynī (fol. 110a–b) repeat much of this

Sharaf al-Dīn ibn Khaṭīr was very disconcerted by the arrival of such a large Mongol force. It was clear, for the time being at least, that the Pervāne was back in the Mongol camp, and had abandoned his flirtation with Baybars. Ibn Khaṭīr considered resisting, but was persuaded to abandon such an idea, given the overwhelming size of the Mongol force. He then fled to one of the forts under his control, Qalʿat Lu'lu', in the hope of fortifying himself in it. Its commander, however, proved treacherous, and handed him over to the Mongols. Tudawun held a trial (*yarghu*) for all those involved in the contacts with Baybars. Ghiyāth al-Dīn was absolved after he claimed that due to his young age he had been manipulated. Ibn Khaṭīr was executed after being beaten; his organs were cut up and circulated around the Seljuq kingdom. Turantay, whose ambivalent attitude toward Ibn Khaṭīr's actions must have been recognized, was able to buy his freedom for a large fee. Some personages got themselves off the hook by claiming that they had feared suffering the same fate as Güyü if they resisted Ibn Khaṭīr. Other officers were too unequivocally implicated and were thus executed. During his interrogation, Ibn Khaṭīr had accused the Pervāne of having initiated the conspiracy and maintained contact with Baybars. The Pervāne, slippery as ever, was able to get him to rescind his accusations, and once again escaped punishment. The Pervāne then made an attempt to restore order in the country. The effect on the rebellious Türkmen, however, was evidently minimal.[38]

The pro-Mongol sources have a general idea of the Pervāne's communication with Baybars, although without details or specific dates. Ibn Bībī writes that envoys came from Syria every day and visited Sharaf al-Dīn b. Khaṭīr, bringing word that Baybars would soon come to Rūm with a large army.[39] Waṣṣāf, after describing the incident of the ring,[40] reports how the Pervāne lost his faith in Abagha and began to correspond with Baybars, asking him to come to Rūm.[41] Rashīd al-Dīn only writes that in 674/1275–6, Ḍiyā' al-Dīn b. Khaṭīr and the son of the Pervāne went to Baybars and incited him to attack Rūm.[42] Bar Hebraeus tells that King Leon of Lesser Armenia warned the Mongols several times that the "Egyptians" were planning to attack Rūm. The Pervāne, however, either because he was in league with the Egyptians or out of hatred for the Armenian king, called this information spurious, and was able to lull the Mongols into a false sense of security.[43] It is evident, in light of

information in a different form, and add details. Tudawun (sometimes written Tudun) was the grandfather of Chuban, the strongman in the first half of Abū Saʿīd's reign (up to AD 1327); Rashīd al-Dīn, ed. ʿAlīzādah, 3:102.

38 Ibn Shaddād, *Ta'rīkh*, 162–5; Yūnīnī, 3:171–3; Ibn Bībī, 313–16; Thorau, *Baybars*, 237–8; Cahen, *Pre-Ottoman Turkey*, 288–9. Āqsarāyī, 103–4, has Abagha's brother, Qonghurtai, together with Toqa and Tudawun at this time, and later (p. 106), they spend the winter together near Dalūja (today Delice, ca. 100 km east of Ankara); Smith, "Qīshlāqs," forthcoming. Qonghurtai is not mentioned in any other source at this juncture, and it thus seems that Āqsarāyī is mistaken in placing him here. 39 Ibn Bībī, 313. 40 See ch. 6, p. 147.

41 Waṣṣāf, 86, who places this, along with Baybars's offensive to Rūm, before the Mongol attack against al-Bīra (671/1272); *ibid.*, 87–8. 42 Rashīd al-Dīn, ed. ʿAlīzādah, 3:143–4.

43 Bar Hebraeus, 456–7 (= Ibn al-ʿIbrī, 501–2); Canard, "Arménie," 243.

what has been seen above along with further developments, that the Mongol commanders in Rūm also had a fairly clear idea of these contacts.

The campaign of 675/1277

During the winter of 675/1276–7, Baybars finally decided to launch his offensive. Professor Cahen has suggested that the Sultan may have been motivated by a desire to keep the support of those remaining military elements in Rūm who had expressed their loyalty to him. Perhaps, Baybars believed that even after the defeat of his imprudent supporters, he still enjoyed significant support among the Türkmen, some Rūmī amirs and even the Pervāne himself. With this support, and together with his own forces, Baybars may have thought that by invading Rūm he could wrench it away from the Mongols.[44] The advantages to be gained from a successful campaign to Rūm are clear: the northern border of the Sultanate would be secured, resources would be denied to the Mongols, Lesser Armenia would be cut off from its patron, the Mongols would lose their outlet to the sea, and last, but not least, an Islamic country would be saved from the Mongol yoke.

It is possible, however, that Baybars's goals were more modest from the beginning. Perhaps this campaign was conceived as nothing more than a large-scale raid, whose aim was to cause damage and confusion among the Mongols. Another object of this campaign may have been the desire to test both the Mongol reaction and the performance of his own troops.[45] As the Mamluk historians left us no record of Baybars's goals for the campaign, all of this must remain speculative.

On 20 Ramaḍān 675/25 February 1277, Baybars set out from Cairo with the majority of the Egyptian army. Five thousand troops were left in the capital under Aq Sunqur al-Fāriqānī, as was the heir apparent, al-Malik al-Saʿīd. Passing through Damascus, Baybars entered Aleppo on the first of Dhū 'l-qaʿda/6 April. The next day, he continued his march to the north. Evidently most of the Syrian armies joined him on this campaign, except for the Aleppan army under the governor Nūr al-Dīn ʿAlī b. Mujallā, which was sent to the Euphrates near al-Sājūr, in order to prevent any Mongol incursions into Syria. Nūr al-Dīn was joined by the leader of the Syrian bedouins, ʿĪsā b. Muhannā. The Mongol commanders in the area received word of the arrival of this force at the Euphrates, and sent a group of Khafāja bedouin to attack it. Nūr al-Dīn, however, was ready for them, and they were defeated.[46]

Meanwhile, the Sultan, together with most of the army, was moving north.

[44] Cahen, *Pre-Ottoman Turkey*, 288; see also Khowaiter, *Baibars*, 71–2.

[45] I am grateful to Professor Ayalon for this suggestion.

[46] Ibn Shaddād, *Ta'rīkh*, 159–61; Yūnīnī, 3:175–6; Ibn al-Ṣuqāʿī, 109–10. Except for Yūnīnī, the various writers who generally base their reports on Ibn Shaddād (Ibn al-Dawādārī, Qirtay, Dhahabī, Kutubī, Ibn Kathīr, Mufaḍḍal, Ibn Taghrī Birdī, ʿAynī) will usually not be cited in the following discussion unless there is a variant account. The narrative in Ibn al-Furāt is found for some reason in MS. Vienna, fols. 161a–174b, although this should be in *ibid.*, 7:68.

Leaving his heavy baggage at Ḥaylān, a village near Aleppo, Baybars advanced north via ʿAyn Tāb and Dulūk, until he reached Kaynūk (Ḥadath al-Ḥamrāʾ = Başpınar, in the area of Gölbaşı). From there, the Mamluk army reached the Gök Su, or al-Nahr al-Azrak, which was crossed with some difficulty, probably on Monday, 6 Dhū 'l-qaʿda/12 April. Having spent the night at the river, the Mamluks advanced on 7 Dhū 'l-qaʿda/13 April to the part of the Taurus now called the Nuruhak Dağ, entering a pass called Aqcha (Arabic: Aqjā/Aqshā) Darband ("The Whitish Defile").[47] The pass, the identity of which will be discussed below, was crossed albeit with some hardship, and the army came out onto an open area (*waṭʾa*) and spread out.[48]

This opening seems to have been merely a widening in the pass, and the Mamluks had still to advance through the mountains. An advance force under Sunqur al-Ashqar was sent ahead. On the 9th (15 April), Sunqur's force encountered a Mongol cavalry detachment (*katība*), numbering 3000 troops, under Karay. The Mongols were driven back and some prisoners were taken. News then reached the Sultan that the Mongol (*al-mughul*) army under Tudawun, along with the Pervāne and Rūmī troops, were close by and was camped at the Jayḥān, that is, near the town of Abulustayn. The Mamluks spent the night of 10 Dhū 'l-qaʿda (still 15 April), in the hills, and the next morning were ready to descend into the plain of Abulustayn. From the heights, the Mamluk soldiers looked down upon the Mongol army arranged on the plain.[49]

Ibn ʿAbd al-Raḥīm, Ibn Wāṣil's continuator who accompanied the Mamluk army into Rūm, tells a slightly different story: the Muslims having reached Aqcha Darband, a lightly armed force (*jarāʾid*) was sent ahead to the outlet of the pass, so as to prevent the Mongol *yazak* (vanguard) from taking up position there. The Mamluk force indeed managed to get there first, and

[47] This name must have been well known by contemporaries. Both Hetʿum (2:179: "le pas Blanc") and Rashīd al-Dīn (ed. ʿAlīzādah, 3:144), mention it in their descriptions of the events this year in Rūm.

[48] In modern Turkish this should be Akça Boğazı, but I did not find such a name on the map. The most detailed map I was able to consult was 1:200000 Turkey (South African Survey Co., Aug. 1941, based on a map from 1931), sheet F.11, Elbistan.

[49] *Rawḍ*, 456–8; the folios of the first part of this letter were lost in the MS., but the passage is cited in Qalqashandi, 14:142–3, and thus the editor of *Rawḍ* rectified the lacuna. The passage is also cited, with changes and omissions, in ʿUmarī's section on Rūm, edited by F. Taeschner as *Al-ʿUmarī's Bericht über Anatolien in seinem Werke Masālik al-abṣār fī mamālik al-amṣār* (Leipzig, 1929), 3–6; see the review by R. Hartmann, in *Orientalische Literaturzeitung*, 34/11 (1931), 972. Ibn Shaddād, *Taʾrīkh*, 171 (whence Yūnīnī, 2:176; Mufaḍḍal, 257–9), basically relates the same information, shorn of flowery prose, and with additional details. Also Nuwayrī, fol. 258a–b; Ibn al-Furāt, MS. Vienna, fol. 163b; Maqrīzī, 1:628. It is difficult to determine the exact relationship between Ibn Shaddād's account of the events leading up to the battle and that of Ibn ʿAbd al-Ẓāhir, who accompanied the Sultan in this campaign. It would seem that the former author used the latter's report, but he also inserts details from other sources. Cf. Thorau, *Baybars*, 238. The plain of Abulustayn is referred to in *Rawḍ*, 458 (cf. ʿUmarī, ed. Taeschner, 6; Maqrīzī, 1:628 and n. 6) as *saḥrāʾ h-w-n-i*. This can be identified with Hono Deresi, a valley north of the modern town of Efsus, which runs into the northwest of the plain that stretches north of Abulustayn; see also Sinclair, *Eastern Turkey*, 2:488.

defeated the Mongols, who withdrew to a location called *Ra's al-ᶜUyūn* (location unidentified), where the rest of the Mongol forces joined them.[50]

An examination of the modern map[51] suggests that the Mamluks took a route which more-or-less follows the present-day road: this generally led north from Kaynūk, crossing the Gök Su after some 15 km, and proceeded north on the eastern side of this stream. On the other hand, T. Sinclair's comprehensive work on eastern Turkey contains a map which shows an early medieval road on the west side of the Gök Su, which crosses the stream about 25 km from Kaynūk.[52] In both cases, the road continues to the northwest for a few kilometers, and then turns to the west. The Mamluks could have then followed a route which works its way to the northwest through the mountains to Abulustayn. Before it reaches the plain of Abulustayn, the road splits, so the Mamluks could have approached the Abulustayn plain from the south or the southeast. Between the Gök Su and Abulustayn there are two places where the passage widens out to form an open area. Either of these could be the *waṭ'a* referred to in the sources. Somewhere along this pass through the mountains must have been the Aqcha Darband of the Mamluk sources. Perhaps a remnant of this name is found in Derbent Deresi, a valley about 25 km southeast of Abulustayn, although this may be just a generic name applied to this particular defile.[53] Assuming that the Mamluks took the first suggested route (i.e., crossing the Gök Su after some 15 km), the whole route from crossing the river to the plain of Abulustayn would have been about 70 km, which the Mamluks could have covered in the three days which the sources give for this march.[54]

The Mongol commanders in Rūm, Toqa and Tudawun, had received word from Lesser Armenia of the impending Mamluk offensive, and also it would seem of its intended route. These two commanders, as well as Toqa's brother Uruqtu, moved with their troops towards Abulustayn from their *qıshlaq* (winter camp) at Qirshehir (140 km north of Nigde).[55] It seems that Tudawun exercised overall command. At some point they were joined by the Pervāne and Rūmī troops. Al-ᶜUmarī writes that the night before the battle, the Mongols camped at Nahr Zamān, the source (*aṣl*) of the Jayḥān river. This

[50] ᶜAbd al-Raḥīm, in Ibn Wāṣil, MS. 1703, fol. 186b.

[51] See the map cited in n. 48 above. Başpınar, the modern name of Kaynūk, does not appear on the map, but rather the village of Aksaray, which Sinclair, *Eastern Turkey*, 4:79, says is a former name for Başpınar.

[52] Sinclair, *Eastern Turkey*, 4:78; see also 2:452–3. On 4:77, Sinclair writes: "In recent times a track climbed northward directly from the site of Hadath toward the Elbistan plain .... Not far to the north-east of Hadath, moreover, a track from the Elbistan plain joined the medieval road to Malatya ..." See also *ibid.*, 2:478–9.

[53] Hartmann (review of ᶜUmarī, ed. Taeschner, 972), seems to be referring to this Derbent. Cf. Krawulsky, *Iran*, 389, who identifies Aqcha Darband with the modern Akçadağ (38° 22' N, 37° 58' E), which seems unlikely, as this mountain is about 70 km in a straight line to the northwest of Abulustayn.

[54] This suggested path appears to be identical to Ḍarb al-Ḥadath/al-Salam, an earlier name for a pass through the Nuruhak Dağ; see Ory, "al-Ḥadath," *EI*[2], 3:19–20.

[55] Āqsarāyī, 113 (see Smith, "Qīshlāqs," n. 70); Rashīd al-Dīn, ed. ᶜAlīzādah, 3:144.

might be identified with the Khurman stream (Hormān Cayi), which flows into the Jayḥān from the northwest;[56] the Mongols were thus riding into the Abulustayn plain from that direction. The Mongol troops (*al-mughul*) were arranged in eleven *ṭulbs* (squadrons), each with a thousand horsemen, or slightly more. A Georgian contingent – numbering 3000 men according to Bar Hebraeus – was organized as a separate *ṭulb*. Thus, Baybars al-Manṣūrī states that the Mongols had twelve divisions. The Rūmī troops, whose numbers are not given, were stationed away from the Mongol army. The Mongol commanders did not trust them and feared that they would act treacherously in the battle. It is not clear why they actually brought them along to the battlefield. Perhaps they thought that this was the best way of keeping an eye on them. The story reported by Bar Hebraeus and Ahrī that the Pervāne succeeded in getting the Mongol commanders drunk on the eve of the battle would seem to be mere slander, belied by the spirited fighting they and their soldiers demonstrated during the battle.[57]

It is worth dwelling on the size of the Mongol army. Previously, the Mamluk sources had spoken of the 30,000 troops which these commanders had brought with them to Rūm earlier that year. The Mongol army at this battle, however, was much smaller. It is unclear where the remainder of the Mongol army had been found. Perhaps part of the army had returned to the east. Alternatively, it was stationed elsewhere in Rūm. There is information that Qutu, the grandson (*sibṭ*) of Baiju, commanded a force which had a winter camp at Nigde, and was not present at the battle.[58] The fact that there is no more information on Qutu or his force in Rūm may indicate that this contingent was not very significant. Possibly, the original figure of 30,000 was simply inflated. Interestingly enough, Rashīd al-Dīn writes that Toqa, Uruqtu and Tudawun each commanded a *tümen*.[59] It would seem, however, that Uruqtu – Toqa's brother – was subordinate in rank, since he is not mentioned by either the Mamluk or other Persian sources in this or any other capacity during the battle. In either case, this evidence is an indication that in reality a *tümen* does not automatically equal 10,000 soldiers. Shāfiᶜ b. ᶜAlī, in his biography of Qalawun, states that the Mongols only had 5000 horsemen in this battle.[60] This figure can be rejected as an attempt by this author to belittle the achievement of Qalawun's predecessor. As Baybars had with him the majority of the Egyptian and Syrian army, he thus probably enjoyed a numerical superiority of some degree over his opponents, who numbered some 14,000 troops all told (not counting the

[56] Instead of *Z-M-'-N*, *R-M-'-N* is read, from which *khurmān* (> Horman in modern Turkish) can be reconstructed; see Hartmann, review of ᶜUmarī, ed. Taeschner, 971; see also Sinclair, *Eastern Turkey*, 2:484–5.

[57] *Rawḍ*, 458–9; ᶜUmarī, ed. Taeschner,6; Ibn Shaddād, *Ta'rīkh*, 171–2; Yūnīnī, 3:176; *Zubda*, fol. 83a; Bar Hebraeus,457 (= Ibn al-ᶜIbrī, 502); Ibn Bībī, 316–17; Ahrī, *Ta'rīkh-i shaykh uways*, ed. van Loon, 138. [58] Āqsarāyī, 108; Smith, "Qīshlāqs," forthcoming.

[59] Rashīd al-Dīn, ed. ᶜAlīzādah, 3:144.

[60] *Faḍl*, fol. 55b. Ibn Abd al-Raḥīm, in Ibn Wāṣil, MS. 1703, fol. 187a, gives the Mongols 7000 men; Ibn al-Fuwaṭī, 389, has that the Mongols numbered only 3000 horsemen.

Plate 3. Plain of Abulustayn (Elbistan), as seen from the east edge of the plain, just where land begins to rise. The picture faces south; on the left are the hills to the east (photograph: T.A. Sinclair)

Rūmīs, who did not participate in the fighting). Until the battle was joined, it would seem – at least according to Ibn ʿAbd al-Ẓāhir – that the Mongol commanders did not realize either the large size of the Mamluk army, or that the Sultan himself was leading the campaign.[61]

The battle began on Friday 10 Dhū 'l-qaʿda/15 April 1277. According to Ibn Shaddād (and those who follow him) the Mongols started the fighting by launching a concerted attack of their Left and smashing the Sultan's standard-bearers (*sanjaqiyya*). A group of Mongols succeeded in penetrating this unit and reached as far as the Mamluk Right. It would seem then that the Mamluk army had not had time to organize itself, because otherwise it is difficult to understand why the Sultan's standard-bearers were positioned in front of the Right. Dr. Thorau, on the other hand, suggests that this information can be interpreted to mean that the Mongols had smashed through the Mamluk Center (where the standard-bearers normally should have been) to the Mamluk Right. In any case, Baybars saw the severity of the situation, and set off himself, presumably accompanied by at least a few troops, to deal with the Mongols. In the midst of this, Baybars saw that the Mongol Right was giving the Mamluk Left a beating and the situation was critical. He thus ordered a

[61] *Rawḍ*, 458 (cf. ʿUmarī, ed. Taeschner, 6, in which this information is missing); Ibn al-Furāt, MS. Vienna, fol. 165a.

force from the army of Hama to reinforce his Left.[62] It was probably during the initial, critical stage of the battle that the bedouin irregulars in the Mamluk army melted away.[63] The situation having been stabilized, the entire Mamluk army then counter-attacked. Here perhaps the numerical advantage of the Mamluks began to influence the course of the battle, which now turned against the Mongols. Rather than retreating, the Mongol troops dismounted. Perhaps the reason for this move was that the Mongol horses had been exhausted, although it seems more likely that the Mongols were staying put in order to fight to the death.[64] The Mongols put up a fierce fight, but it was no use and in the end they were defeated. Some Mongols escaped and took up position in the hills. When these Mongols were surrounded, they also dismounted, and fought until they were killed.[65]

Most of the elements of the above account are found in Ibn ʿAbd al-Ẓāhir's version of the battle. According to him, however, the Mamluks poured out of the hills and attacked the Mongols first, led by some of the personal mamluks of the Sultan and others of his entourage.[66] Only subsequently are the Mamluks' difficulties mentioned, and then briefly and in an unclear manner. This is certainly a deliberate rewriting of events to present the Sultan in a positive light. Presumably, to write that the battle initially did not go in his favor would have been deemed improper. Unlike Ibn ʿAbd al-Ẓāhir's work, Ibn Shaddād's biography is sympathic to its subject without being obsequious. There is no reason why he would have invented Baybars's difficulties. The general concurrence of his account with some of the Persian sources only strengthens the conclusion that Ibn ʿAbd al-Ẓāhir suppressed information that might have been considered unflattering.[67]

In spite of the fact that the Rūmī army had been placed off to the side, and evidently had not taken part in the fighting, a number of Rūmī amirs were taken captive. Others came of their own volition and submitted. The Pervāne himself escaped and headed for Qaysāriyya (see below), but his son Muhadhd-hab al-Dīn was captured. A number of Mongol officers were also taken prisoner, and some were freed. Toqa was killed, while there is some disagreement as to whether Tudawun was captured or killed in battle. Ibn ʿAbd al-

62 Thus in Ibn Shaddād, etc. Mufaḍḍal, 260, states that it was the prince of Hama himself who ordered this movement of troops. Ibn al-Dawādārī, 8:199, writes that Baybars ordered this prince to go to the aid of the Mamluk Left. It would seem that Mufaḍḍal changed the account in his source.

63 Nuwayrī, MS. 2m, fol. 259a. In general, Nuwayrī abridges *Rawḍ*, 476–8, but he adds this information that is not found in the original.

64 On dismounting as a Mongol tactic, see below and ch. 10, p. 223.

65 Ibn Shaddād, *Ta'rīkh*, 172; Yūnīnī, 3:176; Mufaḍḍal, 259–61; Kutubī, MS. Köprülü, fols. 52b–53a. Ibn Bībī, 317, writes of how the Mongols initially succeeded in splitting the Mamluk lines. Rashīd al-Dīn, ed. ʿAlīzādah, 3:144, tells how the Mongols fought dismounted. Cf. the reconstruction of the battle in Thorau, *Baybars*, 238–9, and Martinez, "Īl-Xānid Army," 156–8, which is based on D'Ohsson, *Histoire*, 3:482–9.

66 *Rawḍ*, 259–60; Ibn al-Furāt, MS. Vienna, fol. 165b; Maqrīzī, 1:268–9.

67 For a decidedly unflattering account of Baybars's behavior during the battle, see Yūnīnī, 3:273 (s.a. 676).

Ẓāhir writes that some of the Mongol amirs were spared, while others were put to death. The captive Mongol common soldiers were spared, two of whom – Qipchaq and Salār – became mamluks of Qalawun and subsequently rose to become important Mamluk amirs.[68]

Rashīd al-Dīn and Ibn Bībī report that most of the Mongol troops were killed in the battle. Bar Hebraeus states that 5000 Mongols and 2000 Georgians died in the fighting. Ibn Duqmaq writes that half of the Mongol force was killed while the remainder fled the battlefield. An interesting figure is provided in Ibn Shaddād. Some two weeks later, when Baybars was on his way home from Rūm, he passed by the battlefield and ordered a count of Mongol dead. The number was 6770 Mongols (*min al-mughul*). It appears that Mamluk casualties were relatively few.[69]

The day after the battle Baybars set off for the Seljuq capital of Qaysāriyya. During the march, there had been some apprehension of a Mongol ambush. Precautions were taken, but these proved unnecessary. Sunqur al-Ashqar had already set off in that direction immediately after the battle in pursuit of those Mongols who had succeeded in escaping the carnage. He came upon a group of Mongols, who evidently had not participated in the battle, and their families. Some Mongols were captured, but under cover of the approaching night the remainder were able to escape. Sunqur reached Qaysāriyya, bringing an *amān* (guarantee of safety) for the local inhabitants and orders that markets be set up outside the city. Dirhams carrying the name of Baybars were also to be struck, signifying his rule over the country.[70] The Sultan and the main part of the army reached the city on Wednesday, 15 Dhū 'l-qaʿda/20 April, where they were warmly received by the population. Baybars spent the next few days in impressive ceremonies, but he was surely aware that he was still a long way from gaining real control over Rūm.[71]

The Pervāne, who had done so much to bring Baybars to Rūm, now kept his distance. Either immediately after the defeat or even during the fighting itself, he fled to Qaysāriyya. Taking the Sultan Ghiyāth al-Dīn, he made his way to his stronghold of Dokat. From there, he wrote to Baybars, now in Qaysāriyya, congratulating him on his sitting on the Seljuq throne. Baybars in turn sent back and called on the Pervāne to present himself, in order that he could be rewarded and reconfirmed in his position. The Pervāne answered that he would arrive in fifteen days. Ibn Shaddād adds that the Pervāne's intention

68 *Rawḍ*, 461–3; Ibn Shaddād, *Ta'rīkh*, 173–4, 336–7 (for the fate of the Rūmī prisoners); *Zubda*, fols. 83b–84a. On Tudawun's fate, see below.

69 Rashīd al-Dīn, ed. ʿAlīzādah, 3:144; Ibn Bībī, 317; Bar Hebraeus, 457 (= Ibn al-ʿIbrī, 502); *Rawḍ*, 460; Ibn Duqmaq, 282. Ibn Shaddād, *Ta'rīkh*, 172–3, 178; cf. Mufaḍḍal, 268, who adds that the number of Rūmī and Georgian dead almost equaled that of the Mongols.

70 As far as I know, no exemplars of Baybars's dirhams struck in Rūm have come to light.

71 *Rawḍ*, 463–7; Ibn Shaddād, *Ta'rīkh*, 175–6 (whence Yūnīnī, 3:180). These two sources give detailed, but not identical itineraries of Baybars's march to Qaysāriyya. Ibn al-Furāt, MS. Vienna, fols. 167b–169b (whence Maqrīzī, 1:629–31), conflates these two accounts (also later for the Sultan's return, see below). See also: Hartmann's review of ʿUmarī, ed. Taeschner, 972–3.

was to keep Baybars in Rūm until Abagha could arrive with a large army and deal with the invaders. Baybars, however, was not taken in. The same author recounts that the Mongol general Tudawun, now in Mamluk captivity, was interviewed by Sunqur al-Ashqar and informed him of what the Pervāne had in mind. It is not clear, however, why a Mongol officer would have wanted to tip off his opponent to a plan that might have led to rectifying the recent Mongol defeat. In addition, some sources report his death in the battle. In any event, it is clear that Baybars understood that he could expect no assistance from the Pervāne, as originally hoped.[72]

At first glance, the Pervāne's behavior seems difficult to explain. Granted that Baybars's invasion had caught him off guard, and he had no choice but to accompany the Mongol commanders off to battle. But Rūm was now rid of the Mongol overlords, and Baybars was ostensibly willing to recognize the Pervāne in his former position, as *de facto* ruler of the kingdom. Perhaps the Pervāne found the reality of Baybars's lordship too chafing. Or possibly, and this would seem to be more likely, the Pervāne saw that even in the short run Baybars would be unable to hold Rūm, and one way or the other the Mongols would regain the country. The Pervāne thus thought it best to ingratiate himself with the Īlkhān by drawing the Mamluks into a confrontation with a fresh Mongol army.[73]

Besides the failure of the Pervāne to rally to the Sultan's banner, other no less important factors caused Baybars to withdraw from Qaysāriyya. Supplies were running low, equipment was in need of repair and the prospect of the imminent arrival of a new Mongol army while he was far from his bases convinced Baybars that he should return to Syria soon. On Tuesday, 20 Dhū 'l-qaʿda/25 April, the Mamluk army set off for home. En route, the commander of the Mamluk vanguard, ʿIzz al-Dīn Aybeg al-Shaykhī, deserted to the Mongols. The reason given for this desertion was Aybeg's desire to revenge himself for a beating which Baybars had earlier dealt him. Aybeg later provided Abagha with information on the battle. While marching, Baybars received another letter from the Pervāne calling on him to delay his departure. The Sultan's answer was full of reproaches for the Pervāne's failure to fulfill his part of the agreement. At the same time, Baybars let it be known that he was heading for Sīwās, so as to mislead the Pervāne (and thus the Mongols) as to his true intentions. Instead, the Mamluk army marched quickly to the southwest, taking a different route than before, probably in order to find fresh foodstuffs. On the way, Taybars al-Wazīrī was sent with a force to raid an Armenian town called al-Rummāna (?, location unknown), whose inhabitants had hidden some Mongols there when the Mamluks had earlier marched this way. Baybars passed the battle site at Abulustayn, and soon reached the pass

72 Ibn Shaddād, *Ta'rīkh*, 176–7 (whence Yūnīnī, 3:181–2; Ibn al-Furāt, MS. Vienna, fols. 169a–170b; Maqrīzī, 1:631). The account in *Rawḍ*, 467–8 is substantially the same, but some details differ.

73 See the comments in Cahen, *Pre-Ottoman Turkey*, 287, 289; Thorau, *Baybars*, 239.

by which he had originally entered the country. The Sultan remained with the rearguard until the army entered the pass.[74] The march through the pass was accomplished with some difficulty. By 6 Dhū 'l-ḥijja/16 May, the army was at Ḥārim, where it rested and reorganized. At this point, envoys of Muḥammad Beg, the chief of the Qaramanid Türkmen, reached the Sultan. These Türkmen, having earlier declared their loyalty to Baybars, had raised the banner of revolt against the Mongols and succeeded in taking Konya. Baybars was certainly in no position to assist them now except with words of encouragement. After celebrating ʿĪd al-Aḍḥā (10 Dhū'l-ḥijja/20 May), Baybars moved south and reached Damascus in early Muḥarram 676/early June.[75]

Abagha, having received word of the Mongol defeat from both the Pervāne and Mongol survivors, soon came to Rūm at the head of a large army. On the other hand, Rashīd al-Dīn states that the Īlkhān set out only in Ṣafar 676 (ca. July 1277). He contradicts himself, however, by saying that this was in the spring. The events described in Ibn Shaddād also belie this chronology. When he arrived in the country, Abagha was met by the Pervāne and Ghiyāth al-Dīn. Any doubts that Abagha harbored as to the Pervāne's treachery were removed when the Mamluk renegade Aybeg al-Shaykhī informed him of the details of his contacts with Baybars. For the time being, however, Abagha suspended judgement on the Pervāne, perhaps – as Professor Cahen suggests – because he realized that no one else could rule Rūm as efficiently as he. Surveying the battlefield, Abagha was furious. In revenge, he ordered the massacre of the Muslim civilian population in eastern Rūm and large numbers were killed. According to Ibn al-Shaddād, Abagha sent an army of 30,000 towards Syria, but upon comprehending the size of Baybars's army (again, from information received from Aybeg al-Shaykhī), he called his forces back. Rashīd al-Dīn writes that Abagha contemplated sending an army to Syria that summer, but his officers persuaded him to wait until the winter; this expedition, of course, was never sent. Abagha's army was having logistical difficulties of its own, and this prompted the Īlkhān to call back his troops and subsequently to withdraw from the country with a good deal of his army. To restore order, which included putting down the Qaramanid rising, Abagha entrusted the country to his brother Qonghurtai and Shams al-Dīn Juwaynī, the *ṣāḥib-dīwān*. Abagha

[74] In al-Anṣārī's military guide (*A Muslim Manual of War*, ed. and tr. G.T. Scanlon [Cairo, 1961], 57), Baybars's wait at the pass for the completion of his army's entrance through it is given as an example of behavior to be adopted by commanders in similar circumstances. Hetʿum, 2:179, wishfully writes that at this point the Mamluks were attacked and defeated by a Mongol force.

[75] Ibn Shaddād, *Ta'rīkh*, 177–9 (whence Yūnīnī, 3:182–3); *Rawḍ*, 467–71. Ibn al-Furāt, MS. Vienna, fol. 172a, writes that it was reported that Baybars only ordered that his dead be buried, while Maqrīzī, 1:632, reports this, adding that this was done to give the impression that only a few Mamluk soldiers were killed relative to the many fallen Mongols. For the Qaramanid uprising, see: Ibn Shaddād, 177, 179–81; Cahen, *Pre-Ottoman Turkey*, 289; Ibn Bībī, 321–6. Ibn al-Furāt, MS. Vienna, fol. 172b (whence Maqrīzī, 1:633) adds information about the envoys from the Qaramanids not found in Ibn Shaddād.

then returned to his *ordo*, along with the Pervāne. At first Abagha evidently intended to turn a blind eye to the Pervāne's crimes, but the unequivocal evidence and the outcry from among the Mongol nobles and, especially, the noblewomen, convinced him to have him put to death. Ibn Shaddād states that the execution took place during the first ten days of Muḥarram 676/4–14 June 1277; Rashīd al-Dīn dates it at the beginning of Rabīᶜ II/ca. early September. According to Hetᶜum, as an act of revenge, the Pervāne's flesh was eaten by Abagha and the senior Mongols.[76]

The actions of Aybeg al-Shaykhī would seem to have served Mamluk interests quite well. The information he conveyed blackened the Pervāne even more in Abagha's eyes. This could have been Baybars's retribution for the Pervāne's disregard for the deal between them. Likewise, Aybeg's intelligence on the size of the Mamluk army conveniently helped to convince the Īlkhān to call back his army. Rashīd al-Dīn throws some more light on this character: Aybeg [al-]Shāmī came in Ṣafar 676/ca. July 1277 with ten men. After a warm reception, he was made governor of Malaṭya. When he arrived there, however, he expropriated a large amount of money from the population and fled back to Syria.[77] Perhaps, therefore, Aybeg's desertion had been staged by the Sultan, in order to feed specific information to the Īlkhān. Aybeg having accomplished his mission, took the first opportunity to return to the Sultanate. The fact that Aybeg was one of Baybars's cronies as early as 657/1258–9 does lend some credibility to this story.[78] In lieu of more concrete evidence, however, this remains not much more than an intriguing hypothesis.

Ibn Bībī and Rashīd al-Dīn state that when Abagha arrived in Rūm he sent a threatening and disparaging letter to Baybars, in which the Sultan was challenged to a battle with the Mongol army.[79] The Mamluk sources make no mention of this letter. Perhaps in the confusion after Baybars's death the letter was lost in the shuffle. It is difficult to imagine that two independent, albeit pro-Mongol, sources would simultanously fabricate a letter. On the other hand, the veracity of Rashīd al-Dīn's detailed answer from Baybars, who conveniently blamed the Pervāne for the invasion of Rūm, might well be doubted, since had the letter arrived, been read by the Sultan and been answered, it could be expected that some record would have been found in at least one of the Mamluk sources.

Baybars, soon after the return to Damascus, had received word that the Mongols were planning an invasion of Syria. After consulting with the senior amirs, the decision was taken to prepare the army for an expedition to the

[76] Cahen, *Pre-Ottoman Turkey*, 289–92; Ibn Shaddād, *Ta'rīkh*, 181–4; cf. Ibn al-Furāt, MS. Vienna, fols. 172a–173a, who has additional information; *Zubda*, fol. 85a; Mufaḍḍal, 271 and n. 1; Rashīd al-Dīn, ed. ᶜAlīzādah, 3:144–7; Bar Hebraeus, 457–8 (= Ibn al- Ibrī, 502–3); Ibn Bībī, 318–20; Boyle, "Īl-Khāns," 361; Hetᶜum, 2:180.

[77] Rashīd al-Dīn, ed. ᶜAlīzādah, 3:147, who seems to be consistently several months behind Ibn Shaddād.

[78] Ibn al-Dawādārī, 8:38; Ibn Taghrī Birdī, 7:100.

[79] Rashīd al-Dīn, ed. ᶜAlīzādah, 3:145–6; Ibn Bībī, 319.

north. Before any real action could be taken, news came that Abagha had called off his campaign and thus Baybars did the same. The Sultan could now relax with a clear mind after the exertions of the previous months. His death on 28 Muḥarram 676/1 July 1277 took everybody by surprise, and occasioned a cloud of rumor and innuendo which has yet to be completely dispersed.[80]

[80] Thorau, *Baybars*, 240–3, 268; Irwin, *Middle East*, 57–8.

CHAPTER 8

Baybars's posthumous victory: the second battle of Homs (680/1281)

Mengü Temür [brother of Abagha] was wounded at the battle [of Homs in AH 680], and he was greatly saddened for what had happened to him and his army, when he had been so close to victory.

Ibn al-Furāt[1]

Baybars did not live to see the long-expected Mongol invasion of Syria, which led to the confrontation north of Homs in Rajab 680/October 1281. Professor Ayalon has written: "Though this battle was won by Ḳalāwūn, the real architect of the victory was undoubtedly Sultan Baybars, who, in the seventeen years of his rule . . . built a war-machine which, in spite of the decline it underwent during the four years following his death, proved to be strong enough to beat one of the mightiest armies which the Mongol Īlkhāns ever put into the field."[2]

The Mamluks after Baybars's death

The Mamluk–Īlkhānid front was relatively quiet in the first years after Baybars's death. The lack of an external danger meant that the Mamluk elite could indulge in factional squabbling and jockeying for power with relative impunity. When the Mongol threat again became a reality in 679/1280, the Mamluk factions were able, if not to reconcile their differences, at least to find a *modus vivendi.* Those members of the military society who persisted in plotting against Qalawun were eliminated.

Baybars's son al-Malik al-Saʿīd Berke Khan succeeded his father without any problems. Once on the throne, al-Saʿīd set about limiting the power of the Ṣāliḥī amirs, that is, his father's *khushdāshiyya*, and other senior amirs, including those of the Ẓāhiriyya (the mamluks of Baybars). Bilig al-Khaznadār, his father's trusted mamluk and *nā'ib al-salṭana* (viceroy), who had seen to

[1] 7:234.

[2] D. Ayalon, "Ḥimṣ, Battle of," *EI*², 3:402. See also the comments in Ayalon, "Yāsa," pt. C1, 128–9.

al-Saᶜīd's accession to the throne, soon died under suspicious circumstances. Other important amirs were thrown in jail, although some were soon released. In their place al-Saᶜīd promoted his own mamluks, although as *nā'ib al-salṭana* he appointed Küvendük al-Sāqī, a mamluk of Baybars who had been educated with him. It is not surprising that the veteran amirs were not pleased by this development and reacted accordingly. This personal change and the resulting reaction of the senior officers is an example of the recurring pattern in Mamluk society of new sultans attempting to strengthen their own position by cultivating their personal mamluks at the expense of the established amirs.[3]

At the instigation of his *khāṣṣakiyya*, al-Saᶜīd sent off Qalawun and Baysari, perhaps the two most powerful Ṣāliḥī amirs, to raid Lesser Armenia in the spring of 677–8/1279. Al-Saᶜīd's intention was to remove these two, along with other Ṣāliḥī amirs, from the center of affairs. He planned to consolidate his power at their expense during their absence, and to have them arrested on their return.[4] Qalawun and Baysari must certainly have been aware of the reasons for their dispatch to the north. This did not, however, prevent them from executing their orders. Each commander had some 10,000 troops under him; Qalawun was to raid Cilicia, while Baysari was to take Qalᶜat al-Rūm. Qalawun reached as far as Ṭarsūs. He remained in the country for thirteen days, engaging in looting, killing and the taking of prisoners. Baysari raided the environs of Qalᶜat al-Rūm, but was unable to take the castle.[5]

Al-Saᶜīd, however, did not succeed in realizing his designs for these amirs. The *nā'ib* Küvendük fell out with the Sultan and his *khāṣṣakiyya*, and was removed from his post. He thereupon sent to Qalawun and Baysari to inform them of the plans to have them arrested. Upon their return, Küvendük made common cause with them, and together they succeeded in forcing the abdication of al-Saᶜīd, who was sent off to Karak (Rabīᶜ II 678/August 1279). Qalawun, however, was not yet powerful enough to make himself sultan; Baybarsid sentiment was still too strong, and other Ṣāliḥī amirs may have set their sights on the throne. Another son of Baybars, the seven-year-old Sulamish, was declared sultan with the title al-Malik al-ᶜĀdil. Qalawun, however, was named his *atabeg* (guardian), and in this capacity was the true ruler of the Sultanate. Sunqur al-Ashqar became governor of Damascus, while ᶜIzz al-Dīn Aybeg al-Afram was named the *nā'ib al-salṭana* in Egypt. This situation was not to last long. "The amirs and *khāṣṣakiyya* were prepared to be compliant, having experienced Kalavun's bountiful patronage. There was,

[3] Irwin, *Middle East*, 62–3; Holt, *Crusades*, 99–100. On this general phenomenon, see Ayalon, "Studies on the Structure," pt. 1, 108–10; Little, *Introduction*, 116.

[4] *Zubda*, fols. 90b–92a; Ibn al-Furāt, 7:117, 140; Maqrīzī, 1:650. Shāfiᶜ (*Faḍl*, fol. 16a) states that the idea for this raid was initially raised by Qalawun himself. This must be an attempt to portray Qalawun as a loyal officer, and not a disposer of sultans.

[5] Ibn Shaddād, *Aᶜlāq*, ed. Eddé, 319–20; *Faḍl*, fol. 16a; Yūnīnī, 3:297; Nuwayrī, MS. 2m, fol. 271b; Ibn al-Furāt, 7:141; Maqrīzī, 1:652; Bar Hebraeus, 461–2, provides details of Baysari's campaign, and writes that the Muslims entered Cilicia in order to conduct the leader of the Qaramanid Türkmen, who feared the Mongols and Armenians, to Syria; see also Irwin, *Middle East*, 63.

therefore, no opposition when on 21 Rajab 678/27 November 1279, he proposed that the state required a ruler of mature years. Al-ʿĀdil was thereupon deposed, and sent to al-Karak to join his brother. Kalavun then became sultan with the title of al-Malik al-Manṣūr."[6]

One of Qalawun's first tasks was to consolidate his power by placing his mamluks in positions of authority, and limiting the power of the mamluks of his predecessors. He did not move against the senior Ṣāliḥī amirs in Egypt, perhaps because of a mixture of *khushdāshiyya* feelings, respect for their power and experience and the need for their support in both external and internal affairs. In fact, he commissioned (or recommissioned) as amirs several Ṣāliḥīs who had been languishing in obscurity.[7] The problem was primarily the Ẓāhiriyya, the mamluks of Baybars, who were the backbone of the Mamluk army[8] and harbored much antipathy towards Qalawun and his Manṣūrī mamluks. Qalawun knew he could not depend upon them, and began to eliminate them from the ranks of the amirs and the army at large. Qalawun had started arresting particularly troublesome Ẓāhirīs while *atabeg*.[9] The thinning out of the ranks of the Ẓāhiriyya must have continued after he became sultan, although it is impossible to give numbers for those arrested at this time or later.[10] The process was not unambivalent: once the Ẓāhiriyya was broken, some of the Ẓāhirī amirs were released from prison after Qalawun became sultan; a few had their commission returned to them. In addition, some Ẓāhirīs who had never been amirs received their first commission.[11] Qalawun must have hoped that these new amirs would remain loyal to him out of gratitude. It is clear that Qalawun could not completely dispense with these first-rate troops, desirable as it might have been from the point of view of internal Mamluk politics. In spite of the massive acquisition of new mamluks[12] and the enrolment of the sons of the Baḥriyya in the army,[13] it would take years before the Ẓāhiriyya would be replaced. The Mongols, of course, would not necessarily wait so long.

Qalawun's more pressing problem, however, was the revolt of Sunqur al-Ashqar in Damascus. Taking the title al-Malik al-Kāmil, Sunqur declared

[6] Quote from Holt, *Crusades*, 100–1. See L. Northrup, "A History of the Reign of the Mamluk Sultan al-Manṣūr Qalāwūn (678–689 AH / 1279–1290 AD)," Ph.D. diss., McGill Univ. (Montreal, 1982), 122–30; Irwin, *Middle East*, 63–5.

[7] Ibn al-Furāt, 7:150; Maqrīzī, 1:658. See Northrup, "Qalāwūn," 130–3.

[8] "They were the majority of the army in Egypt": Yūnīnī, 4:8; Kutubī, MS. Köprülü, fol. 111b. This statement is, of course, not literally true, because of the presence of the large *ḥalqa*, the amirs' units and other royal mamluks. But the Ẓāhiriyya, because of its numbers, training and experience, was the most important unit in the army.

[9] *Tuḥfa*, 90; Ibn al-Furāt, 7:150; Maqrīzī, 1:658.

[10] Qirtay, fol. 106b, writes that after Qalawun became sultan he arrested and killed a group of Ẓāhiriyya and Saʿīdiyya (mamluks of al-Saʿīd), and thus "the gate of the Citadel was empty of troops." This is surely an exaggeration, but it gives a sense of the extent of the purges.

[11] Ibn al-Furāt, 7:150; Maqrīzī, 1:658, 671–2.

[12] On Qalawun's massive purchase of mamluks over his reign, see Nuwayrī, MS. 2n, fol. 45a.

[13] Ibn al-Furāt, 7:150; Maqrīzī, 1:658; Ibn al-Dawādārī, 8:303 (in Qalawun's obituary); Qirtay, fol. 106b; Ayalon, "Bahriya," 139.

himself an independent ruler. His authority extended to southern Palestine, and initially he had the backing of both the governor of Aleppo and al-Manṣūr of Hama. He also enjoyed the support of the bedouin leaders ᶜĪsā b. Muhannā (*amīr al-ᶜurbān* in the north and east) and Aḥmad b. Ḥujjā (of the Āl Mirā, *amīr al-ᶜurbān* in the south). Sunqur, however, was unable to translate this support into military success. His troops were worsted in an engagement with a pro-Qalawun force at Gaza in Muḥarram 679/May 1280. Qalawun then sent an army under Sanjar al-Ḥalabī, who ironically had led a similar revolt some twenty years before, to Damascus. Sunqur met Qalawun's army near Damascus in Ṣafar/June. During the fighting, he was abandoned by the troops from Aleppo and Hama. Sunqur was defeated and fled to the Syrian desert with ᶜĪsā b. Muhannā. The majority of Muslim Syria now came under Qalawun's control.[14]

Sunqur and ᶜĪsā went to al-Raḥba, but they failed to win over its governor. Isolated in the desert and expecting the approach of Qalawun's troops, Sunqur despaired. Seeing no other alternative, he and ᶜĪsā thereupon wrote to Abagha, informing him of the disunity in the kingdom, and called on him to invade Syria and offered their support. The years which Sunqur spent with the Mongols in relatively comfortable captivity might have contributed to his willingness to turn to them in his hour of need. It seems that other officers with Sunqur also wrote to Abagha at this time.[15] Sunqur then rode to the fortress of Ṣahyūn (Saone) in northern Syria, where he had already sent his wealth and family. Having control over several nearby fortresses, he essentially created a small principality in the area. Sunqur now waited to see how matters would develop. ᶜĪsā b. Muhannā meanwhile remained on the eastern fringes of the Syrian desert.[16]

It is possible that Sunqur's decision to go to Ṣahyūn was prompted by a last-minute recoil from going over to the infidel enemy. According to Ibn al-Dawādārī, Sunqur wrote not to Abagha but to ᶜAṭā' Malik Juwaynī, the Mongol governor of Baghdad (and famous historian). Juwaynī sent to inform Abagha of this development. Pending further instructions from the Īlkhān, he sent to Sunqur to calm him. Thereupon, ᶜĪsā b. Muhannā rebuked Sunqur for the disaster he was about to cause Islam, and suggested that he should wait upon events in one of his Syrian castles. Mufaḍḍal relates this account with some differences: both Sunqur and ᶜĪsā wrote to Juwaynī, and it was *fuqahā'* (Muslim jurists) who prevailed on Sunqur to desist from anti-Muslim activi-

14 Northrup, "Qalāwūn," 134–6; Irwin, *Middle East*, 65–6; Holt, *Crusades*, 65. On the role of the bedouin in this revolt: Ibn al-Furāt, 7:169–70; Maqrīzī, 1:674–7; Yūnīnī, 4:36, 40–1.

15 Maqrīzī, 1:697 (s.a. 680), writes that after the battle of Homs, a Mongol letter case was captured containing letters to the Mongols from Sunqur and other amirs connected to him, in which the Mongols are encouraged to invade Syria; no letter from ᶜIsa is mentioned. These letters would appear to date from around the time of Sunqur's stay in the desert. The ultimate source of this information is unclear.

16 *Zubda*, fols. 104a, 105a; Nuwayrī, MS. 2n, fols. 4b–5a; Ibn al-Furāt, 7:170, 172; Maqrīzī, 1:677–8; Irwin, *Middle East*, 66. Cf. Northrup, "Qalāwūn," 144–6. Ibn ᶜAbd al-Raḥīm, in Ibn Wāṣil, MS. 1703, fol. 189a, notes that Sunqur wrote to Abagha after he reached Ṣahyūn.

ties.[17] Both of these versions are problematic. Ibn al-Dawādārī's account is contradicted by both Bar Hebraeus and Waṣṣāf, who categorically state that ʿĪsā was a party to this correspondence.[18] On the other hand, it seems improbable that Sunqur and others would run into *fuqahā'* in the middle of the desert, even in a bedouin encampment. But perhaps these accounts give a somewhat imaginative expression to Sunqur and ʿĪsā's Muslim consciences getting the better of them, and thus they were prevented from taking the final step of joining the Mongols. For what it is worth, Waṣṣāf states that it was Juwaynī himself who initiated the contact with Sunqur and ʿĪsā, after news reached him of their arrival in the environs of ʿĀna and Ḥadītha.

The Mongol invasion of 679/1280

The letter or letters that Sunqur al-Ashqar, ʿĪsā and possibly others sent to the Mongols helped prompt Abagha to take advantage of the infighting among the Mamluks and to intervene in Syria. Perhaps Abagha had been tempted by earlier reports of instability,[19] but he had his own problems to deal with before he could turn his attention to Syria: in the winters of 677/1278–9 and/or 678/1279–80, Negüderi Mongols from present-day Afghanistan raided Fārs and Kirmān; in the latter year, fighting flared up on the border with the Golden Horde;[20] the same year, some type of epidemic affecting men and livestock swept Iraq, the Jazīra and parts of Iran.[21]

Sunqur al-Ashqar's letter would have reached Abagha just as he put these problems behind him. The prospect of the Mamluks in disarray and a large chunk of the local military class willing to assist him was too good an opportunity to pass up, and thus in the summer of 679/1280 Abagha sent a large army into Syria. According to the Arabic sources, the Mongol army was organized in three corps: the first, from Rūm under Samaghar, Tanji (?) and Taranji (?);[22] the second, from the east (the Jazīra evidently), under his nephew Baidu, along with the ruler of Mārdīn; and the third and major part of the army under Mengü Temür (direction unspecified). The last mentioned were evidently also to go through Rūm. An Armenian force joined the Mongols as well. Bar Hebraeus, on the other hand, writes that the Mongols were led by Qonghurtai, another younger brother of Abagha. The impression gained is that the actual forces which participated in the offensive were relatively modest

[17] Ibn al-Dawādārī, 8:237–8; Mufaḍḍal, 315–17; cf. Qirtay, fol. 111a, who also states that ʿIsa convinced Sunqur not to flee to the Mongols.

[18] Bar Hebraeus, 463 (= Ibn al-ʿIbrī, 503); Waṣṣāf, 103. The chronology of the material in Waṣṣāf is confused: the Sunqur al-Ashqar affair is described after the battle of Homs of 680/1281 (*ibid.*, 89–90).

[19] *Faḍl*, fol. 27b, states that on hearing of Qalawun's accession the Mongols made plans to enact revenge for earlier defeats.

[20] See above, ch. 4, p. 88. Ibn Kathīr, 13:287, has some knowledge of these conflicts.

[21] Ibn al-Fuwaṭī, 407–8.

[22] Perhaps Tanji is a distorted form of Taiju (see below, p. 195), or even Nabji (Ibn Shaddād, *Ta'rīkh*, 156).

in size. Perhaps only an advanced force actually penetrated into northern Syria. When the Mongols saw that Sunqur al-Ashqar was staying put in Ṣahyūn (see below), the offensive was called off, but not before heavy damage was inflicted on the country. Mongol troops gained temporary possession of ʿAyn Tāb, Baghrās and al-Darbassāk, and reached as far as Aleppo, which had been abandoned by its garrison and most of its inhabitants. From 21 to 23 Jumādā II/27–9 October, they looted the city and put many buildings to the torch, including the main mosque.[23]

News of the Mongol invasion reached Syria at the beginning of Jumādā II 679/late September 1280. The Egyptian expeditionary corps in Syria and Syrian troops gathered near Hama. They were joined by the force which had been besieging the castle of Shayzar, where Sunqur al-Ashqar's confederate al-Ḥājj Özdemür was holed up; this force discontinued the siege and fell back, upon hearing of the Mongol advance. The army of Aleppo, having retreated before the Mongols (as in previous similar cases), also met up with this force at Hama. In the middle of Jumādā II, scouts were dispatched to discover the whereabouts of the Mongols. Meanwhile, refugees from north Syria poured into Damascus and the Baalbek area. It is reported that only those who were incapable of travelling remained in the north. The commanders of the force at Hama wrote to Sunqur at Ṣahyūn, berating him for having induced the Mongols to come by the disunity which he had brought about. (Evidently, the letters of Sunqur etc. to the Mongols were not yet known.) They called upon him to join them in order to repulse the Mongols. Sunqur agreed in principle and along with al-Ḥājj Özdemür took up position outside their castles to see what would happen next. Sunqur may have regretted his earlier actions and have seen the need to resist the Mongols, but he still did not trust Qalawun's officers. When word of the Mongol withdrawal from the country reached Sunqur, he returned to his castle. The amirs at Hama responded to this news by sending forces in different directions: one rode to ʿAyn Tāb, while others went to the Euphrates and al-Bīra. After reconnoitering the country, the forces returned in mid-Rajab/ca. mid-November 1280 to the south.[24]

Shāfiʿ b. ʿAlī tells that Qalawun initially received word of the expected Mongol invasion from his informants (*mukātibūn*) and his intelligence agents (*quṣṣād akhbārihi*). Baybars al-Manṣūrī confirms this information, although he speaks only of *quṣṣād*.[25] This might well explain how the Mamluks knew of the names of the Mongol commanders and organization of their army. When news of the actual raid arrived from Syria, the Sultan made ready to set out. He

[23] *Zubda*, fols. 104b–105a, 108a, 140a (King Leon set fire to mosque in Aleppo); *Tuḥfa*, 94–5; Ibn al-Furāt, 7:185; Maqrīzī, 1:681; Yūnīnī, 4:45–6; Dhahabī, MS. Laud 279, fol. 64b (cites Yūnīnī by name); *Faḍl*, fol. 28a–b; Ibn al-Fuwaṭī, 412, who writes of 50,000 Mongol horsemen sent under Mengü Temür; Bar Hebraeus, 463 (= Ibn al-ʿIbrī, 503); cf. Runciman, *Crusades*, 3:390. Waṣṣāf, 103, would seem to be referring to this expedition, but his chronology is confused; see above, n. 18, and below.

[24] Yūnīnī, 4:44–5; Dhahabī, MS. 279, fol. 64a; Kutubī, MS. Köprülü, fol. 124a; *Zubda*, fol. 105a; Ibn al-Furāt, 7:185–6; Maqrīzī, 1:682–3, 697; Northrup, "Qalāwūn," 147–9.

[25] *Faḍl*, fol. 28b; *Zubda*, fol. 105a.

also had his son al-Malik al-Ṣāliḥ ᶜAlī declared as his heir-apparent. Qalawun left for Syria on 29 Jumādā II 679/2 November 1280. Upon reaching Gaza some two weeks later, the Sultan received word that the Mongols had withdrawn from the country, so he returned to Egypt. Baybars al-Manṣūrī's claim that it was the news of the Sultan's departure for Syria that convinced the Mongols to withdraw from there is nothing more than an attempt to laud his patron's power: the Mongols left Aleppo several days before Qalawun set out from Cairo.[26]

On 1 Dhū 'l-ḥijja 679/23 March 1281, Qalawun again left Egypt with his army for Syria. Possibly, he had decided that the time had come to inspect Damascus and personally to assert his authority in that city. It seems also likely, however, that he had a premonition, perhaps via his intelligence service, that another Mongol offensive was imminent. The length of his stay in Damascus and the presence then of most of his army with him lend strength to this latter supposition.

By the 17th of the month (8 April), Qalawun was at al-Rūḥā', near Acre. There he received the hitherto rebellious bedouin chief ᶜĪsā b. Muhannā, who now submitted to the Sultan. Qalawun pardoned him and apparently at this time returned the title of *amīr al-ᶜurbān* to him, along with his *iqṭāᶜ*. During the period of ᶜĪsā's rebellion, his command and *iqṭāᶜ* had been split up among other chiefs. This arrangement must have proved less than satisfactory, since ᶜĪsā's transgressions were so summarily forgiven. Like Baybars before him, Qalawun must have realized that no one could rule the bedouin as well as ᶜĪsā, and that it was impossible to control them while ᶜĪsā was in rebellion. The other major bedouin leader who participated in Sunqur al-Ashqar's rebellion, Aḥmad b. Ḥujjā, had already submitted to the Sultan's forces immediately after Sunqur's defeat, and evidently had then been reconfirmed as *amīr al-ᶜurbān* in the south.[27]

On 10 Muḥarram 680/1 May 1281, Qalawun moved inland to Lajjūn, where he received Frankish envoys who returned with his own envoys who had been in Acre. A truce (*hudna*) for ten years and ten months was agreed upon with the Hospitallers in Acre, in spite of the raid that their comrades from Marqab had launched the previous year at the time of the Mongol incursion, and the defeat they had subsequently administered to a Mamluk force.[28] Another truce was signed with Bohemond VII, the ruler of Tripoli, for the same period of time.[29]

26 *Tuḥfa*, 95; *Zubda*, fols. 105a, 108a–b; Ibn al-Furāt, 7:190–1; Maqrīzī, 1:682–3; Yūnīnī, 4:46, 52; Ibn al-Dawādārī, 8:239; Ibn Kathīr, 13:292; *Faḍl*, fol. 29a (Shāfiᶜ's chronology for this year is confused).

27 Ibn al-Furāt, 7:171, 177, 195, 200; Maqrīzī, 1:677, 679, 684; Yūnīnī, 4:54; Kutubī, MS. Köprülü, fol. 125a; Ibn Kathīr, 13:292.

28 On this raid, see: *Tuḥfa*, 95; Yūnīnī, 4:52–3; Ibn al-Dawādārī, 8:239; Ibn al-Furāt, 7:195; Maqrīzī, 1:684 (he writes that the Franks helped the Mongols); Bar Hebraeus, 463 (not in Arabic version); Runciman, *Crusades*, 3:390.

29 Prawer, *Histoire*, 2:520, citing Marino Sanudo, *Secreta Fidelium Crucis*, in Bongars, *Gesta Dei per Francos* [Hanover, 1611], 228, suggests that perhaps Franks from Tripoli attacked the Biqāᶜ at the time of the Mongol raid.

Qalawun's willingness to reach an agreement with the Franks, in spite of their truculent behavior, is an additional indication that he feared another Mongol invasion into Syria, and thus wanted to guard himself against Frankish intervention from the Mongols' side. Although the *hudna* arranged by Baybars in 670/1272 with Acre still had another year to run, negotiations were also held to renew it, and evidently some type of formula was agreed upon.[30]

At some point before Qalawun arrived in Palestine, a Mongol embassy had arrived in Acre seeking Frankish support. According to a letter to Edward I, dated 5 October 1280, from Geoffrey, Bishop of Hebron, this envoy stated that the Mongols would soon invade Syria with 50,000 cavalrymen plus infantry. The Franks were called upon to assist with provisions and men.[31] There is no record of any response from the Frankish leaders to this offer and their subsequent actions indicate that they decided to adopt a neutral course. For the Franks, this was perhaps a missed opportunity. The presence of several hundred armed knights with the Mongols or, even more importantly, somewhere behind the Mamluk lines might well have caused great difficulties to Qalawun at the time of the Mongol offensive.

During the negotiations with the leaders of Acre, the Sultan received word from his informants in that city[32] that there was a conspiracy in his own camp: Küvendük al-Khaznadār had joined together with a number of Ẓāhirī amirs and had written to the Frankish leaders, calling on them not to agree to the Sultan's terms, because he would shortly be killed and the Franks would receive what they wanted. Qalawun reacted vigorously. He confronted many of the conspirators, who did not deny the charges. Küvendük and many other amirs were executed. Others, however, fled to Sunqur al-Ashqar along with some 300 horsemen.[33]

Qalawun entered Damascus on 19 Muḥarram 680/10 May 1281. Soon afterwards, an army was dispatched to the north to besiege Shayzar, which was controlled by Sunqur's ally al-Ḥājj Özdemür. But with continuing reports of an imminent Mongol offensive (see below), Qalawun saw it was best to reconcile Sunqur. Envoys went back and forth between Ṣahyān and Damascus, and by 4 Rabīʿ I/23 June, a *ṣulḥ* (peace) was agreed upon. Sunqur was to surrender Shayzar, but in exchange he was to receive several towns and forts.

[30] *Tuḥfa*, 96; Yūnīnī, 4:86; Dhahabī, MS. 279, fol. 64b; Ibn Kathīr, 13:292–3; Ibn al-Furāt, 7:204–5; Maqrīzī, 1:685; Prawer, *Histoire*, 2:520–1; Runciman, *Crusades*, 3:390–1; Northrup, "Qalāwūn," 149–50.

[31] Cited in R. Röhricht, "Les batailles de Hims (1281 et 1299)," in "Études sur les derniers temps du royaume de Jérusalem," *AOL* 1 (1881):638 n. 20. See also Runciman, *Crusades*, 3:390–1; Prawer, *Histoire*, 2:520.

[32] See Amitai, "Espionage," 178. Shāfiʿ (*Faḍl*, fol. 59b) names the informant (*mukātib*) as "Jawān Khāndak." Runciman (*Crusades*, 3:391), whose source is not clear, reports that Roger of San Severino, Charles of Anjou's representative in Acre, sent to Qalawun to inform him of Küvendük's letter.

[33] *Zubda*, fol. 110a; *Tuḥfa*, 97; Nuwayrī, MS. 2m, fol. 20b; Yūnīnī, 4:86–7; Kutubī, MS. Köprülü, fol. 134b; Ibn al-Furāt, 7:206–7, who writes that Saʿīdī amirs were also involved, as were Tatars, i.e. *wāfidiyya*; Maqrīzī, 1:685–6; Northrup, "Qalāwūn," 152.

His control of the other castles already in his hands was recognized. Sunqur was also given *iqṭāʿāt* for 600 horsemen; presumably, these land-holdings were not only in his own "principality." Around the same time, Qalawun reached an agreement with al-Malik al-Masʿūd Khaḍir, Baybars's son who ruled Karak (al-Saʿīd Berke Khan having died in Dhū 'l-qaʿda 678/March 1280), in which Khaḍir's autonomy was recognized.[34]

Thus, on the eve of the Mongol invasion, Qalawun had rectified some of the damage of the preceding years. Due to purges, the army was perhaps smaller than it had been in Baybars's heyday and, more importantly, an unknown number of experienced Ẓāhirī amirs and mamluks had been eliminated. The confusion of al-Saʿīd Berke Khan's reign and even the initial period of Qalawun's rule had certainly not been conducive to the orderly training and strengthening of the army. But at least differences within the military society had been papered over, if not actually solved. No less important, a working relationship with the leaders of the Syrian bedouin had been reestablished. Given the events of the previous years, the Mamluks were probably as ready as they could have been to meet their enemies.

The battle of Homs[35]

Qalawun must have had a fairly good idea that another Mongol invasion of Syria was in the offing, because there is no other reason to explain his remaining in Damascus with most of the Egyptian army throughout the first third of AH 680 (which began on 22 April 1281). Most likely, the source of much of this information was the intelligence service that Qalawun had inherited from Baybars.[36] At the end of Rabīʿ II and the beginning of Jumādā I (ca. mid-August 1281), *quṣṣād* arrived bringing more exact intelligence: Mengü Temür, the brother of Abagha, had come to Rūm at the head of the Mongol army and was currently somewhere between Qaysāriyya and Abulustayn. Subsequent reports from *quṣṣād* spoke of a Mongol army of troops heading for Syria. Scouts were ordered out from ʿAyn Tāb to reconnoiter to the north. Near Abulustayn, these scouts ran into a Mongol reconnaissance force, defeated them and captured a senior Mongol officer. The captive was brought before Qalawun at Damascus on 20 Jumādā I/6 September, and related detailed information on the Mongol numbers and commanders.

34 *Zubda*, fols. 111a–112a; *Tuḥfa*, 97–8; Yūnīnī, 4:88–9; Ibn al-Furāt, 7:208–10; Maqrīzī, 1:686–8; Holt, *Crusades*, 141.

35 For previous reconstructions of the battle, see: Ayalon, "Ḥimṣ," 402–3; J. Glubb, *Soldiers of Fortune: The Story of the Mamlukes* (New York, 1973), 111–15; Runciman, *Crusades*, 3:391–2; D'Ohsson, *Histoire*, 3:525–32; Weil, *Geschichte*, 1:125–8; Röhricht, "Études," 638–41; F.Ḥ. ʿĀshūr, *al-ʿAlāqāt*, 116–22; Northrup, "Qalāwūn," 156–9; Smith, "ʿAyn Jālūt," 329 n. 63; Martinez, "Īl-Xānid Army," 159–65.

36 Shāfiʿ (*Faḍl*, fols. 28b, 29b, 40a, 43b–44a) provides information on the activities of intelligence operatives and informants in the period from Qalawun's accession to the battle of Homs. The confused chronology of the events described therein makes it difficult to place some of this evidence in its proper context.

Baybars al-Manṣūrī writes that he gave the figure of 80,000 Mongols (*al-mughul*) and added that the Mongol offensive was to start in early Rajab (ca. mid-October). Shāfiᶜ b. ᶜAlī tells that the captive's information tallied with intelligence which had arrived via a secret letter (*mulaṭṭaf*) from Diyār Bakr.[37]

The Sultan ordered preparations for the battle, and the units began leaving Damascus for the assembly point on the plain outside the city. A contingent of 4000 bedouin of the Āl Mirā tribe under Aḥmad b. Ḥujjā arrived. Other bedouins, groups of Syrian Türkmen and a contingent from al-Masᶜūd Khaḍir of Karak came to join the army, as did the portion of the army which had remained in Egypt. By 26 Jumādā II/12 October, the entire army was assembled and ready to march.[38]

The question was to where. A major disagreement over strategy erupted between Qalawun and the senior amirs. The Sultan wanted to wait for the Mongols near Damascus, while the majority of amirs were for advancing to Homs. The reasoning of each side is not completely clear. Shāfiᶜ b. ᶜAlī reports that the Sultan thought the proximity of Damascus's citadel would be an advantage in case of a defeat. Perhaps, as Blochet has suggested, the Sultan wanted to be in a better position to flee to Egypt if the Mongols were victorious. The amirs, on the other hand, may have been averse to abandoning all of northern Syria to Mongol depredations. Qalawun eventually conceded to the opinion of the amirs. Certain early fourteenth-century writers would have us believe that this decision was not exactly reached through compromise. When many of the amirs – led by Sanjar al-Ḥalabī and Baysari – saw that Qalawun was unwilling to move to the north, they struck camp, saying that they would fight the Mongols at Homs with or without the Sultan; in the latter case Taybars al-Wazīrī would lead them. Bektash al-Fakhrī counselled Qalawun that if he did not act decisively at this point, he would lose his kingship. Qalawun saw that he had no choice and set out to join the amirs. The whole army advanced to Homs, where it waited for the arrival of the Mongols.[39] While this story does not correspond to the usual image of Qalawun's resolute leadership, it should not be rejected outright. It is clear

[37] Kutubī, MS. Köprülü, fol. 135b; Mufaḍḍal, 324–6; Ibn al-Dawādārī, 8:241–2; *Tuḥfa*, 98; *Zubda*, fol. 112b (thus Nuwayrī, MS. 2n, fols. 7b–8a; whence Ibn al-Furāt, 7:212–13; shorter version in Maqrīzī, 1:690); *Faḍl*, fols. 44a–46b, who writes that Mengü Temür himself was almost captured by the Mamluk scouts.

[38] Yūnīnī, 4:91. ᶜUmarī, ed. Krawulsky, 142, describes in detail the dazzling finery of Aḥmad's bedouin (whence Qalqashandī, 4:209–10, Maqrīzī, 1:690–1 [not in parallel passage in Ibn al-Furāt, 7:213]). See *Faḍl*, fol. 40a–40b, who tells *inter alia* that even bedouin from Egypt were ordered to come, a doubtful assertion.

[39] Jazarī, fol. 16a, whence: Kutubī, MS. Köprülü, fols. 135b–136a; Ibn al-Dawādārī, 8:241–2; Mufaḍḍal, 325–6 (see Blochet's comment, 326, n. 5). *Faḍl*, fols. 41b–42a, describes the disagreement, but not the amirs' insubordination. Baybars al-Manṣūrī (and those who follow him: Nuwayrī, Ibn al-Furāt and Maqrīzī) make no mention of this incident. Ibn Taghrī Birdī, 7:302, reports that Qalawun sent his army before him and then he himself followed at the end of Jumādā II.

that opinions were sharply divided among the leadership of the military society, and it would seem that Qalawun's rule was still far from absolute. In addition, this may well be an indication of an anti-Qalawun strain in Mamluk historiography.

The Mongols were already advancing into north Syria. Some of the Mamluk sources tell a story in Abagha's obituary (*s.a.* 680) that Abagha was against sending an army into Syria, but that he had been convinced by his younger brother Mengü Temür to give him an opportunity to conquer the country.[40] This anecdote is not very credible. Abagha's long-term plans for Syria are clear from his repeated attempts to launch a joint offensive against the country with the Franks (see chapter 4). Rashīd al-Dīn writes that the reason behind this offensive was the Īlkhān's desire to exact revenge for Baybars's invasion of Rūm and other "disorders" that the Mamluks had caused.[41] Finally, it is difficult to believe that Abagha would have committed a good part of his army to a campaign that he really did not want in the first place. Abagha sent his army into Syria because he wished to defeat the Mamluks and conquer Syria. The actual command of this army was not entrusted to Mengü Temür, "who [according to Rashīd al-Dīn] was still a youth and inexperienced in war," but to two senior officers, Tukna and Dolabai.[42] Why Abagha, who had led Mongol armies on several occasions in the past, now chose not to command the invading force personally remains an unanswered question.

The Mongol army advanced from Abulustayn to Marᶜash, and from there to ᶜAyn Tāb, which they reached towards the end of Jumādā II (ca. the first half of October). Continuing south, they bypassed Aleppo, which had again been abandoned by its troops and inhabitants. The Mongol army, according to intelligence reports that the Sultan received, numbered 80,000 men, of whom 50,000 were Mongols (*al-mughul*) and the rest Georgians, Seljuq troops from Rūm, Armenians, Franks and "renegades" (*murtadda*). The Armenian and Georgian contingents were led by their kings, Leon and Dmitri respectively. The Franks may have been members of the military orders from the castles in Lesser Armenia, knights from Tripoli, or just mercenaries. As for the "renegades", these may have been the troops of the Muslim rulers of the Jazīra or elsewhere who were subservient to the Mongols. These renegades could also have been equivalent with the (Muslim) Persians (*al-aᶜjam*) mentioned by Shāfiᶜ and Abū 'l-Fidā'. The Mongol army advanced slowly through Syria, which some writers remark was unusual for the Mongols. The large size of the army appears to have necessitated a deliberate and thorough foraging effort. The Mongols also by-passed Hama, although they wrought havoc in the surrounding agricultural area. Al-Manṣūr and his army had withdrawn to

[40] Yūnīnī, 4:101; Ibn Kathīr, 13:297; Ibn al-Furāt, 7:234.
[41] Rashīd al-Dīn, ed. ᶜAlīzādah, 3:162. [42] *Ibid.*; Boyle, "Īl-Khāns," 363.

Homs before the arrival of the Mongols. In their march through Syria, the Mongol commanders were assisted by the knowledge of "the weak spots [in the positions] of the Muslims" (*ᶜawrāt al-muslimīn*) provided by a Mamluk deserter.[43]

Abagha chose to remain close to Syria, but not to enter the country itself. With a small force of perhaps 3000 men, he took up position across the Euphrates from al-Raḥba on 26 Jumādā II/12 October. From this vantage point, Abagha planned to wait for news of the outcome of the battle. Qalawun, upon hearing of the arrival of Mongol troops near al-Raḥba (he did not know that the Īlkhān was with them), sent a reconnaissance force out to investigate the situation. Shāfiᶜ adds that the Sultan also ordered that ᶜĪsā b. Muhannā take his bedouins to the Euphrates, but later rescinded this order.[44]

There is some disagreement as to when Qalawun reached Homs: Shāfiᶜ says two weeks before the battle; al-Yūnīnī states this was on Sunday 3 Rajab 680/ 18 October 1281, while Baybars al-Manṣūrī has Monday 11 Rajab/ 26 October. Perhaps the earlier dates represent Qalawun's arrival in the area of Homs, while the later one is when Qalawun took up position in the plain to the north of the city. Having reached the location of the prospective battle, the Sultan concerned himself with preparations. The Sultan was joined by ᶜĪsā b. Muhannā and his bedouins, al-Manṣūr and the army of Hama, and the army of Aleppo under its governor, Sanjar al-Bashqardī al-Ṣāliḥī. Units which had been dispatched to the north before Qalawun had left Damascus probably rejoined the main army at this time. Either on 8 or 12 Rajab/23 or 27 October, Sunqur al-Ashqar arrived from the north, along with al-Ḥājj Özdemür, Etmish al-Saᶜdī and other amirs who had joined him. Sunqur had made it a condition of his joining the Sultan that after the battle he should be permitted to return to Ṣahyūn. The sources give the impression that Qalawun wrote to Sunqur only upon reaching Homs, but surely negotiations must have commenced previously.[45]

During the time that Qalawun was waiting for the arrival of the Mongols, he received more precise intelligence of the battle order and size of the Mongol

[43] *Faḍl*, fols. 41a, 42b–43a, 44a, 53a; *Zubda*, fol. 113a–b; *Tuḥfa*, 98–9; Ibn al-Furāt, 7:213–15; Maqrīzī, 1:691–2; Yūnīnī, 4:91; Abū 'l-Fidā', 4:16; Brosset, *Histoire de la Géorgie*, 594; Bar Hebraeus, 564 (AD 1281, but 681 in Ibn al-ᶜIbrī, 504). On the appearance of Frankish soldiers in Mongol armies, see: J. Richard, "An Account of the Battle of Hattin Referring to the Frankish Mercenaries in Oriental Moslem States," *Speculum* 27 (1952):173–4. For the continued, albeit reduced, presence of Franks in Lesser Armenia, see Riley-Smith, "The Templars and the Teutonic Knights in Cilician Armenia," in Boase, *Cilician Kingdom*, 116–17. On the possibility that Hospitallers from Marqab may have participated in this campaign, see Amitai-Preiss, "Mamluk Perceptions," 59–60.

[44] *Faḍl*, fols. 41a–b, 43a–b, who claims that the Mongols surrounded the castle; *Zubda*, fol. 112b; *Tuḥfa*, 99, who states that Abagha was accompanied by the lord of Mārdīn; Ibn al-Furāt, 7:214; Maqrīzī, 1:691; Yūnīnī, 4:91; Ibn Kathīr, 13:294; Rashīd al-Dīn, ed. ᶜAlīzādah, 3:162, who writes of fighting with the defenders of al-Raḥba; Ibn al-Fuwaṭī, 415.

[45] *Zubda*, fol. 113a; *Tuḥfa*, 99; Nuwayrī, MS. 2n, fol. 8a; Ibn al-Furāt, 7:213–14; Maqrīzī, 1:691; Yūnīnī, 4:92; *Faḍl*, fols. 42b–43a.

army.[46] A Mongol soldier had fled to Hama and told the governor that al-Manṣūr had left in his stead, that the Mongol army numbered 80,000, of which 44,000 were in the Center (*qalb*) and would be heading for the Mamluk Center; in addition, the Mongol Right was strong. The deserter's advice was that the Sultan should strengthen his Left wing and guard his banners (*sanājiq*). This information was sent to Qalawun by pigeon post.

With this information, Qalawun arranged his army in the plain north of Homs. The modern map shows a network of irrigation canals extending from Homs to the northwest, along the east bank of the Orontes. If these canals existed in some form in the thirteenth century, and it can be assumed that they did to some degree, then that would mean that the Mamluk army was arranged to the north and northeast of the city. Qalawun reinforced his Left, as the Mongol deserter suggested. Baybars al-Manṣūrī provides us with a detailed breakdown of the Mamluk order of battle. The unique nature of such evidence in early Mamluk historiography justifies its presentation here (see Fig. 1). In the Mamluk Right were al-Manṣūr and the army of Hama;[47] Lachin al-Manṣūrī, the governor of Damascus, and its army (*ᶜaskar al-shām*, which refers here only to Damascus); Baysari; Aydegin al-Bunduqdār; Taybars al-Wazīrī; Aybeg al-Afram; Kushtoghdi al-Shamsī; plus all the amirs of 40 and 10, and *ḥalqa* commanders and troops assigned to them. In the flank (see below) of the Right were the Syrian bedouin commanded by ᶜĪsā b. Muhannā, who included the Āl Mirā led by Aḥmad b. Ḥujjā. In the Mamluk Left, which had been strengthened, were Sunqur al-Ashqar and his supporters from among the Ẓāhiriyya; Etmish al-Saᶜdī; Bilig al-Aydemürī; Bektash al-Fakhrī; Sanjar al-Ḥalabī; Bajka (?) al-ᶜAla'i; Bektüt al-ᶜAlā'ī; Jabrak (?) al-Tatarī; and others (presumably amirs of 40, 10, etc.) assigned to them. In the flank of the Left were the Türkmen and the army of Ḥiṣn al-Akrād (led by its governor Balaban al-Ṭabbākhī). In the *jālīsh* (vanguard) of the Mamluk Center were the *nā'ib al-salṭana* Turantay and his soldiers (along with the amirs and soldiers assigned to him), Abaji *al-ḥājib* and Bektash b. Geremün (the son of the *wāfidī* leader), along with the royal mamluks of the Manṣūrīyya (i.e. personal mamluks of Qalawun). The Sultan himself took up position behind this vanguard, with some of his mamluks, his entourage (*al-alzām*) and various office holders.[48] According to al-Maqrīzī, whose source is unknown,

[46] Qalawun also received intelligence on Mongol troops coming in from the direction of Tripoli, but this turned out to be a false alarm; see Amitai-Preiss, "Mamluk Perceptions," 60.

[47] Abū 'l-Fidā', 4:26, writes in his description of the siege of Acre (s.a. 690) that the normal location of the forces of Hama was in the extreme Right (*bi-ra's al-maymana*) of the Mamluk army. See below for this expression.

[48] *Tuḥfa*, 99–100; *Zubda*, fols. 113b–114a; whence Nuwayrī, MS. 2n, fol. 8a–b (cites Baybars al-Manṣūrī by name); Ibn al-Furāt, 7:215 (also names Baybars's *Zubda* as source); Maqrīzī, 1:692–3; Dhahabī, MS. Laud. 279, fol. 65b (= MS. Aya Sofya 3014, fol. 98a), also gives most of this information, albeit in a different fashion. Martinez, "Īl-Xānid army," 161–2, analyzes some parts of Ibn al-Furāt's rendition of Baybars al-Manṣūrī's passage, but makes several mistakes: first, there is no justification for reading instead of *jālīsh* the word *jāwīsh*, which he

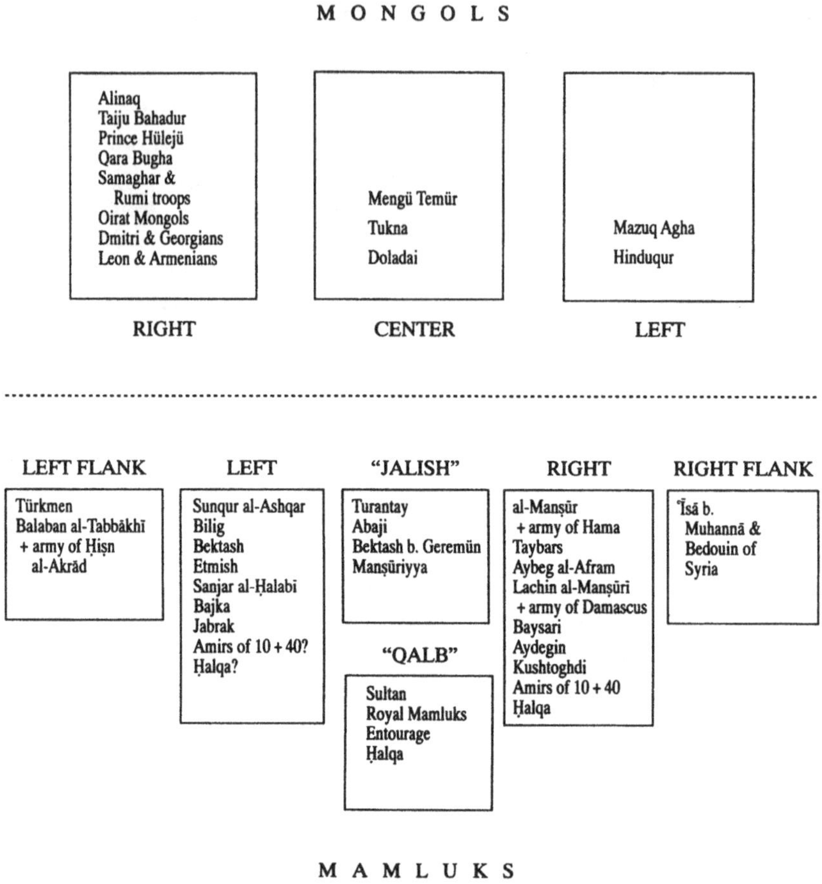

MONGOLS

RIGHT	CENTER	LEFT
Alinaq Taiju Bahadur Prince Hülejü Qara Bugha Samaghar & Rumi troops Oirat Mongols Dmitri & Georgians Leon & Armenians	Mengü Temür Tukna Doladai	Mazuq Agha Hinduqur

LEFT FLANK	LEFT	"JALISH"	RIGHT	RIGHT FLANK
Türkmen Balaban al-Tabbākhī + army of Ḥiṣn al-Akrād	Sunqur al-Ashqar Bilig Bektash Etmish Sanjar al-Ḥalabī Bajka Jabrak Amirs of 10 + 40? Ḥalqa?	Turantay Abaji Bektash b. Geremün Manṣūriyya	al-Manṣūr + army of Hama Taybars Aybeg al-Afram Lachin al-Manṣūrī + army of Damascus Baysari Aydegin Kushtoghdi Amirs of 10 + 40 Ḥalqa	ʿĪsā b. Muhannā & Bedouin of Syria
		"QALB" Sultan Royal Mamluks Entourage Ḥalqa		

MAMLUKS

Fig. 1. Line of battle at Homs (680/1281)

the Sultan had with him 800 royal mamluks and 4000 *ḥalqa* troops; then the Sultan took up position on a nearby hill (*tall*) with 200 of his mamluks. If he saw that any squadron (*ṭulb*) was in a difficult position, he planned to reinforce it with a force of 300 royal mamluks. Al-Maqrīzī also mentions that Kurdish amirs were present, but does not specify their exact location.[49] Most of Qalawun's own mamluks must have been fairly young and inexperienced,

understands to be "sargeant" [*sic*]. In the Mamluk armies there was nothing resembling a "battalion of sargeants." The term *jālīsh* is frequently found, makes perfect sense here, and is clearly read, in both Baybars al-Manṣūrī and Ibn al-Furāt. On p. 165, Martinez must be referring to these so-called "sargeants" when he writes that the Mamluk Center had a "screen of infantry." This last statement is completely unjustified. Secondly, there is no basis for the statement that the troops of Ḥiṣn al-Akrād "were apparently similar to the Turcomans and hence made up of Kurds as the place name implies." The name of the fort had nothing to do with its garrison. Thirdly, ʿIsa b. Muhannā (head of the *ʿurban*, not *ʿarbān* as written), was not present at the next battle of Homs in AH 1299, since he died in 683/1284; rather his son, Muhannā b. ʿIsa, was there.

[49] Maqrīzī, 1:693.

since the majority of them were surely purchased after he had become sultan.[50] The location of those royal mamluks whom Qalawun had inherited from his predecessors and elsewhere is not specified, although they were probably found in both the *jālīsh* of the Center and the force with the Sultan. The locations of the armies of Aleppo and Homs are not specified in the sources.

The placement of the Türkmen (along with the contingent from Ḥiṣn al-Akrād) and bedouin in the Left and Right flank respectively is not without problems. Baybars al-Manṣūrī writes that these two groups were at the "head" (*ra's*) of the wings. Al-Dhahabī, however, who evidently had an independent source, says that the bedouin and Türkmen were at the extreme end of the Right and Left wings. In addition, Baybars al-Manṣūrī had earlier spoken of how the Sultan had organized his army into Center, Right wing, Left wing and two flanks (*janāḥayn*). Later, when he provides details, he does not mention the *janāḥayn*. Perhaps, then, he intended that *ra's al-maymana* meant *janāḥ al-maymana*, and so on.[51] Finally, ʿĪsā b. Muhannā's subsequent attack on the flank of the Mongol Left (see below) suggests that he was placed to the east of the Mamluk Right.

Whatever the exact number of troops with the Sultan, it would seem that the major portion of the Center was actually in its *jālīsh*. Possibly, the *jālīsh* was flush with the Left and Right wing, while the force with the Sultan was actually a reserve behind the front. It seems that the Center, *jālīsh* and all, was relatively weak compared to the two wings. This seems strange considering the intelligence that the Sultan had received of the strength of the Mongol Center. However, as will be seen, the battle was fought over a wide front. Rather than stretch his army too thin, Qalawun may have thought to concentrate his forces in the Left and Right. It is unclear if any one officer had command over either of the wings, but according to the contemporary Hospitaller Joseph de Cancy, Sunqur al-Ashqar was commander of the Left while Aybeg al-Afram had charge of the Right.[52]

It is impossible to determine the exact number of the Mamluk army. No specific figures are provided by the Mamluk sources. Certain writers, however, state that the Mamluks numbered half of the Mongol army, which they give at 100,000 men. This figure may well have originated in Qalawun's victory announcement to Damascus, and seems to be exaggerated.[53] Half of this

[50] In *Zubda*, fol. 115b, it is reported that later in the battle Qalawun was surrounded only by a small group of young mamluks. In *ibid.*, fols. 98b–99a, Baybars al-Manṣūrī lists thirty-nine mamluks, including himself, who belonged to Qalawun before he became sultan.

[51] Dhahabī, MS. Laud 279, fol. 65b (= MS. Aya Sofya 3014, fol. 98a).

[52] Joseph de Cancy, in W.B. Sanders, "A Crusader's Letter from 'the Holy Land'," *Palestine Pilgrim's Text Society* 5 (1896):7. Dhahabī (as cited in previous note) writes that Baysari was at the "head" (*ra's*) of the Right, while Sunqur al-Ashqar was at the "head" of the Left. As seen above, this would seem to refer to their positioning on the respective wings, i.e., at the far end, rather than to the command over the wings.

[53] Yūnīnī, 4:93, 95; Ibn al-Dawādārī, 8:243; Kutubī, MS. Köprülü, fol. 136a; Ibn al-Furāt, 7:216. ʿAbd al-Raḥīm, in Ibn Wāṣil, MS. 1703, fol. 189b, also mentions 100,000, but MS. 1702, fol. 442a, has 120,000. Cf. Maqrīzī, 1:693.

number would be 50,000, which is the figure offered by Joseph de Cancy for the Mamluk army.[54] One wonders about the source of Joseph's information. I would suggest that the appearance of this figure in de Cancy and the indirect figure in the Mamluk sources was merely a coincidence, and that neither figure is credible. Without attempting to quantify the size of the Mamluk army at Homs, I will limit myself to stating that it represented virtually the entire military capability of the Sultanate and probably numbered several tens of thousands.

On the eve of Thursday 14 Rajab/29 October (still Wednesday, 28 October), the Mongols left Hama and began moving to the south. The Mongols advanced over a large front. Rashīd al-Dīn says that the troops were spread over four farsakhs (ca. 24 km), while Baybars al-Manṣūrī states that the Mongol Right was at Hama while that flank of their Left was at Salamiyya, a slightly longer distance. Perhaps this front may have been reduced as the Mongols drew closer to their enemy. Professor Smith appears to be correct that this "over-dispersal" was a result of a need to forage for food and pasture the horses. It also led to confusion on the battlefield, as the commanders in both wings had no idea what was happening on the rest of the battlefield. The Mamluk commanders had the same problem.[55]

There is a wide disparity in the sources about the size of the Mongol army. As mentioned before, the Mamluk sources variously give the figures of 100,000 and 80,000, although in one place al-Maqrīzī (his source is unknown) says that Abagha sent 25,000 picked troops with Mengü Temür. The pro-Mongol sources provide the following figures: Bar Hebraeus – 50,000; Joseph de Cancy – 40,000; Hetʿum – 30,000; Waṣṣāf – three *tümens*.[56] The lower figures of 25–30,000 may perhaps be rejected, because it is difficult to believe that Abagha would attempt the conquest of the country with such a modest army, seemingly smaller than what Qalawun could put in the field.[57] Possibly, however, these lower figures represent the numbers of actual Mongols (and Turkish nomads) in the Mongol army. The highest figure of 100,000 can be rejected as an attempt by Mamluk authors and secretaries to magnify the Mamluk achievement by exaggerating Mongol numbers. The figure of 80,000 also seems to be an exaggeration, in spite of its repeated appearance in Mamluk intelligence reports, not least because of the great difficulty a Mongol army of this size would have had in feeding itself.[58] We are left then with the figure of 40–50,000 Mongol troops, including auxiliaries.[59] These figures, of

[54] Joseph de Cancy, 7.

[55] Rashīd al-Dīn, ed. ʿAlīzādah, 3:162; *Zubda*, fol. 113b; Smith, "ʿAyn Jālūt," 239 n. 68.

[56] Maqrīzī, 1:693; Bar Hebraeus, 464 (= Ibn al-ʿIbrī, 504); Joseph de Cancy, 7; Hetʿum, 182; Waṣṣāf, 89 (cf. Āyatī, 55, who writes "30,000 horsemen").

[57] Cf. Smith, "ʿAyn Jālūt," 329 n. 63, who accepts a figure of 25–30,000.

[58] See the discussion in the next chapter.

[59] Both Weil, *Geschichte*, 1:127 n. 2 and d'Ohsson, *Histoire*, 3:525–6, thought the figure of 80,000 was exaggerated. Weil suggests that Mengü Temür led 30,000 Mongols and 15–20,000 allied troops, while D'Ohsson offered the figure of 45,000 troops altogether.

course, are far from certain, but seemingly they give an approximate idea of the size of the Mongol army.

In spite of the tip that Qalawun received from the Mongol deserter on the size of the Mongol Center (44,000 Mongols), this division, curiously, is hardly mentioned in the subsequent fighting. This is another reason to doubt the figure of 80,000 Mongols, which supposedly contained the 44,000. It must be concluded that either the information was intentionally false,[60] or that the Mongols subsequently changed their battle formation. Rashīd al-Dīn names the commanders of the Mongol army: in the Right wing were Mazuq Aqa and Hinduqur; in the Left were Alinaq, Taiju Bahādur (< Baghatur), "prince" Hülejü and Qara Bugha;[61] in the center were Tukna and Doladai, evidently the real commanders of the expedition, along with Mengü Temür.[62] There is some confusion here: from subsequent events, it is clear that the Mongol "Left" of Rashīd al-Dīn is the Mongol "Right" of the Mamluk sources, as well as of Bar Hebraeus and Waṣṣāf, while Rashīd al-Dīn's Mongol "Right" is the Mongol "Left" of the other sources. To prevent confusion, henceforth the divisions of the Mongol army will be called as they appear in the Mamluk sources. Another Mongol commander not mentioned by Rashīd al-Dīn was Samaghar, who must have come with the Rūmī contingent. From Joseph de Cancy we learn that he was also in the Mongol Right with 3000 Rūmī troops, along with 2000 "Tartars," 1000 Georgians and an unspecified number of Armenians under their king. Bar Hebraeus states that there were 5000 Georgians (presumably under their King) in the Right, as was the Armenian army under King Leon and a contingent of Oirat Mongols. Waṣṣāf places Alinaq in the Mongol Right, together with an officer named Ayaji. Hetʿum writes that the Armenian King was in the Mongol Right, but has "Halinac" (Alinaq) commanding the Mongol Left; the latter was probably in the Right as suggested by Rashīd al-Dīn (which he called "Left") and Waṣṣāf.[63] The Mongol order of battle is also shown on figure 1.

The two armies met early Thursday morning, 14 Rajab/29 October, somewhere between Homs and Rastān, a distance of some 25 km. The

[60] Thus suggests Glubb, *Soldiers of Fortune*, 113, but the Mongol deserter's advice regarding the Mamluk Left was certainly for the Mamluks' good. Qalawun's strengthening of this wing, however, was not sufficient to prevent its defeat. On the Mongol use of false information to weaken the will of the enemy, see H.D. Martin, "The Mongol Army," *JRAS* 1943: 46.

[61] In text: Buqāy. This Qara Bugha may be identified with the Mongol commander in Baghdad, who defeated the Caliph al-Mustanṣir's army in 660/1261. See ch. 3, p. 58.

[62] Rashīd al-Dīn, ed. ʿAlīzādah, 3:162–3.

[63] Bar Hebraeus, 464 (= Ibn al-ʿIbrī, 504); Joseph de Cancy, 8; Hetʿum, 183; Waṣṣāf, 89–90, who first mentions that Mengü Temür came with three officers: Alinaq, Ayaji and Arghasun (?) commanding 3 *tümens*; the last-mentioned is not heard of again. On p. 90, Waṣṣāf mentions Qurmushi, in the Center with Mengü Temür. Waṣṣāf's confused chronology (see above, nn. 18 and 23) detracts from the credibility of his account and the names which he mentioned; perhaps he has added the names of commanders who took part in the raid of AH 679 into the events of the subsequent year. On the other hand, as Rashīd al-Dīn does not mention Samaghar, who was surely at the battle, it is conceivable that these officers mentioned only in Waṣṣāf were also present in 680.

Mongols and their horses must have been quite tired since they had probably ridden most of the night. The Mamluk troops on their part had spent the night in full gear. Essentially there were two separate battles which had little to do with each other. To the west, the Mongol Right (what Rashīd al-Dīn calls the Left) under Alinaq, launched an attack against the Mamluk Left, in which Sunqur al-Ashqar *et al.* were found. The Mamluk Left broke under the force of the Mongol attack and fled. The extreme left flank of the Mamluk Center was also defeated. Retreating Mamluks reached as far as Damascus, Safad, Gaza and even Egypt. Some of the amirs, however, succeeded in rejoining the Mamluk Center and are mentioned later in the battle. The Mongol Right pursued the defeated Mamluk troops past Homs, killing people (including commoners, volunteer infantry and grooms [*ghilmān*]) found outside its walls and looting baggage on their way. The pursuing Mongols reached as far south as the Lake of Homs, where they dismounted and rested. Expecting their comrades to join them soon, they had no idea that the fighting had not also gone in favor of the rest of the Mongol army.[64]

Professor Martinez has attributed this victory of the Mongol Right to the presence of non-Mongol troops in this division, and the fact that these auxiliary troops were of a heavier nature than the Mongols themselves.[65] There are several problems with this suggestion. First, there has been little research on the Armenian, Georgian and Seljuq armies, and therefore the basis for this comparison is unclear.[66] Secondly, the Armenian troops, at least, had often met the Mamluks in the past, and had almost invariably been bested. There is no reason to think that they contributed to the victory now. Finally, the numbers given by the various sources above show that the numbers of the auxiliary troops were not large (several thousand at the most), while the names of Mongol commanders which Rashīd al-Dīn provides hint at the great number of Mongol troops in the Mongol Right.[67] In fact, it is the apparent large size of the Mongol Right which appears to have led to the Mongol victory at this side of the battle.

The Mamluks were faring better on the other side of the battlefield. The initial attack of the Mongol Left had rocked the Mamluk Right, but the Mamluks held firm. The Mamluks then counter-attacked and drove back the

[64] Rashīd al-Dīn, ed. ʿAlīzādah, 3:162; Bar Hebraeus, 464 (= Ibn al-ʿIbrī, 504); Hetʿum, 183; Joseph de Cancy, 8–9; *Zubda*, fol. 115a–b; *Tuḥfa*, 100; Nuwayrī, MS. 2n, fols. 8b–9a; Ibn al-Furāt, 7:216, 220; Maqrīzī, 1:693–4; Jazarī, fol. 16a; Yūnīnī, 4:93; Dhahabī, MS. Laud 279, fol. 65b; Kutubī, MS. Köprülü, fol. 136a–b. Ibn al-Furāt, 7:218, cites Ibn Mukarrim's lost work, *Dhākhirat al-kātib*, who reports that the Mamluk Left fled without even a fight. *Faḍl*, fol. 47b, noted that when Qalawun saw the retreat of his Left, he went after it (to stop its rout). This is, of course, nonsense. [65] Martinez, "Īl-Xānid Army," 162–5.

[66] *Ibid.*, 163, writes that a Danishmandid contingent was present at the battle, and that they "were probably medium-to-heavy cavalry." No evidence is adduced for either part of this statement. Martinez (*ibid.*) makes another unsubstantiated assumption: "From the point of view of weight, the majority of the Mongols were probably somewhere in between the Western or Westernized auxiliaries and the Turcomans, though nearer to the former than to the latter."

[67] I assume, following Smith ("ʿAyn Jālūt," 310), that when Rashīd al-Dīn mentions a commander, he is referring to a *tümen* commander.

Mongols. There is some disagreement in the Mamluk sources on how this came about. Baybars al-Manṣūrī, who was in the Center (although it is not clear if he was in the *jālīsh* or with the Sultan), writes of how the Mongol squadrons (*aṭlāb*) charged one after the other. The Mamluk Right counter-attacked and drove the Mongols towards the Mamluk *jālīsh*. Thereupon, the Sultan ordered an unspecified force, evidently those troops in his vicinity (including Baybars al-Manṣūrī), to follow him. The Mamluks attacked, protecting the Sultan and routing the Mongol Left. This led to the demoralization of the Mongol Center, where Mengü Temür was found, and its withdrawal.[68]

No other version mentions the Sultan at this point, and it would seem that Baybars al-Manṣūrī may have been less than truthful in his attempt to laud his patron's bravery. In fact, some Mamluk sources state that throughout the battle Qalawun "stood firm" under his banners. Al-Jazarī goes even further, and writes that Qalawun had the banners furled, and his location was not known. This historian reveals himself to have a distinctly non-panegyric view of Qalawun in this battle. Whether this was as a result of "objective" reporting or an anti-Qalawun bias is unclear.

After the Mamluk Right stood its ground and repelled the Mongol attack, a group of amirs were (supposedly) inspired by Qalawun's stand to lead a counter-attack against the Mongol Right. These amirs included those of the Mamluk Right (Baysari, Taybars), the Center (Turantay), and even from the recently defeated Left (Sunqur al-Ashkar, Bektash al-Fakhrī, Etmish al-Saʿdī). During this assault (or possibly assaults), ʿĪsā b. Muhannā arrived with his bedouin and attacked the Mongols on the flank. This brought about the final rout of the Mongol Left. A variant of this story is that ʿĪsā raided the baggage of the Mongol Left. The Mongols turned around, and were then attacked in the rear by the Mamluks and routed. The Mamluks then continued on to the Mongol Center.[69]

It was in the Mongol Center that the fate of the battle was decided. Hetʿum comments on Mengü Temür's inexperience, as does Rashīd al-Dīn, and on how he was nonplussed upon seeing a column of bedouin heading his way. The Mamluk sources relate the story differently: one version has it that Mengü Temür panicked at some point and was then thrown from his horse and injured. Another version of events is that the Mamluk amir, al-Ḥājj Özdemür (Sunqur al-Ashqar's confederate), made out as if he were deserting to the Mongols. When brought before Mengü Temür, he struck and wounded him

[68] *Zubda*, fol. 115a; cf. the version in *Tuḥfa*, 100, which is more rhetorical and less detailed.

[69] Jazarī, fol. 16a; Yūnīnī, 4:93–4; Dhahabī, MS. Laud 279, fol. 65b; Ibn al-Furāt, 7:216–18, who also cites Jazarī, who in turn quotes the *amīr jandar* Shams al-Dīn Ibn al-Maḥaffdār (Ibn al-Furāt: Ibn al-Jumaqdār); Maqrīzī, 1:693. For the second version of ʿIsā's attack, see: Jazarī, fol. 16a, whence: Ibn al-Dawādārī, 8:243; Kutubī, MS. Köprülü, fol. 136b; Mufaḍḍal, 327–8. Bar Hebraeus, 464 (= Ibn al-ʿIbrī, 504), tells of a bedouin ambush on the Mongol Left. Joseph de Cancy, 8–9, has the Mongol Left, under Mengü Temür himself, driving back the Mamluk Right; this is contradicted by all other sources.

before he himself was killed. The first account is more credible, as the second version has too much of a legend about it. In either case, it is clear that Mengü Temür was wounded, and this caused confusion in the Mongol Center. The Mongols then dismounted, either to attempt a stand around the wounded prince or because their horses were exhausted. The latter reason seems unlikely, since the Mongol Center had yet to participate in any real fighting. At this point, the Mamluks, seeing the dismounting of the Mongols (and sensing their weakness), attacked and routed the enemy. The Mongols withdrew, taking Mengü Temür with them.[70]

The majority of the Mamluk Center and Right went off in pursuit of the fleeing Mongols, leaving Qalawun behind with a relatively small force numbering some 300 or 1000 troops. At this point, the victorious Mongol Right returned to the scene of the battle. These Mongols, who had been waiting leisurely south of Homs for the arrival of the rest of their army, had become uneasy when it did not appear. Scouts were sent back, and they returned to report the Mongol defeat. The commanders of the Mongol Right had no choice but to turn back in order to join the main Mongol army. Heading for Rastān,[71] their path brought them close to Qalawun's position. Seeing the approaching Mongols, and aware of his own precarious position, the Sultan ordered that his banners be furled and the drums stay silent. The Mongols passed by without perceiving the Sultan's presence, thus letting slip the opportunity for turning the tables on the Mamluks.

The Mamluk sources are not unanimous about subsequent events. Some, including Baybars al-Manṣūrī, state that the Mongols passed by and the Sultan watched them join the Mongol exodus from the battlefield. Others, e.g. al-Yūnīnī and Ibn al-Furāt, describe how Qalawun seized the opportunity and launched an attack with his small force to the rear of the Mongol Right. They were routed and fled the field in disorder. Thus, by nightfall, the Mongol defeat was complete.[72] It appears that the second version is less credible. It is hard to believe that Baybars al-Manṣūrī would pass over in silence such a courageous

[70] Het'um, 183; Jazarī, fol. 16a; Ibn al-Dawādārī, 8:243–4; Kutubī, MS. Köprülü, fols. 136b, 143b; Ibn al-Furāt, 7:217, 236–7; Mufaḍḍal, 329, states that Özdemür continued his attack until he reached Mengü Temür, whom he wounded before he himself was killed. *Faḍl*, fol. 48a, states that Mengü Temür was wounded by an arrow in the neck, while Waṣṣāf, 90, reports that he was hit while already retreating. Waṣṣāf, who does not mention that the Mamluk Right had previously attacked the Mongol Left before moving on to the Mongol Center, does report that the Mamluk Right was composed of the army of Hama and "bedouin archers" (*rumāt-i ʿarab*). Rashīd al-Dīn, ed. ʿAlīzādah, 3:162–3, writes merely that Mengü Temür panicked and fled.

[71] *Tuḥfa*, 101.

[72] A few troops with the Sultan, who does not attack the Mongols: *Zubda*, fol. 115b; Nuwayrī, MS. 2n, fol. 8b. 300 troops with the Sultan, who does not attack the Mongols: Jazarī, fol. 16a–b; Kutubī, MS. Köprülü, fol. 136b; Mufaḍḍal, 329–30; Ibn al-Dawādārī, 8:243–4. 1000 troops with the Sultan, who does attack the Mongols: Yūnīnī, 4:94; Dhahabī, MS. Laud 279, fol.66a; Ibn Kathīr, 13:295 (the drums keep beating and the Mongols attack the Sultan); Ibn al-Furāt, 7:217–18; Maqrīzī, 1:695. Shāfiʿ (*Faḍl*, fols. 48b–49) describes this episode differently: Qalawun orders the banners unfurled and the drums beaten, and then launches an attack against the Mongols. Shāfiʿ, it seems, was particularly interested in presenting the Sultan in a heroic light.

action by his patron had it really happened. It is also difficult to accept that other authors would deliberately suppress information of a complimentary nature to the Sultan, even if they might have had an anti-Qalawun bias. Neither Hetᶜum nor Bar Hebraeus mentions Qalawun's attack on the Mongol Right (although the latter writes of a subsequent skirmish between them and Mamluk troops), but rather describes their withdrawal as fairly organized.[73] The only conclusion which can be drawn is that certain authors, or rather one who was later copied, invented a story to present the Sultan in a more heroic role. In the eyes of this writer or writers, this might well have been necessary, since Qalawun had actually done very little in the battle itself.

The Mongol army split up into smaller groups, each trying to make its way out of the country. Some Mongols and their allies went to the north, while others headed east via Salamiyya and the desert. The retreat soon turned into a rout. Pursued by both regular Mamluk troops and nomadic irregulars, harrassed by local inhabitants and plagued by hunger, thirst and exhaustion, many of the Mongol soldiers were killed in the retreat. Ibn al-Furāt tells of a melée between retreating Mongol and Georgian troops, ostensible allies, over horses, in which many troops from both groups were killed. At the Euphrates, numerous Mongols either drowned in the river or were caught hiding in reedbeds, which were set on fire at the Sultan's orders. The garrisons of al-Bīra and al-Raḥba attacked groups of Mongols passing their way, inflicting heavy casualties and capturing many. At Baghrās, the Mamluk garrison attacked and virtually annihilated a large group of Armenians. Baybars al-Manṣūrī (followed by other authors) may well be correct when he writes that more Mongols were killed during the retreat than in the battle itself. Even more Mongols would have been killed were it not for Khafāja bedouins who showed them the way through the desert and fords over the Euphrates.[74]

Mamluk losses were evidently much lower than those sustained by the Mongols, although perhaps the figure of 200 Muslim dead given in one account is too low. Ibn al-Furāt gives us the names of eleven amirs killed in the battle, while two more are found in the obituaries in al-Yūnīnī and al-Dhahabī's chronicles.[75] Among the wounded was the scribe (and later historian), Shāfiᶜ b. ᶜAlī, who had been present at the battle and was subsequently wounded in the temple by an arrow, and thus blinded for the rest of his life.[76]

There is no single reason why the Mamluks had been victorious at Homs. One contributing factor was the evident fatigue of the Mongol troops and

[73] Bar Hebraeus, 464 (= Ibn al-ᶜIbrī, 504); Hetᶜum, 183.

[74] *Tuḥfa*, 101; *Zubda*, fols. 116a–117a; Nuwayrī, MS. 2n, fol. 9a; Ibn al-Furāt, 7:218, 221–2; Maqrīzī, 1:695–6, 698; Yūnīnī, 4:97; Ibn al-Dawādārī, 8:244; Mufaḍḍal, 330; *Faḍl*, fol. 51a–b; Bar Hebraeus, 464 (= Ibn al-ᶜIbrī, 504); Hetᶜum, 183–4; de Cancy, 9–10, who has the Rūmīs under Samaghar robbing the Armenians during the retreat.

[75] Ibn al-Furāt, 7:219; Maqrīzī, 1:696, 705 (who mentions some civilian casualties not found in Ibn al-Furāt); Yūnīnī, 4:96, 108, 120; Dhahabī, MS. Laud 279, fols. 66a, 116a.

[76] Ṣafadī, *Aᶜyān*, MS. 2964, fol. 53.

horses, who had been on the move all night. An additional reason was Mengü Temür's inexperience, along with the apparent lack of a single authoritative commanding figure among the Mongol officers. The failure of the officers of the Mongol Right to maintain contact with the rest of the army, and thus the lack of assistance they could have provided at a critical juncture, should also be mentioned. The Mamluks on the other hand had been at the site of the battle for at least three days, probably longer. Thus they had had an opportunity to rest and prepare themselves. While Qalawun's part in the battle, both in the actual fighting and as a commander, was somewhat limited, he may have had an important symbolic role: some writers state that his stand on a hill behind the frontline under his banners inspired his troops and officers alike. Al-Jazarī's evidence, however, casts some doubt on this information. The Mamluks had luck on their side, because the Mongol Right, upon passing Qalawun on their return, did not see him (or perhaps ignored him). Had they attacked, the result might well have been different. There is also the morale factor: the Mamluks were fighting on home territory for the survival of their kingdom; evidence of this fervor is seen in the amirs' desire to move north from Damascus to meet the Mongols. The Mongols may well have wanted to conquer Syria and avenge previous defeats, but a reverse would not have endangered their kingdom. As at ʿAyn Jālūt, the Mamluks were probably driven by the feeling that they were fighting for their lives, their kingdom and their religion.

Qalawun remained on the battlefield for several days. News of the victory was sent to Damascus and Cairo. The day after the battle he dispatched a force to the north. The armies of Hama and Aleppo subsequently set out for their cities. Sunqur al-Ashqar also left for Ṣahyun, although several of the amirs who had been with him elected to remain with the Sultan. On 22 Rajab/6 November, Qalawun entered Damascus to great acclaim, as droves of Mongol prisoners were paraded before him.[77] With the Mongol danger thus removed, at least for the forseeable future, the Sultan could now turn his attention to other matters, not the least of which was the further reduction of the Frankish possessions.

There is some disagreement over Abagha's whereabouts during the battle. Rashīd al-Dīn and Waṣṣāf report that the Īlkhān left al-Raḥba for the east by the end of Jumādā II/15 October, after occupying himself with hunting. On the other hand, the Mamluk sources tell that Abagha remained at al-Raḥba, waiting for the results of the battle. Fighting broke out with the defenders of the castle, although the description in some sources of a Mongol siege is surely exaggerated. The earliest news of Mengü Temür's defeat was brought by the first Mongol survivors who reached him. Some Mamluk writers tell that Abagha realized that the celebrations inside al-Raḥba (its inhabitants had received word via pigeon post) could only be a result of good tidings – from a

[77] *Zubda*, fol. 117a; Ibn al-Furāt, 7:218; Maqrīzī, 1:696; Yūnīnī, 4:94–6.

Muslim point of view – from the front. In either case, the Īlkhān withdrew from al-Raḥba to Hamadhān. While *a priori* it would seem that the Persian historians should have had a better idea of Abagha's actions during this period, some of the Mamluk writers report that their source for this information was the Mongol deserters who subsequently fled to the Sultanate, reaching Damascus on 23 Shaʿbān 680/7 December 1281.

Whatever Abagha's exact timetable, he was furious at the Mongol defeat and planned another offensive the next year to exact revenge. His death later in 680/1282 prevented the realization of this plan.[78] Amost twenty years were to pass before another Īlkhān attempted again to invade Syria.

[78] Yūnīnī, 4:101; Ibn al-Furāt, 7:221–2, 234–5; Maqrīzī, 1:698; *Zubda*, fol. 117a; Rashīd al-Dīn, ed. ʿAlīzādah, 3:162, who has Abagha leave al-Raḥba long before the news of the battle reached him; Waṣṣāf, 98; Boyle, "Īl-Khāns," 363–4. During the month after the battle, 200 Mongol *wāfidiyya* arrived in Damascus, bringing news that Mengü Temür had died, and of how Abagha had been at al-Raḥba and subsequently withdrawn; Ibn al-Dawādārī, 8:248; Mufaḍḍal, 334. These *wāfidiyya* might have been the the source of other information on the battle.

CHAPTER 9

The Mamluk–Īlkhānid frontier

The entire population of some provinces, because they were frontier [regions] and were traversed by armies, was either killed or fled, such as . . . parts of Abulustayn and Diyār Bakr: thus Ḥarrān, Ruḥā, Sarūj and Raqqa, as well as most of the cities on this and that side of the Euphrates, were completely uncultivated and abandoned.

Rashīd al-Dīn[1]

The frontier region

In this section, a number of generalizations will be drawn about the nature of the Mamluk–Īlkhānid frontier. Much of the discussion will be based on the findings in chapter 5, in which the course of the border war was examined in some detail.[2] Each kingdom's frontier, its defence and the strategy adopted towards the other side will be examined separately.

The Mamluk border defence was based first on the two great fortresses on the bank of the Euphrates, al-Bīra and al-Raḥba.[3] During Baybars's reign, the former was more prominent, as it suffered most of the Mongol attacks. It withstood every attack and siege attempt, in no small degree thanks to the Sultan's prompt dispatch of relief. These forts were well supplied and garrisoned, and were connected to the center of the Sultanate by several means of rapid communication (*barīd*, pigeon-post and bonfires). Al-Bīra and al-Raḥba served several important functions: they guarded the fords, served as forward-warning stations and would withstand the first shock of a Mongol offensive. In addition, they acted as centers for the gathering of intelligence on the Mongols,[4] and as bases for raids into Mongol-controlled territory.[5] With justice, Shāfiʿ b. ʿAlī referred to al-Bīra as "the lock of Syria" (*wa-hiya qufl al-*

[1] Ed. ʿAlīzādah, 3:557–8; cited in I.P. Petrushevsky, "The Socio-Economic Condition of Iran under the Īl-Khāns," *CHIr*, 5:491. Ruḥā, called al-Ruhā in the Arabic sources, is Edessa; see Krawulsky, *Īrān*, 452.

[2] I will thus dispense with most of the documentation of material covered in ch. 5.

[3] On these two forts, see: E. Honigman, "al-Raḥba," *EI*[1], 3:1100–3; M. Streck-[V.J. Parry], "Bīredjik," *EI*[2], 1:1233–4; Krawulsky, *Īrān*, 585, 595–6, 614.

[4] *Ḥusn*, 87: information about the Mongols was gathered at al-Bīra.

[5] Yūnīnī, 3:132–3: raids launched from al-Raḥba by its governor.

shām).[6] The Mongols must also have understood the importance of these two forts to the Mamluks, because in the sixty years of the war they subjected both of them to numerous raids and attacks.

Important as they were, however, these forts would have had little value without the rapid reaction of Baybars. At the first word of an expected Mongol offensive or raid, he would begin organizing an expeditionary force, which he himself often commanded personally. In some cases, the knowledge that a Mamluk force was approaching was enough to cause the withdrawal of the Mongols; the Mongol commanders were evidently not looking for a major confrontation. Besides the obvious need of repulsing the Mongol attackers, Baybars's resolute response served another purpose. By showing that he was a capable and decisive ruler, who protected soldiers and common people alike, the morale of the officers and soldiers in the Syrian army, not least in the border fortresses, was strengthened.

The Āl Faḍl bedouin, who were found in the Syrian side of the Euphrates, patrolled the area and served as an additional source of intelligence on Mongol intrusions into Syria. Given the far-flung frontier and the lack of a large concentration of Mamluk troops permanently stationed in the area, these bedouin were an important component in the defense of the Euphrates frontier. They also raided, perhaps not always at the request of the Mamluk authorities, over into the Mongol side of the border.

To the east and northeast, the cities of Syria were protected to some extent by the expanse of the Syrian desert. Defending the northern frontier from the Mongols and Armenians was more of a problem. Because of the smaller distance, there was less advanced warning of an attack, unless the Mamluks received intelligence information. The situation was especially critical before Baybars regained a number of fortresses in 666/1268 on the border with Lesser Armenia (al-Darbassāk, Baghrās, etc.). The conquest of Antioch that year also helped improve security in the region.

The approaches to Aleppo were protected by the fortified towns of ʿAyn Tāb and ʿAzāz. On the former, Ibn Shaddād writes that it was "a watch-post (*raṣad*) for fresh developments coming from the land of the Armenians and Rūm."[7] Baybars maintained governors and some type of forces at Tall Bāshir, Burj al-Raṣāṣ and Ḥārim, but their fortifications had not been repaired since the Mongols had destroyed them.[8] It is clear that Mamluk forces in this area were spread very thin. To help alleviate this situation, every year a corps of the Syrian army was sent north to patrol the frontier region, a practice seemingly continued at least to the end of the century.[9]

There was little that the Sultan could do about Mongol raids coming from Seljuq territory into north Syria, except to respond quickly. Lesser Armenia was a different matter. The numerous attacks and raids from that direction early in Baybars's reign, albeit not overly successful, prodded the Sultan into

[6] *Ḥusn*, 87. [7] Ibn Shaddād, *Aʿlaq*, ed. Eddé, 376, 382, 385. [8] *Ibid.*, 378, 380, 386–7.
[9] Ibn Shaddād, *Ta'rīkh*, 155; Mufaḍḍal, 554–5 (s.a. 700/1300–1).

action. His motives are clear: to punish the Armenians and their king, and to neutralize the danger from that direction. Possibly, Baybars sought to damage the transit trade from the Īlkhānid realm to the West, but this is only speculation. In a series of devastating campaigns, Baybars achieved his goals.

It is difficult to assess the harm caused to the population and economic life of northern Syria by the Mongol raids, which compounded the damage sustained during the Mongol occupation of 658/1260. Ibn Shaddād, in his *al-Aʿlāq al-khaṭīra* (written ca. 679/1280–1),[10] provides important information on the devastation wrought on the Mamluk side of the border running along the Euphrates River. Both Bālis and Manbij were destroyed during the Mongol occupation and abandoned by their inhabitants. The latter was occupied by a few Türkmen. Al-Ruṣāfa, about 50 km to the southwest of al-Raqqa, had originally been granted a pardon by Hülegü, but subsequently all its inhabitants left and settled in Salamiyya, Hama and elsewhere.[11] The situation was not unequivocally bad: Ṣiffīn on the river, and al-Bāb and Buzāgha further west were inhabited and seem to have enjoyed some prosperity.[12] The countryside around al-Bīra was cultivated, at least until the Mongol attack of 663/1265, when it was severely damaged.[13] It is unclear if the land was subsequently cultivated. If so, this story probably repeated itself in subsequent attacks.

Conditions were similar in the regions of northern Syria bordering Armenian and Seljuq territory. Some towns – Tall Bāshir, Ḥārim and Burj al-Raṣāṣ – were virtually uninhabited except for Mamluk garrisons and some Türkmen. On the other hand, the fortifications of ʿAyn Tāb and ʿAzāz had been rebuilt and these towns were populated and thriving.[14] Further to the south, in the environs of Aleppo, the situation was somewhat better. Ibn Shaddād tells that Sarmīn, Ḥāḍir Qinnasrīn and Khunāṣira, all south of Aleppo, were populated by peasants, although none of the towns any longer had fortifications (perhaps a legacy of the Mongol occupation).[15] Aleppo itself was slow in recovering from the effects of 658–9/1260–1. The fortifications of the city, as well as the great mosque and the citadel were damaged during the first Mongol occupation. The last mentioned was further demolished by the Mongol raiders in 659/1261, while the mosque suffered during the Mongol raid of 679/1280, when it was burnt again. The great mosque and the citadel, the symbols of authority in a major provincial capital, were rebuilt only years later: the mosque in 684/1285–6 and the citadel in the reign of al-Ashraf Khalīl b. Qalawun (689–93/1290–3).[16] Ibn Shaddād reports that when he left Aleppo in 657/1259, there were hundreds of baths. In the 670s, only ten were still in use.[17] The process of

[10] See, e.g., *Aʿlāq*, 3:510. [11] Ibn Shaddād, *Aʿlaq*, ed. Eddé, 294, 394, 397.
[12] *Ibid.*, 373–5, 396. [13] Abū Shāma, 233. [14] See above, nn. 6 and 7.
[15] Ibn Shaddād, *Aʿlaq*, ed. Eddé, 391–4.
[16] Ibn al-Shiḥna, 36, 54–8, 64, 68–9; Maqrīzī, 1:774–5; see also J.Sauvaget, "Ḥalab," *EI*², 3:88. The fortifications of Aleppo were repaired only at the end of the fourteenth century.
[17] Cited in Ibn al-Shiḥna, 134.

rehabilitation was certainly not helped by the news of Mongol raids, real and imagined, and the resulting panic and damage.

Each wave of rumors about another impending Mongol advance into northern Syria usually occasioned a flurry of refugees to the south. There is no indication, however, that the majority of these refugees did not return to their homes when the danger had past. From the little explicit evidence that we have, it appears that there was not the massive depopulation in the province of Aleppo that we find on both sides of the Euphrates, albeit evidently to a lesser degree on the Mamluk side.[18]

It is worth noting in this connection the behavior of the Aleppan army whenever the Mongols raided north Syria. Invariably, these forces would withdraw to the south, joining up with the armies of Homs and Hama, and together they would meet up with reinforcements from the south. Never did the Aleppan army attempt to stop the Mongols alone. Perhaps this was the drill dictated by the Sultan, who realized that the Aleppan army alone would not be able to deal with even a relatively modest body of Mongol raiders, and that it was wiser to combine forces.

Baybars also brought the war into the enemy camp. Besides carrying out raids against the Armenians, Mamluk forces, usually from northern Syria and often accompanied by Syrian bedouins (who also raided by themselves), struck across the Euphrates River. The purpose of these raids was to act as diversions, to keep the enemy off balance, to reconnoiter and to strengthen morale in the army and the civilian population. Besides these raids, there are records of specific reconnaissance parties setting out.[19] Some of these operations must have been at the Sultan's direct order. Others may have been the initiatives of local commanders, although it is clear that they were acting under the guidelines of the Sultan.

Al-ʿUmarī (d. 749/1349), writes that the Mamluks employed operatives who laid waste to the border regions, particularly on the Mongol side of the border, including the area around Mosul and Sinjār. The Mongols did not bring fodder with them, but grazed their horses as they advanced, so if the fields and grasslands were burned, then their progress in Syria would have been made difficult if not impossible. The "bravest men" (*ajlad al-rijāl*) who carried out this work either stayed with local contacts (*nuṣṣāḥ*)[20] in Mongol territory or hid out in mountains or valleys. When the conditions were ripe, i.e. windy days, the "burners" would release wild foxes, with burning rags tied to their tails. To spread the fire, hungry dogs were released that chased after the foxes.[21] Perhaps the last part of this account is a little tongue in cheek. It is

[18] Cf. the comments in Irwin, *Middle East*, 46.

[19] Ibn al-Furāt, MS. Vienna, fol. 77a, under Badr al-Dīn Bilig al-Fāyizī (s.a. 663/1264–5); Yūnīnī, 3:132–3, dispatched by governor of al-Raḥba; *ibid.*, 3:229, Shams al-Dīn Aq Sunqur al-Fāriqānī, some time early in his career.

[20] For this term, see ch. 6, p. 143. It is possible that the intention here is to refer not to local informers, but just contacts willing to help Mamluk operatives.

[21] ʿUmarī, *Taʿrīf*, 201–3; whence Qalqashandī, 1:127–8; also 14:401–2.

difficult to conceive of operatives moving around the Jazīra with foxes and hungry dogs in tow, and remaining under cover for long.[22] A man on a horse with a torch would have been no less effective in setting fields on fire. Still, even if this passage might contain some exaggeration or untruths, we can accept the information about the existence of these "burners." Such activities were described in 660/1262, and in 670/1272 we read of "burners" (*al-munawwirūn*) being sent out with scouts by Baybars.[23] Yet a number of questions remain unanswered. Were these operatives permanently stationed over the border or did they only go there in response to news of a Mongol advance? If the former, did they execute "preventative" incitements or only when the Mongols were advancing towards Syria? What would the "burners" do in the winter, when the grasslands were wet? (Both known cases were in the autumn.) Unfortunately, the chronicles do not provide more details on this subject.

The Mongol frontier defence was arranged differently than that of the Mamluks. There were no major fortresses on their side of the frontier similar in size and function to al-Bīra and al-Raḥba. The Mongol garrisons which the Mamluk raiders encountered in Ḥarrān and Qarqīsiyā seem to have been quite small. The only times that large Mongol forces were present in the western Jazīra were during offensives against the Mamluks. The sources do not make clear where the closest large concentration of Mongols was found. The relative impunity with which Mamluk raiders and scouts traversed the Jazīra leads to the conclusion that the region was not brimming with Mongol troops.

In Lesser Armenia, the Mongol presence was also minimal, although there seem to have been some Mongols at al-ʿAmūdayn. During Baybars's raid on Cilicia in 673/1275, Mongol women and children were found, indicating that Mongol men could not have been too far away. As for the Armenians, their king, secure at first in his belief of Mongol superiority and support, raided Mamluk northern Syria. When the Mamluks responded by launching their first large-scale raid to Cilicia in 664/1266, he made an attempt to resist, by fielding his army and fortifying the pass that the Mamluk army was to traverse. This attempt ended in disaster, and in the following years the Armenians made no substantial attempt to hold the frontier, and the Mamluks had no trouble breaching it.

The Mongol side of the Euphrates was full of abandoned and ruined cities. Some of these may have been devastated during Hülegü's conquest, others by the border war, still others by Mongol misrule. Ibn Shaddād provides important information on the sorry state of several of the cities and towns of Diyār Muḍar and its environs: al-Raqqa was destroyed when the Mongols took it over and nobody lived there.[24] The Mongols destroyed the citadel of al-Ruhā (Edessa) after ʿAyn Jālūt, and its inhabitants fled; only a few Türkmen

[22] This method is reminiscent of that employed by Samson against the Philistines, as told in Judges 15, 4–5. Perhaps this story is merely a topos, which ʿUmarī inserted to liven up the narrative. [23] *Rawḍ*, 396. [24] Ibn Shaddād, *Aʿlaq*, 3:82.

remained.[25] Qalʿat Jaʿbar was handed over to the Mongols by its *wālī* (governor) without a siege. They destroyed it and its surrounding countryside. Only a few wretched souls remained and they eventually left.[26] The Mongols also destroyed Qalʿat Najm at some point, probably soon after they had gained control of the city in 658/1259–60; its population subsequently left.[27] Sarūj was abandoned by the Mongols in 663/1264–5; its population had been massacred in 658/1260.[28] The decline and final ruin of Ḥarrān by the Mongols has been mentioned above.[29] It comes as no surprise, as Rashīd al-Dīn informs us, that the destruction of the towns was accompanied by the steep decline of agriculture in the area.[30]

Some of the population must have fled to the Sultanate, although there is little explicit evidence to confirm a mass movement of civilian refugees. We know that in Ḥarrān there were successive waves of emigration to Syria until the city was finally razed by the Mongols, and the remainder of its population was evacuated to other places in the Jazīra. After the Mamluk raid on Sharmūshāk in 667/1268–9, peasants were brought back and resettled in north Syria.

The Mongol excursions into Syria proper during Baybars's reign were raids and probes. The attacks, on the other hand, against al-Bīra were usually serious attempts to capture the fort, but because of the determined resistance of the defenders, the approach of a relieving force and lack of supplies, these sieges failed. Only with the invasion of 680/1281, did the Mongols attempt something more than a raid into Syria or an attack along the border.

Open borders and trade in a time of war

It is reasonable to assume that the state of war and the fighting along the border would have adversely affected commercial and other civilian traffic between Syria and the lands now under Īlkhānid control.[31] The occasional evidence at our disposal tends to strengthen this supposition, although there are fairly clear indications that as early as Baybars's reign there was some trade and other contact over the border. Evidently, these commercial endeavors did

[25] *Ibid.*, 98–9; see also Krawulsky, *Īrān*, 452.

[26] *Ibid.*, 119. This place was rebuilt and resettled by the governor of Syria, Tankiz al-Nāṣirī, in 735/1334–5; Ibn al-Dawādārī, *Kanz al-durar*, vol. 9, ed. H.R. Roemer (Freiburg-Cairo, 1960), 400; Ibn Kathīr, 14:173; Maqrīzī, 2:385–6.

[27] Ibn Shaddād, *Aʿlaq*, ed. Eddé, 292 and 3:119; see also Krawulsky, *Īrān*, 614.

[28] Ibn Shaddād, *Aʿlāq*, 3:103; Krawulsky, *Īrān*, 454.

[29] See also Ibn Shaddād, *Aʿlāq*, 3:40, 60–3. In 662/1263–4, the governor of Damascus appointed governors for Ḥarrān and al-Raqqa. These must have been merely paper appointments. *Rawḍ*, 186–7; Ibn al-Furāt, MS. Vienna, fol. 39a; Maqrīzī, 1:505–6.

[30] See the passage cited at the beginning of this chapter.

[31] Spuler, *Iran*, 358, makes such an assumption, and does not discuss the matter further; see also J.Ḥ. Khiṣbāk, *al-ʿIrāq fī ʿahd al-mughūl al-īlkhāniyya* (Baghdad, 1968), 136; Irwin, "Supply of Money," 76; Ashtor, *Social and Economic History*, 263. On the relatively prosperous Syrian–Iraqi trade before Hülegü's invasion, see the general comments in *ibid.*, 239–41. The economic relations between these countries during the Ayyūbid period has yet to be investigated in detail.

not enjoy official Īlkhānid approval, although perhaps they turned a blind eye to some activities; otherwise it is difficult to see how even limited commercial relations could have existed. Baybars seems to have had a more favorable attitude, the extent of which, however, is hard to gauge. Whatever evidence we have relates to the import of strategic items (mamluks and horses) from Īlkhānid-controlled territory, particularly from Anatolia, to the Sultanate, and it is clear that he had an interest in such a trade. There is no evidence, however, that he evinced any desire to export to Īlkhānid territory, and there is no report of such activity.

Two pieces of information lead to the conclusion that there was a lack of regular Īlkhānid–Mamluk commercial traffic in Baybars's reign. The first is an anecdote found in al-Yūnīnī's obituary of this sultan (676/1277). At an unspecified date, merchants from Iran (*bilād al-ᶜajam*) headed for Baybars's court via Ayās in Lesser Armenia. The Armenian king, however, detained them and sent to Abagha to notify him of this matter. Abagha wrote to keep them under guard and send them to him. However, a mamluk, evidently in the process of being imported to the Sultanate, escaped to Aleppo and word was sent to Baybars of the incident. Baybars then dispatched a threatening message to the Armenian King, who thereupon had the merchants released. The Armenian King then placated (*ṣānaᶜa*) Abagha by sending him much money.[32] Two conclusions can be tentatively drawn from this passage. First, the route over the Euphrates was blocked or too dangerous to be considered by merchants, although it could be argued that from certain sections of Iran it was easier to go to Ayās and from there by boat to Egypt than via Iraq or the Jazīra. Secondly, the detention of the merchants and Abagha's reaction show that from the Mongol point of view trade with the Mamluks was not acceptable and seemingly was officially forbidden. Professor Ashtor understood this evidence as an indication of the occasional swerving of trade from the trans-Euphrates route via Lesser Armenia, whenever Īlkhānid disapproval of such activities became too strong.[33] Such a conclusion, however, is unwarranted by this passage.

Secondly, we have the evidence of the Īlkhān Aḥmad Tegüder (680–3/1282–4) on the subject of trade. In a letter sent to Qalawun in 681/1282–3, in which he attempted to effect a rapprochement with the Mamluks, Aḥmad states that he unilaterally ordered his officials to permit the free movement of merchants going back and forth.[34] This indicates that previous to this time commercial traffic was restricted. From this specific passage it is impossible to decide the extent of this restricted trade, although the use of the expression *al-tujjār al-mutaraddidūn* ("the merchants who go back and forth") hints at the existence of some type of trade via the Euphrates, the Red Sea or Lesser Armenia (or a

[32] Yūnīnī, 3:254. The author's intention was to illustrate the fear and awe that Baybars generated, both in his own kingdom and among his neighbors.

[33] Ashtor, *Social and Economic History*, 263.

[34] *Zubda*, fol. 132b; edited in appendix to Maqrīzī, 1:979. Cf. Ibn al-Fuwaṭī, 425.

combination of these), even when their activities were discouraged and the tension on the border was unpropitious for regular trade.

There exist additional indications of some type of possible commercial activity. In 670/1271–2, the head Ḥanbalī qadi of Cairo, Shams al-Dīn Ibn al-ʿImād, was arrested and removed from office, when it became clear that he had mishandled deposits of money (*waḍāʾiʿ*) given over to his care by merchants from Damascus, Ḥarrān and Baghdad.[35] While it is tempting to see this as clear proof of the existence of trade with Mongol Iraq and the Jazīra,[36] it is possible that these deposits were left before the Mongol conquest of Baghdad or previous to the battle of ʿAyn Jālūt.

Another example, albeit from a different direction, is s.a. 671/1273. "Türkmen merchants," bringing horses and mules to Baybars, were intercepted by Armenians from the fortress of Kaynūk (Ḥadath al-Ḥamrāʾ).[37] Ibn Shaddād, evidently referring to the same episode, writes of the waylaying (*taʿarruḍ*) of caravans coming from Rūm.[38] The exact identity of these Türkmen merchants is unclear. However, the mention of this information about such merchants in such an incidental manner leads to the conclusion that this was not the only occurrence of such trade. The existence of such trade can be explained by the fact that the Türkmen were only nominally, if at all, under Īlkhānid domination, and that Mongol forces in this area were relatively few in number and spread rather thin, thus permitting clandestine livestock trading.

For all the problems that the Armenians were making for the transient trade passing through their country on the way to the Sultanate, there was plenty of trade emanating from their own port of Ayās. Recent research by C. Otten-Froux, based on the records of the Genoese notaries in Ayās from 1274, 1277 and 1279, indicates the extent of this trade. Commerce took place directly between Ayās and Egypt, or followed the Ayās–Syria–Egypt (or Egypt–Syria) triangular route. Goods exported from Cilicia were wood, iron and tin, but the sources are silent as to what products were brought back.[39] It is also unclear if the exported goods from Ayās originated from the territory of Lesser Armenia or were brought from further inland. Naturally, the Genoese notaries would only have recorded the activities of Genoese citizens, who may have represented only a fraction of those engaged in what must have been a quite lucrative trade.

Another possible indication of commercial activity in this period may be the biographies of travelling merchants (singular: *tājir saffār*), especially those from Iraq or other Mongol-controlled territories. The problem is, however, that among those who travelled between the Mamluk Sultanate and Īlkhānid

[35] Yūnīnī, 2:470–1; Ibn al-Furāt, MS. Vienna, fol. 209a–b; Maqrīzī, 1:602–3. For an analysis of this affair, see J.H. Escovitz, *The Office of Qāḍī al-Quḍāt in Cairo under the Baḥrī Mamluks* (Berlin, 1984), 229–1.

[36] Labib, *Handelsgeschichte*, 72, adduces this as proof of Īlkhānid–Mamluk trade at this time.

[37] *Rawḍ*, 417; Ibn al-Furāt, 7:2. See above, ch. 5, p. 132.

[38] Ibn Shaddād, *Aʿlaq*, ed. Eddé, 321. [39] Otten-Froux, "L'Aïas," 160–7.

territory, either by land or by sea, the dates of their trips are usually not specified, so these trips could have been either before ʿAyn Jālūt, or somewhat after Baybars's reign. Also, it is sometimes not clear whether these merchants came to the Sultanate to trade, or had fled and had opened up shop in their new homeland.[40]

One example, however, is more certain and quite interesting, and deserves mention here. In 681/1282–3, an envoy arrived at Qalawun's court from the Rūmī lord of Amāsiyya, Sayf al-Dīn Turantay. This envoy was sent with Abagha's approval; his mission was to arrange the release of Turantay's son, who was a prisoner of the Sultan. What is relevant to our purposes here is that this envoy was a merchant, and had often come to the Mamluk court before (i.e., during at least part of the period covered here), importing mamluks and other goods.[41] This information is reported in passing, and was evidently not regarded as anything unusual. It suggests that, in spite of the war, perhaps some type of traffic in mamluks was going on via Mongol-controlled Anatolia and/or Lesser Armenia, even before Qalawun's treaty of 684/1285 with the Armenian king secured this trade.[42] One wonders if this trade in mamluks was clandestine. On the one hand, it is difficult to understand how such a trade could have received the permission of the Īlkhāns and their local agents. Yet, on the other hand, it is hard to see how it could have been conducted without the tacit approval of these same Mongols. This paradox will have to be resolved by further research.

J.Ḥ. Khiṣbāk has suggested that the use of Baghdādī paper in Egypt for official documents (he adduces only one example, from 661/1262–3) is proof of an ongoing trade between the two kingdoms.[43] This, however, is far from being conclusive for trade in this particular commodity, let alone for regular commercial activity. S.Y. Labib has written that the Mongol–Mamluk war had little serious effect on trade between their two kingdoms, but adduces virtually no evidence to prove this assertion.[44] Professor Rogers asserts that trade via land between Iraq and Syria continued unabated throughout the period of the Mongol–Mamluk wars, but cites no examples for the years of Baybars's reign.[45] Instead of such blanket statements, I would suggest the following: in spite of the enmity between the two kingdoms and the fighting on the border, some trading continued. The curtailment of trade probably had its origin in several reasons. First, the ongoing warfare on both sides of the border must have made travelling in the area risky, both to life and merchandise.

40 Since these are far from unequivocal examples, I have not listed them here.

41 *Zubda*, fol. 128b. See ch. 8 for Turantay and his son.

42 See Ayalon, "Mamlūk," *EI*², 6:315a–b; Irwin, "Supply of Money," 3–4. See also the comments in Ehrenkreutz, "Slave Trade," 336.

43 Khiṣbāk, *al-ʿIrāq*, 143, citing Maqrīzī, 1:497; cf. Ashtor, *Social and Economic History*, 262.

44 Labib, *Handelsgeschichte*, 70, 72.

45 J.M. Rogers, "Evidence for Mamluk–Mongol Relations," *Colloque international sur l'histoire du Caire, 1969* (Cairo, [1974]), 399.

Secondly, it seems that to a certain degree the Īlkhānids discouraged commercial activity. Thirdly, while Baybars was happy to receive certain commodities of strategic importance, it would appear that he did not encourage exports out of his kingdom to Mongol-controlled territory. Fourthly, both sides had a fear, not unjustified (see chapter 6), of spies being sent in the guise of merchants. Khiṣbāk may have been correct when he suggested that internal Mongol factors, such as the lack of a unified currency throughout the Īlkhānid realm and the expropriation of money from the rich, may have also adversely affected trade with Mamluk territory or merchants arriving from there.[46] That commerce continued under these conditions testifies to the profits that were probably to be made, and the intrepidity of the merchants who set out to make them.

In the subsequent decades after Baybars's death, trade between Mamluk Syria and Mongol Iraq becomes increasingly more discernible in the sources. Early in Qalawun's Sultanate there is a clear indication of what seems to be some type of bilaterally sanctioned commercial activity.[47] This was perhaps the only tangible result of Aḥmad Tegüder's ill-fated attempt to end the state of war. It is interesting, and possibly more than a coincidence, that the contemporary Baybars al-Manṣūrī writes that in 682/1283–4 there were embassies from both the King of Ceylon and the Īlkhān Aḥmad which arrived in Syria from Iraq, via the "frequented road" (*al-jadda al-maslūka* and *al-tarīq al-maslūka*).[48] Through the next decade, the situation is less clear, but evidence of some trading activity exists.[49] The increasing evidence of trade from the last decade of the seventh/thirteenth century would appear to indicate the growth and establishment of this activity.[50]

A telling indication of the continued existence of trade over the Mamluk–Īlkhānid border in the first decade of the eighth/fourteenth century is the Armenian historian Hetᶜum's complaint to the Pope in his memoir: the Pope must send messages to the Īlkhān Khudābanda (Öljeitü) to have him forbid the export of merchandise to his enemies, the Mamluks.[51] Given what we have seen of the extent of Mamluk trading through the Armenian port of Ayās, Hetᶜum's lament is not without a note of gratuitous self-righteousness.

[46] Khiṣbāk, *al-ᶜIrāq*, 144. On the other hand, it can be remembered that Mongol leaders traditionally were sympathetic to trade and merchants; Petrushevsky, "Socio-Economic Condition," 506–10.

[47] Bar Hebraeus, 467 (not in the Arabic version); Kutubī, MS. Köprülü, fol. 159a (s.a. 682).

[48] *Zubda*, fols. 142a–b, 147a–b. For translation of *maslūk*, see Dozy, 1:677a.

[49] See Jazarī, cited by M. Jawād, "Tijārat al-ᶜirāq fī ᶜuṣūr al-ḥukm al-mughūlī," pt. 3, *Majallat ghurfat tijārat baghdād* 7 (1944):64; *Zubda*, fol. 176a (s.a. 691).

[50] See the chapter on trade in Amitai, "Holy War," 70–5. Since completing that study, I have found numerous additional pieces of evidence relating to commercial relations during the second half of the Mamluk–Īlkhānid war. It is beyond the scope of this chapter to go into these examples. Ashtor, *Social and Economic History*, 262, speaks of the improvement of trade only at the beginning of the fourteenth century.

[51] Hetᶜum, 2:242; cited also in Howorth, *Mongols*, 578.

Non-commercial civilian traffic over the border

Non-commercial movement over the Mongol–Mamluk frontier was probably greatly reduced during the initial period of the war. The border, however, was not impermeable. Occasionally we find a reference in the sources indicating that during a certain year news arrived about an occurrence on the other side of the frontier, which hints at the arrival of some individuals from across the border.[52] Mention has already been made of the mainly one-way traffic of military refugees, Mongol and otherwise, to the Mamluk Sultanate. Finally, there were religious figures and other civilian refugees who made their way across the border.[53]

The most important manifestation of non-commercial traffic was the Iraqi pilgrimage caravan, although this did not generally affect the Syrian heartland directly. The Iraqi *ḥajj* caravan was renewed in 666/1267–8.[54] By that time, things must have settled down enough in Mongol-controlled Iraq to permit the sending out of the caravan. As overlord of Mecca and Medina, Baybars had a direct interest in permitting Iraqi Muslims to perform the *ḥajj*, thereby increasing his prestige. It certainly would not have looked good had he forbidden their participation in the *ḥajj*. Possibly, Baybars's agents used the opportunity to make contacts among Iraqi Muslims which might be useful to Mamluk espionage work. From the Mongol point of view, or at least that of the senior Muslim officials who served them, the equipping of the *ḥajj* caravan might lend them more legitimacy in the eyes of their Muslim subjects. The role of ʿAlāʾ al-Dīn Juwaynī in dispatching the caravans of AH 666 is mentioned by Ibn al-Fuwaṭī, and hints at such a motive. Additional *ḥajj* caravans set out from Baghdad in 667/1269, 669/1271 and 678/1280.[55] This occasional record of *ḥajj* caravans may have been a result of a selective mentioning by our main source, Ibn al-Fuwaṭī, or due to these caravans only having set out in certain years. There is, at least as far as I can tell, no obvious cause why the Iraqi caravan did not set out every year, or what was the reason that it set out when it did. In any event, in 686/1287–8 the Iraqi caravan is mentioned again, and it was continued regularly until 689/1290–91, when it was mysteriously discontinued.[56] The on-again, off-again nature of the Iraqi *ḥajj* in the subsequent decades is beyond the scope of this study.

[52] See, e.g.: Ibn al-Furāt, MS. Vienna, fol. 36a (s.a. 661, not in Maqrīzī); Qirtay, fol. 100a (s.a. 671); Ibn al-Dawādārī, 8:272 (AH 684). Of course, Mamluk intelligence agents may also have been the source of such reports.

[53] Ibn al-Fuwaṭī, 360 (s.a. 666): Shaykh ʿAfīf al-Dīn Yusūf b. al-Baqqāl from Syria to Iraq. Bar Hebraeus, 452 (s.a. 673–4/1275): *faqīrs* from Syria to Cilicia (and suspected as spies). Ibn Shaddād, *Taʾrīkh*, 333; Bar Hebraeus, 455, 464; Cahen, *Pre-Ottoman Turkey*, 277 (unknown date): Shaykh ʿĪsā ibn ʿĀdī and sons from eastern Anatolia to Syria. Ibn Shaddād, *Taʾrīkh*, 221 (AH 676): the chief qadi of Diyār Bakr. Other civilian refugees are mentioned in *ibid.*, 331.

[54] Ibn al-Fuwaṭī, 358; al-Fāsī, in F. Wüstenfeld, *Akhbār makka al-musharrafa* (rpt., Beirut, 1964), 2:271. [55] Ibn al-Fuwaṭī, 361, 368, 411; al-Fāsī, in Wüstenfeld, 2:272.

[56] Ibn al-Fuwaṭī, 453, 456, 461, 462.

We have only a single, but important, piece of evidence on the traversing of Syria by Rūmī pilgrims on their way to the *ḥajj*. In the summer of 669/1270–1, these pilgrims, possibly joined by those from Iran and Iraq, were camped in the square (*maydān*) of Damascus, when they were caught by a flash flood; most of them were killed.[57] Again, the incidental nature of the mention of Rūmī pilgrims, and possibly others, in the Syrian capital leads to the tentative conclusion that in other years additional groups of Rūmīs and others from the Īlkhānid domain may have made their way to the Hijaz via Syria. Baybars probably had no choice but to permit these pilgrims to pass, in his capacity as ruler of Mecca, but this permission left Syria open to Mongol spies, although he himself could avail himself of the opportunity to make contacts among Rūmī Muslims for his own purposes.

The above discussion refers to the overland route from the north or east over the frontier to Syria. The sea route, via the Persian Gulf and the Red Sea, or from Lesser Armenia to Acre and from there to Mamluk territory, or even directly from Lesser Armenia to Alexandria, was also a possibility. We know of Georgian pilgrims in Syria[58] and Armenian merchants in the Sultanate (see above). This is in addition to unspecified "Christian pilgrims" from the east who came to Jerusalem. They may have come by either the land or the sea route.[59] It may be assumed that non-commercial traffic, like its mercantile counterpart, increased towards the end of the thirteenth century.

[57] Yūnīnī, 2:451; Kutubī, 20:402; Ibn Kathīr, 13:259. Ibn al-Furāt, MS. Vienna, fol. 194a mentions also people from Iran. Mufaḍḍal, 196, and Ibn al-Dawādārī, 13:160, note only pilgrims from Iran and Iraq, and do not mention the Rūmīs.

[58] See ch. 6, pp. 150–1, 154.

[59] See ch. 6, p. 154.

CHAPTER 10

Mamluks and Mongols: an overview

Now it is the custom of the Tartars never to make peace with men who kill their envoys, until they have taken vengeance on them.

John of Plano Carpini[1]

In this study, the origins and early course of the Mamluk–Īlkhānid war have been examined through narrative history interspersed with chapters of a monographic nature. Having looked at the war in some detail, it is appropriate to conclude this study with an overview of the subject, keeping in mind two paramount questions: why did this war continue, and why were the Mamluks successful in stopping the Mongols?

In recent studies, Professor J.M. Smith, Jr.[2] and Dr. D.O. Morgan[3] have offered fresh insights into the nature of the Mamluk–Mongol war. Professor Smith, in a wide-ranging article, analyzes the weaponry and tactics of both sides, and embarks on a technical discussion on the strengths and limitations of the Mongol and Mamluk horses. In the first section of this chapter, his approach will be considered and elaborated upon. In the second section, the question of the logistical problems encountered by the Mongols in Syria, as raised independently by Professor Smith and Dr. Morgan, will be examined. In the final section, I will suggest explanations for both the ongoing war and the Mamluk success in stopping the Mongols.

Troops and tactics compared

Professor Smith's discussion, the most detailed and systematic study of the subject yet attempted, can be summarized as follows:[4] the Mongol army was a people's army, that is, all Mongol adult males were enlisted. Since these soldiers, however, were not professionals, they had undergone a somewhat haphazard training. The majority of Mongol troops were armed with

[1] In Dawson, *Mission to Asia*, 68 (= ed. Van den Wyngaert, 125–6).
[2] "ʿAyn Jālūt," 307–45. [3] "The Mongols in Syria," 231–5.
[4] Smith, "ʿAyn Jālūt," 314–20. This summary cannot do full justice to Smith's detailed analysis.

mediocre, homemade weapons, and most carried only bows and arrows, along with axes and clubs. Because of this lack of weapons appropriate for hand-to-hand combat and their inferior training, the Mongols were hesitant to engage in frontal attacks, preferring instead to depend on their archery and mobility. In order to maintain this mobility, each Mongol troop would lead a string of mounts, small steppe horses,[5] when they set out on campaign. While on march, they could thus change mounts when necessary. During the battle itself, the Mongols would remount at frequent intervals, and thus so maintain their famed mobility. The small steppe horse, really a pony, would quickly tire, thus necessitating rapid changes of mounts. The tactics of the Mongols reflected their dependence on archery and mobility:

> The Mongols ... sent unit after unit galloping at the enemy as fast as could be with each man shooting one heavy arrow from as close as possible; each unit would then turn away and out of the path and line of fire of the next unit, which could follow almost on its heels. Thus the enemy would be repeatedly pounded by the Mongols' best shots, delivered by a quick and confusing succession of attacking units, each concealing the next until the last moment. Each unit would charge, shoot, turn and gallop away, and then circle into position for another charge, in this way making several attacks... The attacking units would then give place to fresh forces and retire to rest, rearm, and remount.[6]

The aim of such tactics, together with efforts at outflanking, was to wear down the enemy. If the Mongols faced cavalry, it was hoped that they could provoke a pursuit, with the Mongols shooting to the rear (the so-called Parthian shot) as they rode off. This would lead to the exhaustion of the opponents' horses. At some point, the Mongols, either on fresh horses or reinforced by additional troops, would turn against their pursuers, dealing them a crushing blow or harassing them as they withdrew. In general, the Mongols tried to avoid hand-to-hand combat,[7] because of their lack of personal arms and armor.

The Mamluk army was also based on mounted archers, but the equipment of its troops and its tactics were different. The Mamluk trooper was heavily armed with bow and arrow, sword, dagger, axe or mace, lance, shield and body armor. His horse, a large Arabian steed, was fed primarily on fodder. However, due to the expense of maintaining a horse in a sedentary society, most Mamluks only had one mount. The Mamluks were picked troops and thus on the whole were better raw material for soldiers than their Mongol

[5] On the Mongol horse, see *ibid.*, 331 n. 75. For an appreciative view of this horse, see J.R. Sweeney, "Thomas of Spalato and the Mongols: A Thirteenth-Century Dalmatian View of Mongol Customs," *Florilegium* 4 (1982):168; also in J. Richard, "Les causes des victoires mongoles d'après les historiens occidentaux du XIIIe siècle," *CAJ* 23 (1979):111–12.

[6] Smith, "ʿAyn Jālūt," 318–19. Previously, Smith wrote that a Mongol horse-archer could not fire more than one effective shot, as he charged his opponent; this arrow was let loose at a distance of about 30 meters.

[7] *Ibid.*, 319, citing Plano Carpini, Dawson, *Mission to Asia*, 37 (= ed. Van den Wyngaert, 82); Marco Polo, tr. Latham, 101 (= tr. Yule, 1:262).

counterparts, who were just average men. In addition, the Mamluks underwent thorough, long-term training. Of particular importance in their training was shooting while galloping, which was regularly practiced in the hippodromes.

The battlefield tactics of the Mamluks also differed from those of the Mongols. As they had only one mount, they could not compete with the mobility of the Mongols, each of whom had several horses at his disposal. Rather, they exploited their better-quality bows and arrows and their rigorous training. Mounted on standing horses, the Mamluks would let off a succession of deadly shots when the Mongols attacked. "Unless the Mongols could use their greater mobility to outflank and surround the Mamluks, or superior numbers to wear them down, Mamluk archery would balance and overbalance the Mongols' horsepower."[8] Although Professor Smith does not explicitly say so, it would seem, according to this suggestion, that the Mamluks having repelled a Mongol assault, would then attack, bringing into play their heavier shock power.

There is much that is convincing in this model, the first systematic attempt to compare the fighting abilities and tactics of the Mamluks and Mongols. I would suggest, however, that it must be modified to some degree by additional evidence from sources of various provenance. First, the Mongols may have been better equipped than has been suggested. While John of Plano Carpini and William of Rubruck describe poorly equipped regular troopers, having only bows, arrows and axes,[9] their contemporary, Thomas of Spalato, writes that the Mongols carried helmets, swords and bows.[10] Sibṭ ibn al-Jawzī reports that the Mongols used swords in their battles with the Khwārazm-shāh Jalāl al-Dīn.[11] Marco Polo, describing the situation later in the thirteenth century, states that the Mongols had sword and mace, and even shields.[12] In addition, it must be remembered that the Īlkhānids and their Mongol soldiers were no longer wandering about on the Eurasian steppes, but now had possession of an extensive empire encompassing major centers of urban civilization. This surely must have influenced the quality and variety of the arms that the Mongol soldier now carried. It would seem that the Īlkhāns and their officials by then had enough skilled craftsmen at their disposal to produce some high-quality weapons and other accessories for the Mongols.[13] Cer-

[8] Smith, "ʿAyn Jālūt," 320–6; see *ibid.*, 331 n. 75, for the Mamluk horses.

[9] Smith, "ʿAyn Jālūt," 319, citing Plano Carpini, 33 (= ed. Van den Wyngaert, 77), and William of Rubruck, ed. Dawson, 210–11 (= tr. Jackson, 259–60).

[10] Sweeney, "Thomas of Spalato," 164. There are some scattered references to swords and lances in the *Secret History*; see R.W. Reid, "Mongolian Weaponry in *The Secret History of the Mongols*," *Mongolian Studies* 15 (1992):88.

[11] Sibṭ ibn al-Jawzī, 8:671.

[12] Marco Polo, tr. Yule, 1:260, 2:460.

[13] Marco Polo (tr. Yule, 1:90 and n. on 96) praises the craftsmen of Kirmān for the implements of war which they manufactured, including swords, bows, quivers and "arms of every kind." One example of the Mongols, albeit from the Chaghatayid Khanate, employing local craftsmen in the 1260s to make military equipment is found in Waṣṣāf, 68; cited in Pumpian-Biran, "Battle of Herat," 7.

tainly, throughout the empire there were armorers who had made weapons for the pre-Mongol armies. This capacity would now be turned over for the use of the Mongols. All of this was in addition to military stores that the Mongols seized whenever they conquered a new area.[14] It might also be mentioned in passing that the skills of the Mongol nomads themselves in producing weapons and other implements of war were perhaps underestimated in the previous discussion.[15]

The occupation of greater Iran may have had a second possible influence. The Mongols could now supplement the diet of their horses with either grazing on cultivated fields or grains collected through taxes or expropriated in other ways.[16] This would lead to the strengthening of their horses. While there is no explicit evidence that the Mongols adopted the larger horses found in the areas under their control, there is information that they had shown an interest in both the horses used by local nomads[17] and those ridden by the Armenians.[18] In short, the Mongols of the Īlkhānid state may well have ridden on smaller horses and been less equipped for receiving and delivering frontal assaults than their Mamluk enemies, but perhaps the difference was not as great as suggested above.

The Mamluk troops were not quite the supermen they have been portrayed as. Certainly they were not all cut from the same cloth. Only the royal mamluks were usually given the first-rate training of the Sultan's military schools. The amirs' mamluks had an inferior military education.[19] In addition, during the early years of the Mamluk period, the period under discussion here, many of the troopers in the amirs' units were not even mamluks, but rather free horsemen. These could have been Kurds, refugee Muslim military personnel (including mamluks), and Mongol *wāfidiyya*.[20] The *ḥalqa*, then an important part of the Mamluk army, was mainly composed of these non-mamluk elements.[21] Some of the *ḥalqa* was actually quite similar to the Mongols in ethnic origin and military techniques.

Care should even be taken with regard to the royal mamluks, those

[14] See Allsen, *Mongol Imperialism*, 210–16, for a discussion on how the Mongols organized craftsmen in their empire. Smith ("ʿAyn Jālūt," 322–3 n. 47), writes that the Mongols "also developed a 'military-industrial complex' to supply weapons," but possibly only in Ghazan's time. On the use of captured equipment, see Richard, "Les causes," 109.

[15] "The Mongols were very adept at such work as blacksmithing and production of armor and weapons." Jagchid and Hyer, *Mongolia's Culture*, 316. I might add that I was impressed during my own visits to nomads in Mongolia by the high quality of their metal and leatherwork, although – as far as I could tell – no weapons are being produced today. Cf. the comments in Plano Carpini, tr. Dawson, 18 (= ed. Van den Wyngaert, 50).

[16] For the effect of controlling settled areas on nomads' horses, see Lattimore, "The Geography of Chingis Khan," 2.

[17] In 658/1260, the Mongols seized horses from the bedouin in Trans-Jordan; Abū Shāma, 206. In 668/1269, the Mongols raided north Syria, looting the livestock of the bedouin in the area; *Rawḍ*, 270.

[18] Kirakos, tr. Bedrosian, 226: the Mongols constantly seized the horses of the Armenians.

[19] Ayalon, "Studies on the Structure," pt. 2, 460. [20] See ch. 5, pp. 108–9.

[21] See Ayalon, "Studies on the Structure," pt. 2, 448–51; *idem*, "Ḥalḳa," *EI*², 3:99.

mamluks bought and raised by the Sultan.[22] At the battle of ʿAyn Jālūt, Qutuz had been Sultan less than a year, certainly an inadequate period in which to build a large unit of personal mamluks. In fact, the first decade of Mamluk rule (1250–60) had been characterized by instability, in-fighting and changes of rulers, hardly conducive to the orderly establishment of a strong corps of royal mamluks. At the battle of Homs in 680/1281, the majority of Qalawun's personal mamluks were young and inexperienced, while the body of veteran royal mamluks – the Ẓāhiriyya – had been weakened by Qalawun's purges.

There is no doubt that with time the royal mamluks received thorough training in swordsmanship, horsemanship, lancework, and archery on the ground and from a galloping horse. Having mastered horsemanship and the lance game, the young mamluks were sent to the hippodrome, where they received "cavalry training proper, i.e. coaching in teamwork. The mamluks did group exercises, learning how to enter, come out, turn right or left, advance or retreat together and to know, in any fight, their own place as well as that of their fellows."[23] It would seem that this training was of relatively small tactical units. There was nothing to indicate that maneuvers of large-scale units in the field were undertaken, as with the Mongols during their hunts.[24]

It is worth dwelling on the Mamluk horses. First, not all of their horses were of Arabian stock. A major source of Mamluk mounts was Cyrenaica (*al-barqa*). These horses were very strong and were something between an Arabian horse and a pack-horse, with the latter's sturdy legs; they were thus well suited to rough terrain.[25] Second, the Mongols were not alone in maintaining remounts. The Mamluks also brought with them to battle reserve horses, the *janā'ib* (plural of *janīb*). Al-ʿUmarī states that the amirs brought with them *janā'ib*, the number of which varied, depending on the wealth of each amir and the importance he attributed to this matter.[26] It is unclear if the regular Mamluk troops, be they royal mamluks, or the mamluks of amirs and *ḥalqa* troopers, had recourse to spare mounts, but it appears that their use was not as widespread as among the Mongols.

On the basis of the above discussion, it can be suggested that the Mamluks and Mongols may have been more evenly matched than proposed by Professor Smith. While experienced royal mamluks may have had few equals among the

[22] The royal mamluks (*al-mamālīk al-sulṭāniyya*) were composed of the sultan's personal mamluks, those of former sultans, and mamluks of deceased or *declassé* amirs. See *ibid.*, pt. 1, 204–22.

[23] See: H. Rabie, "The Training of the Mamlūk Fāris," in V.J. Parry and M.E. Yapp, eds., *War, Technology and Society in the Middle East* (London, 1975), 153–63, esp. 157; Ayalon, *L'esclavage du mamelouk* (Jerusalem, 1951), 12–13.

[24] On the Mongol hunt, see Morgan, *Mongols*, 84–5; Allsen, *Mongol Imperialism*, 6 and n. 17; Jagchid and Hyer, *Mongolia's Culture*, 27–37. Both Baybars and Qalawun went hunting, but it would seem that these were small-scale affairs involving the sultan and his entourage; see the sources cited in D. Ayalon, "Ḥarb, iii. Mamlūk Sultanate," *EI*², 3:188a.

[25] Ayalon, "System of Payment," 263–4; ʿUmarī, ed. Sayyid, 101.

[26] *Ibid.*, 33; for the *janā'ib* of the sultan, see *ibid.*, 38; Dozy, 1:221a–b.

Mongols (or any other army of the time), such troops did not form the majority of the Mamluk army, much of which was composed of less thoroughly trained amirs' mamluks, along with various non-mamluk troops, including Mongol *wāfidiyya*. On the other hand, after the consolidation of Īlkhānid rule the Mongol army was probably better equipped and perhaps better mounted than they had been when they came off the steppe. Even assuming that the training of the average Mongol was less rigorous than that of his Mamluk counterpart,[27] the Mongols enjoyed a clear advantage in the training of large-scale units.

The Mamluks themselves do not seem to have been aware of any great advantage over their Mongol adversaries. The resources, time and energy which the Mamluks devoted to training and expanding their army, along with the strengthening of border fortresses and the development of the espionage system, show how seriously they considered Mongol military prowess. The large-scale mobilizations of the Mamluk army at the slightest hint of a Mongol raid, let alone offensive, also indicate that the Mamluks did not disparage their enemy.

A compelling piece of evidence regarding the Mamluk view of the Mongols is found in Ibn ʿAbd al-Raḥīm's continuation of Ibn Wāṣil's chronicle. The writer, a Mamluk official, accompanied Baybars's expedition to Rūm in 675/1277, and recorded the following incident: when the Mamluk army left Rūm, it camped near Ḥārim to rest. When ʿĪd al-Aḍḥā ("Sacrificial Feast") arrived, the Sultan forbad the beating of the "drums of good tidings" on the holiday. When the amirs asked for an explanation. He replied:

> How can I rejoice? I had believed that if 10,000 horsemen of my army were to meet 30,000 Mongols, I would defeat them. But I met 7000 [Mongols] with all my army. [The Mongols] aroused panic and [my] army lost heart. [The Mongols] defeated the [Muslim] Left. Without Allāh's grace, they would have defeated us. If I met them, and they were equal to the [Muslims in size], or larger than they, then [the matter] would not have turned out well.[28]

There is nothing in this story that rings false; Ibn ʿAbd al-Raḥīm was in a position to record this incident. Even if it is apocryphal, it may well reflect the Mamluk perception of their strength *vis-à-vis* the Mongols. One thing is certain: a relatively small Mongol force (although apparently more than the number given here)[29] had given the Mamluk army, which included a large corps of experienced Ẓāhirī royal mamluks, a tough battle before they were defeated. This last fact, more than anything else, should call into question the idea that on a man-to-man basis the Mamluk army was inherently vastly superior to its Mongol counterpart.

[27] Smith, "ʿAyn Jālūt," 325–6. For a different appraisal of the archery of the nomads and the training they underwent, see J.D. Latham, "Notes on Mamluk Horse-Archers," *BSOAS* 32 (1969):258–9.

[28] Ibn ʿAbd al-Raḥīm, in Ibn Wāṣil, MS. 1703, fol. 187a; MS. 1702, fol. 439b.

[29] See ch. 7, pp. 171–2.

I am in general agreement with Professor Smith's discussion of Mongol and Mamluk tactics, although this can be perhaps refined by specific information in the Mamluk sources. I must admit, however, that a number of questions present themselves for which clear-cut answers have yet to be found. It is true that Marco Polo describes how the horses of the Mongols "are trained so perfectly that they will double hither and thither, just like a dog would do."[30] Yet it is difficult to imagine Mongol troops riding forth towards the Mamluks and letting loose a volley at a short distance (ca. 30 meters), then wheeling round and galloping back. All of this while the Mamluks, perched on their horses, were letting off shot after shot. It is also unclear what happens next. Did the Mongols then ride past the side of the next unit coming up to launch an attack? Or did the new unit open up and let the previous force pass through it? It is clear that the succeeding unit could not launch its attack until the preceding one was well out of the way. Finally, the idea that the Mongol troopers would then go to replace their mounts is hard to picture. In the tumult of the battle, they would have to search out their mounts (were they with grooms, other soldiers?), certainly a far from simple task given the general confusion that accompanies any battle.[31]

As will be seen, there is some evidence that the Mongols did attack in waves, but it would seem this was not executed as easily as has been suggested. In addition, it appears that this was not the only tactic adopted by the Mongols. A fourteenth-century Mamluk military manual describes the Mongol attack thus:

> The Mongols [*al-mughul*] from among the Turks[32] customarily form one squadron [*kurdūs*], in order to push one another against the enemy [*li-yatadāfaʿa ʿalā al-ʿudūw*], [in order] to prevent all of them from retreating and withdrawing.[33]

This passage is problematic. There is sufficient evidence that the Mongols actually did divide their armies into separate squadrons (*aṭlāb* or *karādis*) in battle, as in the first and second battles of Homs as well as at Abulustayn (see below). But it is possible that on occasion at least, the Mongols adopted the tactic of a concerted, mass attack straight into the enemy formation (surely shooting as they went), eschewing the tactic of wave-after-wave of hit-and-run archery.

It has been suggested that the Mongols let off only one volley as they approached the Mamluk enemy, perhaps as close as 30 meters. Yet even the heavier type of Mongol arrow was effective to some degree at a longer distance, possibly to 150 yards. In addition, as both *The Secret History* and Marco Polo report, the Mongols had lighter arrows, which could be used for

[30] Marco Polo, tr. Yule, 1:262.

[31] See Smith, "ʿAyn Jālūt," 316–19, for these suggestions of Mongol tactics, and *ibid.*, 322, for the Mamluk response.

[32] Muslim writers tended to see the Mongols as part of the Turkish peoples; see, e.g., Ibn al-Athīr, *al-Kāmil fī al-ta'rīkh* (Beirut, 1965–6), 12:361.

[33] Anṣārī, 77 (Arabic text); cf. translation, 103.

shooting either longer distances or over the heads of forward ranks.[34] In the light of Plano Carpini's statement that when the Mongols attack, each one shoots "three or four arrows at their adversaries,"[35] it is possible to suggest that they let loose a volley or even volleys of these light arrows at a trajectory while still some distance away. As they were shooting at a large body, these volleys would appear to have had some effect. They would certainly be disconcerting to those under attack, making it difficult for them to return fire. In any case, the Mongol attackers would still have time to prepare for another volley, using heavier arrows at close quarters.[36]

Archery was certainly critical for the Mongols but not sufficient for them to win. As R.C. Smail wrote of the Turks (apparently referring to both mamluks and Türkmen): "The mobility and archery of the Turks alone were usually insufficient to give them victory. By such means they weakened the enemy, but his final defeat on the battlefield could be achieved only by the fight at close quarter with lance, sword, and club."[37] This applies *mutatis mutandis* to the Mongols. At some point, the Mongols would have had to throw themselves on the Mamluks armed with axes, maces,[38] and – as has been seen – swords.

The Mamluks, of course, did more than wait on their horses for the Mongols to attack, responding only by shooting from their bows. The intensive practice which the Mamluks underwent in the hippodrome in shooting while at full gallop[39] indicates that they were trained to launch a frontal attack at the right time, letting off arrows (whether or not in concert is another question) at their enemy. Then, relying on their heavier horses, armor and weapons, they would bear down on the enemy line, hoping to drive them back.

Thus it was in theory. What were the actual tactics and fighting methods used by the armies in the four pitched battles on an open field examined in this study: ʿAyn Jālūt (658/1260), the first battle of Homs (659/1260), Abulustayn (675/1277) and the second battle of Homs (680/1281)?[40] Unfortunately, as has been seen, the sources are usually less than explicit about the actual fighting methods employed in the battles. We find such expressions describing Mamluk attacks: "[Qutuz] himself and those with him launched a brave assault (*ḥamla ṣādiqa*)";[41] "they launched against them a concerted attack

[34] Smith, "ʿAyn Jālūt," 314–16, who dismisses the use of light arrows or shooting over forward ranks; Marco Polo, tr. Latham, 314; Reid, "Mongolian Weaponry," 85–6.

[35] Tr. Dawson, 36 (= ed. Van den Wyngaert, 81). Cf. Smith, "ʿAyn Jālūt," 318.

[36] These thoughts are based on a reading of "The Tartar Relation," ed. and tr. G.D. Painter, in R.A. Skelton *et al.*, *The Vinland Map and the Tartar Relation* (New Haven, 1965), 98, par. 58, which includes information not found in the report by Plano Carpini.

[37] R.C. Smail, *Crusading Warfare* (Cambridge, 1956), 82.

[38] For the importance of these weapons, see Richard, "Les causes," 111; L. Mayer, *Mamluk Costume* (Geneva, 1952), 45–6.

[39] Rabie, "Training," 160; Latham, "Notes," 258–62; Smith, "ʿAyn Jālūt," 320–4.

[40] The battle at the Euphrates in 671/1272 is not included, because of its unusual nature (the Mongols taking up position behind a palisade; the Mamluks attacking after fording the river).

[41] Maqrīzī, 1:631: ʿAyn Jālūt; cf. Ibn al-Furāt, MS. Vatican, fol. 247b: *wa-ḥamala fī sabīl allāh*.

(*ḥamalū ʿalayhim ḥamlat rajul wāḥid*)";[42] "the [Mamluk] armies in their entirety attacked together (. . . *fa-ḥamalat al-ʿasākir bi-rummatiha ḥamlat rajul wāḥid*)."[43] For that matter, there is little mention of the use of bows and arrows by both sides, apparently because it was obvious to all authors that this was the way these armies fought.[44]

Information of a more exact nature, however, does exist: at the second battle of Homs[45] and possibly at ʿAyn Jālūt,[46] it is recorded that the Mamluks launched a series of attacks until the Mongols were defeated. It is also important to note that in three of the four battles the Mongols opened up the fighting by attacking first. The exception was the first battle of Homs, which in any case was actually won by a Syrian Ayyūbid army, albeit probably composed to a large degree of Ayyūbid mamluks.

Taking the above into consideration along with Professor Smith's research, the following general remarks on Mamluk tactics against the Mongols can be made: the Mamluks absorbed the initial Mongol attack, probably maintaining a steady fire of arrows as they approached.[47] If the Mamluks held their position and repulsed the Mongols, they would then go over to the offensive, launching a concerted, all-out attack, the front rank (at least) shooting as they rode until they reached the enemy lines, where they would then bring into play maces, axes, swords and perhaps lances. On occasion, it seems, the Mamluks employed repeated attacks, perhaps hit-and-run archery barrages (reminiscent of the Mongol tactics) in order to soften up the enemy.

As for the Mongols, we have two pieces of information that might confirm Professor Smith's suggestion for standard battle procedure: first, at the first battle of Homs, the Mongols were organized in eight squadrons (*aṭlāb*), one after another, as if they were ready to launch a series of successive attacks.[48] Second, during the second battle of Homs – according to Baybars al-Manṣūrī – when the Mongol Left attacked the Mamluk Right, "[The Mongols] were organized as squadrons (*aṭlāban*) in [the attack] and followed one another as groups (*tarādafū aḥzāban*)."[49] Although this is not unequivocal (there is no mention of a rapid succession of squadrons letting off volleys of arrows and wheeling off to the rear), there is nothing that contradicts Professor Smith's thesis and this evidence could be seen to complement it.

[42] Yūnīnī, 1:435: first battle of Homs. [43] Ibn Shaddād, *Ta'rīkh*, 172: Abulustayn.

[44] Explicit mention of the use of bows and arrows (by the Mongols) is made in the descriptions of ʿAyn Jālūt (Rashīd al-Dīn, ed. ʿAlīzādah, 3:74), and the second battle of Homs (*Faḍl*, fol. 47b; Rashīd al-Dīn, ed. ʿAlīzādah, 3:162–3).

[45] Yūnīnī, 4:94: "[The amirs] counter-attacked against the Mongols, and launched several assaults against them, and totally defeated them."

[46] Ibn Taghrī Birdī, 7:79; ʿAynī, fol. 76b. The ultimate source of this report is unclear.

[47] The Mamluks were not necessarily mounted on their horses. Ibn Khaldūn (1:229) writes: "[The Turks] divide their army into three lines, one placed behind the other. They dismount from their horses, empty their quivers on the ground in front of them, and then shoot from a sitting position. Each line protects the one ahead of it against being overrun by the enemy ... "; translation from *Muqaddimah*, tr. Rosenthal, 2:81. Ibn Khaldūn could be referring to Mamluks or Turkish (and by extension Mongol) nomads in general.

[48] See ch. 3, p. 51. [49] *Zubda*, fol. 115a.

At the battle of Abulustayn, however, things were different. There, the Mongols launched a frontal attack against the Mamluks, penetrating the enemy lines.[50] This may be an instance of the Mongol tactic of the concerted attack, described in the above-cited Mamluk military manual, although the Mongols were not organized here as one squadron, but at least initially were arranged as separate tactical units. As for ʿAyn Jālūt, we have no clear information beyond that the Mongols attacked first; for what it is worth, al-Maqrīzī tells us that the two sides "slammed into each other *(iḍṭarabat)*."[51]

Taken altogether, I would offer the following model for Mongol behavior on the battlefield. The Mongols sought to attack first. As the forward squadrons drew close, they let off as many arrows as possible. The Mongols were prepared to launch successive waves of archers, but if they caught the Mamluks in a state of relative disorganization, as at Abulustayn, then they plunged straight into the Mamluk lines.

At both Abulustayn and the second battle of Homs, the Mongols dismounted when the battle began to go against them. This tactic was not an innovation from the war with the Mamluks: the Mongols had dismounted in their battles with the Khwārazm-shāh Jalāl al-Dīn.[52] The Mongols may have dismounted because their horses were exhausted, although it is more likely that this was a more effective defensive maneuver: the Mongol troops could let off more accurately aimed arrows when standing than on horseback. In the case of Abulustayn at least, the Mongols realized that the battle was lost, and in effect declared their willingness to fight to the end by dismounting.[53] There are no examples of the Mamluks dismounting during battle.[54] At their one defeat at Wādī al-Khaznadār in 699/1299, the Mamluks, rather than fight to the death, for all their "professionalism" fled the battlefield in complete disarray.[55]

In the above discussion it has been suggested that in the long run, the Īlkhānid army may have been influenced by its control of a large, rich and settled country such as Iran, primarily in the size of the horses and the quality and type of weapons (and perhaps armor). It is difficult, however, to determine the rate and extent of this change, and how much of it occurred as a result of deliberate policy on the part of the Īlkhāns and the senior officers. In a recent article, Professor A.P. Martinez has suggested a thought-provoking thesis

50 Ibn Shaddād, *Ta'rīkh*, 172. 51 Maqrīzī, 1:431. See ch. 2, p. 41.

52 Sibṭ ibn al-Jawzī, 8:671. I am grateful to Prof. Ayalon for this reference. The formation adopted by the Mongols when they dismounted may be similar to that suggested by Ibn Khaldūn (above, n. 47) for the Turks.

53 At the battle of Wādī al-Khaznadār (699/1299), the Mongol army was caught unprepared by the Mamluk attack, and a part received the Mamluk assault dismounted, taking cover behind their horses; Smith, "ʿAyn Jālūt," 324 and n. 53; C.E. Bosworth, "Ḥarb, v. Persia," EI^2, 2:198. A full discussion on Mamluk and Mongol tactics should take into consideration this battle and Marj al-Ṣuffar (702/1303), but this is beyond the scope of the present study.

54 Examples of dismounting during battle are found in the early Muslim period; Ayalon, "Ḥarb," 3:188a. 55 Irwin, *Middle East*, 100; Amitai, "Mongol Raids," 243.

that, in fact, the Īlkhāns themselves initiated a transition from light cavalry to heavy cavalry, and that this transformation began quite early on and reached its height in the reign of Ghazan. This innovation in the military sphere was connected to the terrain over which the Mongols now had to fight and the nature of their main enemies, the Mamluks, as well as to the changes in the Mongol society of the Īlkhānid state.[56] These are major subjects which transcend the limitations of the present study. In the following discussion, therefore, I will concentrate on examining the evidence of a possible transition having occurred from light to heavier cavalry in the Īlkhānid army within the period covered by this work (1260–81).

I must say from the outset that within this narrow framework I am not in full agreement with Professor Martinez's conclusions. One shortcoming of his study is the lack of a discussion of the battle of ʿAyn Jālūt. Taking this battle into consideration, we can see that the following statement cannot be made:

> The battle of Elbistan [i.e., Abulustayn in 675/1277 – R.A.] is significant because it marks a further stage in the development of tactical weight by the Īl-Xānid army. During it, for the first time, Īl-Xānid Mongol forces charged the Mamluk calvary [*sic*] and dismounted to receive their attack and to subject the onrushing enemy cavalry to an intensive barrage of projectile fire. However, that the Mongols had not yet achieved sufficient weight is evident from the thoroughness of their defeat. . . .[57]

It has been clearly shown in chapter 2 that the Mongols attacked first at ʿAyn Jālūt, so this cannot be taken as an indication of any development within the Īlkhānid army. If anything, there are clear indications that this was standard Mongol practice.[58] In addition, it has also been seen above that dismounting was a tactic used by the Mongols as early as their conflict with the Khwārazm-shāh Jalāl al-Dīn, so this too cannot be taken as evidence for a change of tactics and equipment. Finally, the "thoroughness of their defeat" was probably due to the fact that the relatively small Mongol force was facing almost the entire Mamluk army. Several reservations were raised in chapter 8 regarding Professor Martinez's reconstruction and analysis of the second battle of Homs. There too, it was shown that there is little basis for the claim that the Īlkhānid army was in the midst of a deliberate reorganization on a massive scale.[59]

Professor Martinez discusses one other battle which falls within the timespan of my study, although it is outside its purview: the battle of Herat between Abagha and Baraq in 668/1270 (not 1269 as Martinez writes).[60] I will limit myself to several brief comments on his discussion. First, Martinez mainly bases his reconstruction on Sayf-i Harawī's *Ta'rīkh-nāma-i harāt* and to a lesser extent on Waṣṣāf's history. A look at Rashīd al-Dīn as well as the

[56] Martinez, "Īl-Xānid Army," 129–242. [57] Martinez, "Īl-Xānid Army," 158.

[58] Besides the example of the three battles given above in this chapter, see also Plano Carpini, tr. Dawson, 36 (= ed. Van den Wyngaert, 81): "when they come in sight of the enemy they attack at once . . ." [59] See ch. 8, n. 48 and p. 196. [60] Martinez, "Īl-Xānid Army," 152–6.

Mamluk sources might lead to a different reconstruction.[61] Second, the battle was fought well to the south of Herat, on an open plain,[62] and not "outside the town of Herat," with the associated implications which Martinez makes. Thirdly, although the Mongol elite guard, the *bahādurs*, may well have carried spears or lances of some type, as Waṣṣāf suggests,[63] there is no indication that this is something new. It is possible that the Mongol imperial guard – either of the Qa'an or the various khans – had long carried lances;[64] it certainly seems that these troops had more sophisticated arms or armor than the average Mongol. The presence of such troops at the battle of Herat cannot be seen as a tactical shift of the whole Mongol army. Fourthly, here – as at the second battle of Homs – Martinez may be overestimating the importance of the Georgian contingent at Herat. We have no idea what was the size of this unit, and what exact role it played.[65] In this connection, it is worth citing the words of Dr. Bedrosian:

> Because the Mongols considered their subject people expendable, they usually designated them as advance attackers. This was not, as the *History of K'art'li*[66] and Grigor Aknerc'i would have us believe, because the Armeno-Georgian troops were such excellent warriors, but first precisely because the Caucasians were expendable and second, because desertion was impossible with foreign troops fighting in front or in detachments surrounded by Mongols.[67]

The logistical limitations of Syria

Recent research has suggested that the Mongol failure to capture and hold Syria was not only a result of military losses at the hands of the Mamluks. Rather, it was also directly related to logistical problems encountered by the Mongols in Syria, namely the country did not have the capacity to feed a large Mongol army. This had a twofold affect on the Mongols. First, the Mongols were unable to bring with them all the troops that they would have liked, so as to increase the chances of defeating the Mamluks. Second, when they did succeed in conquering the country, the Mongols were unable to leave a large enough force to maintain their conquest.

The two proponents of this approach reached their conclusions independently and via different methods. Dr. Morgan found several references in

[61] This has already been done by Pumpian-Biran, "Battle of Herat."

[62] Boyle, "Īl-Khāns," 360.

[63] Waṣṣāf, 75; it is not impossible that Waṣṣāf's *ba-asnān-i nīzah* is merely a product of his literary imagination.

[64] Plano Carpini, tr. Dawson, 34 (= ed. Van den Wyngaert, 79), writing in the 1240s, reports that some of the Mongol troops had "lances which have a hook in the iron neck, and with this, if they can, they will drag a man from his saddle."

[65] The evidence of the Georgian Chronicle edited by Brosset cannot be taken too seriously, as this source tends to exaggerate the importance of the Georgian contribution to the Mongol war effort.

[66] Translated in Brosset's *Histoire de la Géorgie*.

[67] R. Bedrosian, "The Turco-Mongol Invasions and the Lords of Armenia in the 13th-14th Centuries," Ph.D. diss., Columbia Univ. (New York, 1979), 194–5.

historical sources which gave evidence of difficulties the Mongols encountered in Syria trying to feed their troops and especially their horses.[68] Professor Smith tackled the problem from a different angle. He first calculated the logistical needs of Mongol armies, and then applied the result to Syria.

It is worth going over Professor Smith's calculations. His starting point was that each Mongol trooper set out on campaign with five horses. This figure seems justified on the basis of the evidence that Smith adduces and other information.[69] An army of, say, 60,000 Mongols would thus mean about 300,000 horses. Each horse needed some 9.33 lb (dry weight) of grass per day, so 300,000 horses required about 2.8 million lb (dry weight) of grass per day. Professor Smith does not have figures for Syrian pastures, but good Inner Asian pastures provide 534 lb of grass per acre per year, although actual figures depend on season and climate. Thus, 300,000 horses would need 5243 acres or about 8 square miles of grazing land each day. This is during the optimal growing season. In reality, the Mongols would probably have required more land to feed their horses.[70]

A second problem was water. A small horse or pony needs 5 (U.S.) gallons of water per day, so an army of 60,000 needs 1.5 million gallons of water a day. Some of this would be provided by the grass the horses consumed (up to half at the peak growing season), but in the summer this would be a problem. Likewise, the flow of water in the rivers of Syria would be sharply reduced in the summer: the Quwayq near Aleppo falls from an average of 167 million gallons in the winter to 1.8 million gallons per day, while the Orontes (ʿĀṣī) falls from 89 million to 7.1 million.[71]

It must be mentioned that these calculations are directly connected to Professor Smith's thesis which was discussed in the previous section. If the "amateur" Mongols were inferior soldiers to the "professional" Mamluks, then the only way that the latter could be defeated was by bringing a much larger army in to Syria. The Mamluks would thus be crushed by numbers, if not by skill and equipment. However, the problems of feeding and watering such an enormous army and its horses were so great that the Mongols were unable to concentrate enough troops to gain numerical superiority over the Mamluks at a given battle, and thus were condemned to defeat. If the Mongols did manage to defeat the Mamluks, as at Wādī al-Khaznadār (699/1299), then they soon had to withdraw most of their army from Syria due to the lack of adequate pastureland.[72]

[68] See n. 3 above.

[69] "ʿAyn Jālūt," 314 n. 18, to which can be added Rashīd al-Dīn, ed. ʿAlīzādah, 3:85 (three horses per man in the campaign against Aqqush al-Barlī in 660/1262); ʿUmarī, ed. Lech, 79 (five horses in campaign of Golden Horde); Plano Carpini, tr. Dawson, 47 (= ed. Van den Wyngaert, 91; apparently three or four horses). See also D.O. Morgan, "The Mongol Armies in Persia," *Der Islam* 56 (1979):85–6.

[70] Smith, "ʿAyn Jālūt," 336–9. On p. 332, Smith remarks that 50,000 horses would require 250 tons of hay and barley per day. Smith's figures are based on a number of technical works on horses and pasture economy. [71] *Ibid.*, 339–40. [72] Smith, "ʿAyn Jālūt," 344–5.

These calculations, especially when complemented by Dr. Morgan's study, are compelling. I would suggest, however, that the picture has perhaps been overdrawn, and the logistical situation as faced by the Mongols was not as bad as Professor Smith and Dr. Morgan have suggested; thus the logistical factor was not the dominant reason for the Mongol failure decisively to defeat the Mamluks.

Let us start with the question of the total number of horses that the Mongols brought with them on campaign. The figure of five horses per Mongol trooper mentioned by Professor Smith seems to be correct, although in note 69 there is an indication that the Mongols on occasion may have been satisfied with less. In addition, not all soldiers in the Mongol army, however, were Mongols (or nomadic Turks). For example, in 680/1281, Mengü Temür's army contained a number of Armenians, Georgian and other auxiliary cavalryman; it can be assumed that these troops had with them only one horse (albeit bigger than the Mongol horse) per man. Some of the non-Mongols may have been infantrymen. All together these "allies" may have been more than a third of the Mongol army.[73] Thus, there may have been somewhat less horses all told for Mengü Temür's army than initially thought.

This, however, is only a minor reservation. More importantly, the Mongols did not have to rely only on pasturelands for feeding their horses when they invaded Syria. First and foremost, they gained possession of the various stores of grains and other foodstuffs when they marched into the country. For example, in 680/1281, it is related that when the garrison and inhabitants fled Aleppo, "they abandoned crops, granaries and foodstuffs."[74] These supplies could then be used by the Mongol invaders had they chosen to do so. In addition, there is no reason why the Mongols would have limited themselves to grazing their horses on pasturelands. While on campaign, and perhaps afterwards, they would certainly have had little compunction against pasturing their horses in agricultural fields, areas traditionally off-limits to nomads. The Mamluk practice of burning grasslands would not have adversely affected the Mongols here, because this organized incitement – when it happened – was limited to the frontier region and the Mongol side of the border. There is no indication that the agricultural areas of northern and central Syria were ever intentionally or otherwise set ablaze.[75]

The Mongols would also have had few scruples in grazing their horses on the pasturelands of Syria's indigenous nomads, be they bedouin or Türkmen. Professor Smith himself has shown that in modern Syria (ca. 1950), these lands had the capacity to support 80,000 nomads (= troops) with herds.[76] These

[73] See ch. 8, pp. 194–5; the actual number of Armenian and Georgian troops given in the pro-Mongol sources was not very large.
[74] Yūnīnī, 4:91; Ibn al-Furāt, 7:213; Ibn Taghrī Birdī, 7:302.
[75] See ch. 9, pp. 205–6; cf. Morgan, "The Mongols in Syria," 233–4.
[76] Smith, "ʿAyn Jālūt," 309 n. 3, based on figures from: Syria, Ministry of National Economy, Dept. of Statistics, *Statistical Abstract of Syria, 1950*, 158–9.

pasturelands should have been able to contribute greatly to the maintenance of the Mongol horses in the months of the Mongol campaign. In the long run, had the Mongols been successful in occupying Syria, they could have taken possession of at least the better pasturelands of these nomads. This, it can be mentioned in passing, may help explain why the Syrian Türkmen and bedouin were so willing to join the Mamluks against the invaders. In addition, in none of their campaigns into Syria, including the successful one of 699/1299–1300, did the Mongols fully exploit the "logistical capacity" of all of greater Syria. Even discarding the marginal areas unsuitable for pastoral nomadism of the Turco-Mongolian type, there would have been large areas – both agricultural areas and pastureland of indigenous nomads – suitable for grazing their horses in the pasture areas in the regions today contained in Israel, Lebanon and Jordan. This argument has already been made with regard to 658/1260.[77] Although the campaign of 699/1299–1300 is beyond our concern here, it is worth dwelling on it to demonstrate this point. The Mongols, except for a large raiding party sent through Palestine, did not exploit the grazing areas of Lebanon, the Syrian coast, the Plain of Jezreel and the Jordan valley.[78]

The lack of water does not seem to have been an insurmountable strategic problem for the Mongols. They usually arrived in Syria during the winter, that is, the rainy season, when the riverbeds were full and the grass contained a high percentage of water. The campaign of 680/1281 was an exception, as it was fought in the mid-fall. However, the proximity of the battlefield to the Orontes would certainly have alleviated this problem to a great degree.

There are two additional arguments against the logistical thesis. First, during this period, a large number of Türkmens settled in Syria with their families and herds, particularly in the north of the country.[79] This shows that the nomadic pastoralism of the Turco-Mongolian tribes could be practiced to some degree in at least part of the country. The problem was first gaining permanent possession of Syria.

Second, if the Mongols were unable to surmount the difficulties of feeding their horses, and were thus limited in the size of the army they could bring and the time they could remain with a large force in Syria, why did they keep coming back?[80] After the debacle of ʿAyn Jālūt, the Mongols made four concerted efforts to invade the country (AD 1281, 1299, 1300–1, 1302). Given the awareness of logistical problems that Professor Smith credits to the Mongols,[81] this behavior is inexplicable. Since, according to this view, logistical considerations prevented the dispatch of a large enough army to deal with the Mamluks, the Mongols were essentially dooming themselves to defeat

[77] See ch. 2, pp. 28–9.

[78] See Amitai, "Mongol Raids," 243–7; *idem*, *Holy War*, 30–1. Rashīd al-Dīn, ed. ʿAlīzādah, 3:338, writes that Ghazan withdrew because of the approaching warm season, an indication that Ghazan was indeed concerned with logistical problems. But Hetʿum, 196, writes that the Mongol ruler left because of an offensive of (Chaghatayid) Mongols on his eastern border.

[79] See ch. 3, pp. 69–70.

[80] For this comment, I must thank Dr. Morgan himself.

[81] Smith, "ʿAyn Jālūt," 344.

time after time. This is difficult to accept. The Mongols invaded Syria with the reasonable hope of conquering it. We must thus conclude that either the Mongols were not as logistically conscious as suggested and/or their logistical problems were not as overwhelming as have been proposed. In light of the above discussion, it would seem that at least the latter statement is correct.

This does not mean that logistical considerations among the Mongols were non-existent. Certainly, the Mongols refrained from setting out on a campaign in the summer, most likely from such considerations. Usually, the pro-Mongol sources euphemistically speak only of the hot weather,[82] although it would seem that the problem was not merely one of discomfort, but also of dearth of pasture and water. One indication of the interaction between hot, summer weather and the welfare of Mongol horses is seen in the following: Ibn Bībī reports that Abagha, having come to Rūm at the head of an army after the battle of Abulustayn, did not invade Syria because it was summer. Ibn Shaddād, describing these same events, reports that the reason behind Abagha's decision not to invade was that most of his horses had perished.[83] There may be some exaggeration here, but it is clear that the Mongol horses were in a sorry state, perhaps from the forced march in the summer, with all the attendant difficulties of procuring adequate food and water for the horses.

Taken as a whole, the Mongols were not significantly inferior soldiers to their Mamluk enemies, in spite of certain differences in arms, horses and tactics. Logistical problems did not prevent the Mongols from invading Syria with large forces, nor do they fully explain the withdrawal of most of the Mongol forces in the two instances when the Mongols did succeed in occupying the country. The reasons behind Mamluk success and Mongol failure must be sought elsewhere.

The dynamics of the Mamluk–Īlkhānid war[84]

The Īlkhānids of Persia were primarily responsible for the ongoing war with the Mamluks. It was the Mongols who launched most of the offensives and raids. Their aggressive attitude toward the Mamluks and their aspiration to conquer Syria are further seen in their repeated attempts to persuade the Western Christian powers to launch a concerted effort against their common enemy, along with the belligerent tone found in the many letters to the Mamluk sultans. Another indication of the long-term intentions of the

[82] Bar Hebraeus, 407 (Yasa'ur's attack against Aleppo in 1244; cited in Morgan, "The Mongols in Syria," 234); Kirakos, tr. Dulaurier, 487 (Hülegü's campaign against Baghdad), 506 (Īlkhānid wars against Golden Horde); Het'um, 198, 245 (Mongol difficulties in Syria in 1300, because of the heat of summer).

[83] Ibn Bībī, 319; Ibn Shaddād, *Ta'rīkh*, 182 (whence Yūnīnī, 4:186).

[84] Some of the ideas expressed in this section have been enlarged upon in R. Amitai-Preiss, "Aims and Motivation of Īlkhānid Strategy towards Syria and the Mamluks," in D. Morgan *et al.* (ed.), *The Mongol Empire and its Legacy*, forthcoming. Several paragraphs here also appear there in a similar form.

Mongols towards Syria is the repeated attempts made to take the border fortress of al-Bīra. These efforts can be seen as an attempt to establish a bridgehead in Mamluk territory and to eradicate a possible obstacle to a future invasion. If the Mongols were interested merely in raiding, then they would not have taken such trouble to conquer this fortress.

The above generalization should be qualified. For all the importance attributed by the Mongols to the conquest of Syria and the defeat of the Mamluks, it must be remembered that this was only one of the many foreign policy concerns of the Īlkhāns. Throughout the period under consideration in this study, and afterwards, the Īlkhānid Mongols often fought with other Mongol groups. These wars were usually more crucial for the future of the Īlkhānid kingdom than the war with the Mamluks.

The Mamluks were not without responsibility for the continuing hostilities. Baybars sent his share of raiders across the border, and engaged in all kinds of surreptitious activity in the Īlkhānid kingdom. Rather than waiting passively for Mongol attacks, Baybars brought the war into the territories of the enemy camp and its allies. These activities destabilized the enemy to a certain degree and weakened his ability to launch attacks. At the same time, the Mamluk soldiery gained experience and morale was improved. There is no doubt that Baybars would have liked to have seen the Mongols pushed out of Iraq and even further back, out of the Islamic lands altogether. Yet for all his bluster and *jihādī* rhetoric, Baybars did virtually nothing to realize these abstract goals, if we discount the rather symbolic and not very effective efforts from his early reign, and the large-scale raid into Rūm before his death. Baybars, ever the political realist, surely understood that liberating Iraq from the Mongols was beyond his capabilities.

The dynamic of the conflict can be summed up as follows: the Mongols under the rule of Hülegü and his descendants wanted to occupy Syria. The Mamluks, under Qutuz, Baybars and Qalawun, refused to oblige. Thus, the Mongols tried various means to oust the Mamluks, who continued to resist and succeeded in keeping the Mongols at bay.

In light of the above, it would be reasonable to ask what drove the Mongols to fight the Mamluks over Syria. One suggestion was that the Mongols were looking for an outlet to the sea (presumably, in order to encourage and profit from trade). The "indirect" route via Asia Minor and Lesser Armenia was not sufficient.[85] This explanation can be rejected as a major reason for Mongol aggression. If anything, Ayās and Antioch were the most logical outlets for goods coming out of the Jazīra, north-west Iran and perhaps even Baghdad.[86] The origin of Mongol enmity towards the Mamluks must be sought elsewhere.

The original impetus for the Mongol expansion into southwest Asia was Mongol imperial designs, that is, to widen the territory under Mongol control. As has been discussed at the beginning of this study, these designs were a

[85] Spuler, *Iran*, 54; see also Labib, *Handelsgeschichte*, 71; cf. Morgan, "Eastern Mediterranean," 198. [86] Ashtor, *Social and Economic History*, 264–5.

mixture of traditional nomadic desires to expand and gain control over settled areas along with the Mongol belief that they had a right to conquer the world and place it under the aegis of Chinggis Khan and his descendants. I am suggesting that to a great degree these same imperial ideals continued to propel the Mongols to attempt to take Syria from 1260 onward. There can be no doubt that these ideals had taken a beating since the highwater mark of Hülegü's conquest in 1260: a Mongol army had been defeated at ʿAyn Jālūt; the Mongols were worsted in the border war; and, Mongol unity had been shattered in the civil wars after Möngke's death and the Īlkhānid–Golden Horde war. In addition, the tone of the letters to the Western Christian rulers became increasingly conciliatory; in order to woo the Franks, Mongol claims to world domination had to be eschewed, at least publicly.

Yet, there are clear indications that to some degree the Mongol imperial ideal still remained the official ideology of the Īlkhānid state. Thus, we find in the oral message from Abagha delivered to Baybars (before the written letter was handed over) in 667/1269, the following unequivocal statement:

> When the King Abagha set out from the East, he conquered all the world. Whoever opposed him was killed. If you go up to the sky or down into the ground, you will not be saved from us. The best policy is that you will make peace between us. You are a mamluk who was bought in Sīwās. How do you rebel against the kings of the earth?[87]

A second example is from 675/1277, when – according to Rashīd al-Dīn – after the battle of Abulustayn, Abagha wrote to Baybars, and *inter alia* declared that God had given the earth to Chinggis Khan and his descendants.[88] An additional indication of the continued belief in imperial mission is seen in numismatic evidence. We find on Abagha's coins such titles as: "lord of the world (*pādishāh-i ʿālam*)" and "ruler of the necks of the nations (*mālik riqāb al-umam*)."[89]

The presence of such expressions on such official documents as royal letters and coins leads to the conclusion that the Īlkhān at least maintained some belief in the traditional heaven-inspired manifest destiny of the Mongols. Whether this belief continued to percolate down the Mongol ranks is unclear, although I would hazard a guess that it did, at least among the higher echelons.[90] And it was the Mongol elite, together with the Īlkhān, that made the decisions.

[87] Yūnīnī, 2:407; Ibn al-Dawādārī, 8:139–40; Maqrīzī, 1:573–4; see ch. 5, pp. 121–2, for the relation of this message to the accompanying letter.

[88] Rashīd al-Dīn, ed. ʿAlīzādah, 3:145, the Mamluk sources do not mention this letter; see ch. 7, p. 177.

[89] İ. and C. Artuk, *İstanbul Arkeoloji Müzerleri Teşhirdeki İslâmî Sikkeler Kataloğu* (Istanbul, 1971–4), 2:768; S. Lane-Poole, *Catalogue of Oriental Coins in the British Museum* (London, 1881), 6:23. The second example is not itself unequivocal, because it seems to have had some currency with other Muslim rulers of this time. Thus we find it twice in two inscriptions of Baybars: *RCEA*, 12:63 (no. 4485), 214 (no. 4723).

[90] Cf. A.K.S. Lambton, "Concepts of Authority in Persia: Eleventh to Nineteenth Centuries AD," *Iran* 26 (1988):100. For the continuation of this idea after Abagha's reign, see Amitai-Preiss, "Aims," forthcoming.

The objection can be raised, that if the Mongols of Persia, or at least their ruler, continued to believe in the Mongol imperial ideal, why did they only aim their expansion efforts against Syria and the Mamluks? The Īlkhāns could not very well head for the the northeast (Transoxania) or north (the Caucasus), since the Chaghatayid Mongols and Gorden Horde were already there. The Īlkhāns had enough trouble holding off invaders from these directions without going off on an offensive (notwithstanding the occasional probe against these adversaries). The Negüderi Mongols in Afghanistan, unwilling to accept Īlkhānid authority, made expansion to the east difficult after AD 1262.[91] In addition, India was seemingly unsuited climatically and geographically for Mongol-style nomadism.[92] The indigenous rulers of southern Persia and much of Afghanistan had submitted to the Mongols, so there was no reason to march against them. Perhaps, also for climatic reasons, the Mongols were not attracted to southern Persia, although recent research shows that some Mongol settlement might have occurred in this region.[93] In Asia Minor, the Seljuqs and the Armenians of Cilicia had submitted and their realms were satellite countries. It is true that the Byzantine Emperor had not submitted, yet a *modus vivendi* had been worked out with Michael Palaeologus. Perhaps Hülegü and Abagha had not wanted to put too much pressure on Michael, out of fear of pushing him firmly into the Mamluk–Golden Horde camp. Thus, the only direction the Īlkhāns could go was west into Syria.

Yet the continual Mongol designs on Syria were not merely because there was nowhere else to go. Only in that direction did someone have the temerity not only to reject the Mongol call for submission, but to resist and even to succeed, and to keep on doing so. In 1260, the Mamluks had killed the Mongol envoys and had defeated the Mongol armies at ʿAyn Jālūt and Homs. This in itself was cause enough for revenge. To add insult to injury, the Mamluks thwarted all Mongol attempts to breach the border, and continued to launch raids across it with impunity, virtually entering at will Lesser Armenia, always loyal to the Mongols. Without a doubt, the desire to revenge defeats and punish provocations was an additional reason behind Īlkhānid policy towards Syria.[94] This was not just a question of revenge for specific defeats or raids. The continued existence of a strong Mamluk state in Egypt and Syria was an affront in Mongol eyes and a challenge to the whole Mongol imperial *raison d'être*. The Mamluks refused them any legitimacy, and called on them to withdraw from the Islamic countries.[95] It is perhaps not too extreme to suggest

[91] Aubin, "Qaraunas," 79–88; Jackson, "Dissolution," 238–44; *idem*, "Chaghatayid Dynasty," *EIr*, 5:344–5.

[92] Khazanov, *Nomads*, 67–8, 191. I am not claiming that this ecological difficulty was the main cause for the lack of Īlkhānid initiative in the direction of India, but suggest it in addition to the one previously given.

[93] Spuler, *Mongol Period*, 32–3; A.K.S. Lambton, "Mongol Fiscal Administration," 82–4.

[94] On the other hand, Krawulsky, *Īrān*, 586, may attribute too much importance to this particular reason; see Amitai-Preiss, "Aims," forthcoming.

[95] See, e.g., Baybars's reply to Abagha's call to submit in 667/1268, in ch. 5, p. 122.

that another motivation of the Īlkhāns in their war against the Mamluks was to punish and destroy those who were audacious enough to question the Mongol imperial dream.

Old ideals of imperial glory were probably hard to discard. The desire for Mongol expansion carried on through inertia, even if in reality it was no longer viable. Vestigial expansionist ideology combined with the desire for revenge felt against the Mamluks after ʿAyn Jālūt. The embers of Mongol imperial dreams were kept alive by the raids and occasional offensives into Syria.

Other reasons beyond the continual Īlkhānid antipathy towards the Mamluks and the desire to conquer Syria present themselves. First, there might have been the Īlkhānid dread of a joint Mamluk-Golden Horde attack. In order to defuse this potential danger, the Īlkhāns would have attempted to disrupt the border region, and weaken the Mamluks by taking Syria, and if possible destroy them. Secondly, the sultans were the leaders of the Muslim world, who had resurrected the ʿAbbāsid Caliphate. The Mongol leaders may have feared the impact of a strong Muslim state, outside their control and offering resistance, on their own subject population, the vast majority of which was Muslim.[96] A third reason may have been the fact that Syria was included in the territories originally granted to Hülegü by Möngke, or so at least the pro-Īlkhānid sources claim.[97] The Īlkhānids thus thought they had a right to the country, and they tried to realize this right. Finally, the raids and campaigns, if nothing else, kept the tribesmen busy, and indulged their desire for adventure and booty. Of the latter, the Mongols must have been particularly interested in horses and other forms of livestock.[98]

Neither these explanations nor the ones already mentioned contradict each other, and it is possible that Īlkhānid designs on Syria and the Mamluks may have been inspired by several reasons. One matter is clear: the Īlkhāns kept their sights on Syria and hoped to defeat the Mamluks. Thus they sought to keep up pressure on the border and from time to time the Īlkhāns launched offensives when they thought the conditions were right. It was to take the Mongols some sixty years after ʿAyn Jālūt to realize that they could not defeat the Mamluks and officially to renounce the ideal of Mongol manifest destiny.

Why did the Mongols fail to realize their designs towards Syria and the Mamluks? It was not because they were vastly inferior soldiers, nor because Syria could not feed their horses. Rather, the root of their failure is to be sought elsewhere. I would propose the following reasons: (1) the building-up of the Mamluk military machine; (2) Baybars's dynamic leadership; (3) the morale of the Mamluks and the importance they attributed to the war; (4) the Īlkhānid war with the Golden Horde and other Mongols; (5) the failure to reach an understanding with the West.

96 I would like to thank Prof. Ayalon for suggesting to me these two reasons.

97 Dr. Jackson suggested this possibility; on this mandate from Möngke, see ch. 1, p. 12. On the importance the Toluids attributed to Möngke's edicts, see Ayalon, "Yāsa," pt. B, 168.

98 See n. 17 above.

The first two reasons are obviously connected. Under Baybars's rule, the army – like that of the Mongols, based on mounted archers of steppe origin – was expanded and rigorously trained; fortifications were put in order; the bedouins firmly brought into line; an effective espionage system was established; administration was organized; Syria was integrated into the kingdom; rapid communications were established throughout the state; the Caliphate was reestablished in Cairo, providing him with legitimation; and, relations were opened up with Hülegü's enemy, Berke. The army reacted swiftly to the slightest rumor of a Mongol offensive, and Baybars himself either led the troops or was right behind them. The continuing war also strengthened his rule, because in the face of the Mongol danger Baybars would brook no disloyalty. In general, his policies were continued by Qalawun, although, in the part of his reign covered by this study, Qalawun's leadership was not as yet fully felt, at least as regards the war with the Mongols. As has been seen, the battle of Homs (680/1281) was won more by the army that Baybars had built up than by the generalship of Qalawun.

The Mamluks also had the advantage of morale over their enemy. They were fighting (usually) on home territory, for their religion, their kingdom, and their lives. They were also defending their status as a ruling caste. To their mind, they had no choice but to win. The sultans did their best to inculcate these feelings in their followers. The Mongols may have been fighting for an abstract imperial ideal, for personal honor, and for booty, but they could not compete with the Mamluks for motivation.

The contrast in importance attributed by each side to the struggle is seen in the different treatment of the border war and other aspects of the conflict in the respective sources. The Mamluk sources are full of references to this war, because for them it was a matter of life and death, while the pro-Mongol sources, especially the semi-official Persian works, are usually laconic to an extreme when it comes to reporting the struggle with the Mamluk enemy, and their silence is only broken on the occasion of a major confrontation. It has been suggested that this terseness may be due in part to the fact that for the Mongols the war with the Mamluks was only one of many conflicts with external enemies, and not necessarily always the most pressing one.

All of Baybars's efforts might have been useless without the wars the Īlkhāns had to wage against their various Mongol neighbors, especially the Golden Horde. Without these distractions, it is quite possible that the Persian Mongols would not have waited twenty-odd years to return in force to Syria, thereby permitting the Mamluks to build up their army. Certainly, this is what the authors of some Mamluk and Mongol sources thought might well have happened if Hülegü's attention had not been turned elsewhere.[99] Additional

[99] Rashīd al-Dīn, ed. ʿAlīzādah, 3:77; Hetʿum, 176; Maqrīzī, 1:474 (not in parallel passage in Ibn al-Furāt, MS. Vienna, fol. 7a); Ibn Khaldūn, 5:430–1.

confirmation is provided by Abagha himself: in his 667/1268 letter to Baybars, it was stated that the reason that (his) Mongols had not attacked Syria was that the Mongols had disagreed amongst themselves.[100]

The Īlkhāns sought to compensate themselves for their preoccupation with the Golden Horde and other Mongols by opening up a second front of their own. They initiated communications with the Pope and other Western rulers. That these exchanges came to naught was not out of a lack of interest on the part of Hülegü and Abagha: the vast distance between the Īlkhāns and the West militated against the negotiations coming to fruition. And yet at the one time when real cooperation was possible, in 1271, Abagha failed to exploit the opportunity to the full. In a sense, this failure helped to lay the stage for the Mongol defeat at Homs a decade later.

[100] *Rawḍ*, 340; see ch. 5, p. 121. A similar claim was made by Abagha in his letter to the Council of Lyon in 1274; Roberg, "Tartaren," 300–1; Lupprian, *Beziehungen*, 227. Berke is reported to have remarked that his war with Hülegü led to the cessation of Mongol conquests; see above, ch. 4, p. 80.

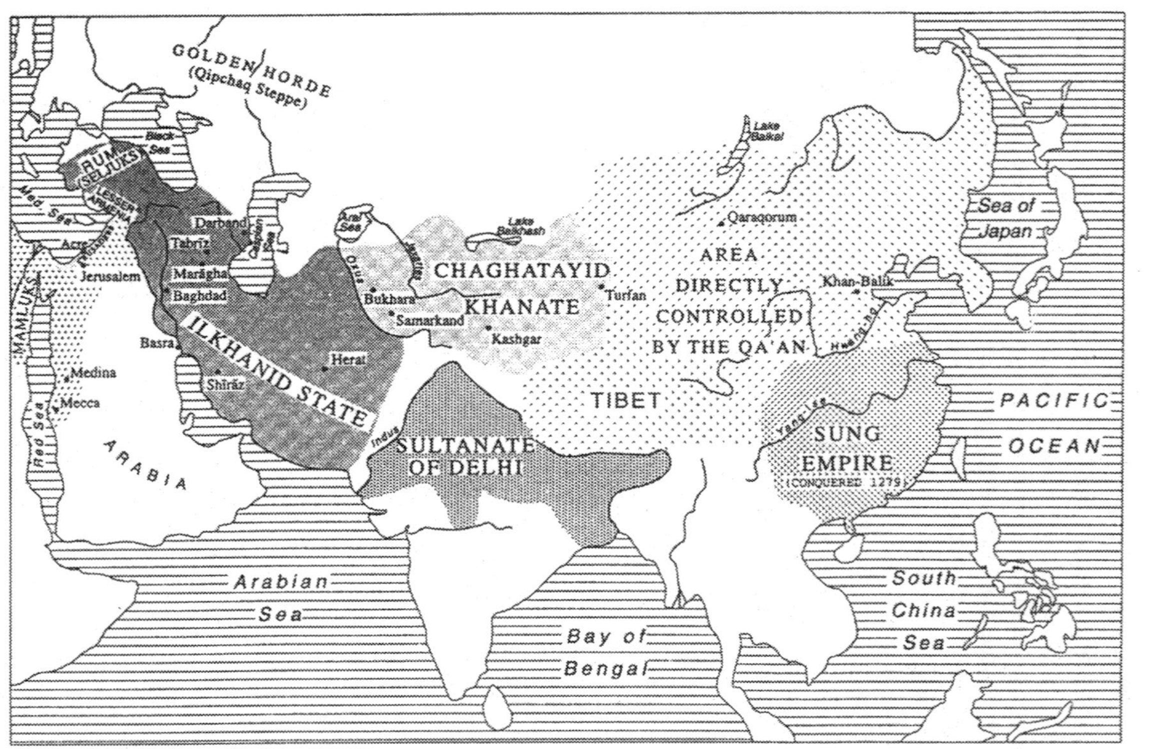

Map 1. Asia after AD 1260, showing territory under Mongol control and the Mongol Khanates (after J.J. Saunders, *The History of the Mongol Conquests* [London, 1971], 90)

Map 2. Palestine and its environs, ca. AD 1260

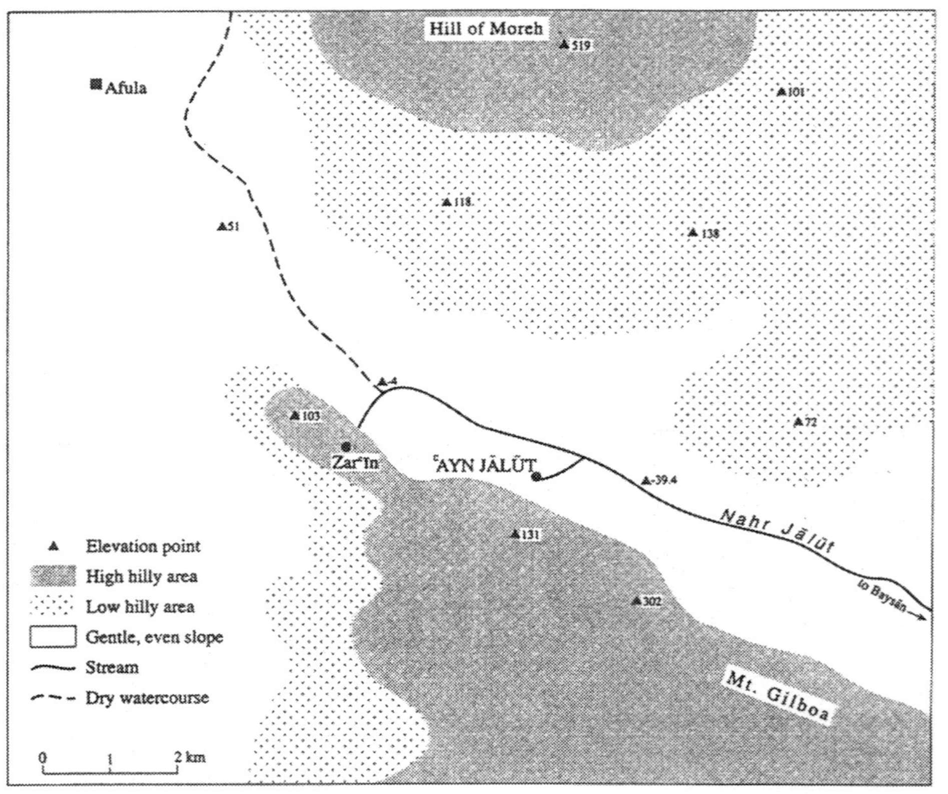

Map 3. The area of ʿAyn Jālūt, ca. AD 1260

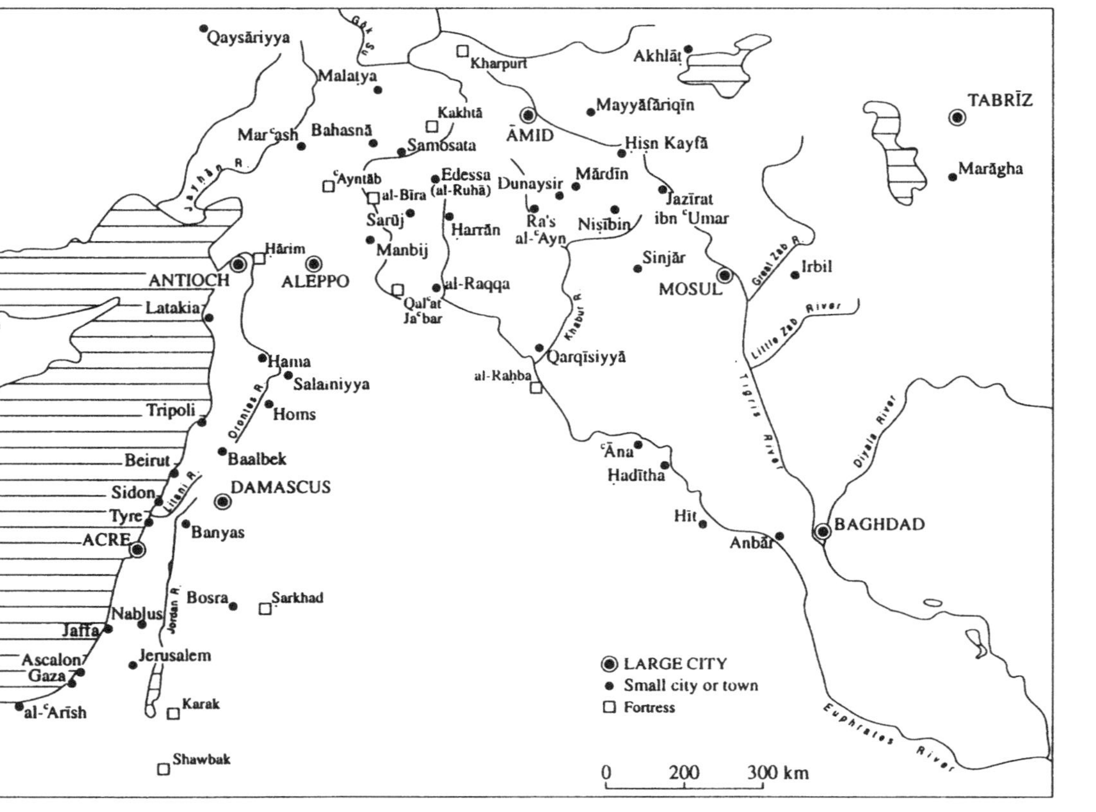

Map 4. The Fertile Crescent, ca. 13th century AD

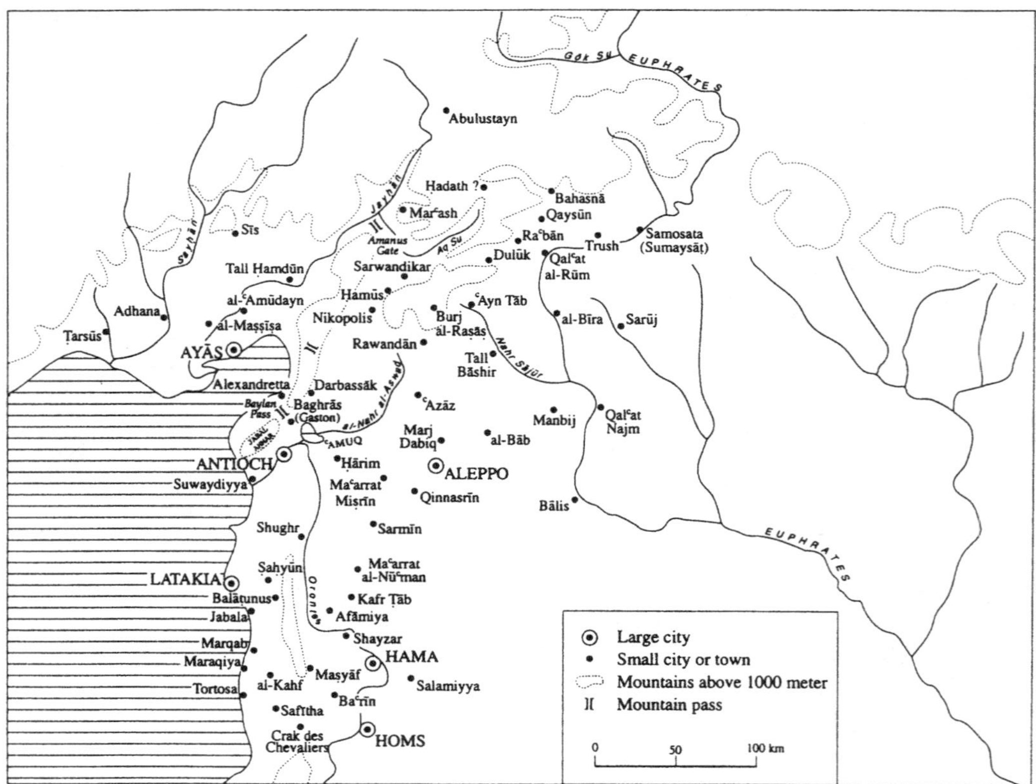

Map 5. Northern Syria and southeastern Anatolia, including Cilicia, ca. 13th century AD

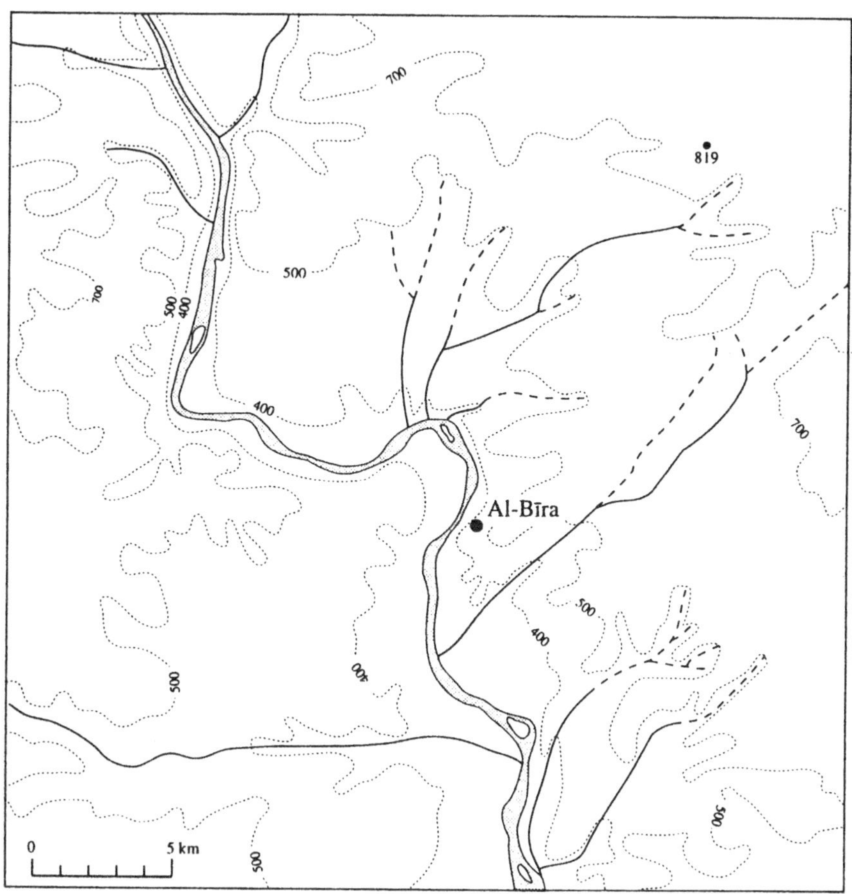

Map 6. Al-Bīra (Birecik), ca. AD 1940

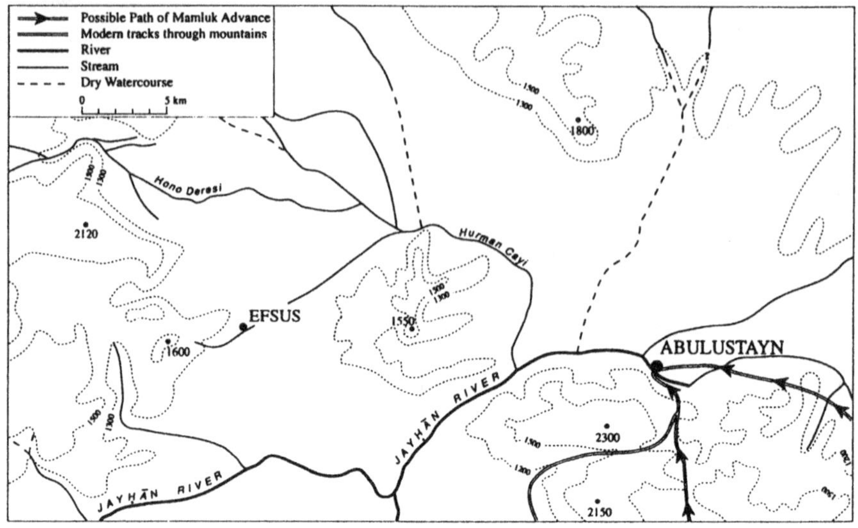

Map 7. The Plain of Abulustayn (Elbistan), ca. AD 1940

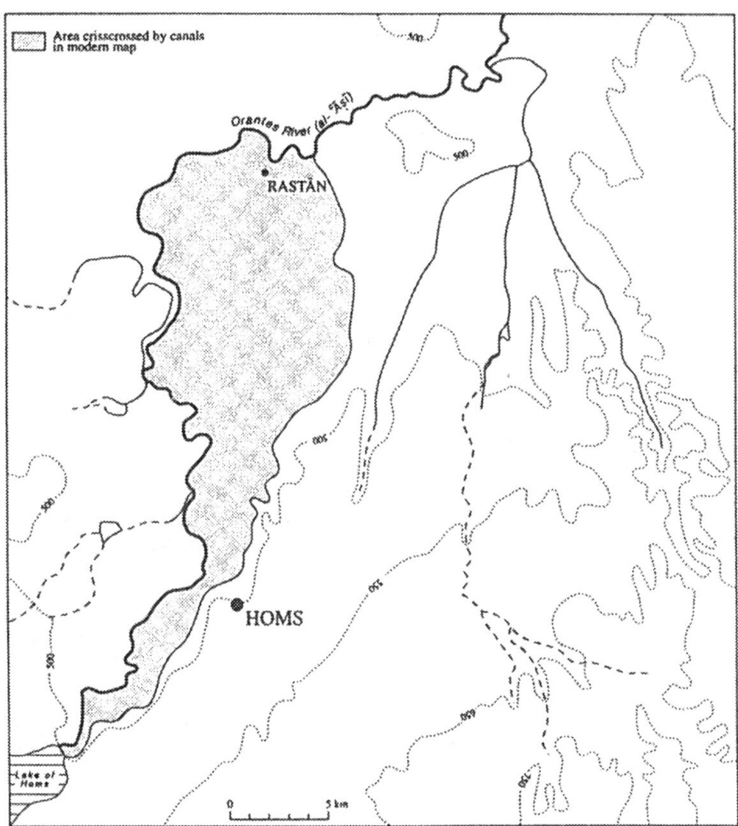

Map 8. Homs and its environs, ca. AD 1940

Dynastic and genealogical tables

648/1250	Shajar al-Durr
648/1250	al-Muʿizz Aybeg al-Turkmanī
655/1257	al-Manṣūr ʿAlī b. Aybeg
657/1259	al-Muẓaffar Qutuz
658/1260	al-Ẓāhir Baybars al-Bunduqdārī
676/1277	al-Saʿīd Berke Khan b. Baybars
678/1279	al-ʿĀdil Sulamish b. Baybars
678/1279	al-Manṣūr Qalawun b. Alfī
689/1290	al-Ashraf Khalīl b. Qalawun
693/1293	al-Nāṣir Muḥammed b. Qalawun (first reign)
694/1294	al-ʿĀdil Ketbugha
696/1296	al-Manṣūr Lachin
698/1299	al-Nāṣir Muḥammad b. Qalawun (second reign)
708/1309	al-Muẓaffar Baybars al-Jāshnakīr
709/1310	al-Nāṣir Muḥammad b. Qalawun (third reign)
741/1340	Various descendents of al-Nāṣir Muḥammad (until 784/1382)

1 Mamluk Sultans until 741/1340

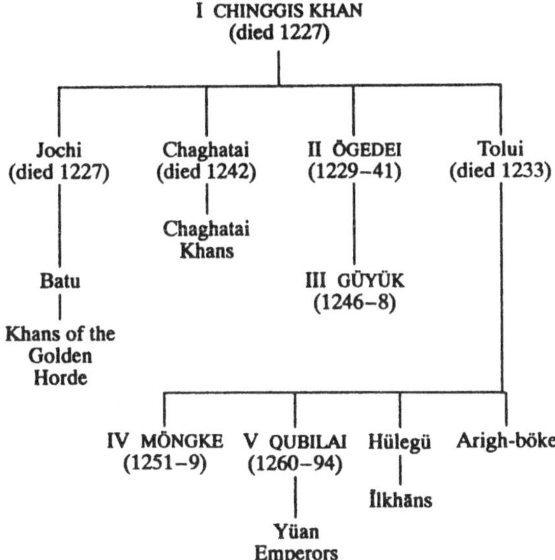

2 The Great Khans (Qa'ans)

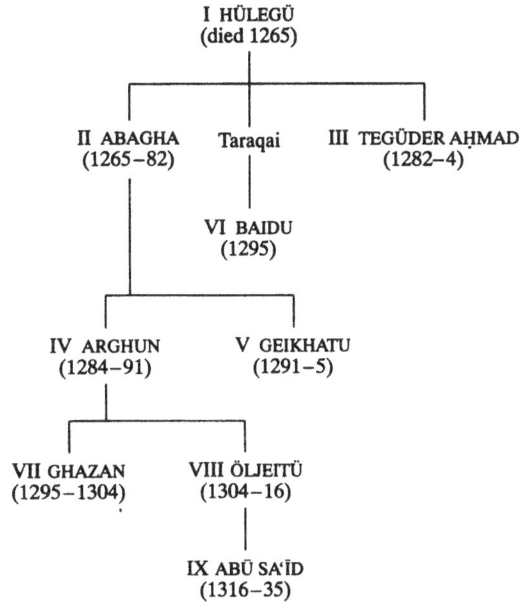

3 Īlkhāns of Persia

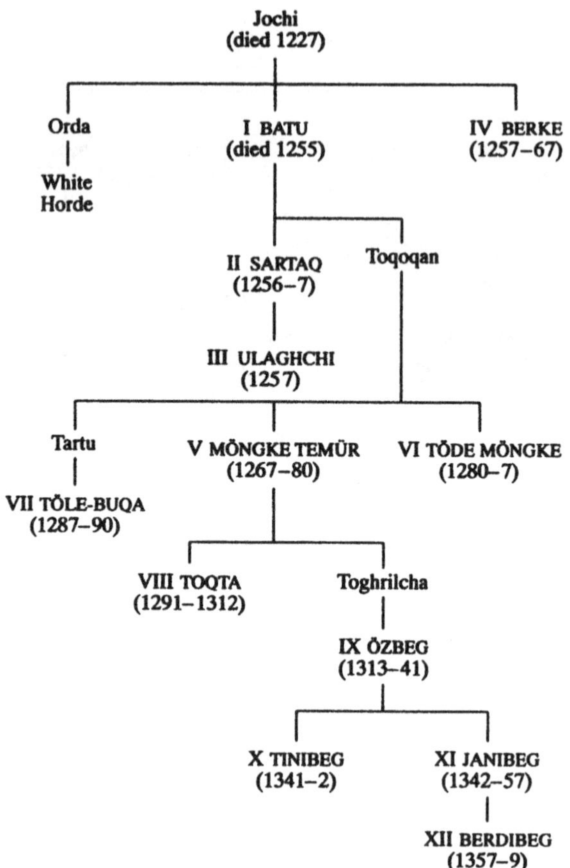

4 Khans of the Golden Horde

Glossary

Note: The following definitions apply only to the period and geographical area covered in this study. In earlier or subsequent periods, as well as other areas in the Islamic world or Inner Asia, these terms may have had other meanings. The following abbreviations are used: Ar. = Arabic; Mo. = Mongolian; Per.- = Persian; Tu. = Turkish.

amīr	Mamluk officer (Ar.).
amīr al-ʿarab/ ʿurbān	Leader of Syrian bedouin (Ar.).
ʿarab	Bedouins; also called *ʿurbān* (Ar.).
atabeg	Guardian of young prince and (at times) commander-in-chief of army (Tu.).
Baḥriyya	Mamluk regiment, founded by al-Ṣāliḥ Ayyūb, in which Baybars and Qalawun both originally served (Ar.).
bahādur	Hero; elite Mongol trooper (Ar. and Per. < Mo. *baghatur* < Tu.).
barīd	Mamluk postal system based on horse relays (Ar.).
bayʿa	Oath of allegiance to caliph or sultan (Ar.).
bulgha	State of being unsubmitted, i.e. rebellious, to the Mongols (Mo. < Tu.); see *yaghı*.
dawādār	Mamluk official, always an officer, who supervised matters relating to correspondence, *barīd*, and possibly espionage (Ar. and Per. hybrid).
Golden Horde	Mongol state north of the Black Sea.
ḥalqa	Non-mamluk cavalry formation in Mamluk army (Ar.).
īl	State of being in peace with the Mongols, by unconditionally submitting (Ar. and Per. < Mo. *el*).
īlchī	Mongol envoy or ambassador (Ar. and Per. < Mo. *elchi*).
īlkhān	Title of the Mongol ruler in Iran; often translated as "subject *khān*" (s.v.) (Ar. and Per. < Mo. *elkhan* < Tu. *eligkhan* ?).
imra	Rank of amir (Ar.).

iqṭāʿ — Allocation of revenues from a rural area to a Mamluk officer, for the maintenance of his household and unit (pl. *iqṭāʿāt*; Ar.).

Jazīra — The area between the upper Euphrates and the Tigris, today comprising northern Iraq, northeastern Syria and southeastern Turkey.

jihād — Muslim holy war (Ar.).

khan — Mongol ruler (Mo. and Tu.).

khaznadār — Treasurer of sultan (Ar. and Per. hybrid).

khushdāsh — Fellow mamluk of the same patron (pl. *khushdāshiyya*; Ar. < Per. [suffix ultimately derived from Tu.]).

khuṭba — Sermon recited at Friday service in mosque (Ar.).

ordo — Camp of Mongol ruler or member of the royal family (Mo. < Tu.).

qa'an — The supreme Mongol ruler, i.e. "the Great Khan" (Mo. < *qaghan* = Tu. *khaghan*).

qāḍī — Muslim judge (Ar.).

qaraghul — Mongol road or border patrols (Mo. > Ar. *qarāwūl*).

Qipchaq — Turkish tribes living in the steppe north of the Black Sea. Also applied as the name of this steppe.

qāṣid — Envoy; more specifically Mamluk intelligence agent. (pl. *quṣṣād*; Ar.).

qıshlaq — Winter camp of the Mongols (Tu.).

Ṣāliḥiyya — The mamluks of al-Ṣāliḥ Ayyūb; the Baḥriyya were the major component of the Ṣāliḥiyya (Ar.).

shaḥna — Mongol commissioner in a subject city (Ar.); equivalent to *basqaq* (Tu.) and *darugha[chi]* (Mo.).

ṣulḥ — State of being in peace (Ar.).

taqlīd — Deed of office (Ar.).

ṭulb — Cavalry squadron (pl. *alṭāb*; Ar. of unknown origin).

tümen — A Mongol unit of (theoretically) 10,000 men (Mo. < Tu.).

ʿurbān — Bedouin; equivalent to *ʿarab* (Ar.).

ustādār — Major-domo of the household of sultan or senior amir (Per.).

wāfidiyya — Refugees from the Īlkhānate to the Mamluk Sultanate (Ar.).

yaghı — State of being unsubmitted, i.e. rebellious, to the Mongols; the Mongols used it as the functional equivalent of *bulgha* (Tu.).

yarligh — Command or order (Tu. = Mo. *jarligh*).

yasa — Command, decree or law. Also applied to the Law Code attributed to Chinggis Khan (Tu. < Mo. *jasagh*).

Bibliography

Note: Abbreviations are found above on pp. xiii–xiv. Authors of primary sources have been arranged alphabetically (in English) by the name by which they are best known by modern scholars; the definite article *al-* before names has been disregarded in this arrangement.

Primary sources

Arabic sources

Abū 'l-Fidā', al-Malik al-Mu'ayyad ʿImād al-Dīn Ismāʿīl b. ʿAlī. *Al-Mukhtaṣar fī ta'rīkh al-bashar*. Istanbul, 1286/1869–70. 4 vols. [There is a partial translation by P.M. Holt. *Memoirs of a Syrian Prince*. Wiesbaden, 1983.]

Abū Shāma, Shihāb al-Dīn ʿAbd al-Raḥmīn b. Ismāʿīl. *Tarājim rijāl al-qarnayn al-sādis wa'l-sābiʿ al-maʿrūf bi'l-dhayl ʿalā al-rawḍatayn*. Ed. M. al-Kawtharī. Cairo, 1947. [Cf. MS. British Library Or. 1539.]

al-Anṣārī, ʿUmar b. Ibrāhīm al-Awsī. *A Muslim Manual of War, being Tafrīj al-kurūb fī tabdīr al-ḥurūb*. Ed. and tr. G.T. Scanlon. Cairo, 1961.

al-ʿAynī, Badr al-Dīn Maḥmūd b. ʿAlī. *ʿIqd al-jumān fī ta'rīkh ahl al-zamān*. MS. Topkapı Sarayı, Ahmet III 2912.

Baybars al-Manṣūrī al-Dawādār, Rukn al-Dīn. *Kitāb al-tuḥfa al-mulūkiyya fī 'l-dawla al-turkiyya*. Ed. ʿA-R.S. Ḥamdān. Cairo, 1987.

Zubdat al-fikra fī ta'rīkh al-hijra. MS. British Library Add. 23325.

al-Dhahabī, Shams al-Dīn Muḥammad b. ʿUthmān. *Al-Mukhtār min ta'rīkh al-jazarī*. MS. Köprülüzade 1147.

Ta'rīkh al-islām. MSS. Bodleian Laud 279, 305; MSS. Aya Sofya (Süleymaniye) 3014–15.

al-Fāsī, Tāqī al-Dīn Muḥammad b. Aḥmad. *Shafā' al-gharam bi-akhbār al-balad al-ḥaram*. Ed. F. Wüstenfeld, in *Die Chroniken der Stadt Mekka* (reprinted as *Akhbār Makka al-musharrafa*). Rpt., Beirut, 1964. 2:55–324.

Ghāzī b. al-Wāsiṭī. *Kitāb radd ʿalā ahl-dhimma wa-man tabaʿahum*. Ed. and tr. Gottheil, in "An Answer to the Dhimmis." *JAOS*. 41 (1921):383–457.

Ibn ʿAbd al-Raḥīm al-Anṣārī, Nūr al-Dīn ʿAlī. Continuation of Ibn Wāṣil, *Mufarrij al-kurūb*. See there.

Ibn ʿAbd al-Ẓāhir, Muḥyī al-Dīn ʿAbd Allāh. *Al-Rawḍ al-zāhir fī sīrat al-malik al-ẓāhir*. Ed. ʿA-ʿA. al-Khuwayṭir. Riyad, 1396/1976.

Tashrīf al-ayyām wa'l-ʿuṣūr fī sīrat al-malik al-manṣūr. Ed. M. Kāmil. Cairo, 1961.

Ibn al-ʿAmīd, al-Makīn Jirjis. *Kitāb al-majmūʿ al-mubārak*. Ed C. Cahen, in "'La Chronique Ayyoubides' d'al-Makīn b. al-ʿAmīd." *BEO*. 15 (1955–7):109–84.

Ibn al-Athīr, ʿIzz al-Dīn ʿAlī. *Al-Kāmil fī 'l-ta'rīkh*. Beirut, 1965–6. 13 vols.

Ibn al-Dawādārī, Abū Bakr b. ʿAbd Allāh. *Kanz al-durar wa-jāmiʿ al-ghurar*. Vol. 8: *al-Durra al-kanziyya fī akhbār al-dawla al-turkiyya* (*Der Bericht über die frühen Mamluken*). Ed. U. Haarmann. ("Quellen zur Geschichte des islamischens Ägypten," vols. Ih–Ii). Freiburg-Cairo, 1971. Vol. 9: *al-Durr al-fākhir fī sīrat al-malik al-nāṣir* (*Der Bericht über den Sultan al-Malik an-Nāṣir Muḥammad ibn Qalāʾūn*). Ed. H.R. Roemer. Freiburg-Cairo, 1960.

Ibn Duqmaq [Duqmāq], Ṣārim al-Dīn Ibrāhīm b. Muḥammad. *Kitāb al-jawhar al-thamīn fī siyar al-khulafā' wa'l-mulūk wa'l-salāṭīn*. Ed. S.ʿA-F. ʿĀshūr. Umm al-Qurā [Mecca], n.d. [cf. MS. Bodleian Digby Or. 28.]

Ibn al-Furāt, Nāṣir al-Dīn ʿAbd al-Raḥmān b. Muḥammad. *Ta'rīkh al-duwal wa'l-mulūk*. MS. Vatican Ar. 726; MS. Vienna 814.

Ta'rīkh [= *Ta'rīkh al-duwal wa'l-mulūk*]. Vol. 7. Ed. Q. Zurayk. Beirut, 1942.

Ayyubids, Mamlukes and Crusaders. Selections from the Tārīkh al-Duwal wa'l-Mulūk of Ibn al-Furāt. Tr. U. and M.C. Lyons; intro. and notes J.S.C. Riley-Smith. Cambridge, 1971. 2 vols.

Ibn al-Fuwaṭī, Kamāl al-Dīn Abū 'l-Faḍl. *Al-Ḥawādith al-jāmiʿa wa'l-tajārib al-nāfiʿa fī'l-mi'a al-sābiʿa*. Ed. M. Jawād. Baghdad, 1351/1932–3. [There is some doubt as to whether this work is actually by Ibn al-Fuwaṭī; see *EI*², 3:769.]

Ibn Ḥajar al-ʿAsqalānī, Aḥmad. *Al-Durar al-kāmina fī aʿyān al-mi'a al-kāmina*. Hyderabad, 1348–50/1929–32. 5 vols.

Ibn al-ʿIbrī, Abū 'l-Faraj. *Ta'rīkh mukhtaṣar al-duwal*. Ed. A. Ṣāliḥānī. Beirut, 1890. [See also Bar Hebraeus under Miscellaneous sources.]

Ibn al-Kathīr, Abū 'l-Fidā' ʿAbd Allāh. *Al-Bidāya wa'l-nihāya fī'l-ta'rīkh*. Rpt., Beirut, 1977. 14 vols.

Ibn Khaldūn, ʿAbd al-Raḥman. *Kitāb al-ʿibar wa-dīwān al-mubtada' wa'l-khabar fī ayyām al-ʿarab wa'l-ʿajam wa'l-barbar*. Bulāq, 1284/1867–8. 7 vols.

The Muqaddimah, an Introduction to History. Tr. F. Rosenthal. 2nd ed. Princeton, 1967. 3 vols.

Ibn al-Nafīs, ʿAlā' al-Dīn ʿAlī b. Abī 'l-Ḥaram. *Kitāb Fāḍil ibn Nāṭiq*. Ed. and tr. M. Meyerhof and J. Schacht, as *The Theologus Autodidactus of Ibn al-Nafīs*. Oxford, 1968.

Ibn Shaddād al-Ḥalabī, ʿIzz al-Dīn Muḥammad b. ʿAlī. *Al-Aʿlāq al-khaṭīra fī dhikr umarā' al-shām wa'l-jazīra*. Vol. 1, pt. 1: *Ta'rīkh ḥalab*. Ed. D. Sourdel. Damascus, 1953.

Al-Aʿlāq al-khaṭīra ... Vol. 2, pt. 2: *Ta'rīkh lubnān, al-urdunn wa-filasṭīn*. Ed. S. Dahhān. Damascus, 1963.

Al-Aʿlāq al-khaṭīra ... Vol. 3: *Ta'rīkh al-jazīra*. Ed. Y. ʿAbbāra. Damascus, 1978. 2 parts.

Al-Aʿlāq al-khaṭīra [North Syria exclusive of Aleppo = part of vol. 1]. Ed. A.-M. Eddé, in "La description de la Syrie du Nord de ʿIzz al-Dīn ibn Šaddād." *BEO*. 32–3 (1981–2):265–402.

Ta'rīkh al-malik al-ẓāhir (*Die Geschichte des Sultans Baibars*). Ed. A. Ḥuṭayṭ. ("Bibliotheca Islamica," vol. 31.) Wiesbaden, 1983.

Ibn al-Shiḥna, Muḥibb al-Dīn Abū 'l-Faḍl Muḥammad. *Al-Durr al-muntakhab fī ta'rīkh mamlakat ḥalab*. Ed. Y. Sarkīs. Beirut, 1909.

Ibn al-Ṣuqāʿī, Faḍl Allāh b. Abī Fakhr. *Tālī kitāb wafayāt al-aʿyān*. Ed. and tr. J. Sublet. Damascus, 1974.

Ibn Taghrī Birdī, Abū 'l-Maḥāsin. *Al-Nujūm al-zāhira fī muluk miṣr wa'l-qāhira*. Rpt. [n.d.] of Cairo, 1930–56. 16 vols.

Ibn Wāṣil, Jamāl al-Dīn Muḥammad b. Sālim. *Mufarrij al-kurūb fī akhbār banī ayyūb*. MSS. Bibliothèque Nationale ar. 1702–3. [Two separate MSS of the same work.]

Mufarrij al-kurūb. Vols. 4 and 5. Ed. Ḥ.M. Rabīʿ and S.ʿA-F. ʿĀshūr. Cairo, 1972 and 1977.

al-Jazarī, Shams al-Dīn Muḥammad. *Ḥawādith al-ẓamān*. MS. Gotha 1560.

al-Kutubī, Muḥammad b. Shākir. *Fawāt al-wafayāt*. Bulāq, 1299/1881–2. 2 vols.

ʿUyūn al-tawārīkh. MS. Köprülüzade 1121.

ʿUyūn al-tawārīkh. Vol. 20. Ed. F. Sāmir and N. Dāwūd. Baghdad, 1980.

al-Maqrīzī, Taqī al-Dīn Aḥmad b. ʿAlī. *Kitāb al-sulūk li-maʿrifat duwal al-mulūk*. Ed. M.M. Ziyāda and S.ʿA-F. ʿĀshūr. Cairo, 1934–73. 4 vols. in 12 parts.

Histoire des sultans mamlouks de l'Égypte. Tr. M.E. Quatremère. Paris, 1837–45. 2 vols. in 4 pts.

Mufaḍḍal Ibn Abī 'l-Faḍā'il. *Al-Nahj al-sadīd wa'l-durr al-farīd fīmā baʿda ibn al-ʿamīd (Histoire des sultans mamlouks)*. Ed. and tr. E. Blochet. (*Patrologia Orientalis*, vols. 12, 14, 20). Paris, 1919–28.

al-Muqrī, Aḥmad b. Muḥammad al-Fayyūmī. *Nathr al-jumān fī tarājim al-aʿyān*. MS. Chester Beatty Arabic 4113.

al-Nuwayrī, Shihāb al-Dīn Aḥmad b. ʿAbd al-Wahhāb. *Nihāyat al-arab fī funūn al-adab*. MS. Leiden University, Codex Or. 2m and 2n. [Part of MS. 2m was published in 1992 as vol. 31 of the Cairo edition. I was, however, unable to obtain this volume in time to use it for the present study.]

Nihāyat al-arab. Vol. 27. F.Ḥ. ʿĀshūr, ed. Cairo, 1984.

al-Qalqashandī, Shihāb al-Dīn Aḥmad. *Ṣubḥ al-aʿshā fī ṣināʿat al-inshā'*. Cairo, 1913–19. 14 vols.

Qirtay [Qirṭāy] al-ʿIzzī al-Khaznadārī. *Ta'rīkh al-nawādir mimmā jāra li'l-awā'il wa'l-awākhir*. MS. Gotha 1655.

al-Ṣafadī, Ṣalāḥ al-Dīn Khalīl b. Aybeg. *Aʿyān al-ʿaṣr wa-aʿwān al-naṣr*. MSS. Aya Sofya (Süleymaniye) 2962–70; MS. Emanet Hazinesi (Topkapı Sarayı) 1216.

Al-Wāfī bi'l-wafayāt. Ed. H. Ritter *et al.* Wiesbaden, 1931–. 20 vols. to date.

Al-Wāfī bi'l-wafayat. MS. British Library Add. 23359.

Ṣāliḥ b. Yaḥyā. *Ta'rīkh Bayrūt*. Ed. L. Cheikho. Beirut, 1927.

Ṣārim al-Dīn Özbeg, in G. Levi della Vida, ed. and tr. "L'Invasione dei Tartari in Siria nel 1260 nei ricordi di un testimone oculare." *Orientalia*. 4 (1935):253–76.

Shāfiʿ b. ʿAlī al-Kātib, Nāṣir al-Dīn. *Al-Faḍl al-ma'thūr min sīrat al-sulṭān al-malik al-manṣūr*. MS. Bodleian Marsh 424.

Ḥusn al-manāqib al-sirriyya al-muntazaʿa min al-sīra al-ẓāhiriyya. Ed. ʿA-ʿA. al-Khuwayṭir. Riyad, 1976.

Sibṭ ibn al-Jawzī. *Mir'at al-zamān fi ta'rīkh al-aʿyān*. Vol. 8. Hyderabad, 1370/1951.

al-Suyūṭī, Jalāl al-Dīn ʿAbd al-Raḥmān b. Abū Bakr. *Ta'rīkh al-khulafā'*. Miṣr [Cairo], 1351/1932.

History of the Caliphs. Tr. H.S. Jarrett. Calcutta, 1881.

Tiesenhausen, W. de (ed.). *Recueil de matériaux relatifs à l'histoire de l' Horde d'Or*. Vol. 1. St. Petersburg, 1884.

al-ʿUmarī, Aḥmad b. Yaḥyā ibn Faḍl Allāh. *Masālik al-abṣār fī 'l-mamālik al-amṣār:*

mamālik miṣr wa'l-shām wa'l-ḥijāz wa'l-yaman. Ed. A.F. Sayyid. Cairo, 1985.
Masālik al-abṣār fī 'l-mamālik al-amṣār: qabā'il al-ʿarab fī 'l-qarnayn al-tāsiʿ wa'l-thāmin al-hijriyyayn. Ed. D. Krawulsky. Beirut, 1985.
Das Mongolische Weltreich: al-ʿUmarī's Darstellung der mongolischen Reiche in seinem Werk Masālik al-abṣār fī 'l-mamālik al-amṣār. Ed. and tr. K. Lech. ("Asiatische Forschungen," vol. 14). Wiesbaden, 1968.
Al-ʿUmarī's Bericht über Anatolien in seinem Werke Masālik al-abṣār fī 'l-mamālik al-amṣār. Ed. F. Taeschner. Leipzig, 1929.
Al-Taʿrīf fī al-muṣṭalaḥ al-sharīf. Cairo, 1312/1894–5.
Yāqūt al-Rūmī. *Muʿjam al-buldān*. Ed. F. Wüstenfeld. Leipzig, 1866–73. 6 vols.
al-Yūnīnī, Quṭb al-Dīn Mūsā b. Muḥammad. *Dhayl mir'at al-zamān fī ta'rīkh al-aʿyān*. Hyderabad, 1954–61. 4 vols.
al-Ẓāhirī, Khalīl b. Shāhīn. *Kitāb zubdat kashf al-mamālik*. Ed. P. Ravaisse. Paris, 1894.

Persian sources

Ahrī, Abū Bakr al-Qaṭbī. *Taʾrīkh-i shaykh uways*. Ed. and tr. J.B. van Loon. The Hague, 1954.
Āqsarāyī, al-Karīm. *Musāmarat al-akhbār*. Ed. O. Turan. Ankara, 1944.
Āyatī, ʿA-M. *Taḥrīr-i ta'rīkh-i waṣṣāf*. Tehran, 1346/1967.
Ibn Bībī, al-Ḥusayn b. Muḥammad. *Tawārīkh-i āl saljūq (Histoire des Seldjoucides d'Asie Mineure)*. Ed. T. Houtsma. Leiden, 1902.
Die Seltschukengeschichte des Ibn Bībī. Tr. H.W. Duda. Copenhagen, 1959.
Juwaynī, ʿAlā' al-Dīn Aṭā Malik. *Ta'rīkh-i jahān gushā*. Ed. M.M. Qazwīnī. London and Leiden, 1912–37. 3 vols.
The History of the World Conqueror. Tr. J.A. Boyle. Manchester, 1958. 2 vols.
Jūzjānī, Minhāj al-Dīn. *Ṭabaqāt-i nāṣirī*. Ed. ʿA. Ḥabībī. Kabul, 1964–5. 2 vols.
Tabaḳāt-i-nāṣirī. Ed. and tr. H.G. Raverty. London, 1881. 2 vols.
Mustawfī, Ḥamd Allāh Qazwīnī. *Ta'rīkh-i guzīda*. Ed. A. Nawā'ī. Teheran, 1958–61.
Naṭanzī, Muʿīn al-Dīn. *Muntakhab al-tawārīkh-i muʿīnī*. Ed. J. Aubin. Teheran, 1957.
Rashīd al-Dīn, Faḍl Allāh Abū 'l-Khayr. *Jāmiʿ al-tawārīkh*. Vol. 3. Ed. ʿA. ʿAlīzādah. Baku, 1957.
Histoire des Mongols de la Perse. Ed. and tr. M.E. Quatremère. Paris, 1836.
Djami el-Tévarikh. Vol. 2. Ed. E. Blochet. Leiden and London, 1911.
The Successors of Genghis Khan. Tr. J.A. Boyle. London and New York, 1971.
Waṣṣāf, ʿAbd Allāh b. Faḍl Allāh. *Ta'rīkh-i Waṣṣāf (= Tajziyat al-amṣār wa-tazjiyat al-aʿṣār)*. Rpt., Teheran, 1338 S./1959–60 of ed. Bombay, 1269 H./1852–3. [See also Āyatī above.]

Miscellaneous sources

W. Abramowski, "Die chinesischen Annalen des Möngke. Übersetzung des 3. Kapitel des Yüan-chih," *Zentralasiatische Studien*. 13 (1979):7–71.
Bar Hebraeus. *The Chronography of Gregory Abû 'l-Faraj*. Ed. and tr. E.A.W. Budge. London, 1932. Vol. 1: translation. [See also under Ibn al-ʿIbrī.]
Brosset, M., tr. *Histoire de la Géorgie*. Vol. 1. St. Petersburg, 1849.

Budge, E.A.W., tr. *The Monks of Ḳûblâi Khân Emperor of China*. Rpt., New York, 1973, of London, 1928. [See also below under Chabot.]

Chabot, J.B. "Histoire du patriarche Mar Jabalaha III et du moine Rabban Çauma." *ROL*. 1 (1893):567–610; 2 (1884):73–142, 235–305.

Dawson, C., ed. ("Translated by a Nun of Stanbrook Abbey"). *The Mission to Asia* [rpt. of *The Mongol Mission*]. London, 1980.

"L'Estoire de Eracles Empereur," in *RHC, Occ*. 2:1–481.

Gestes des Chiprois, in *RHC, Ar*. 2:737–872.

Grigor of Akanc' [Akner], in R.P. Blake and R.N. Frye, ed. and tr. "History of the Nation of the Archers." *HJAS*. 12 (1949):269–399.

Het'um [Hayton/Hethoum]. "La Flor des estories de la Terre d'Orient," in *RHC, Ar*. 2:111–253.

James of Aragon. *The Chronicle of James I of Aragon*. Tr. J. Forster and P. de Gayngos. London, 1883.

Jean Dardel. "Chronique d'Arménie," in *RHC, Ar*. 2:1–109.

Joseph de Cancy, in W.B. Sanders, tr. "A Crusader's Letter from 'the Holy Land'." *Palestine Pilgrim's Text Society*. 5 (1896).

Kirakos of Gandzak, in E. Dulaurier, ed. and tr. "Des Mongols d'après les historiens arméniens." *JA*. 5 Ser., 11 (1858):481–508.

History of the Armenians. Tr. R. Bedrosian. New York, 1986.

Marco Polo. *The Book of Ser Marco Polo*. Tr. and ed. H. Yule. 3rd ed. revised by H. Cordier. London, 1921. 2 vols.

The Travels. Harmondsworth, 1958; rpt., 1986.

"MS. de Rothelin" ("Continuation de Guillaume de Tyr de 1221 a 1261 dité du Manuscript de Rothelin"), in *RHC, Occ*. 2:485–639.

Painter, G.D., ed. and tr. "The Tartar Relation." In R.A. Skelton *et al*., ed. *The Vinland Map and the Tartar Relation*. New Haven, 1965.

Simon de Saint-Quentin. *Histoire des Tartares*. Ed. J. Richard. Paris, 1965.

Smpad, in S. Der Nersessian, tr. "The Armenian Chronicle of Constable Smpad or of the Royal Historian." *DOP*. 13 (1959):141–68.

La Chronique attribuée au Connétable Smbat. Tr. G. Dédéyan. Paris, 1980.

Step'anos Orbellian. *Histoire de la Siounnie*. Ed. and tr. M. Brosset. St. Petersburg, 1860–4. 2 vols.

Vardan, in E. Dulaurier, ed. and tr. "Les Mongols d'après les historiens arméniens." *JA*. 5 Ser., 16 (1860):273–322.

In R.W. Thomson. "The Historical Compilation of Vardan Arewelc'i." *DOP*. 43 (1989):125–226.

William of Rubruck, in P. Jackson, tr. and ed., and D. Morgan, ed. *The Mission of Friar William of Rubruck*. London, 1990.

Wyngaert, A. Van den. *Sinica Fransciscana*. Vol. 1: *Itinera et relationes Fratrum saeculi XIII et XIV*. Quaracchi-Firenze, 1929.

Modern studies

Abel, F-M. *Géographie de la Palestine*. Paris, 1933. 2 vols.

Abel-Remusat, J. "Mémoires sur les relations politiques des princes chrétiens, et particulièrement des rois de France, avec les empereurs mongols." *Mémoires de l'Institut Royal de France, Académie des Inscriptions et Belles-Lettres.* 6 (1822):396–469; 7 (1824):335–438.

Alban, J.R. and C.T. Allmand, eds. "Spies and Spying in the Fourteenth Century," in C.T. Allman, ed. *War, Literature and Politics in the Later Middle Ages.* Liverpool, 1976. Pp. 73–101.

Allen, W.E.D. *A History of the Georgian People.* London, 1932.

Allsen, T.T. "Changing Forms of Legitimation in Mongol Iran," in G. Seaman and D. Marks, eds. *Rulers from the Steppe: State Formation on the Eurasian Periphery.* Los Angeles, 1991. Pp. 223–41.

Mongol Imperialism: The Policies of the Grand Qan Möngke in China, Russia and the Islamic Lands. Berkeley, 1987.

Amedroz, H.F. "Three Arabic MSS on the History of the City of Mayyāfāriqīn." *JRAS.* 1902:785–808.

Amitai, R. "From Holy War to Reconciliation: The Relations between the Mongols of Iran and the Mamluks during the Reign of al-Nāṣir Muḥammad b. Qalāwūn" [Hebrew]. MA thesis, Hebrew Univ. of Jerusalem, 1984.

"Mamlūk Espionage among Mongols and Franks." *AAS.* 22 (1988):173–81.

"Mongol Raids into Palestine (AD 1260 and 1300)." *JRAS.* 1987:236–55.

"The Rise and Fall of the Mamlūk Military Institution: A Summary of David Ayalon's Works," in M. Sharon, ed. *Studies in Islamic History and Civilization in Honour of Professor David Ayalon.* Jerusalem and Leiden, 1986. Pp. 19–30.

Amitai-Preiss, R. "Aims and Motivation of Īlkhānid Strategy towards Syria and the Mamluks," in D. Morgan *et al.*, eds. *The Mongol Empire and its Legacy.* Forthcoming.

"An Exchange of Letters in Arabic between Abaγa Īlkhān and Sultan Baybars (AH 667/AD1268–9)." *CAJ.* 38 (1994):11–33.

"ʿAyn Jālūt Revisited." *Tārīh.* 2 (1991):119–50.

"Hülegü and the Ayyūbid Lord of Transjordan (More on the Mongol Governor of al-Karak)." *AEMA.* Forthcoming.

"In the Aftermath of ʿAyn Jālūt: The Beginnings of the Mamlūk–Īlkhānid Cold War." *Al-Masāq: Studie Arabo-Islamica Mediterranea.* 3 (1990):1–21.

"Evidence for the Early Use of the Title *īlkhān* among the Mongols." *JRAS.* 3rd ser., 1 (1991):353–62.

"Mamluk Perceptions of the Mongol–Frankish Rapprochement." *MHR.* 7 (1992):50–65.

Amitai-Preiss, N. and R. Amitai-Preiss. "Two Notes on the Protocol on Hülegü's Coinage." *Israel Numismatic Journal.* 10 (1988–89 [1991]):117–28.

Artuk, İ. and C. *İstanbul Arkeoloji Müzerleri Teşhirdeki İslâmî Sikkeler Kataloğu.* Istanbul, 1971–4. 2 vols.

Ashtor, E. *Levant Trade in the Later Middle Ages.* Princeton, 1983.

A Social and Economic History of the Near East in the Middle Ages. London, 1976.

ʿĀshūr, F.Ḥ. *Al-ʿAlāqāt al-siyāsiyya bayna al-mamālīk wa'l-mughūl fī al-dawla al-mamlūkiyya al-ūlā.* Cairo, 1976.

ʿĀshūr, S.ʿA-F. *Al-ʿAṣr al-mamālīkī fī miṣr wa'l-shām.* Cairo, 1965.

Aubin, J. "L'ethnogénèse des Qaraunas." *Turcica.* 1 (1969):65–94.

Ayalon, D. "Aspects of the Mamlūk Phenomenon: Ayyūbids, Kurds and Turks." *Der Islam.* 54 (1977):1–32. [Rpt. in *Mamlūk Military Society*, no. Xb.]

"The Auxiliary Forces of the Mamluk Sultanate." *Der Islam*. 65 (1988):13–37.
"Dawādār." *EI*². 2:172.
"Egypt as a Dominant Factor in Syria and Palestine during the Islamic Period," in A. Cohen and G. Baer, eds. *Egypt and Palestine: A Millennium of Association (868–1948)*. Jerusalem and New York, 1984. Pp. 17–47. [Rpt. in *Outsiders*, no. II.]
L'esclavage du mamelouk. Jerusalem, 1951. [Rpt. in *Mamlūk Military Society*, no. I.]
"The European Asiatic Steppe: A Major Reservoir of Power for the Islamic World." *Proceedings of 25th Congress of Orientalists – Moscow, 1960*. Moscow, 1963. 2:47–52. [Rpt. in *Mamlūk Military Society*, no. VIII.]
"The Great Yāsa of Chingiz Khān. A Re-examination." *SI*. Pt. A, 33 (1971):97–140; pt. B, 34 (1971):151–80; pt. C1, 36 (1972):113–58; pt. C2, 38 (1973):107–56. [Rpt. in *Outsiders*, no. IV.]
"Ḥalḳa." *EI*². 3:99.
"Ḥarb, iii.-The Mamlūk Sultanate." *EI*². 3:184–90.
"Ḥimṣ, Battle of." *EI*². 3:402–3.
"Mamlūk." *EI*². 6:313–21.
"The Mamluks and Naval Power: A Phase of the Struggle between Islam and Christian Europe." *Proceedings of the Israel Academy of Sciences and Humanities*. 1/8 (1967):1–12. [Rpt. in *Studies on the Mamlūks*, no. VI.]
The Mamlūk Military Society: Collected Studies. London, 1979.
Outsiders in the Lands of Islam: Mamluks, Mongols and Eunuchs. London, 1988.
"Notes on the Furūsiyya Exercises and Games in the Mamlūk Sultanate," in U. Heyd, ed. *Studies in Islamic Civilisation and History = Scripta Hierosolymitana* (Jerusalem). 9 (1961):31–62. [Rpt. in *Mamlūk Military Society*, no. II.]
"On One of the Works of Jean Sauvaget." *IOS*. 1 (1971):298–302. [Rpt. in *Mamlūk Military Society*, no. VII.]
"Regarding Population Estimates in the Countries of Medieval Islam." *JESHO*. 28 (1985):1–19. [Rpt. in *Outsiders*, no. V.]
"Le régiment Bahriya dans l'armée mamelouke." *REI*. 19 (1951):133–41. [Rpt. in *Studies on the Mamlūks*, no. III.]
Studies on the Mamlūks of Egypt (1250–1517). London, 1977.
"Studies on the Structure of the Mamlūk Army." *BSOAS*. 15 (1953):203–28 (pt. 1), 448–76 (pt. 2); 16 (1954):57–90 (pt. 3). [Rpt. in *Studies on the Mamlūks*, no. I.]
"Studies on the Transfer of the ʿAbbāsid Caliphate from Baġdād to Cairo." *Arabica*. 7 (1960):41–59. [Rpt. in *Studies on the Mamlūks*, no. IX.]
"The System of Payment in Mamlūk Military Aristocracy." *JESHO*. 1 (1958):37–65, 257–96. [Rpt. in *Studies on the Mamlūks*, no. VIII.]
"The Wafidiya in the Mamluk Kingdom." *Islamic Culture*. 25 (1951):89–104. [Rpt. in *Studies on the Mamlūks*, no. II.]
Balog, P. *The Coinage of the Mamlūk Sultans of Egypt and Syria*. New York, 1964.
Barthold, W. *An Historical Geography of Iran*. Tr. Svat Soucek, ed. C.E. Bosworth. Princeton, 1984.
Turkestan down to the Mongol Invasion. 4th ed. London, 1977.
Bedrosian, R. "The Turco-Mongol Invasions and the Lords of Armenia in the 13th-14th Centuries." Ph.D. diss., Columbia Univ. New York, 1979.
Boase, T.S.R., ed. *The Cilician Kingdom of Armenia*. Edinburgh, 1978.
"The History of the Kingdom," in Boase, *The Cilician Kingdom of Armenia*. Pp. 1–33.

Bosworth, C.E. "Ḥarb, v. Persia." *EI²*. 2:194–8.

"Recruitment, Muster and Review in Medieval Islamic Armies," in V.J. Parry and M.E. Yapp, eds. *War, Technology and Society in the Middle East*. London, 1975. Pp.59–77.

Boyle, J.A. "The Death of the Last ʿAbbāsid Caliph: A Contemporary Muslim Account." *JSS*. 4 (1961):145–61. [Rpt. in J.A. Boyle. *The Mongol World Empire 1206–1370*. London, 1977. Art. no. XI.]

"Dynastic and Political History of the Īl-Khāns." *CHIr*. 5:303-421.

"The Il-Khans of Persia and the Princes of Europe." *CAJ*. 20 (1976):25–40.

Brinner, W. "Some Ayyūbid and Mamlūk Documents from Non-archival Sources." *IOS*. 2 (1972):117–43.

Brunel, C. "David d'Ashby auteur méconnu des Faits des Tartares." *Romania*. 79 (1958):39–46.

Cahen, C. "La Djazira au milieu du treizième siècle d'après ʿIzz al-Din Ibn Chaddad." *REI*. 8 (1934):109–28.

Pre-Ottoman Turkey. Tr. J. Jones-Williams. London, 1968.

"Quelques textes négligés concernant les turcomans du Rūm au moment de l'invasion mongole." *Byzantion*. 14 (1939):131–9.

La Syrie du nord. Paris, 1940.

Canard, M. "Djāsūs." *EI²*. 2:487.

"La royaume d'Arménie-Cilicie et les Mameloụks jusqu'au traité de 1285." *Revue des études arméniennes*. 4 (1967):217–59. [Rpt. in M. Canard. *L'expansion arabo-islamique et ses repercussions*. London, 1974. Art. no. VII.]

"Un traité entre Byzance et l'Egypte au XIIIe siècle et les relations diplomatiques de Michel VIII Paléologue avec les sultans mamlûks Baibars et Qalâ'ûn," in *Mélanges Gaudefroy-Demombynes*. Cairo, 1937. Pp. 197–224. [Rpt. in M. Canard. *Byzance et les musulmans du Proche Orient*. London, 1973. Art. no. IV.]

Conder, C.R. and H.H. Kitchener. *The Survey of Western Palestine: Memoirs of the Topography, Orography, Hydrography and Archaeology*. Vol. 2: *Samaria*. London, 1882.

Der Nersessian, S. "The Kingdom of Cilician Armenia," in K.M. Setton, gen. ed. *History of the Crusades*. Vol. 2: R.L. Wolff and H.W. Hazard, eds. Philadelphia, 1962. Pp. 630–59.

Doerfer, G. *Türkische und mongolische Elemente im Neupersischen*. Wiesbaden, 1963–75. 4 vols.

D'Ohsson, A.C.M. *Histoire des Mongols*. Rpt., Tientsin, China, 1940, of The Hague, 1834. 4 vols.

Edbury, P.W., ed. *Crusade and Settlement*. Cardiff, 1985.

Edwards, R.W. *The Fortifications of Armenian Cilicia*. Washington, 1987.

Ehrenkreutz, A. "Strategic Implications of the Slave Trade between Genoa and Mamluk Egypt in the Second Half of the Thirteenth Century," in A.L. Udovitch, ed. *The Islamic Middle East, 700–1900: Studies in Economic and Social History*. Princeton, 1981. Pp. 335–46.

Ellenblum, R. "The Crusader Road from Lod to Jerusalem" [Hebrew], in Y. Ben-Arieh *et al.*, eds. *Historical–Geographical Studies in the Settlement of Eretz Israel*. Jerusalem, 1988. Pp. 203–18.

Erdal, M. "Die Türkisch-mongolischen Titel *elxan* und *elči*." *Proceedings of the Permanent International Altaistic Conference (Berlin, 1991)*. Forthcoming.

Escovitz, J.H. *The Office of Qāḍī al-Quḍāt in Cairo under the Baḥrī Mamluks*. Berlin, 1984.

Fletcher, J.F. "The Mongols: Ecological and Social Perspective."*HJAS*. 46 (1986):11–50.

Gaudefroy-Demombynes, M. *La Syrie à l'époque des Mamelouks*. Paris, 1923.

Geanakoplos, D.J. *Emperor Michael Palaeologus and the West*. Cambridge, MA, 1959.

Glubb, J. *Soldiers of Fortune: The Story of the Mamlukes*. New York, 1973.

Golden, P. "Cumanica II: The Ölberli (Ölperli). The Fortunes and Misfortunes of an Inner Asian Nomadic Clan." *AEMA*. 6 (1986 [1988]):5–29.

Grousset, R. *L'Empire des steppes*. Rpt., Paris, 1949. Translated by N. Walford as *The Empire of the Steppes*. New Brunswick, 1970.

Histoire des croisades et du royaume franc de Jérusalem. Paris, 1934–6. 3 vols.

Haarmann, U. *Quellenstudien zur frühen Mamlukenzeit*. Freiburg, 1970.

Hambis, L. "La lettre mongole du governeur de Karak." *Acta Orientalia Academiae Scientarum Hungaricae*. 15 (1962):143–6.

Hartmann, R. Review of F. Taeschner, *Al-ʿUmarī: Bericht über Anatolien in seinem Werke Masālik al-Absār* (Leipzig, 1929), in *Orientalische Literaturzeitung*. 34/11 (1931):970–4.

Herde, P. "Taktiken muslimischer Heere von ersten Kreuzzug bis ʿAyn Djālūt (1260) und ihre Einwirkung auf die Schlacht bei Tagliacozzo (1268)," in W. Fischer and J. Schneider, eds. *Das Heilige Land in Mittelalter*. Neustadt an der Aisch, 1982. Pp. 83–94.

Heyd, W. *Histoire du commerce du Levant au moyen âge*. Rpt., Leipzig, 1936, of 1885–6 ed. 2 vols.

Hiyari, M.A. "The Origins and Development of the Amīrate of the Arabs during the Seventh/Thirteenth and Eighth/Fourteenth Centuries." *BSOAS*. 38 (1975):509–24.

Hodgson, G.S. "The Ismāʿīlī State." *CHIr*. 5:422–82.

Holt, P.M. *The Age of the Crusades: The Near East from the Eleventh Century to 1517*. London, 1986.

"Mamluk-Frankish Diplomatic Relations in the Reign of Baybars (658–76/1260–77)." *Nottingham Medieval Studies*. 32 (1988):180–95.

"Mamluk-Frankish Diplomatic Relations in the Reign of Qalāwūn (678–89/1279–90)." *JRAS*. 1989:278–89.

"Some Observations on the ʿAbbāsid Caliphate of Cairo." *BSOAS*. 47 (1984):501–7.

"Some Observations of Shāfiʿ b. ʿAlī's Biography of Baybars." *JSS*. 29 (1984):123–30.

"Three Biographies of al-Ẓāhir Baybars," in D.O Morgan, ed. *Medieval Historical Writing in the Christian and Islamic Worlds*. London, 1982. Pp. 19–29.

Honigman, E. "Al-Raḥba." *EI*[1]. 3:1100–3.

Howorth, H.H. *The History of the Mongols from the 9th to the 19th Century*. Rpt., New York, [1965] of London, 1876–1927. 4 vols. in 5 parts.

Hsiao Ch'i-ch'ing. *The Military Establishment of the Yuan Dynasty*. Cambridge, MA, 1978.

Humphreys, R.S. "The Emergence of the Mamluk Army." *SI*. 45 (1977):67–100; 46 (1977):147–82.

From Saladin to the Mongols: The Ayyubids of Damascus 1192–1260. Albany, 1977.

Irwin, R. "The Image of the Byzantine and the Frank in Arab Popular Literature of the Late Middle Ages." *MHR*. 4 (1989), 226–42.
"The Mamluk Conquest of the County of Tripoli," in P. Edbury, ed. *Crusade and Settlement*. Cardiff, 1985. Pp. 246–50.
The Middle East in the Middle Ages: The Early Mamluk Sultanate, 1250–1382. London, 1986.
"The Supply of Money and the Direction of Trade in Thirteenth-Century Syria," in P.W. Edbury and D.M. Metcalf, eds. *Coinage in the Latin East. The Fourth Oxford Symposium on Coinage and Monetary History*. (BAR International Series, no. 77). Oxford, 1980.
Jackson, P. "Abaqa." *EIr*. 1:61–3.
"Chaghatayid Dynasty." *EIr*. 5:343–7.
"The Crisis in the Holy Land in 1260." *English Historical Review*. 95 (1980): 481–513.
"The Dissolution of the Mongol Empire." *CAJ*. 32 (1978):186–244.
Review of P. Edbury, *Crusade and Settlement* (Cardiff, 1985), in *BSOAS*. 50 (1987):552.
Jagchid, S. and P. Hyer. *Mongolia's Culture and Society*. Boulder and Folkestone, 1979.
Jawād, M. "Tijārat al-ʿirāq fī ʿuṣūr al-ḥukm al-mughūlī." *Majallat ghurfat tijārat baghdād*. 4 (1943):436–40, 597–602; 7 (1944):64–8, 258–65.
Khazanov, A.M. "Characteristic Features of Nomadic Communities in the Eurasian Steppes," in W. Weissleder, ed. *The Nomadic Alternative*. The Hague, 1978. Pp. 119–26.
Nomads and the Outside World. Tr. J. Crookenden. Cambridge, 1984.
Khiṣbāk, J.H. *Al-ʿIrāq fī ʿahd al-mughūl al-īlkhāniyya*. Baghdad, 1968.
Khowaiter, A.A. *Baibars the First: His Endeavours and Achievements*. London, 1978.
Koch, Y. "ʿIzz al-Dīn ibn Shaddād and his Biography of Baybars." *Annali dell'Istituto Universitario Orientale* (Naples). 43 (1983):249–87.
Krader, L. "The Cultural and Historical Position of the Mongols." *Asia Major*. NS, 3 (1952–3):169–83.
Krawulsky, D. "Die Dynastie der Ilkhâne. Eine Untersuchung zu Regierungsbeginn, Dynastie- und Reichsname," in *idem*. *Mongolen Ilkhâne und Ideologie Geschichte* [*sic*]. Beirut, 1989. Pp. 87–112. [Correct title: *Mongolen und Ilkhane: Ideologie und Geschichte*.]
Īrān – Das Reich der Īlḫāne: Eine topographische-historische Studie. Wiesbaden, 1978.
Kwanten, L. *Imperial Nomads*. Philadelphia, 1979.
Labib, S.Y. *Handelsgeschichte Ägyptens in Spätmittelalter (1171–1517)*. Wiesbaden, 1965.
Lambton, A.K.S. "Concepts of Authority in Persia: Eleventh to Nineteenth Centuries AD" *Iran*. 26 (1988):95–103.
"Mongol Fiscal Administration in Persia." *SI*. 64 (1986):79–99; 65 (1987):97–123.
Lane-Poole, S. *Catalogue of Oriental Coins in the British Museum*. Vol. 6. London, 1881.
Latham, J.D. "Notes on Mamluk Horse-Archers." *BSOAS*. 32 (1969):257–67.
Lattimore, O. "The Geography of Chingis Khan." *The Geographical Journal*. 129/1 (1963):1–7.

Review of F. Grenard, *Genghis-Khan* (Paris, 1935), in *Pacific Affairs* (New York). 10/4 (Dec. 1937):462–8.

Lawrence, A.W. "The Castle of Baghras," in Boase, *The Cilician Kingdom of Armenia*. Pp. 34–83.

Levanoni, A. "The Mamluks' Ascent to Power in Egypt." *SI*. 72 (1990):121–44.

Lewis, B. "ʿAyn Djālūt." *EI*². 1:786.

Islam: From the Prophet Muhammad to the Capture of Constantinople. New York, 1974. 2 vols.

Lindner, R.P. "What Was a Nomadic Tribe?" *Comparative Studies in Society and History*. 24 (1982):689–711.

Lippard, B.G. "The Mongols and Byzantium, 1243–1341." Ph.D. diss., Indiana Univ. Bloomington, 1983.

Little, D.P. *An Introduction to Mamlūk Historiography*. Wiesbaden, 1970.

Lockhart, L. "The Relations between Edward I and Edward II of England and the Mongol Il-Khans of Persia." *Iran*. 6 (1968):22–31.

Lopez, R.S. "Fulfillment and Diversion in the Eight Crusades," in B.Z. Kedar, H.E. Mayer, R.C. Smail, eds. *Outremer: Studies in the Crusading Kingdom of Jerusalem Presented to Joshua Prawer*. Jerusalem, 1982. Pp. 16–26.

Lupprian, K-E. *Die Beziehungen der Päpste zu islamischen und mongolischen Herrschern im 13. Jahrhundert anhand ihres Briefwechsels*. Vatican City, 1981.

Marshall, C. *Warfare in the Latin East, 1192–1291*. Cambridge, 1992.

Martin, H.D. "The Mongol Army." *JRAS*. 1943:46–85.

Martinez, A.P. "Some Notes on the Īl-Xānid Army." *AEMA*. 6 (1986):129–242.

Mayer, L. *Mamluk Costume, A Survey*. Geneva, 1952.

Meyvaert, P. "An Unknown Letter of Hulagu, Il-Khan of Persia, to King Louis IX of France." *Viator*. 11 (1980):245–59.

Morgan, D.O. "The 'Great *Yāsa* of Chingiz Khān' and Mongol Law in the Īlkhānate." *BSOAS*. 49 (1986):163–76.

"The Mongols and the Eastern Mediterranean." *MHR*. 4 (1989):198–211.

"The Mongol Armies in Persia." *Der Islam*. 56 (1979):81–96.

The Mongols. Oxford, 1986.

"The Mongols in Syria, 1260–1300," in Edbury, *Crusade and Settlement*. Pp. 231–5.

"Persian Historians and the Mongols," in D.O. Morgan, ed. *Medieval Historical Writing in the Christian and Islamic Worlds*. London, 1982. Pp. 109–24.

Mostaert, A. and F.W. Cleaves. "Trois documents mongols des archives secrètes vaticanes." *HJAS*. 15 (1952):419–506.

Mutafian, C. *La Cilicie au carrefour des empires*. Paris, 1988. 2 vols.

Northrup, L.S. "A History of the Reign of the Mamluk Sultan al-Manṣūr Qalāwūn (678–689 AH/1279–1290 AD)." Ph.D. diss., McGill Univ. Montreal, 1982.

Ory, S. "Al-Ḥadath." *EI*². 3:19–20.

Ostrogorsky, G. *History of the Byzantine State*. Tr. J. Hussey. New Brunswick, 1957.

Otten-Froux, C. "L'Aïas dans le dernier tiers du XIIIe siècle d'après les notaires génois." *AAS*. 22 (1988):147–71.

Patton, D. *Badr al-Dīn Lu'lu' Atabeg of Mosul, 1211–1259*. Seattle and London, 1991.

Pelliot, P. *Notes on Marco Polo*. Paris, 1959–63. 2 vols.

Petech, L. "Les marchands italiens dans l'empire mongol." *JA*. 250 (1962):549–74.

Petrushevsky, I.P. "The Socio-Economic Condition of Iran under the Īl-Khāns." *CHIr*. 5:483-537.

Poliak, A. "La caractère colonial de l'état mamelouk dans ses rapports avec la Horde d'Or." *REI.* 9 (1935):231–45.

Feudalism in Egypt, Syria, Palestine, and the Lebanon, 1250–1900. London, 1939.

"The Influence of Chingiz Khan's Yāsa on the Mamlūk State." *BSOAS.* 10 (1942):862–72.

Prawer, J. *Histoire du royaume latin de Jérusalem.* Tr. G. Nahon. Paris, 1970. 2 vols.

Pritsak, O. "Two Migratory Movements in the Eurasian Steppe in the 9th-11th Centuries," in *Proceedings of the 26th International Congress of Orientalists, New Delhi 1964.* Vol. 2. New Delhi, 1968. Pp. 157–63.

Pumpian-Biran, M. "The Battle of Herat (668/1270)" [Hebrew]. M.A. seminar paper, Hebrew Univ. of Jerusalem, 1991.

Rabie, H. "The Training of the Mamlūk Fāris," in V.J. Parry and M.E. Yapp, eds. *War, Technology and Society in the Middle East.* London, 1975. Pp. 153–63.

de Rachewiltz, I. *Papal Envoys to the Great Khans.* London, 1971.

"Some Remarks on the Ideological Foundations of Chingis Khan's Empire." *Papers on Far Eastern History* (Canberra). 7 (1973):21–36.

"The Title Činggis Qan/Qaγan Re-examined," in W. Heissig and K. Sagaster, eds. *Gedanke und Wirkung: Festschrift zum 90. Geburtstag von Nikolaus Poppe.* Wiesbaden, 1989.

Ratchnevsky, P. *Genghis Khan: His Life and Legacy.* Tr. T.N. Haining. Oxford and Cambridge, MA, 1991.

Reid, R.W. "Mongolian Weaponry in *The Secret History of the Mongols.*" *Mongolian Studies.* 15 (1992):85–96.

Richard, J. "An Account of the Battle of Hattin Referring to the Frankish Mercenaries in Oriental Moslem States." *Speculum.* 27 (1952):168–77.

"Une ambassade mongole à Paris en 1262." *Journal des Savants.* 1979:299–300.

"Les causes des victoires mongoles d'après les historiens occidentaux du XIIIe siècle. *CAJ.* 23 (1979):104–17.

"La conversion de Berke et les débuts de l'islamisation de la Horde d'Or." *REI.* 35 (1967):173–84.

"Le début des relations entre la papauté et les Mongols de Perse." *JA.* 237 (1949):291–7.

"The Mongols and the Franks." *Journal of Asian History.* 3 (1969):45–57.

"Ultimatums mongols et lettres apocryphes: l'occident et les motifs de guerre des Tartares." *CAJ.* 17 (1973):212–22.

Riley-Smith, J.S.C. "The Templars and the Teutonic Knights," in Boase, *The Cilician Kingdom of Armenia.* Pp. 92–117.

Roberg, B. "Die Tartaren auf dem 2. Konzil von Lyon 1274." *Annuarium Historiae Conciliorium.* 5 (1973):241–302.

Rogers, J.M. "Evidence for Mamluk–Mongol Relations," in *Colloque internationale sur l'histoire du Caire.* Cairo, 1974. Pp. 385–403.

Röhricht, R. "Études sur les derniers temps du royaume de Jérusalem." *AOL.* 1 (1881):617–52.

"Der Kreuzzug des Königs Jacob I. von Aragonien (1269)." *Mittheilungen des Instituts für Oesterreichische Geschichtsforshung* (Innsbruck). 11 (1890):372–95.

Rosenthal, F. "Ibn al-Fuwaṭī." *EI*[2]. 3:761.

Rossabi, M. *Khubilai Khan: His Life and Times.* Berkeley, 1988.

Runciman, S. *A History of the Crusades*. Rpt., Harmondsworth, 1971, of Cambridge, 1951–54. 3 vols.
The Sicilian Vespers. Harmondsworth, 1960.
Sagaster, K. "Herrschaftsideologie und Friedensgedanke bei den Mongolen." *CAJ*. 17 (1973):223–42.
Saunders, J.J. *The History of the Mongol Conquests*. Rpt., London, 1977.
"The Mongol Defeat at Ain Jālūt and the Restoration of the Greek Empire," in *idem*. *Muslims and Mongols*. Christchurch, NZ, 1977. Pp. 67–76.
Sauvaget, J. "Halab." *EI*². 3:88.
La poste aux chevaux dans l'empire des Mamelouks. Paris, 1941.
Schamiloglu, U. "Tribal Politics and Social Organization in the Golden Horde." Ph.D. diss., Columbia Univ. New York, 1986.
Schein, S. *Fideles Crucis: The Papacy, the West and the Recovery of the Holy Land*. Oxford, 1991.
Sinclair, T.A. *Eastern Turkey: An Architectural and Archaeological Survey*. London, 1987–90. 4 vols.
Sinor, D. "Central Eurasia," in D. Sinor, ed. *Orientalism and History*. 2nd ed., Bloomington, 1970. Pp. 93–119. [Rpt. in Sinor, *Inner Asia*, art. no. I.]
"Horse and Pasture in Inner Asian History." *Oriens Extremus*. 19 (1972):171–84. [Rpt. in Sinor, *Inner Asia*, art. no. II.]
Inner Asia and its Contacts with Medieval Europe. London, 1977.
"The Mongols and Western Europe," in K.M. Setton, gen. ed. *A History of the Crusades*. Vol. 3: H.W. Hazard, ed. Madison, 1975. Pp. 513–44. [Rpt. in Sinor, *Inner Asia*. Art. no. IX.]
"On Mongol Strategy," in Ch'en Ch'ieh-hsien, ed. *Proceedings of the Fourth Altaistic Conference*. Tainan, Taiwan, 1975. Pp. 238–49. [Rpt. in Sinor, *Inner Asia*. Art. no. XVI.]
Smail, R.C. *Crusading Warfare (1097–1193)*. Cambridge, 1956.
Smith Jr., J.M. "ʿAyn Jālūt: Mamlūk Success or Mongol Failure?" *HJAS*. 44 (1984):307–45.
"Mongol Manpower and Persian Population." *JESHO*. 18 (1975):271–99.
"Mongol Nomadism and Middle Eastern Geography: Qīshlāqs and Tümens," in D.O. Morgan *et al*., eds. *The Mongol Empire and its Legacy*. Forthcoming.
"Turanian Nomadism and Iranian Politics." *Iranian Studies*. 11 (1978):57–81.
Spuler, B. *Die Goldene Horde: Die Mongolen in Rußland, 1223–1502*. Wiesbaden, 1965.
Die Mongolen in Iran: Verwaltung und Kultur der Ilchanzeit. 1220–1350. 4th ed. Leiden, 1985.
The Muslim World. Vol. 2: *The Mongol Period*. Leiden, 1960.
Steingass, F. *Persian-English Dictionary*. Rpt. London, 1977.
Streck, M. and V.J. Parry. "Bīredjik." *EI*². 1:1233–4.
Strothmann, R. "Al-Ṭūsī." *EI*¹. 4:980–1.
Sweeney, J.R. "Thomas of Spalato and the Mongols: A Thirteenth-Century Dalmatian View of Mongol Customs." *Florilegium*. 4 (1982):156–83.
Ṭarāwina, T.T. *Mamlakat ṣafad fī ʿahd al-mamālīk*. Beirut, 1402/1982.
Thorau, P. "The Battle of ʿAyn Jālūt: A Re-examination," in Edbury, *Crusade and Settlement*. Pp. 236–41.
The Lion of Egypt: Sultan Baybars I and the Near East in the Thirteenth Century. Tr. P.M. Holt. London and New York, 1992.

"Die Burgen der Assassinen in Syrien und ihre Einnahme durch Sultan Baibars." *Die Welt des Orients*. 18 (1987):132–58.

Tritton, A.S. "Tribes of Syria in the Fourteenth and Fifteenth Centuries." *BSOAS*. 12 (1948):567–73.

Turan, O. "The Idea of World Domination among the Medieval Turks." *SI*. 4 (1955):77–90.

Vernadsky, G. *The Mongols and Russia* (vol. 3 of his *A History of Russia*). Rpt., New Haven, 1966, of 1953 ed.

"The Scope and Contents of Chingiz Khan's Yasa." *HJAS*. 3 (1938):337–60.

Voegelin, E. "The Mongol Orders of Submission to European Powers, 1245–1255." *Byzantion*. 15 (1940–1):378–413.

Weiers, M., ed. *Die Mongolen: Beiträge zu ihrer Geschichte und Kultur*. Darmstadt, 1986.

Weil, G. *Geschichte des Abbasidenchalifats in Egypten*. Stuttgart, 1860–2. 2 vols.

Wickens, G.M. "Naṣīr al-Dīn Ṭūsī on the Fall of Baghdad: A Further Study." *JSS*. 7 (1962):23–34.

Wu, Pai-nan Rashid. "The Fall of Baghdad and the Mongol Rule in al-Iraq, 1258–1335." Ph.D. diss., Univ. of Utah. 1974.

Zakirov, S. *Diplomaticheskie Otnosheniia Zolotoi Ordy s Egiptom (XIII–XIV vv.)*. Moscow, 1966.

Index

Note: The definite article *al-* and diacritical marks have been ignored in the alphabetization of the index. Page references to illustrations are in italic.

CPSIA information can be obtained
at www.ICGtesting.com
Printed in the USA
BVHW030238220520
580127BV00001B/28